ISLAM AND ISLAMIC GROUPS

ISLAM AND ISLAMIC GROUPS

A Worldwide Reference Guide

Edited by

FARZANA SHAIKH

ISLAM AND ISLAMIC GROUPS

DPA
DIRECTORY PUBLISHERS
ASSOCIATION

Published by Longman Group UK Limited, Westgate House,
The High, Harlow, Essex CM20 1YR, United Kingdom.
Telephone (0279) 442601
Telex 81491 Padlog
Facsimile (0279) 444501

Distributed exclusively in the United States and Canada by Gale Research Inc.,
835 Penobscot Building, Detroit, Michigan 48226, USA.

ISBN 0-582-09146-2

A catalogue record for this publication is available from the British Library.

Printed and bound in Great Britain by
William Clowes Limited, Beccles and London

Contents

Introduction

This book is the first comprehensive worldwide survey of the current status of Islamic political groups. It reviews developments related to the process of Islamization in Muslim countries and focuses attention on organized political action among Muslim communities in countries where they form a minority.

At a general level, then, the volume seeks to underline the contemporary importance of Islam as the political ideology of almost 1,000 million people representing a fifth of the world's population.

The need for such a survey was generated by current interest in the phenomenon broadly described as Islamic "revivalism" and by the global spread of popular Islamic militancy.

The international significance of Islamic movements today stems less from their novelty than from the nature of their goals. While the great Islamic reform movements of the nineteenth century tended, on the whole, to preach accommodation with the modern world, albeit to win back Islam's ascendancy, current revivalist groups, inspired by the political success of the Iranian revolution, demand nothing less than the creation of full-fledged Islamic states.

Shorn of its traditional affiliation with the exclusive world of religious scholarship, the ideology of contemporary Islamic movements holds wide appeal across the social spectrum, but above all among the Muslim poor.

The importance of Islam in the political life of its adherents is, of course, dictated by their belief that it provides the ultimate framework of action for every condition and circumstance. The tenacity with which present day followers of Islam as against, say, Christianity, continue to abide by this dictum explains why a volume on Islamic political organizations seems more necessary than one dealing with Christian political groups.

Information relating to the structure and organization of radical Islamic groups has been difficult to obtain, let alone substantiate, not least because of the semi-clandestine nature of their activities.

Since conventional methods of data-collection normally employed for an undertaking of this kind, such as questionnaires, were not possible, other sources were used to provide information relating to the activities of semi-clandestine Islamic groups. These included international press reports, investigations by human rights organizations, proscribed publications issued by opposition groups, assistance from established international Muslim bodies and in-depth academic research.

However, the patchiness of the available information requires that all observations concerning militant and/or semi-clandestine groups be regarded as tentative rather than authoritative.

Data on established Islamic political parties, organizations and state-sponsored institutions were by comparison relatively easier to obtain. Even here, however, rapidly unfolding events in the area extending from the former Soviet Union to parts of eastern Europe, notably

Yugoslavia, complicated the task of presenting a coherent picture of existing Islamic political alignments.

Equally problematic was the attempt to establish whether or not there were links between national governments and international organizations engaged in strengthening Islamic identity among Muslims abroad.

The inclusion of some ostensibly non-political Muslim organizations which would normally be beyond the scope of this survey, such as Muslim missionary groups active in parts of western Europe and north America, needs to be explained. For while these groups tend primarily to be engaged in proselytization, their role in heightening Muslim communal identity has acted as the catalyst for organized action in the public domains of education, culture and legal reform.

The coverage of such a wide range of issues and regions would scarcely have been possible without a genuinely co-operative effort. I owe an enormous debt to all my colleagues at CIRCA and am especially grateful to Philippa Youngman, who was responsible for the book's final production.

I am grateful to all the contributors for the hours of hard work they put into this project and for their good-humour as I nitpicked my way through their copy.

Finally, a word of thanks to Patrick and Emile who ensured that I survived what seemed at times to be an improbable venture.

Farzana Shaikh
Cambridge, July 1992

A note on using this book

Each entry consists of a broad introductory survey comprising an historical outline, the distribution of Muslims along sectarian and ethnic lines, salient Islamic issues in the contemporary period, and the involvement of major Islamic organizations.

Organizations indicated in bold in the text are listed separately, where appropriate, in the section immediately following each country survey with details, where available, of their date of foundation, leadership, membership, aims, publications and affiliated organizations.

A final entry provides a listing of major international Islamic organizations and their addresses.

Contributors

Sarah Ansari (SA) is honorary lecturer at Royal Holloway and Bedford New College, University of London. She is the author of *Sufi Saints and State Power: the Pirs of Sind, 1843-1947* (Cambridge University Press, Cambridge, 1992) and is a contributor to the *Encyclopedia of Islam* (E.J. Brill, Leiden, 1991).

Eileen Byrne (EB) is regional editor for north Africa, the Middle East and southern Europe for *Keesing's Record of World Events*.

Tanya Joseph (TJ) is regional editor for Africa for *Keesing's Record of World Events* and a contributor to *The World's News Media* (Longman UK, Harlow, 1992).

Marc Cole-Bailey (MCB) is a researcher at Southampton University specializing in late 18th and 19th century military records and a contributor to *The World's News Media* (Longman UK, Harlow, 1992).

Steve Lewis (SL) is regional editor for north America and the Pacific for *Keesing's Record of World Events*. He is the author of *Illusions of Grandeur: Mosley, Fascism and British Society, 1931-1981* (Manchester University Press, Manchester, 1986) and the editor of *Korea: enduring division* (Longman UK, Harlow, 1988).

Geoffrey Roberts (GR) is a specialist on eastern Europe and the Commonwealth of Independent States. He is the author of *The USSR and the origins of the World War II* (Macmillan, London, forthcoming 1992) and *The Unholy Alliance: Stalin's Pact with Hitler* (I.B. Tauris/Indiana University Press, 1989).

Darren Sagar (DS) is regional editor for south-east Asia and the Middle East for *Keesing's Record of World Events*. He is the author of *Major Political Events in Indo-China 1945-1990* (Facts on File, New York, 1991) and a major contributor to *Cambodia: a Matter of Survival* (Longman UK, Harlow, 1989).

Yunus Samad (YS) is Associate Research Fellow for the Rhodes Chair of Race Relations, Oxford University. He is the author of *Islam, Ethnicity and the State in Pakistan 1937-1958* (Oxford University Press, Oxford, forthcoming) and is co-editor with T. Ranger and Ossie Stuart of *Culture, Identity and Politics: Ethnic Minorities in Britain* (forthcoming).

Farzana Shaikh (FS) is regional editor for international affairs for *Keesing's Record of World Events*. She has written on Indian Islam and is the author of *Community and Consensus in Islam: Muslim Representation in Colonial India, 1860-1947* (Cambridge University Press, Cambridge, 1989).

Wendy Slater (WS) is regional editor for the Commonwealth of Independent States and eastern Europe for *Keesing's Record of World Events* and a contributor to *The World's News Media* (Longman UK, Harlow, 1992).

Emma Wilson (EW) has worked as a researcher for the BBC and Channel 4 specializing on current affairs in the Middle East.

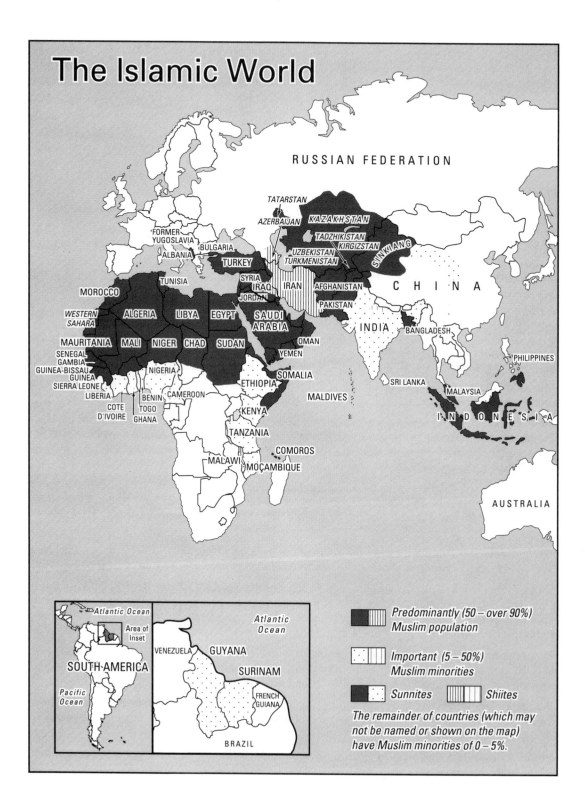

The Islamic World

RUSSIAN FEDERATION

TATARSTAN
AZERBAIJAN
KAZAKHSTAN
TADZHIKISTAN
KIRGIZSTAN
UZBEKISTAN
TURKMENISTAN
SINKIANG

FORMER
YUGOSLAVIA
BULGARIA
ALBANIA
TURKEY
TUNISIA
SYRIA
IRAQ
IRAN
AFGHANISTAN
CHINA
MOROCCO
JORDAN
PAKISTAN
WESTERN
SAHARA
ALGERIA
LIBYA
EGYPT
SAUDI
ARABIA
INDIA
BANGLADESH
MAURITANIA
MALI
NIGER
CHAD
SUDAN
OMAN
SENEGAL
YEMEN
PHILIPPINES
GAMBIA
GUINEA-BISSAU
NIGERIA
SRI LANKA
GUINEA
SOMALIA
MALAYSIA
SIERRA LEONE
ETHIOPIA
MALDIVES
LIBERIA
CAMEROON
COTE
BENIN
KENYA
INDONESIA
D'IVOIRE
TOGO
GHANA
TANZANIA
COMOROS
MALAWI
MOÇAMBIQUE
AUSTRALIA

Atlantic Ocean
Area of
Inset
Atlantic
Ocean
VENEZUELA
GUYANA
SOUTH AMERICA
SURINAM
Pacific
Ocean
FRENCH
GUIANA
BRAZIL

Predominantly (50 – over 90%)
Muslim population

Important (5 – 50%)
Muslim minorities

Sunnites   Shiites

The remainder of countries (which may
not be named or shown on the map)
have Muslim minorities of 0 – 5%.

Afghanistan

Afghanistan, previously a monarchy, was declared a republic following a coup d'état in July 1973 led by Muhammad Daud, the former Prime Minister. A further coup in April 1978, headed by the People's Democratic Party of Afghanistan (PDPA), established the Democratic Republic of Afghanistan, led by a Revolutionary Council and with close ties with the Soviet Union. Opposition to the new regime by pro-Islamic *mujaheddin* guerrillas led the government to call on assistance from the Soviet Union and Soviet troops invaded the country in December 1979. A prolonged civil war between the Soviet-backed government and *mujaheddin* forces engulfed the country for the next 13 years and took a new and dangerous turn in April 1992 after *mujaheddin* forces overthrew the regime of President Najibullah. Within days *mujaheddin* forces were locked in deadly combat with one another as the legitimacy of the newly-established ruling Islamic Jihad Council (IJC) under Imam Seghbatullah Mujjaddedi continued to be bitterly disputed by powerful sections loyal to the leader of the hardline **Islamic Party** (*Hezb-i-Islami*).

Although ethnically diverse, the overwhelming majority (99 per cent) of Afghanistan's population, estimated in 1990 to total 16,600,000, are Muslims; the rest are Hindus, Sikhs and Jews. Most Afghans are Sunnis who follow the Hanafi school of law. Sunnis predominate in among the country's largest and most important ethnic group, the Pashtun, as well as among the Aimaq, Baloch, Brahui, Mughal, the Persian-speaking Tajik and the Turkic-speaking Kirghiz, Turkmen and Uzbek. They also prevail among the Nuristani, the so-called "Kafirs" (unbelievers) of Kafiristan who are said to have converted to Islam in the 19th century, after which the name of their province was changed to Nuristan.

The Shia minority, prevalent among the Farsiwan, Hazara, Qizilbash, Turi and some Tajik, is divided between the Twelver (*ithna ashariyya* sect, representing about 15 per cent of the population), and a small group of Ismailis concentrated in the remote northern province of Badakshan. Among Sufi brotherhoods the best-established is the Naqshbandiyyah order, represented by the Mujjaddedi family, although the Qadiriyyah, headed by the Gailani family, and the Chishtiyyah orders are also widespread.

Islam and the state: developments in the republican era

The emergence of an Islamic opposition in Afghanistan, mainly after the Soviet invasion of December 1979, is a relatively new phenomenon as traditionally Islamic groups had seldom taken an active role. While the central government in Kabul had been careful not to alienate the Muslim religious establishment, avoiding any infringement of traditional interpretations of Muslim law and practice, it did not regard it as a source of active politics. A democratic

Constitution adopted in 1964 secured the continued support of Muslim clerics and scholars (*ulama*) by ensuring that democratic ideas were combined with Islamic religious and political beliefs. However, the formation at this time of the Communist Party of Afghanistan (CPA) is believed to have inspired an Islamic opposition which attacked the regime for its secular modernization and its alleged leniency towards the CPA.

The proclamation of a republic in July 1973 steadily eroded the modus vivendi which had existed between the government and Afghanistan's fiercely traditionalist and deeply devout tribesmen. Under pressure from reform-oriented army officers who had backed the republican coup, the Daud regime moved to introduce social and economic changes, many of which met resistance from sections of the liberal intelligentsia and tribal Muslim opinion.

Impatient with the pace of change, left-wing factions within the PDPA, backed by urban-based Marxist intellectuals, ousted Daud in April 1978 and initiated what came to be known (from the name of the month) as the Saur Revolution. In the months that followed, the new regime's commitment to a Soviet-style revolution underpinned by a systematic secularization of society gradually alienated the country's traditional religious and tribal leadership. In a series of decrees issued between April and November 1978, the government ordered the introduction of radical land reforms aimed at a more equitable distribution of property, abolished usury and rural indebtedness, and replaced Islamic law (*sharia*) by a civil code. At the same time the new regime also sought to effect social change, much of which was deemed by Muslim tribesmen to be un-Islamic, especially provisions raising the minimum age of marriage for women to 16 years and encouraging women to participate in co-educational adult literacy programmes which were secular in orientation.

In May 1978 Islamic and anti-communist parties opposed to the regime joined forces to create the National Rescue Front under the leadership of Burhanuddin Rabbani, a Tajik from Badakshan who had founded the **Islamic Society** (*Jamiat-i-Islami*) . By September there were reports of armed resistance by tribesmen (now calling themselves *mujaheddin* or "holy warriors") in Nuristan, Paktia and Ghazni provinces in the east and in Herat and Farah provinces in the west.

While some within the ruling establishment, including the country's new President, Nur Muhammad Taraki, and the Deputy Prime Minister, Babrak Karmal, appealed for restraint and stressed the need to retain Islamic policies acceptable to the country's tribal leadership, moderate opinion was steadily marginalized. By the autumn of 1979, however, the hardline policies of Hafizullah Amin, who had replaced Taraki as President in September, were proving unsuccessful as the country veered towards civil war in almost all provinces, prompting the mass exodus of Afghan refugees to Pakistan and Iran.

In December 1979 Soviet armed forces intervened, ostensibly to help restore stability. Amin was replaced by Karmal who was in turn replaced by Sultan Ali Keshtmand in June 1981. Riots, strikes and inter-factional strife continued throughout most of 1980-81 along with intensified resistance from Afghan *mujahedddin*, now engaged in a full-scale holy war (*jihad*) against Soviet occupying forces and what was seen as their "puppet regime" in Kabul.

Meanwhile the new government of Babrak Karmal sought to adopt a more conciliatory policy towards Afghanistan's religious leadership. In June 1981 Karmal announced the suspension of laws relating to debts and bride-price while constitutional reform entitled all Afghans to practise and profess Islam. The partial success of the government's policies was indicated in reports in June 1985 alleging that two leading Muslim spiritual leaders, Abdullah Agha and Asmatullah Muslim, had endorsed the reforms.

Between 1984 and 1989 the *mujaheddin* were aided and abetted, militarily and financially, by the United States, the United Kingdom and the People's Republic of China. Many guerrillas established bases across the border in the Pakistani town of Peshawar where they were subjected to constant government bombardment from land and air.

Attempts in 1986 by the government to adopt a policy of reconciliation with *mujaheddin* groups failed after the seven-party *mujaheddin* alliance, the **Islamic Union of Afghan Mujaheddin** (IUAM—*Ittehad-i-Islami Afghan Mujaheddin*), formed in May 1985, refused to accept a ceasefire or to engage in negotiations without the prior, complete and unconditional withdrawal of Soviet forces. The intensification of *mujaheddin* military attacks against government targets in 1988-89 was paralleled by developments on the political front leading to the withdrawal of Soviet troops under the terms of the Geneva Accord, signed in April 1988, and to the formation in February 1989 of the Afghan Interim Government (AIG) in Peshawar. This was composed of representatives from seven Pakistan-based Sunni *mujaheddin* groups. The legitimacy of the AIG, led by Seghbatullah Mujjaddedi, head of the **Afghan National Liberation Front** (*Jebh-i-Nejat-i-Milli Afghanistan*), was however, questioned by *mujaheddin* commanders operating inside Afghanistan and by the Iran-backed alliance of Islamic Shia factions, the Islamic Coalition Council of Afghanistan (ICCA, renamed the **Islamic Unity Party of Afghanistan** (IUPA—*Hezb-i-Wahdat-i-Afghanistan*) in June 1990). In March 1989 the status of the AIG was substantially enhanced after its recognition as the legitimate government of Afghanistan by the Islamic Conference Organization (ICO).

Meanwhile the government of Najibullah Ahmedzai (henceforth Najibullah), who had been elected president in September 1987, made fresh attempts to resolve the political deadlock by reaffirming its commitment to Islamic principles. A new Constitution, adopted in November 1987, declared that "Islam is the religion of Afghanistan and no law shall run counter to the principles of Islam". In an apparent reversal of the socialist objectives of the Saur Revolution, the Constitution also stated that "the hereditary right to property shall be guaranteed according to Islamic law". However, the lack of response to the government's overtures was paralleled by military stalemate, with Soviet and Afghan forces holding on to major cities while *mujaheddin* forces achieved numerous local victories.

Extensive international negotiations in the late 1980s which hoped to put an end to the civil war by drawing up plans for an interim government which would administer free elections failed after *mujaheddin* groups insisted that negotiations be preceded by the removal from office of Najibullah. Difficulties were compounded by increasing disunity, especially after 1989, among *mujaheddin* forces. While Iran-based Shia groups continued to operate independently of the AIG, the Sunni-dominated AIG was itself riven by divisions between Islamic hardliners backed by Saudi Arabia and the fundamentalist *Jamaat-i-Islami Pakistan* (JI), which favoured a military solution, and pro-monarchist moderates who favoured the resumption of political negotiations. In August 1989 these splits intensified after the withdrawal from the AIG of Gulbuddin Hekmatyar, leader of the largest faction of the *Hezb-i-Islami;* in May 1991 the AIG's Interior Minister, Yunus Khalis, leader of the *Hezb-i-Islami* (Khalis faction), resigned, accusing the AIG of "complicity" with the Kabul-based government. These moves came amid widespread reports, some of them subsequently confirmed, of atrocities, including murder, by members of opposing *mujaheddin* factions.

Disillusioned by the lack of progress in negotiations and buoyed by their mutual rapprochement, the USA and the Soviet Union announced in September 1991 that they would cease all military assistance to warring factions and would encourage other countries (Pakistan, Saudi

Arabia and Iran) to do likewise. The move prompted fresh negotiations between the Soviet Union and *mujaheddin* forces which ended in a joint statement in November 1991 endorsing the creation of an interim Islamic government in Afghanistan.

In January 1992 Pakistan, long a backer of hardline *mujaheddin* factions, announced its support for a UN plan aimed at the creation of a broadly-based interim government which would oversee free elections. An offer by Najibullah in March to hand over power to an interim government was followed within days by a major offensive in the north by *mujaheddin* forces loyal to Ahmed Shah Massoud, military commander of the *Jamiat-i-Islami*. On April 15 rival *mujaheddin* forces belonging to the JI and the *Hezb-i-Islami* (Hekmatyar faction) pre-empted a UN-brokered transfer of power when they forcibly removed Najibullah from office and seized all strategic government centres in Kabul.

On April 28 power passed from the republic of Afghanistan to a six-party (excluding the *Hezb-i-Islami* Hekmatyar faction), Islamic Jihad Council, headed by Seghbatullah Mujjaddedi, leader of the moderate **Afghan National Liberation Front** (*Jebh-i-Nejat Milli Afghanistan*). The new regime, although dominated by Pashtun Sunni groups, also included representatives from minority ethnic groups, notably the Tajik-dominated *Jamiat-i-Islami*, whose military chief, Ahmed Shah Massoud (dubbed the Lion of Panjsher), was appointed Defence Minister. In early June the IUPA declared that it would co-operate with the new government, resulting in the control of three Cabinet portfolios by members of the predominantly Shia Hazara ethnic group. Support for the IJC under Mujjaddedi continued, however, to be withheld by *Hezb-i-Islami* forces loyal to Hekmatyar.

The new government, despite being beset by intense factional in-fighting, immediately sought to initiate Islamic reform. On May 6 the 50-member IJC announced that all crimes against "Islamic law" would be tried in "people's courts" and on May 8 it decreed a total ban on the sale and consumption of alcoholic drinks and ordered all women to dress "in Islamic fashion". (Within hours of the *mujaheddin* take-over of Kabul, the price of female Islamic hoods (*burqas*) had tripled.)

The future and the stability of the new government continues to be highly uncertain. Challenged by formidable military opposition from hard-line *mujaheddin* forces, the Pushtu-dominated IJC may still confront stiff political opposition from sectarian (Shia) and ethnic minorities eager to displace the long-established Pushtun-Sunni political dominance.

FS

Major Islamic organizations

Afghan National Liberation Front
Jabh-i-Nejat Milli Afghanistan
Moderate organization, member of IUAM [see below].
Leader. Imam Sebghatullah Mujjaddedi (traditional Islamic scholar and head of Naqshbandiyyah Sufi order in Afghanistan); president of the AIG and subsequently head of the IJC until June 1, 1992.

Membership. 35,000.

Afghani Nasr Organization
Sazmane Nasr
Largest Iran-based Shia organization; part of IUPA [see below].
Leader. Abdul Karim Khalili.
Membership. 50,000.

Afghanistan Party of God

Hezbollah-i-Afghanistan

Government-approved Islamic party founded in Kabul in 1990.

Leader. Alhaj Shaikh Ali Wosoqusalam Wosoqi (chair).

Da'wa Party of Islamic Unity of Afghanistan

Da'wa-i-Ittehad-i-Islami Afghanistan

Shia group; member of the IUAP, with support in Ghazni province.

Guardians of Islamic Jihad of Afghanistan

Pasdaran-i-Jihad-i-Afghjanistan

Shia organization which is a member of Tehran-based IUPA [see below].

Leader. Led collectively by 10-member council.

Islamic Force of Afghanistan

Nehzat-i-Afghanistan

Shia group; a member of IUAP with a wide following in the Jogore area of Afghanistan.

Leader. Collective leadership concentrated in a three-member council.

Islamic Movement of Afghanistan

Harakat-i-Islami Afghanistan

Shia organization whose precise status in relation to its membership of the IUAP [see below] is unclear. Some reports, observing its closeness to the Iranian government, infer its membership while others note the anti-Iranian stance of its leader, reportedly the only Afghan Shia leader with headquarters in Pakistan (Peshawar).

Leader. Ayatollah Aseh Mohseni.

Membership. 20,000.

Islamic Party (Hekmatyar faction)

Hezb-i-Islami (Hekmatyar faction)

Founded in 1979 after a split in the *Hezb-i-Islami*, it is reputed to be the largest and best-organized fundamentalist Islamic party; it has close links with the JIP and the sections of Pakistan army intelligence services handling Afghan affairs. A member of the IUAM, it withdrew from AIG in August 1989 and subsequently refused to co-operate with the *mujaheddin*-dominated Islamic Jihad Council (IJC) established in April 1992.

Leader. Gulbuddin Hekmatyar.

Membership. 35,000.

Aim. The creation of a strict Islamic state in Afghanistan.

Islamic Party (Khalis faction)

Hezb-i-Islami (Khalis faction)

Fundamentalist faction created after a split over personal differences with Gulbuddin Hekmatyar, rival leader of the *Hezb-i-Islami*, in 1979. The group is reported to have a wide following among Afghan refugees in Pakistan and to have received substantial assistance from the US Central Intelligence Agency (CIA). A member of the IUAM [see below], the faction quit the AIG in May 1991 accusing it of complicity with the Kabul-based government.

Leader. Mawlawi Muhammad Yunus Khalis (appointed Interior Minister in the AIG).

Membership. 20,000.

Islamic Party of the People of Afghanistan

Kabul-based, government-approved, Islamic party.

Leader. Alhaj Maulvi Ruhollah Abed.

Islamic Society

Jamiat-i-Islami

Tajik-dominated group founded in 1970. The group's military commander, Ahmed Shah Massoud, who wrested control of the Panjsher Valley from Soviet forces in 1979, is reputed to have been instrumental in forging the Tajik-Pashtun anti-government alliance which finally toppled the Najibullah regime in April 1992. The group is a member of the IUAM and its military chief, Massoud, was allocated the powerful defence portfolio in the IJC in May 1992.

Leader. Burhanuddin Rabbani (a Tajik who took

over from Mujaddedi as head of the IJC in June 1992).

Membership. 20,000.

Aim. The creation of an Islamic state in Afghanistan (on lines less rigid than those advocated by the fundamentalist *Hezb-i-Islami*).

Publication. The party organ is *Afghan News* (in English).

Islamic Struggle for Afghanistan

Narave Islami Afghanistan

Shia organization; member of the IUPA [see below].

Leader. The group's most prominent member is Zaidi Mohazzizi.

Islamic Union of Afghan Mujaheddin (IUAM)

Ittehad-i-Islami Afghan Mujaheddin

Founded in May 1985 as an alliance representing seven Sunni Islamic factions, both moderate and fundamentalist; its headquarters are in Pakistan.

Leader. The organization has a rotating leadership which changes every three months.

Membership. 100,000.

Islamic Unity

Ittehad-i-Islami

Militant Sunni fundamentalist organization representing the puritanical stream of Saudi Arabian-inspired *Wahhabi* Islam, it has had extensive financial and military support from Saudi Arabia (Saudi advisers are believed to have ordered members of the groups to kill all Soviet prisoners-of-war); a member of the IUAM [see above]. The group was involved in pitched street battles with rival Shia factions belonging to the Islamic Unity Party of Afghanistan (*Hezb-i-Wahdat-i-Afghanistan*) following the ousting of the Najibullah government in April 1992.

Leader. Abdul Rasul Sayyaf.

Membership. 15,000.

Aim. The creation of a Sunni Islamic state inspired by Saudi-Arabian Wahhabism.

Islamic Unity Party of Afghanistan (IUPA)

Hezb-i-Wahdat-i-Afghanistan

Founded in June 1990 with headquarters in Tehran; formerly known as the Islamic Coalition Council of Afghanistan (ICCA), it represents a nine-party alliance of Shia groups.

Leader. Rehmat Ullah Mutazawi.

Movement for Islamic Revolution

Harakat-i-Inqilab-i-Islami

Moderate organization; member of IUAM.

Leader. Mawlawi Muhammad Nabi Muhammadi (traditional Islamic scholar known for his anti-Shia views).

Membership. 20,000.

National Islamic Front

Mahaz-i-Milli-Islami

Dubbed "Gucci mujaheddin" by the Western media, this small but visible moderate Pashtun-dominated organization is a member of IUAM [see above] and has consistently favoured the return to Afghanistan of ex-King Zahir Shah.

Leader. Pir Saiyid Ahmed Gailani (head of the Sufi Qadiriyyah order in Afghanistan).

Membership. 20,000.

Party of God

Hezbollah

Militant Shia organization; member of IUAP.

Leader. Qari Ahmed (also known as Qari Yakdasta).

Union of the Companions of the Prophet

Ittehad-i-Ansarollah

Government-approved Islamic party founded in 1988.

Leader. Haji Zafar Muhammad Khadem.

United Islamic Front for Afghanistan

Jabhe Muttahid-i-Afghanistan

Shia organization with strong following among ethnic Hazara; member of Tehran-based Islamic Unity Party of Afghaniatan [see above].

Leader. Collective leadership.

Unity Council

Shoora-i-Ittefaq

Shia organization with broad-based support but concentrated mainly in the Hazarajat area; member of the IUPA.

Albania

Seventy per cent of Albania's population, estimated in mid-1990 to total 3,250,000, are Muslims, making it the only European country with a Muslim majority. (Muslims also form the majority among an estimated 1,900,000 ethnic Albanians living in the province of Kosovo in Yugoslavia.)

Albanian Muslims are mainly Sunnis of the Hanafi school. The heterodox Shia Bektashi sect concentrated in the south is also important, having claimed the support of up to 15 per cent of Albania's Muslims in the pre-war period.

Islam under Communism

The 1950 Constitution, which guaranteed the right to religious freedom so long as churches refrained from political activity, masked the communist regime's hostility to religion. By 1967 Albania's communist party, renamed the Party of Labour of Albania (PLA) in 1948, had succeeded in imposing a ban on the practice of religion and dismantling all religious institutions. Up to 2,000 mosques and churches were reported to have been demolished, the rest converted into museums or sports halls. In 1976 the country's new Constitution formalized the end of religious organizations and reaffirmed Albania's commitment to the creation of an atheistic social and political order.

As a majority, Muslims in Albania have not faced problems of discrimination common to Muslim minorities elsewhere in the Balkans. It should be noted, however, that while the ire of the communist regime may have been directed mainly against the minority Eastern Orthodox and Roman Catholic churches, the country's Islamic links were cynically exploited to lessen Albania's international isolation by promoting closer relations with Muslim states in the Middle East.

The communist era in Albanian history drew to a close in March 1991 following the country's first democratic elections after months of anti-government protests. Fresh elections in March 1992 produced a victory for the opposition Democratic Party which defeated the ruling Socialist Party of Albania (SPA), formerly the PLA).

Islam in the post-Communist era

Freedom for followers of Islam came in December 1990 when President Ramiz Alia lifted the ban on religion and ordered the re-opening of mosques and churches. Although Albania continues to adhere to a secular constitution, provisional legislation adopted in April 1991 grants Muslims, and members of all other religious denominations, "the freedom of religious belief and creates conditions in which to exercise it".

In January 1991 the country's first legal Muslim service in 23 years was held in a Tirana mosque. Around 50 mosques were reported to have been left intact from a pre-war total of 700. In February 1992 a Muslim religious seminary (*madrassa*) was inaugurated at a new mosque in Durrës aimed at training preachers.

The presence at this occasion of representatives from religious associations in Libya and Saudi Arabia was regarded as an indication of Albania's growing ties with the Muslim world abroad. In 1991 some 180 Albanian Muslims, the first in 60 years, were reported to have performed the pilgrimage to Mecca (*hajj*) with financial assistance from Saudi Arabia. In June 1992 King Fahd issued a directive to increase the number of Albanian Muslim pilgrims who were to be accommodated at his personal expense from 150 to 300.

The majority of Albania Muslims today are represented by the *Beshkesia Islamike Shqiptare* (Albanian Islamic Community), founded in Tirana in 1991 under the chairmanship of Hafiz Sabri Koci. The Muslims' spiritual head is the Grand Mufti of Albania, Hafiz Salih Terhat Hoxha.

The Bektashi sect is represented by the World Council of Elders of the Bektashis, founded in Tirana in 1991 under the chairmanship of Reshat Baba Bardhi.

GR

Islamic organizations

There appear to be no specifically Muslim political organizations in Albania although there are a number working for the rights of Albanians abroad. These include the three given below.

Democratic Alliance
Political party representing Albanians in Kosovo.

Forum for the Protection of Rights of Muslims
Civil and religious rights group representing Albanians in Kosovo.

Party for Democratic Prosperity
Representing Albanians in Macedonia.

Algeria

Algeria became independent in 1962 after an eight-year war against French colonial rule. Virtually all Algerians, out of a population estimated in mid-1990 at 24,960,000, are Muslim. About 20 per cent of Algerians are Berber-speakers; the rest are Arabic-speakers. The great majority of non-Arabs are Kabyles while other Berber-speakers are the Tuareg of the Sahara.

Most Algerians follow the Sunni Malikite school of law, although a small number follow Hanafi rites. There is a small community of Ibadites in the M'zab region. Among Sufi orders, the Shadhiliyyah (*tariqa*) and the Qadiriyyah brotherhoods are most strongly represented. In desert villages most adult males belong to the Wazzaniyyah brotherhood which has its centre in Ouezzane, Morocco.

Under French colonial rule Islamic institutions and practice were subject to a number of formal restrictions. A law passed in 1866 required Algerian Muslims eligible for French citizenship to renounce their judicial status as Muslims subject to Islamic law. The measure coincided with increasing curbs on the jurisdiction of Islamic *sharia* courts following the intensification of Christian missionary activity in Kabyle areas.

In 1874 the number of judges (*qadis*) administering Islamic law was reduced by more than half, and Islamic courts were later ordered to hear exclusively cases concerned with family law, making the crucial area of land tenancy the preserve of French courts.

The anti-Sufi Salafiyyah reform movement which became influential in the early 20th century formed the kernel of the Islamic element of Algerian nationalism and, subsequently, of establishment Islam. The pro-Salifiyyah **Association of Reformist Ulama** (religious scholars), founded in 1931 by Shaikh Abd al-Hamid Ben Badis, joined the anti-colonial resistance led by the National Liberation Front (Front de Libération Nationale) (FLN) in 1956.

Islam and the state: Developments since independence

Algeria's Constitution, adopted in 1976, recognized Islam as the state religion but refrained from making Islamic law (*sharia*) an integral part of the country's legal system. Muslim jurists were not accorded an independent role in national legislative matters but were instead subject to centralized control by a Minister of Religious Affairs who had the final authority to appoint or dismiss clergymen, review Friday sermons, administer religious endowments (*awqaf*), control religious publications and set up religious institutions.

Under Ahmed Ben Bella, president from 1962 to 1965, the **Uprising** (*Al-Qiyam*) movement, regarded as a precursor of present-day fundamentalist movements, enjoyed tacit official approval as the opponent of secular, left-wing trends among trades unionists and university students. *Al-Qiyam* was eventually suppressed by Houari Boumedienne, president from 1965 to 1978, and one of the movement's most prominent leaders, Muhammad Khidar, was assassinated.

During the 1970s Islamic radicals were both courted and alienated by the government. In 1970 Mouloud Kassim, Minister of Education and Religious Affairs, launched a campaign against the "deterioration of morals" which was designed to win support from Islamists and in 1971 he initiated steps to promote Arabic as the official language in schools and the civil service. This Arabization campaign (renewed with fresh vigour in 1980), together with the issue of family law, was to continue as focal points of Islamist pressure on the government during the 1980s.

At the same time the government's policy on the nationalization of private property and its rapprochement with sections of the Algerian left were regarded by Islamic radicals as essentially anti-Islamic. The government's Arabization programme, which worked against the employment prospects of an urban under-class with limited linguistic skills, ironically helped to swell the ranks of the Islamist movement.

The **League of the Call** (*Rabitat al-Da'wa*), which rose to prominence in the late 1970s, expressed the dissatisfaction of growing numbers of Algerians with the content and direction of state policy.

In June 1984 Chadli Benjadid, who had succeeded Boumedienne as president in 1979, promulgated the *Code de la Famille* which endorsed polygamy on the terms permitted under Islamic law and upheld the right under Islamic law of the husband (but not the wife) to secure divorce on demand.

Meanwhile Islamic radicals moved to seize control of the country's estimated 9,073 mosques, under the control of the government for two decades, by establishing independent places of worship and appointing their own clerics (*imams*). Clashes between security forces and Islamic factions erupted in Laghouat in 1981 and on the Ben-Aknoun campus of the University of Algiers in November 1982, and ended in a ban on the *al-Da'wa* organization.

With the trend towards greater democratization in Africa and eastern Europe, the government came under increasing pressure from Islamists to introduce the alternative Quranic system of consultation (*shura*). Many pressed for the creation of an Islamic state, in which ultimate sovereignty rested with God rather than with the people and in which the ruler was bound to consult the Muslim community (*umma*) and religious scholars (*ulama*).

Some of the leaders of this as yet loosely defined Islamic movement, including Shaikh Ahmed Sahnoun and Shaikh Abdellatif Soltani of the *al-Da'wa* organization, were clerics and religious scholars from Algeria's traditional religious leadership. Soltani had since the mid-1970s been an outspoken critic of the regime's brand of "socialism" and, like Sahnoun, had been active in the Association of Reformist Ulama. Soltani's burial at an Algiers cemetery in 1984 was the occasion of a large Islamist demonstration.

The Algerian Islamic Movement (*Mouvement Islamique Algérien*), active from 1981 to 1987, represented the transition of the Islamic opposition from non-violent to armed resistance. Shunned by the traditionally-minded *ulama* (religious scholars), under its leader Mustafa Bouyali the movement engaged in a series of armed confrontations with security forces, including a spectacular attack in 1985 on a police barracks in Souma, south of Algiers, which ended in January 1987 with the killing of Bouyali in a police ambush in the Atlas mountains.

In June 1987 200 alleged supporters of Bouyali were tried and four sentenced to death.

Other small Islamic groups active in the late 1980s and early 1990s were also said by the authorities to be preparing for an armed insurrection and to have financial and military assistance from sections of the Afghan *mujaheddin* and from Islamic radicals in Iran, Saudi Arabia and Sudan.

Meanwhile the government attempted to quell Islamic opposition by building new Islamic institutes, schools and teaching centres, and by encouraging the training of a greater number of clerics (*imams*). In 1985 135 alleged Muslim fundamentalists were released from prison and others had their sentences reduced.

Anti-government riots in Algiers in October 1988, in which between 150 and 200 people were reported killed, spread quickly to the Belcours and Bab al-Oued districts of Algiers where thousands of Muslim fundamentalists staged demonstrations. A group calling itself the Movement for Algerian Renewal assumed responsibility for the riots. Following the disturbances, President Benjadid received proposals for a programme of Islamic reform from leading Muslim fundamentalist leaders including Shaikh Sahnoun, Shaikh Ali Bin al-Haj and Shaikh Mahfouz Nanah.

The revised Constitution of 1989 established a Superior Islamic Council (SIC—*Conseil supérieur islamique*) under Shaikh Ab al-Hamid ibn Badis, a central religious institution with advisory powers. The SIC has recommended an increase in religious education in secondary and higher education, greater air-time for religious programmes on television and radio, and the prohibition of the sale of material deemed "harmful" to Muslims.

In February 1989 Algerians approved in a referendum the text of the new Constitution which contained no reference to socialism and only a passing reference to the FLN, and which accorded a more limited role to the military. However, while it recognized the right to create "associations of a political nature", subsequent legislation in July 1989 prohibited the formation of political parties based on religion or claiming to protect or defend Islam.

In local elections held in June 1990, the **Islamic Salvation Front** (*Front Islamique de Salut*—FIS), recognized as a legal political party since February 1989 and led by the radical Shaikh Abbasi Madani and Shaikh Ali Belhadj, won control of a majority of municipal and provincial assemblies, with 55 per cent of the overall vote.

Legislative elections scheduled for June and July 1991 were cancelled after a general strike called by the FIS in May 1991 to demand revisions to the electoral law, early presidential elections and the establishment of an "Islamic state" led to widespread disturbances, the deaths of scores of demonstrators and the imposition of a state of emergency.

With the arrest in June of Madani and Belhadj, the new non-party government installed under Prime Minister Sid-Ahmed Ghozali hoped to secure the co-operation of a less radical current within the FIS leadership led by Said Guechi.

In the first round of voting in the general elections, in December 1991, 231 of the 430 seats in the National Popular Assembly were decided. The FIS won 188 of these, making it almost certain that it would form a majority government after the second round of voting (scheduled for January 16, 1992) and would thus implement its project for an "Islamic state". Neither of the more moderate Islamic organizations, **Movement of the Islamic Society** (Hamas) and the **Renaissance Party** (*En-Nahda*), won seats in the first round, although they were due to contest some constituencies in the second round.

On January 11, 1992, President Benjadid resigned and presidential powers were assumed by a provisional body, the High Committee of State (HCS). The HCS, headed by Mohammed Boudiaf, a veteran leftist dissident of the 1960s, was widely reported to be subservient to the military. In a move designed to placate Islamists, the HCS also included the Algerian-born rector of the Paris Mosque, Tedjini Haddam.

The second round of voting in the legislative elections was cancelled and the following weeks saw violence between the army and demonstrators in Algiers and elsewhere, with casualties and the detention of some thousands of FIS members or sympathizers. The new authorities indicated that by-laws prohibiting political activity in and around mosques would be strictly enforced, and promised immediate measures to alleviate Algeria's worst economic problems.

In February Guechi became Minister of Employment and Vocational Training and Sassi Lamouri, a former FIS supporter, was appointed Minister of Religious Affairs.

In March 1992 the government banned the FIS on the grounds that it violated the July 1989 law on political parties [see above] which forbade the existence of any party created exclusively on the basis of religion. In a measure reportedly aimed at breaking FIS control over municipal councils, the government also approved the suspension of 397 of the country's 1,541 municipalities. In April FIS leaders Madani and Belhadj were formally charged with inciting armed rebellion and sabotage and in May a military court sentenced to death 13 Muslim fundamentalists allegedly linked to the FIS.

EB

Major Islamic organizations

Algerian Islamic Movement
Mouvement Islamique Algérien
Formed in 1961, it was responsible for a number of bomb explosions and guerrilla operations in the Larba region south-east of Algiers, as well as for an armed attack on a police barracks in Souma, south of Algiers. In January 1987 members of the group were ambushed by police at a hideout in the Atlas mountains.
Leader. Unknown; the group's former leader Mustafa Bouyali was killed in the 1987 ambush.
Structure. There are believed to be sixteen cells dedicated to armed opposition to the regime.
Aims. Include establishment of an Islamic state governed by a Quranic Consultative Council.

Association of Muslim Brothers
Jammat al-Ikhwan al-muslimun
Heavily influenced by Egyptian and Syrian fundamentalism, this group was already active in the 1960s. During the government of Houari Boumedienne it denounced state socialism, nationalization and religious reforms and sought greater recognition for religious education.

Association of Reformist Ulama
Formed in 1931 by Shaikh Abdel Hamid Ben Badis (d. 1940), it espoused the ideas of the Salafiyyah reform movement and maintained that the interpretation of Quranic principles in line with contemporary conditions would allow the Muslim community to challenge Western hegemony. In 1956 it joined the anti-colonial resistance led by the FLN.
Aims. Reform of religious and secular education.

Islamic Salvation Front
Front Islamique de Salut (FIS)
al-Jibhat al-Inqath
Officially recognized as a political party in

February 1989, the party was banned in March 1992 on the grounds of having violated a July 1989 law which prohibited political parties formed on a religious basis. The organization rose to prominence after it won 55 per cent of the vote in municipal elections held in June 1990. In December 1991 the FIS won 188 out of 231 seats in the first round of voting to elect members to the National Popular Assembly. (The second round was cancelled.)

Leader. The organization's consultative council (*majlis ash-shoura*) provides for a collective leadership. In June 1991 the FIS's principal spokesmen were Abbasi Madani (b. 1931) and Ali Belhadj (b. 1958), both imprisoned in that month. Abdelkader Hashani led the FIS through the December 1991 elections but was imprisoned in January 1992. A less radical current, led by Abdel Guechi, co-operated with the provisional Higher Committee of State (HSC) under Boudiaf. The organization is reported presently to be under the control of a moderate faction led by Muhammad Said.

Aims. Its supporters among the clergy advocated the creation of an Islamic state run in accordance with the *sharia* and based on the Islamic concept of "consultation" (*shura*). Its party programme, as published in 1991, promised the renovation of social, political and economic life in accordance with Islamic precepts and the historical experience and special characteristics of the Algerian people, the reform of the educational system and the media in conformity with Islamic precepts, a higher level of education and behaviour among women, payment for women involved in childcare at home, improved standards of living for retired people, and accountability for public officials.

Publications. The party organ is *al-Mounquid*.

League of the Call
Rabitat al-Da'wa

An ostensibly non-political organization believed to have been founded in the late 1970s which rose to prominence as an active and organized movement in 1980 under the leadership of Shaikh Sahnoun (who had earlier founded the *Al-Irshad wal-Islah*) and Shaikh Abd al Latif Sultani.

Leader. Shaikh Ahmed Sahnoun (who later went on to found *Hamas* [see below]).

Aims. The promotion of Islamic values and scholarship throughout Algeria and the promotion of observance of the *sharia* legal code.

Movement of the Islamic Society
Harakat al-Mujtamaa al-Islami (Hamas)

Moderate Islamic organization founded in December 1990 in opposition to the FIS and what it deemed to be the FIS's attempt to dominate the Islamic movement in Algeria.

Leader. Shaikh Mahfouz Nanah.

Aims. It offered a less radical Islamic alternative to the FIS, with an emphasis on a reformist interpretation of Quranic precepts, a respect for human rights and for women's rights in the workplace, and a consolidation of the democratization process.

Party of God
Hezbollah

Unsuccessfully applied for recognition as a political party in March 1990. Three alleged members of the group were sentenced to death by a criminal court in Tlemcen in March 1992 on charges of murder in connection with an incident near Tlemcen in July 1990.

Renaissance Party
En-Nahda

Emerged from the independent Islamist movement at the University of Constantine in the late 1970s. In July 1991 its leadership emphasized that it was ready to co-operate with attempts to achieve a national consensus on electoral reform and proposed a "statute of opposition" guaranteeing the rights of opposition parties.

Leader. Abdallah Djaballa.

Aims. The establishment of an Islamic state with

the *sharia* as its legal code, but maintaining respect for political pluralism; continued national ownership of natural resources as well as the encouragement of private initiative.

Repentance and Flight
At-Takfir wal-Hijra
Clandestine organization, said to be linked with Egyptian group of the same name, representing Algerians some of whom reportedly trained with Afghan *mujaheddin* in Afghanistan. From 1982 members became known for their fanaticism in the poorer districts of Algiers. In June 1991 their presence was reported in disturbances in the capital and they were sometimes denounced as *agents provocateurs* by Islamist parties. The group was implicated in an attack on a border post at Guemar, on the Tunisian border, in November 1991. In February 1992 four alleged members of the group were arrested in Blisa, near Algiers.
Leader. Tayeb al-Afghani (according to unconfirmed reports).

Aims. There was no clear information as to its aims, which were assumed to include the overthrow of the FLN-dominated government and the institution of a fundamentalist Islamic regime.

Uprising
Al-Qiyam
Created in 1964 by Malik Bennabi, it was dissolved in 1966 and officially banned in 1970. Professing a Salafiyyah outlook, the organization was also influenced by the ideas of Hassan al-Banna, the founder of the Egyptian Muslim Brotherhood, and his disciple, Sayyid Qutb.
Leader. Al-Hashemi Tijani (president at the time of the party's proscription).
Aims. Implementation of the *sharia* and the establishment of a "single state, with a single leader, founded on Muslim principles".
Publications. The party organ is *Majallat al-Tadhib al-Islami* (Review of Muslim Education).

Argentina

The Federal Republic of Argentina is overwhelmingly European in ethnic composition. The heavy influx of Italian and Spanish immigrants during the early 20th century meant that almost 85 per cent of Argentina's population is of European descent, with the rest claiming *mestizo* (mixed race), Indian and other origins.

The first Muslim immigrants to arrive in Argentina in the 16th century were Spanish Moors (Moriscos). Their culture has generally not survived, though it exerts a considerable influence over Argentinean literature and the arts.

Immigrants from "greater Syria" (Syria and Lebanon) constitute the third largest ethnic group after the Spanish and Italians. However, most "greater Syrians" are Christian, Muslims being a minority amongst them. The predominance of Christian Arabs is a key factor which explains the weakness of Islamic culture in Argentina.

Reliable estimates in 1980 showed that Muslims in Argentina numbered close to 370,000, of a total of 1,500,000 Arabs. Mainly Syrian (65 per cent) and Lebanese (25 per cent) in origin, many migrated to the country in the 1880s, reaching peak numbers between 1918 and 1939. The majority, around 80 per cent, are Sunnis, 10–12 per cent are Shias from Lebanon, and the remainder are Alawis or Druze from "greater Syria". Concentrated in Buenos Aires, where there are estimated to be up to 50,000 Muslims, members of the community tend mostly to be involved in trade and small industry.

Islam has been subjected to severe restrictions in Argentina; historically Muslim officials, including state governors and senior military personnel, have been forbidden to use their Islamic names. It is believed that many Muslims have been baptized into the Roman Catholic faith in order to secure advantages in their economic or professional lives.

Official hostility to Islam has meant that Islamic institutions and organizations have tended, on the whole, to remain under-developed. No mosques existed in Argentina in 1984, although two were planned, for Buenos Aires and Cordova. However, an Islamic centre established in Buenos Aires in 1918 provides Islamic instruction and facilities for Muslim prayers. The centre, which employs a religious leader (*imam*), purchased its own building in 1968. Buenos Aires also enjoys the facility of an Islamic school with an estimated 250 pupils.

More recently there have been indications of political activity among some sections of the Muslim population, which are believed to have established links with radical Islamic factions abroad. In March 1992 the Lebanese-based Shia organization, *Islamic Jihad*, claimed that Abu Yasser, a suicide bomber allegedly responsible for a car-bomb outside the Israeli embassy in Buenos Aires, which killed 28 people and injured 200 others, had been an Argentinean convert to Islam. Other reports indicated that the attack, believed to be a reprisal for the Israeli-endorsed assassination of Sheikh Abbas Musawi, leader of the Lebanese organization, *Hezbollah*, may have been organized by Argentine Muslim groups opposed to the government's involvement during the Gulf War in the allied naval blockade against Iraq—the only Latin American state to do so.

MCB

Islamic organizations

Arab Argentinian Islamic Association (AAIA)
Established in 1960, this association opened the first Muslim school in Argentina.

Australia

Australia is a federal democracy with the British sovereign, represented by a Governor-General, as the head of state. Government is in the hands of a Prime Minister and Cabinet, answerable to a directly elected legislature, although a considerable amount of power is also devolved to the individual states.

An overwhelming majority of Australia's population, estimated at 17,086,000 in mid-1990, is Christian, and although recent waves of immigration have contributed to the emergence of a significant Muslim minority totalling more than 200,000 or just over 1 per cent, its impact on the secular relationship between religion and politics has been minimal.

The first Muslims to visit Australia were probably Arab traders in the 10th century. Later, from the 14th century, Muslims visited Australia's northern shores from the Indonesian islands which had been colonized by Arabs.

Heavy Muslim immigration dates from the mid-19th century with Muslim Malays arriving in northern Australia to work as pearl divers or indentured labourers on sugar cane plantations. They were followed by "Afghans" (a generic term for immigrants drawn from the Indian subcontinent) who were imported by the British for their expertise with camels. Originally used to help explore the vast and arid Australian interior, they later branched into occupations such as camel breeding and haulage contracting. Indian indentured labourers were also brought to Australia in the late 19th century to work in the sugar cane plantations of Queensland.

In the early 20th century the new Australian state adopted a "white Australia" policy designed to exclude non-European immigrants. Nevertheless, from 1920 to 1950 there was a steady flow of Muslims from Albania and from 1948 to 1960 heavy immigration by Yugoslav and Turkish Cypriot Muslims. With the dismantling of the "white Australia" barrier in 1960, the number of non-European Muslim migrants rose, with many arriving from Lebanon, Egypt, Pakistan and Syria.

Although most of the descendants of the pre-1914 Muslim immigrants are no longer adherents of Islam, this is not true of the later waves of immigrants, many of whom raised their children as Muslims.

Organizational developments in the Muslim community

Afghan immigrants, living in small communities on the edge of European towns where they were often subject to severe racial discrimination, were among the first to attempt to found Muslim organizations. The majority of these scattered communities were based in South Australia, but some were also present in the other states.

Mosques were built in most states around the turn of the century, but in most cases Muslim communities remained isolated. Malay Muslims, based in Queensland and West Australia, were even less organized than the Afghans.

By 1948 the Muslim population appeared to be in a state of inexorable decline, with many mosques having fallen into disuse. This trend was halted by the post-war wave of immigrants. Muslim communities were reorganized in most of Australia's major cities in the early 1950s, with mosques being renovated and reopened.

Albanian Muslim societies were founded in Queensland and Victoria in the mid-1950s, and multinational Muslim organizations were established in Sydney and Melbourne in 1957. This trend continued in the 1970s with the rapid growth of new Muslim organizations, and a revival of some of those which had become derelict. Whereas in 1950 there was only one organized Muslim community, the number had risen to 58 in 1983. The states most heavily represented were New South Wales and Victoria with 17 organizations each, and Western Australia and Queensland with eight and seven organizations respectively.

SL

Islamic organizations

Australian Federation of Islamic Councils (AFIC)

Created in 1975, the AFIC was designed to organize Muslim societies on a geographical rather than a racial or sectarian basis.

Structure. Local Islamic societies in each of the country's nine states and territories form an Islamic Council designed to represent all Muslims within the state; the AFIC represents the final tier of this organization by serving as the co-ordinating body for these councils. A 10th council, the Australian Federation of Muslim Students Association (AFMSA), is also represented in the AFIC.

Aims. Securing recognition for Islam at the same level as other religions; liaison between Australian Muslims and the Muslim world community; securing financial stability for Muslim preachers (*imams*) and Australian Muslim societies; securing Islamic education for Muslim children.

Publication. Australian Minaret.

Australian Federation of Islamic Societies (AFIS)

Established in 1963 by the 10 or so organized Muslim societies then in existence in Australia. In 1975 the group was reconstituted as the Australian Federation of Islamic Councils [see above].

Structure. Despite a strong executive, the organization's work was hampered by the ethnic diversity of the Muslim population and the history of local organizations having been founded on a racial basis.

Aims. Initially the primary aim of the AFIS was to co-ordinate the activities of local Muslim organizations. Increasingly there were those within the organization who wished it to function as an Islamic pressure group, and in 1968 its constitution was altered towards this end.

Azerbaijan

(For a broad survey of Islam in the former Soviet Union see separate entry for the Commonwealth of Independent States)

Azerbaijan became a Union Republic in 1920, when Bolshevik forces liberated it from Allied troops, and, after a brief period as a constituent republic in the Transcaucasian Soviet Federal Socialist Republic, became a separate republic in 1936.

With a population of about 7,000,000, Azerbaijan is the only Muslim republic of the CIS with up to three-quarters of its people belonging to the Twelver (*Ithna'ashaariyya*) sect of Shi'ism; the rest adhering to the Sunni Hanafi school.

The most widely used language of administration and instruction in schools is Azerbaijani. In 1979, only 29.5 per cent of Azerbaijanis claimed a good knowledge of Russian as a second language.

The spread of Islam was symbolized by the opening in Baku in 1989 of the first school to teach the Quran for 70 years; 50,000 copies of the Quran in Azerbaijani and Arabic were printed in the same year.

Azerbaijan administers the Nakhichevan Autonomous Republic, created in 1924, and the autonomous region of Nagorny Karabakh. Nakhichevan is an Azerbaijani enclave in (Christian) Armenia bordred on one side by Iran, while Nagorny Karabakh is an enclave in Azerbaijan, inhabited mainly by Armenians. Both have been involved in a bloody civil war which began in 1988.

Azerbaijan's refusal to accede to Armenian demands for control of Nagorny Karabakh unleashed Azeri-led pogroms against Armenians in Sumgait and Baku in February 1988 and January 1990. According to Armenian sources, between 300 and 1,500 Armenians were killed and many more rendered victims of atrocities. Soviet sources claimed that up to 90 people died and a further 1,500 injured, mostly Armenians. The imposition of a series of states of emergency and the despatch of Soviet troops failed to quell communal unrest.

A peace plan negotiated by the Russian and Kazakh Presidents, Boris Yeltsin and Nursultan Nazarbayev, in September 1991, collapsed after reports emerged of continuing atrocities against the population of Nagorny Karabakh following the withdrawal of Russian forces from the region in December.

The conflict has a religious dimension. In October 1988, the then head of Shi'ite Islam and leader of the Spiritual Directorate in Baku, Ayatollah Allah-Shakur Pasha-Zadeh, attacked what he called the "enemies of Islam" and called for the "mobilization and vigilance of the faithful". His appeal was followed by mass demonstrations which coincided with the Islamic month of *Muharram*, traditionally a month of mourning for Shias, during which protestors in Islamic dress carried portraits of Shia leaders, including Iran's former spiritual leader,

Ayatollah Ruhollah Khomeini. The protests, which ended in a compromise settlement in November permitting Muslims to hold mourning ceremonies in private but to refrain from street marches, were instrumental in fuelling religious sentiment including calls for solidarity with Iran's four million Azerbaijanis.

Meanwhile Iran, despite its aid to the enclave of Nakhichevan, is reportedly wary of any further political involvement for fear of encouraging an irredentist movement among its own Azerbaijani population. Azerbaijan is looking increasingly to other Muslims states, notably Turkey and Pakistan, which recognized its independence in November and December 1991, respectively. In June 1992 it became the first of the former Soviet Muslim republics to join the Islamic Development Bank (IDB).

WS

Islamic organizations

National Defence Army
The main Azeri fighting force in Nagorny Karabakh which grew out of the National Defence Council, created in October 1991 by President Ayaz Mutalibov and the radical Azeri leader, Itibar Mehmedov.

National Front
Milli Jibhassi
Founded in February 1989.
Aims. Demands unification with Iranian Azerbaijan.

Popular Front
Khalqu Jibhasi
Leader. Abulfez Elcibey.

Social Democratic Party
Leader. Zardusht Ali Zade.

Bahrain

Bahrain, formerly a British Protectorate, was granted independence in 1971. Like other states of the Persian Gulf, it is characterized by ethnic diversity. According to 1990 estimates, 70 per cent of the population are Bahraini Arabs, 24 per cent Iranians, Indians and Pakistanis, 4.1 per cent other Arabs from elsewhere in the Middle East and North Africa, and 2 per cent European.

Eighty-five per cent of the population, estimated in 1989 at 489,000, is Muslim, of whom almost 60 per cent (according to other estimates 70 per cent) are Shia and just over 40 per cent (or 30 per cent) Sunni. Sectarian sub-sects characterize both major sects.

Bahrain's ruling family, the al Khalifa, are Sunni Muslims who follow the Maliki school of law; the commercial classes are divided into Sunnis, into migrants from southern Iran who follow Shafi rites, and into Twelver Shias, with strong links with Shia centres in Iran and southern Iraq. There are also small groups of Sunnis who adhere to the rigid Hanbali school of law, and Shia Akhbaris, traditionalists who eschew speculation and independent reasoning (*ijtihad*) as sources of law.

Bahrain has an absolute monarchy. The Amir governs with the assistance of an appointed Cabinet. Although the Constitution provides for a popularly elected legislature, the National Assembly was dissolved in 1975 on the grounds that it interfered with the administrative affairs of the government and has not been re-convened.

Islam is the state religion and the legal system is based on a combination of English and Islamic law. There is close consultation between the Amir and the heads of the religious sects, but beneath the surface tranquillity dissent is lively.

Since the suppression of the trade unionists in 1975 and the continuing disarray among left-wing organizations, the most serious opposition to the Bahraini regime has come from the country's Islamic movement, characterized as "populist", in terms both of its egalitarian principles and its commitment to a grassroots mode of organization.

The Islamic movement in Bahrain has taken two distinct forms: one advocating a relatively moderate, reformist social programme, supported by the island's Sunni community, and another, more radical, calling for the overthrow of the existing order, by violence if necessary. Support for the latter comes mainly from militant Shias.

In a country governed by a Sunni Amir, where 60-70 per cent of the population are Shia, Shia activism has been a constant threat, exacerbated by external factors, particularly developments in Iran.

In August 1979 Shia demonstrations on the occasion of the return of a close associate of the leader of the **Islamic Front for the Liberation of Bahrain** (IFLB), Hadi al-Mudarrissi, led to the arrest of 28 protesters and the expulsion of Mudarrissi. The protests had coincided with a call by Iran's religious leadership reviving Iran's historic claim to Bahrain and appealing to

Shias in the Gulf to stage a revolution on the Iranian model.

In April and May 1980 Shias in the capital, Manama, were involved in violent riots following the announcement of the execution of Iraq's Shia leader, Muhammad Baqer al-Sadr.

The most serious incident involving Shia militants occurred in December 1981 after a group of "revolutionary guards", trained in Iran and allegedly organized by the IFLB, attempted to overthrow the government and establish an Islamic state. Observers estimated that between 10 and 40 per cent of the Shia population in Bahrain were in favour of an Iranian-style Islamic republic.

Religiously inspired opposition has continued in more recent years and has included the unearthing in November 1988 of a pro-Iranian underground group with alleged military and financial links with the Lebanon-based *Hezbollah* (Party of God).

Tension has continued, with numerous claims that the Shias are now excluded from any significant role in the administration and government of Bahrain. A report by the human rights group Amnesty International in May 1991 claimed that a campaign of arbitrary arrests had been carried out by the authorities over the previous 10 years with the intention of intimidating various Shia communities in Bahrain. The efficiency of the state security forces in rounding up potential Islamic revolutionaries is such that the indigenous Islamist movement has now been severely weakened.

EW

Major Islamic Organizations

Call of Islam
al Da'wa al Islamiya
Shia grassroots populist organization founded in 1965 by a group of Bahraini students returning from Iraq. During the 1980s the group lost ground to activist Shia groups such as the IFLB, and in December 1983 it was dismantled by the Bahraini government.
Leader. The organization's most prominent figure is Shaikh Isa Qassin.
Aims. The creation of an Islamic state through cultural and political means and the implementation of a reformist social programme.

Islamic Action Organization
Sunni organization whose activist stance during the 1980s is said to have undermined support for the influential, though relatively quietist, Society for Social Reform [see below].

Islamic Enlightenment Society
Founded in 1972 as a Shia self-help group providing educational courses for the community. It was dismantled by the authorities in December 1984 after the discovery by police of a large arms cache.
Leader. Shaikh Isa Qassin.

Islamic Front for the Liberation of Bahrain (IFLB)
The most important clandestine Shia Muslim fundamentalist organization. Founded in Tehran in late 1978 or early 1979, it is known to work in close association with the radical Iraqi underground Shia movement *al Da'wa al-Islamiya* (Call of Islam). Since 1981 the IFLB has been based in Iran.
Leader. Shaikh Hadi al-Mudarrisi, a Shia of Iranian origin exiled by the late Shah of Iran, Muhammad Reza Shah Pehlavi. Deeply impressed by the Iranian revolution of 1979 and

the ideas of the late Ayatollah Khomeini. Mudarrissi was expelled by the Bahraini government in 1979 and again in 1981 following his alleged involvement in an anti-government conspiracy. He is reported to be living in Iran.

Aims. The creation of an Islamic state involving a ban on alcohol and the reintroduction of religious instruction in schools.

Society for Social Reform

Sunni revivalist organisation founded in 1948 which reportedly acts as a front for the Bahrain branch of the *Ikhwan al muslimun* (Muslim Brotherhood).

Aims. Educational and cultural reform along Islamic lines.

Society of the Call

Al Da'wa

Sunni fundamentalist group with a reportedly small following. Members live in imitation of the *salaf* (the first generation of Muslims, considered by later generations to be the most authoritative source for Islamic practice and guidance).

Bangladesh

The People's Republic of Bangladesh, (formerly East Pakistan), was established after a protracted and bloody civil war in 1971 which led to its formal secession from the Islamic Republic of Pakistan of which it had been part since 1947.

The Constitution of the new state, approved in November 1972, was initially based on the principles of nationalism, socialism, democracy, secularism and guaranteed freedom of religious worship. In 1977 a constitutional amendment replaced secularism with Islam and a further amendment in 1988 established Islam as the state religion.

Bangladesh is the largest Muslim country in South Asia. Estimates based on the country's 1981 census show that 86.6 per cent of its population (approximately 90,000,000 in 1981; 106,507,000 in 1989) were Muslim, 12.1 per cent were Hindu and the remaining 1.3 per cent were made up of Buddhists, Christians and followers of indigenous tribal religions.

While most Muslims are Sunnis belonging to the Hanafi school of jurisprudence, in Bangladesh Islam developed a strongly syncretic character, with Sufis employing the idiom of Hindu mythology to produce a distinctive local culture in which saint veneration figures prominently. Although some Bangladeshi Muslims claim non-Bengali Arab, Persian or Central Asian origins, the vast majority are local converts who responded to the appeal of Sufi mystics.

In the period leading up to the partition of India in 1947, Bengali Muslim support was a crucial factor in consolidating the movement for a separate Muslim state. Legislative elections held in the Muslim majority province of East Bengal produced a massive vote for the Muslim League and its campaign for a separate state.

However, by the early 1950s the League had lost its base of support in East Pakistan, winning only nine seats in the 1954 provincial elections. Although there were moves by the province's religious scholars (*ulama*), represented by the **Islamic System** (*Nizam-i-Islam*—NI), founded in 1953), to mobilize opinion in favour of an Islamic regime, the depth of Bengali nationalist feeling left the political initiative firmly in the hands of secular parties.

In the long run the common religious sentiment which had resulted in the creation of Pakistan failed to hold the two parts of the country together. The main reasons for the emergence of Bangladesh were the lack of Bengali participation in central decision-making processes and the steady economic deprivation of the province by a non-Bengali, often West Pakistan-based, commercial and industrial oligarchy.

During the 1960s the Awami League (AL), under the leadership of Shaikh Mujibur Rahman, emerged as the leading party in East Pakistan campaigning for a Six-Point programme which stressed provincial autonomy within a broadly secular framework.

Islamic political organizations did not on the whole support calls for greater autonomy for

East Pakistan. In 1970 the NI criticised the AL's brand of secular Bengali nationalism by emphasising the Islamic bond which held Pakistan together.

Other organizations, including the **Islamic Society** (*Jamaat-i-Islami*—JI, subsequently the *Jamaat-i-Islami Bangladesh*—JIB) and sections of the Muslim League (ML, subsequently **Bangladesh Muslim League**—BML), also denounced the advocates of Bengali nationalism, claiming that their actions were un-Islamic and opposed to the integrity of Pakistan.

In 1970 the AL won 160 out of 162 National Assembly seats allocated to East Pakistan in Pakistan's first genuinely democratic parliamentary election. Resistance by Pakistan's political and military establishment to the outcome of the election and the prospect, for the first time, of a Bengali-dominated government, led directly to the civil war that preceded the creation of Bangladesh.

Islam and the state: developments since independence

The victory of the AL and its ideology of Bengali nationalism, opposed by religious parties prior to the creation of Bangladesh, contributed substantially to the political marginalization of these parties for several years. The new regime banned all Islamic parties on the grounds of their alleged pro-Pakistan stance during the war, and maintained restrictions on their activities until July 1976, well after a coup d'etat which ended with the assassination of Shaikh Mujib in August 1975.

Islamic parties were the among the first to endorse the regime of General Ziaur Rahman, who assumed the office of President in April 1977. They also backed Ziaur Rahman's first act as President when he discarded "secularism" as one of the fundamental principles of the Constitution and abandoned a commitment to the gradual implementation of a secular system. Ziaur Rahman justified these steps as necessary to counteract unwelcome Indian influence in Bangladesh.

A hallmark of Bangladesh's Islamic parties has been their tendency to fragment into smaller groupings. By early 1978 the BML, which had sought to unite all pro-Islamic groups under a broad umbrella organization, was divided by intra-party factionalism over the question of whether or not to join forces with Ziaur Rahman.

Other Islamic parties, namely the JIB, NI, People's Democratic Party (PDP), Imrat Party and Islamic Ganotantrik Dal, which in August 1976 had formed the **Islamic Democratic League** (IDL), also developed differences over the question of the leadership of the IDL. On the eve of the 1979 elections the party split into several smaller groups.

Even the Labour Party, launched in July 1976 by a breakaway section of the ML intending to reconstruct society on the basis of Islamic ideology, was by 1979 divided into competing factions.

Under Ziaur Rahman, however, Islamic parties gradually improved their electoral record. Whereas in the 1970 elections Islamic parties had failed to win a single seat in East Pakistan (and were subsequently, in 1973, prohibited from contesting any seats), in 1979 the BML and the IDL, in alliance, emerged with 20 seats in the *Jatiya Sangsad* (parliament), the third largest political force after Ziaur Rahman's Bangladesh Nationalist Party (BNP) and the AL.

Although the two parties contested the elections under a joint symbol, they campaigned on different manifestos due to differences in their outlook towards Islam. The BML, representative of the modernist view of Islam, tried to appeal to voters' religious loyalties by promising to fight against the enactment of laws repugnant to the Quran and the Sunnah, but generally played down the role of Islam. The IDL, representing a more fundamentalist approach, committed itself to the introduction of an Islamic state. The alliance fared best in urban districts where Bengali Muslims resented the presence of well-established Hindu communities who remained influential in trade and commerce.

The Islamization of the Constitution continued under Ziaur Rahman's military successor, General Mohammad Hussain Ershad, who came to power in March 1982, almost a year after Ziaur Rahman's assassination in May 1981. Under Ershad's military regime, emphasis was laid on the Islamic identity of the country, which he said he would run according to Quranic principles. Critics of Ershad's Islamization policies argued that they were merely an expedient measure to encourage extra financial assistance from other Muslim countries, notably Saudi Arabia.

In the May 1986 general elections, boycotted by the BNP alliance, the JIB emerged as the leading Islamic party and the third largest party, in terms of seats won, after Ershad's *Jatiya Dal* (JD) (National Party), representing the reconstituted National Front, and the AL.

The JIB had earlier joined the opposition BNP and AL in anti-government agitation but had been quietened by promises that Ershad would seek the people's verdict on the issue of Islamization. Although this had succeeded in keeping the JI aloof from anti-government demonstrations, the JI and other Islamic fundamentalist parties continued to press for greater Islamization of the country.

In March 1988 fresh parliamentary elections, boycotted by the opposition, resulted in victory for the JD. In anti-government protests in the period leading up to the elections the JIB had formed part of the opposition alliance and its leaders had been detained alongside other opposition politicians.

During the election campaign Ershad announced that his government intended to introduce a bill "to provide religious identity to the nation by incorporating Islam as a state religion". In June 1988 a constitutional amendment establishing Islam as the state religion was approved by an overall majority in the Jatiya Sangsad. The amendment was, however, criticized by religious organizations including the fundamentalist Islamic Constitutional Movement (ICM) which described the move as "useless" and "hypocritical", and called on Ershad to hand power over to the *ulama* (religious leadership).

On the other hand, religious parties such as the JIB stressed that the amendment should have included a reference to both divine and popular sovereignty, and a commitment to render all laws consistent with the Quran and Sunnah (the example of the Prophet Muhammad). Ironically, the amendment itself was widely interpreted by political commentators as an attempt by the government to undermine the position of the JI.

In May 1990, 55 intellectuals issued a call for all opposition parties, including Muslim fundamentalist groups, to unite against Ershad. At the same time the opposition BNP pursued an active policy of building up links to create an anti-AL alliance, including a rapprochement with the JIB. Relations between secular parties and the JIB, however, remained difficult against the background of continuing violence between rival student supporters of the AL, BNP and JIB.

The forced resignation of Ershad at the end of 1990 led to a general election early in February 1991 which was won by the BNP under Khaleda Zia who was sworn in as the country's first woman Prime Minister in March. Although the BNP government fell short of an absolute majority (subsequently obtained in by-elections in September), it was able to secure pledges of support from smaller parties, notably the JIB which had won 18 seats and which was formally opposed to female leadership.

The post-electoral strength of the JIB was reflected in the election in December 1991 of Golam Azam as *Amir* (chairman) of the party. By publicly acknowledging, and formally rehabilitating, Azam, a Pakistani passport-holder, the JI demonstrated that it had made significant political gains. Azam, still regarded as a pro-Pakistan politician, had opposed the independence of Bangladesh in 1971 and had been stripped of his citizenship. In 1978 he had returned secretly to Bangladesh and had acted as unofficial chief of the party despite criticism from nationalist groups who called on successive governments to expel him from the country.

In April 1991 the government bowed to popular pressure and announced that Azam would be formally tried on charges of heading a political organization while a foreign national. Earlier, in March, more than 100,000 people had participated in a mock trial in Dacca which accused Azam of collaborating with the Pakistani army in the secret execution of thousands of Bengali nationalists, including some of the country's most eminent intellectuals.

SA

Major Islamic Organizations

Bangladesh Muslim League (BML)
Offshoot of the original Muslim League which led the movement for Pakistan in the 1940s. The party is broadly pro-Islamic, though not fundamentalist in that it has refrained from advocating an Islamic state. Although allied to the more fundamentalist IDL during the 1979 elections, the party was keen to maintain its distinct approach to Islamic reform and campaigned on a separate manifesto. In 1985 the BML joined the coalition National Front representing right-wing, pro-Ershad parties. The party is reported since 1988 to have split into rival factions with no single acknowledged leader.
Leader. Kazi Qadir (status disputed by rival factions).
Aims. Supports reform on the basis of Islamic ideals.

Freedom Party
Islamic political party founded in 1987 by retired army officers to oppose the AL.
Leader. Lt.-Col. (retd.) Said Faruq Rahman and Lt.-Col. (retd.) Khandakar Abdur Rashid (co-chairs).

Islamic Democratic League (IDL)
Alliance of Islamic parties including the JIB (which subsequently broke away), NI, PDP, Imrat Party and *Islamic Ganotantrik Dal* (Islamic Democratic League), and formed in August 1976 following the legalization of religious parties the previous year.
Leader. Maulana Abdur Rahim.
Aims. Committed to the introduction of an Islamic welfare state.

Islamic System
Nizam-i-Islam (NI)
Organization of orthodox *ulama* (religious scholars) formed in 1953.
Aims. To establish an administration based on Islamic principles.

Jamaat-i-Islami Bangladesh (JIB)
Islamic fundamentalist organization, an offshoot

of the original organization founded by Abul Ala Maududi in 1941. Opposed Bangladeshi independence in 1971 and was banned (along with other religious parties) until 1975. Following the legalization of religious parties in 1976, it briefly joined the IDL, representing a coalition of Islamic parties. In legislative elections held in May 1986 the JIB emerged as the third largest party after the JD and the AL. In fresh elections held in February 1991 the JIB won 18 seats and constituted the fourth largest party in the Parliament after the BNP, the AL and the JD.

Leader. Golam Azam (*Amir*—chairman); Maulana Matiur Rahman Nizami (secretary-general). From 1978 the JIB was secretly led by Azam, a Pakistani passport-holder and alleged opponent of the state of Bangladesh. In December 1991 Azam's election as *Amir* was met with widespread protests from opposition parties who demanded that he be tried for heading a political organization while remaining a foreign national. In March 1992 Azam was tried at a "mock-trial" in the capital, Dacca, attended by more than 100,000 people, and in April the government announced that it would bring formal charges against him.

National United Front (NUF)
Founded in 1991 as an alliance of 23 nationalist and Islamic parties.
Leader. Khandekar Mushtaq Ahmed.
Aims. Advocates Islamic values, a representative government and the economic emancipation of the people.

Zaker Party (ZP)
Fundamentalist religious party founded in 1989.
Leader. Syed Hasmatullah; Mustafa Amir Faisal (member of the Presidium).
Aims. Supports divine sovereignty and the introduction of an Islamic state.

Belgium

There are an estimated 250,000 Muslims in Belgium, the majority of whom are Moroccan, closely followed by Turks. Representing almost 2 per cent of a total population estimated in 1990 to be around 9,986,975, Belgium's Muslims are immigrants of relatively recent origin who arrived in the first half of the 1960s. Although widely dispersed around urban industrial centres including Anvers (Antwerp), Charleroi, Namur and Liège, Muslims are estimated to form up to 8 per cent of the population of Brussels where their presence has become increasingly manifest in recent years.

In spite of the relative lateness of north African and Turkish immigration, Muslims have acquired an important position in Belgian society due in large part to the rapid rise in the size of the Muslim population. Whereas in 1960 Muslims in Belgium totalled a mere 1,200, and in 1970 some 65,000, by 1985 the number had risen to some 200,000. According to official estimates reported in December 1991, Muslims form just over a quarter of the country's immigrant population totalling around 870,000, and the second largest religious category after Christians.

Muslims in Belgium are predominantly Sunni adhering to Maliki and Hanafi rites. There is reported to be a vast network of religious organizations, some more secret than others. Sections of the Egyptian-inspired *Ikhwan al Muslimun* (Muslim Brotherhood) and the *Association des Étudiants Musulmanes* (Association of Muslim Students), while being primarily interested in educational reform, have sought also to instil a more political approach to Islam, especially in Muslim intellectual circles. The Sufi orientations of the Alawiyyah and Sulaymanci brotherhoods—the latter with its well-established opposition to the Turkish secular state—also have wide support among the Muslim immigrant population.

There are an estimated 130 mosques and Muslim places of worship, more than half of which were established in the early 1980s. The infrastructure of mosques has resulted in a density (in relation to the Muslim population) that is almost comparable to that of the countries of origin of most Muslim immigrants.

While the Belgian Constitution does not acknowledge official religions, certain "recognized" religions are entitled to receive financial and other assistance from the state. A law passed in July 1974 granted Islam official recognition, thus permitting Muslims to benefit from the advantages hitherto reserved for other religions. Under the 1974 law the government is committed to paying salaries of teachers imparting Muslim religious instruction while refraining from intervening in their appointment which is generally left to the authorities of each religion. In 1984-85 more than 300 Turkish and Arabic-speaking teachers of religion were appointed in Belgian schools. Some 20,000 Muslim pupils in primary schools and about 9,000 Muslim pupils in secondary schools attended these courses.

Since 1974 the government has recognized the authority of the **Islamic and Cultural Centre of Belgium** (*Centre Islamique et Culturel de Belgique* —ICCB) in the appointment of religious teachers and the organizations of mosque committees.

Organizational developments in the Muslim community

Organized Islam in Belgium has tended to follow two distinct currents, "popular" as propounded by the ostensibly non-political **Missionary Society** (*Jamaat at- Tabligh*), and "established" as embodied by the Muslim World League (MWL)-sponsored ICCB. Organized Islam, especially the administration of mosques, has also been subject, more or less systematically, to direction by the governments of immigrants' native countries, many of which have sought to maintain tutelage over their expatriate citizens.

By far the most important rival claims to influence over Belgium's Muslim community have come from the *Jamaat at Tabligh* and the ICCB. Established as an offshoot of the similarly named Indian movement founded in the 1920s, the *Jamaat*'s influence in Belgium is said to have derived from the activities of its first *amir* (leader), a Moroccan immigrant who joined the *Tabligh* movement while on a visit to Bangladesh in the late 1960s. Although the movement has publicly refrained from engaging in political debate, it has played an important part in reinforcing symbols of Muslim cultural identity by promoting the wearing of beards and the traditional north African garb, the *djellaba*, as well as by advocating the spatial rearrangement of Muslim households to maintain sexual segregation.

Addressing the needs primarily of the less well-educated, the *Jamaat* has attempted to challenge what it deems the "Islam of the powerful" as embodied in the ICCB, established in 1969 as an outgrowth of the Saudi-backed MWL. Challenging the authority accorded to the ICCB by the government since 1974 [see above], the *Jamaat* in February 1985 inspired the formation of the **Federation of Mosques and Islamic Cultural Associations in Belgium** (FMICAB—*Fédération des Mosquées et des Associations Culturelles et Islamiques de Belgique*), which succeeded within months of its foundation in securing the removal and replacement of the director of the ICCB. In recent years the FMICAB has emerged as a prominent mediating body between the vast majority of ordinary Muslims and the government, and has steadily established its position as a leading representative of the country's mosques. Despite its unofficial links to the Tabligh movement, the FMICAB has been skilful in adopting a neutral position on issues eliciting strong Islamic sentiment as in April 1986, when it chose to distance itself from the radical Islamist posture of some Arab associations which had organized demonstrations to protest against the US bombing of Libya.

Although the *Jamaat* and the FMICAB have attempted to counteract the ICCB by skilful organization, their comparative lack of intellectual and financial resources has rendered them less able to withstand the forces ranged against them. The place occupied by the ICCB in Belgian society is not only enhanced by the official recognition of its authority in all "worldly matters" relating to Islam, but also by the considerable means put at its disposal by the MWL which has delegated the ICCB to act as its European section in charge of promoting the construction of mosques throughout Europe.

These rival claims for the loyalty of the Belgian Muslim community have been paralleled by the activities of the governments of Muslim immigrants' native states. The activities of the

Turkish government's Directorate of Religious Affairs (*Diyanet Baskanligi Isleri*), represented in Belgium by a diplomatic officer, are important in the management of mosques, many of which tend to be organized along national lines. Intervention in the organization of mosques is also periodically, though less efficiently, undertaken by the Moroccan consulate.

In March 1988 the Belgian Royal Commission for Immigration, in consultation with the Belgian government, sought to resolve the problem of competing claims from rival organizations by opting for the creation of a 13-member Supreme Council, dubbed *Conseil des Sages* (Wise Men's Council), consisting of representatives from the ICCB and the wider Muslim immigrant community. In April 1989 the government drafted formal proposals for the establishment of a *Conseil Supérieur des Musulmanes* (Supreme Council of Muslims) to act as a new representative body comprising spokesmen from the MWL, Muslim diplomats accredited to Belgium and persons from within the Muslim immigrant community.

Fears of the gradual emergence of fundamentalist currents were compounded in March 1989 after the director of the ICCB (appointed in 1985) and Imam of the main mosque in Brussels, Abdullah Ahdal, was shot dead, reportedly for not favouring a ban on the novel *The Satanic Verses* by the Indian-born writer, Salman Rushdie. The killing, subsequently claimed by a Lebanese group, Soldiers of Truth, was widely believed to have been committed with the active connivance of radical Islamic groups operating within the Muslim immigrant community.

FS

Islamic organizations

Federation of Mosques and Islamic Cultural Associations in Belgium (FMICAB)

Fédération des Mosquées at des Associations Culturelles et Islamique de Belgique

Founded in February 1985 reportedly at the instigation of the *Jamaat at Tabligh* to express opposition to the appointment of the director of the ICCB [see above], but more generally to counter the officially recognized authority of the ICCB. In 1985 the FMICAB was responsible for securing the dismissal of the ICCB's director who was replaced by Abdullah Ahdal, assassinated in March 1989.

Aims. To defend the resident Islamic community in Belgium; to organize and promote the teaching of Arabic and the Quran as well as teaching Islamic culture, particularly by the creation of Islamic schools; to nominate Muslim clerics *imams*; and to supervise the administration of member mosques.

Islamic and Cultural Centre of Belgium (ICCB)

Centre Islamique et Culturel de Belgique

Founded in 1979 as an offshoot of the Muslim World League (MWL), it is granted legal status by the government as an international organization. The ICCB acts as the European section of the MWL in charge of promoting the construction of mosques in Europe, and has normally accepted the nomination of the Saudi-backed MWL in the selection of its director. Since 1974 the ICCB has been officially recognized as the chief authority in matters relating to the appointment and education of Muslim clerics (*imams*), the administration of mosques and the selection of teachers of Islamic instruction. The ICCB occupies the main mosque in Brussels where its director also acts as the Muslim community's chief Imam.

Leader. Salman al-Rahdi.

Structure. The ICCB's administrative board

includes representatives of the Muslim diplomatic corps in Belgium and is chaired by the Saudi Arabian ambassador.

Missionary Society
Jamaat at-Tabligh

Founded as an offshoot of the popularly oriented Indian missionary movement founded by Muhammad Ilyas in the 1920s, the Belgian branch of the organization (which has an extensive network across Europe) became established in the late 1960s following the return of its then (Moroccan-born) leader (*amir*) from Bangladesh where he had participated in missionary activities. Although not designated a formal organization, its members, often itinerate preachers, tend to be formally grouped in the statutory form of non-profit organizations. The first of these, which still remains the *Tabligh* centre in Belgium, was constituted in 1975. Whilst members have refrained from public involvement in politics, their stress on Muslim cultural symbols, including the wearing of beards and advocacy of sexual segregation in the home, have helped consolidate the idea of a distinct Muslim communal identity.

Aims. "To promote the Islamic faith and the teaching of the Quran among Muslims." The *Tabligh* also organizes self-help social and cultural activities, including the teaching of Arabic as distinct from the Quran, aimed at Muslims in Belgium and elsewhere in Europe.

Benin

The Republic of Benin (known as the People's Republic of Benin from 1975 to 1990) gained independence from France under its former name, Dahomey, in 1960. The country's political history in the post-independence period until 1972 was marked by chronic political instability.

In 1973 a military coup led by Maj. (later Brig.-Gen.) Mathieu Kerekou deposed the civilian government and established a one-party Marxist regime under the *Parti de la révolution populaire du Benin* (PRPB).

In August 1990 the government promulgated a law permitting the registration of political parties (the PRPB having been dissolved and replaced by the *Union des forces du progrès*), and in February 1991 it sanctioned multi-party elections. In March 1991 presidential elections resulted in a victory for the country's former Prime Minister, Nicéphore Soglo, who was sworn in as head of state in April 1991.

An estimated 13-15 per cent of the population of Benin, which totalled around 1,736,000 in 1990, are Muslim. Most are concentrated in the north-west of the country where they are especially predominant among the Yoruba, the Dendi and the Fulani, although the Bariba majority there is largely animist. The north of the country also has numerous Quranic schools.

The spread of Islam in the south, mainly through the activities of Yoruba and Hausa merchants, has been peaceful though it has been hampered by the strong hold of indigenous religions among the local population. In the south adherents of Islam are to be found among the Nagot and Goun ethnic groups, especially in the Porto Novo area.

Except for the Tijaniyyah and Qadiriyyah brotherhoods, Sufi orders are virtually unknown.

Under the Marxist regime of Kerekou the activities of all religious groups were strictly restricted, provoking resistance from the country's influential Roman Catholic Church. Followers of indigenous African religions, who constitute the majority (about 65 per cent) of the population, were subjected to a long, and often violent, campaign of persecution by the regime in 1971-77.

The regime's relations with the Muslim community were calmer, though more ambiguous. Although the 1977 Constitution, the *Loi fondamentale*, did not discriminate between religions in its objection to groups deemed to be "preach[ing] against the Beninois revolution on the pretext of defending a religion or [their] special or peculiar interests", the government's more accommodating posture towards Muslims was generally regarded to have been a consequence of its close, and internationally controversial, relations with Libya during the 1970s.

According to reports (subsequently denied), Kerekou was said to have converted to Islam during a visit to Libya in 1980 and to have adopted the name "Ahmed". He was also reported to have sought the advice of a wealthy Malian businessman and *marabout* (saint or venerated descendant of a saint), Madou Cissé, known as "Djinne" ("the devil").

It is understood that Benin's continued membership of the Islamic Conference Organization (ICO) has also contributed to the regime's reluctance seriously to antagonize the country's Muslim population.

There is no evidence of the emergence of any party or organization with a specifically Islamic agenda and none was known to have contested Benin's last legislative elections.

FS

Brazil

Brazil is a Federal Republic consisting of one Federal District and 25 states. In 1985 Brazil returned to civilian government after 21 years of military rule. In May 1985 a constitutional amendment restored the right of political parties to function and elections were held for the new National Congress which produced a new Constitution, promulgated in 1988.

The first Muslims to arrive in Brazil, in about 1500, were Moriscos (Spanish Moors) who reached the country in spite of attempts by the Portuguese to prevent Muslim migration to Brazil. Muslims continued to arrive throughout the 16th century until the Court of Bahia responded to the migration by instituting the Brazilian Catholic Inquisition against them in 1594. Thousands of Muslims were enslaved or executed and virtually the entire community was destroyed.

In the 17th century the Portuguese brought in Africans as slaves, including Muslims belonging to groups such as the Hausa. Often learned, these Muslims of African descent succeeded in keeping knowledge of Arabic and Islamic culture alive while managing also to proselytize among the Amerindian community. By the 19th century these descendants of slaves, concentrated around Rio de Janeiro, had established mosques, Quranic schools and, in 1835, an Islamic Muslim state, which was swiftly crushed and Muslims widely persecuted.

The third wave of Muslim migrants, beginning in the early 1860s, came from Syria and Lebanon. As in Argentina, however, Muslims were a minority in this movement, mainly of Christian Arabs.

By the early 1980s Muslims in Brazil were reported to number around 500,000. About 40 per cent are of Syrian origin, 20 per cent of Lebanese origin and 20 per cent of Palestinian origin, the other 20 per cent from diverse backgrounds, including African. Of the Muslim population, about 90 per cent are Sunnis and the rest Shias.

Organizational developments in the Muslim community

The historical record of repression explains the lack of Muslim organization on a national level. However, recent years have seen more freedom for Muslims in Brazil than in Argentina. There are reported to be Muslim associations in seven states and in 10 Brazilian cities.

Brazil's first mosque was built in São Paulo in 1950. By the mid-1980s eight mosques were in existence and a further seven under construction, mainly in the south. Brasilia has an Islamic Centre, founded in 1977, and a Federation of Muslim Associations, formed in 1979 and including 20 associations, 10 of which are in São Paulo State.

MCB

Brunei Darussalam

Having gained full self-government in 1971, Brunei became fully independent from the United Kingdom in 1984. The Sultan of Brunei, Sir Hassanal Bolkiah, rules by decree; he is advised by a Council of Cabinet Ministers, a Religious Council and a Privy Council.

The indigenous people of Brunei (estimated to total 249,000 in mid-1989) are mainly Malay (171,300), of whom the majority are Sunni Muslims of the Shafi school, although there is also a sizable Chinese community (44,000) and large numbers of animists.

Islam is the country's official religion and the Sultan is head of the Islamic community. The country's 1959 Constitution permits religious freedom and other faiths are practised by a small minority.

The Sultan is advised on matters relating to Islam by a Religious Council. A Ministry of Religious Affairs, headed by Pehin Dato Dr Haji Mohammad Zain, a graduate of Al-Azhar University in Cairo, is officially responsible for the promotion of the practice and teaching of Islam, seeking thereby to strengthen it at all levels within the country. Religious education in schools is compulsory for every Muslim child.

The Ministry's proselytizing efforts were strengthened in the mid-1980s by the opening of an Islamic Propagation Centre on the outskirts of the capital, Bandar Seri Begawan.

In 1990 the Sultan encouraged the people of Brunei to adopt the concept of *Melayu Islam Beraja* (Malay Islamic Monarchy) as the state ideology. In a major speech delivered in October to mark the Birth of the Prophet, the Sultan declared that *Melayu Islam Beraja* signified "God's will".

The new ideology emphasized strict observance of Islam, the distinctive nature of Brunei culture and the sovereignty of the monarchy. Some commentators claimed that the Sultan's public endorsement of traditional Muslim values was a response to a possible internal security threat posed by rising unemployment and associated social problems, including alcoholism. In January 1991 the government banned the importation of alcohol.

DS

Islamic organizations

Society of Companions [of the prophet Muhammad]
al-Arqam
Muslim organization banned by royal decree in February 1991 for allegedly spreading teachings contrary to Islam.

Bulgaria

The Republic of Bulgaria, (formerly the People's Republic of Bulgaria) proclaimed in November 1990, was in July 1991 defined as a republic with a parliamentary form of government and a directly elected president.

Bulgaria's population, estimated at end-1990 to total 8,989,000, is characterized by ethnic and religious diversity. Most of the population (80 per cent) profess Christianity but there is a significant Sunni-Hanafi Muslim minority (about 13 per cent), most of whom are ethnic Turks in the north-east of the country and eastern Rhodope while the rest are Bulgarian Muslims or Pomaks, descendants of those who adopted Islam under the Ottoman empire but retained local language and customs, of whom there are about 300,000 living in the mountainous regions in the south and south-west.

In addition there are between 600,000 and 1,000,000 gypsies, of whom an estimated 75 per cent are said to follow Islam. Muslims are also reported to form part of Bulgaria's 250,000 "Macedonian" population (an ethnic category still not officially recognised).

Islam under Communism

Turkish-speaking Bulgarians, who constitute the majority of Muslims, were subjected to a policy of discrimination under the Communist regime which was hostile both to Islamic religious practices and to ethnic Turks. During the repression many Muslims emigrated or became assimilated to the dominant culture, at times abandoning their faith.

In the 1970s the Bulgarian authorities became increasingly concerned about the high birth-rate of ethnic Turks and their control of the important tobacco and wheat-growing areas along the border with Turkey. The 1971 Constitution effectively refused to recognise the Turkish (and other) minorities, allowing the government to pursue a "programme of modernization" aimed at Turkish communities and regions.

By the 1980s the Bulgarian Communist Party (BCP) was engaged in a policy of the forced assimilation of ethnic Turks. Turks were forced to adopt Slavic names in advance of the December 1985 census and a ban was imposed on Islamic religious rites. Some 820,000 Turks were said to have changed their names. A number of mosques were closed and many local Islamic leaders were subjected to intimidation and imprisonment, with reports of murders. The policy prompted accusations of the government by the international community of "seeking to eliminate all statistical evidence of [Bulgaria's] ethnic Turks". In 1986 Bulgaria denied allegations by human rights organizations that hundreds of ethnic Turks had been arrested or imprisoned for refusing to accept new identity cards and that many more had been forcibly resettled.

Muslim opposition to the government's policy of assimilation came to a head in May 1989 after violent demonstrations by an estimated 30,000 ethnic Turks in the eastern region which were suppressed by Bulgarian militia units; as many as 30 people were reported to have died.

There had been emigration, at an unofficial level, by ethnic Turks since the late 1940s. Some 250,000 ethnic Turks left Bulgaria primarily in two periods: the late 1940s and early 1950s and the late 1960s and early 1970s. International concern over the question of Bulgarian Muslim emigration to Turkey was revived in August 1989 when reports indicated that more than 310,000 ethnic Turks had been forcibly expelled from their homes. However, Turkey's decision to restrict further immigration and the disillusionment of ethnic Turks with conditions in Turkey led many to return to Bulgaria. The most prominent Muslim organization campaigning for the rights of ethnic Turks is the **Movement for Rights and Freedom** (MRF), established in early 1990.

The government's policy of assimilation also affected the Muslim Pomak population, 6,000 of whom demonstrated in December 1989 to demand religious and cultural freedom.

Meanwhile ethnic Bulgarians, fearful of Turkey's encroachment on Bulgarian territory and of a dilution of Bulgarian culture and national identity, continued to back the government's policy of assimilation. In January 1990 hundreds of Bulgarian nationalists protested in the Kurdzhali district of southern Bulgaria against the government's intention to revoke its assimilationist policy and restore civil and religious rights to ethnic Turks. Inter-ethnic tension continued during much of 1990 and erupted in riots in early 1991 after Bulgarian nationalists denounced the government's plans to introduce the teaching of Turkish in predominantly Turkish-speaking regions. In November 1991, however, the government decreed that Turkish be an optional subject in schools in such areas, thus persuading the MRF to end its call for a boycott of schools in these areas.

The MRF was itself being subjected to political restrictions arising in part from its decision to participate in general elections under the 1991 constitution—a move prompted by some parliamentary delegates who argued that the Constitution forbade political activity by parties based on ethnic and religious lines. A decision by the Supreme Court to lift restrictions on the MRF shortly before the elections was criticised by Bulgarian nationalists.

Islam in the post-Communist era

Despite decades of political repression, Islam in Bulgaria has experienced a notable revival in the post-Communist period. Although the 1991 Constitution declares Eastern Orthodox Christianity to be the "traditional religion in Bulgaria", it guarantees freedom to all religious minorities.

New Islamic institutes and schools have been opened and a number of Muslim papers and magazines have begun publication, the most notable being *Prava i Svobodi*, published weekly as an organ of the MRF. Meanwhile an estimated 300,000 ethnic Turks who fled Bulgaria during the late 1980s are reported to have returned to their homes.

The MRF is flourishing and waged successful election campaigns in June 1990 and October 1991. Towns and villages with an ethnic Turkish majority have elected Turkish councils and mayors.

The country's predominantly Muslim Romany Gypsy population has also begun to organise itself and has become politically active in the post-Communist period. Members of the Pomak minority, who generally consider themselves to be Bulgarian in everything except religion, have tended not to co-operate with their Turkish and Gypsy co-religionists.

GR

Islamic Organizations

Democratic Union of Romanies in Bulgaria (DURB)

Initially known as the Independent Socialist Democratic Union of Romanies in Bulgaria, the organization was renamed in January 1990.

Aims. To represent gypsies in Bulgaria, the majority of whom are said to be followers of Islam.

Movement for Rights and Freedoms (MRF)

Founded in February 1990, it contested the June 1990 general elections, winning 23 seats and 6 per cent of the vote, mainly in areas populated by ethnic Turks. Fresh elections under the new constitution in October 1991 resulted in the MRF becoming the third strongest political force in the Grand National Assembly, with 24 seats representing 7.5 per cent of the vote. In April 1992 it held the balance of power in the Grand National Assembly.

Leader. Ahmed Dogan (president).

Structure. It has 800-900 branches and a membership of 90,000-120,000.

Aims. To represent the Muslim minority in Bulgaria. The MRF is opposed to Islamic fundamentalism and extreme forms of "Turkish" nationalism. Its programme and political activities centre on the human, religious and cultural rights of ethnic Turkish communities in Bulgaria, including the optional teaching of the Turkish language and Islamic theology in schools; the restoration of mosques and the building of new ones; and freedom to conduct Muslim religious rites and observe religious holidays such as festivals associated with the month of fasting (*Ramadan*).

Publication. Prava i Svobodi, published weekly. There is also a Turkish edition.

Roma Democratic Union (RDU)

Founded in March 1990.

Leader. Manush Romanov, the Romany film director.

Aims. To represent gypsies in Bulgaria, the majority of whom are reported to be Muslims.

Supreme Muslim Theological Council (SMTC)

Umbrella organisation representing Bulgarian Muslims and Muslim religious bodies.

Leader. Hadzhi Nedim Khaafuz Ibrachim Gendzhev, who succeeded Mirian Topchiev as chief *Mufti* in November 1988. He is on the editorial board of the daily newspaper *Myusyuimani*, published in Bulgarian and Turkish.

Structure. The Council is composed of an estimated 800 regional religious leaders (*imams*).

Burkina Faso

Burkina Faso (known as Upper Volta until August 1984) gained full independence from France in August 1960. A civilian government elected in 1978 was overthrown in a military coup in November 1980, after which the Constitution was suspended. After a series of military governments, a coup in October 1987 led by a faction of the armed forces calling itself the Popular Front (PF) installed Capt. Blaise Compaoré as head of state. Compaoré was elected President in elections in December 1991. Multi-party legislative elections, originally scheduled for January 1992 under a new Constitution adopted in June 1991, were held in May 1992.

Burkina Faso's ethnically diverse population, estimated in 1990 to total just over 9,000,000, includes the Mossi, Fulani, Lobo Dagari, Mande (Mandingo), Senoufo, Gourounisi, Bissa, and Gourma. The majority (around 55 per cent) of the population follow traditional African religions, with Christian Roman Catholics representing about 10 per cent. Muslims, mainly Sunni following Maliki rites, who numbered 2,514,261 in 1986, predominate among the Fulani and the Mandingo groups and are believed to constitute about 35 per cent of the total population.

Although not generally considered an Islamic stronghold, despite its membership of the Islamic Conference Organization (ICO), Burkina Faso, like its more outwardly Islamic Sahelian neighbours, notably Mali and Senegal, has recently witnessed something of a Muslim resurgence. While this Islamic revivalism has had minimal influence in the political sphere (there are no reports to date of any organizations with a specifically Muslim agenda), its impact in the social field has been considerable, concealing in some instances political resentment against the non-Muslim, Marxist-oriented, *Conseil Nationale de la Révolution* (CNR, replaced by the PF in October 1987).

The CNR's media campaign against Islam soon after assuming power led to the destruction of a number of mosques and to revisions in family law opposed to Islamic provisions and encouraged the emergence of ostensibly non-political Muslim national organizations, notably the Association of Muslim Students of Burkina (AMSB—*Association des Étudiants Musulmans de Burkina*), and Muslim self-help bodies, concentrated in the country's second major city, Bobo-Dioulasso, and concerned with the administration of Muslim ceremonies.

The growing number of Quranic schools (madrassahs) has also led to the rise of an Arabicized counter-elite whose outlook differs markedly from the dominant Westernized elite educated in Roman Catholic teaching establishments. The spread of Arabicization is believed to account for the recent rise of a reformist movement similar to the puritanical, Arabian-inspired, Wahhabi movement.

FS

Cambodia

Cambodia, a former French colony, was granted independence in 1953. During the 1960s and 1970s the Vietnam War was partly fought on Cambodian territory. The end of the war foreshadowed a short period of brutal rule by Pol Pot's *Khmers Rouges*; this in turn was followed by some 13 years of civil war, which finally ended in 1991.

The mainly Buddhist Khmer group account for some 90 per cent of Cambodia's population, estimated in mid-1990 to total 8,246,000.

The Muslim Cham, also known as the "Islamic Khmer", constitute the country's principal minority, numbering around 185,000.

As a non-Khmer minority, the Cham were reported to have been subjected to particularly harsh treatment under the rule of the ultra-nationalist *Khmers Rouges*. Islamic worship was banned by the *Khmers Rouges* in 1975, but was legalized in 1979 following the defeat of the Democratic Kampuchea regime. The pro-Vietnamese government which replaced the *Khmers Rouges* has encouraged the Cham to organize and practise their religion.

DS

Cameroon

Fifty-three per cent of the population of Cameroon, estimated in 1989 to total 11,554,000, profess Christianity; 25 per cent adhere to traditional beliefs, and the remaining 22 per cent are Muslim, mainly followers of the Sunni Maliki school.

The Muslim population is concentrated in the north of the country, on the right bank of the River Sanaga. There is also a sizeable Muslim community in the country's southern cities among the small traders and artisan classes.

The earliest conversions, dating back several generations, occurred among ethnic groups including the Fulbe (Peul, Fulani), Bamum, Tikar, Kotoko, Mandara and Shuwa ("Black Arabs").

Since the end of World War II, the faith has extended swiftly to the Mbum, Duru, Lakka, Kutin, Fali, Mofu, Matakam, Mundang and the Musgum. Not surprisingly there are great differences in the extent and depth of Islamization amongst these groups. Several groups, particularly more recent converts, are Muslim only in terms of dress and certain other external practices. Conversely, a tradition of classical Islamic learning is not uncommon among some of the more well-established Muslim communities.

The three most influential sects (the first two of which are notable Sufi orders) are the Tijaniyyah, the Qadiriyyah and the Mahdists. The Qadiriyyah, whose members claim to be among the oldest Muslim community in Cameroon, has its main centre in Garua and enjoys strong links with the Qadiriyyah brotherhood in Nigeria. However, the Qadiriyyah appear to have few followers outside Garua and are generally thought to be declining in popularity.

Disaffected members of the Qadiriyyah have increasingly changed their allegiance to the Tijaniyyah order, which is now believed to have overtaken the number of Qadiriyyah followers in parts of Garua, and is known to be particularly strong among Muslim communities in the southern cities.

The north is evenly divided between followers of the Tijaniyyah and Mahdists who are predominantly Fulbe.

Cameroonian Muslims maintain links with the Muslim world through Cameroon's membership of the Islamic Conference Organization (ICO).

Islam and the state: developments since independence

Until the adoption in December 1990 of a multiparty system, Cameroon was effectively a one-party state, governed since 1972 by the secular-oriented Cameroon People's Democratic Movement (MDPC).

Nevertheless, an important feature of the development of Islam in Cameroon since independence has been the support lent by the government to religious education. At independence the new government decided to broaden the state education system, based primarily on the French curriculum, by incorporating religious education. One consequence of this move has been the development of Islamic educational and cultural programmes which are regularly broadcast on the national radio network.

Until recently religious strife has been avoided. What religious and political tension there might have been was firmly suppressed by the country's first President, Ahmadou Ahidjo, a Fulani Muslim and a northerner, who resigned in 1984. The potential significance of the religious factor in politics became apparent when, in April 1984, the largely northern and Muslim presidential guard attempted to stage a coup against President Paul Biya, a southerner and a Christian, with the aim of restoring Ahidjo to power.

Signs of Christian-Muslim tension re-surfaced in early 1992 when hundreds of Muslim youths clashed with security forces in the capital, Yaoundé, after protesting about delays in the construction of a new central mosque. The new mosque had been opposed by the city's majority Christian population who claimed that the chosen site was sacred to them. Several weeks of demonstrations, held usually after Muslim Friday prayers, led to a decision by the authorities to seal off the Muslim quarter of the city and to prohibit all demonstrations within it.

Islamic organizations

There are few formal Islamic organizations. Those which exist are attached to mosques and are concerned primarily with the promotion of Quranic teaching and Islamic culture. Although legislation was approved in December 1990 permitting the formation of an unlimited number of political parties, the formation of religious parties is effectively prohibited.

At the time of the legislative elections in March 1992, no religious group had sought to challenge the ban and none of the parties contesting the elections claimed to have the support of any particular religious group.

TJ

Canada

Initially colonized by Britain and France, Canada became a British colony in the mid-18th century. Today, the Dominion of Canada remains a member of the Commonwealth, with the British sovereign as its head of state, represented by a Governor-General. It is a federal democracy, with a Prime Minister and Cabinet who are responsible to the popularly elected legislature. Considerable powers are also delegated to individual provinces.

Of Canada's population (estimated at 26,991,600 in 1991), the majority are of white British or French extraction. The overwhelmingly European heritage of Canadians has been gradually reduced by heavy immigration from non-European countries, particularly since 1945. Nevertheless, Canada's ethnic homogeneity is reflected in the country's overwhelming adherence to Christianity, with around 75 per cent adhering to one of the three main Christian churches: Roman Catholic, United and Anglican. Canada's public life is largely secular, however, with a strong emphasis placed on the separation of church and state.

Canada's Muslim community, estimated to total around 350,000 in 1991, is the product of two distinct waves of immigration. In 1871 the census recorded only 13 Muslim residents within the entire country. This figure grew steadily in the period before 1914. In 1901 there were around 400 Muslims, equally divided between Turks and Syrian Arabs. By 1911 the number had reached 1,500, with Turks constituting two-thirds of the total. Increasing restrictions on non-European immigration in the early-20th century, and the return of many Turks (classified as "enemy aliens" upon the outbreak of war) to their country of origin, meant that for the remainder of the first half of the 20th century there was little expansion of the Muslim community.

In 1951 the Muslim population of Canada was estimated to number 2,000-3,000. This figure rose rapidly as a result of renewed immigration, reaching 64,000 in 1971 and 120,000 by 1982.

Unlike pre-war immigrants, those who arrived in the post-war period were ethnically diverse, including those from the Arab world (particularly Lebanon, Syria, Jordan, Palestine and Egypt), Pakistan, Bangladesh, Turkey, Iran, eastern Europe, east Africa and the Caribbean. Although the majority were Sunni Muslims, some were from different Shia or Shia-related sects, notably Ismailis (from the Indian subcontinent) and the Druze (mostly from Lebanon).

This second wave of Muslim migrants was also educationally and occupationally more heterogeneous. Whereas the early immigrants had tended to be unskilled labourers, those who arrived later included engineers, physicians, scientists, teachers and technicians.

About 50 per cent of the current Muslim population live in the province of Ontario, with most of these resident in the city of Toronto. Other provinces with significant Muslim minorities include Quebec (largely in Montreal), and Alberta (mostly in Edmonton, Calgary and Lac la Bichel). Within these cities, Muslims have tended to disperse rather than to congregate in close-knit communities.

Organizational developments in the Muslim community

Canada's first Muslim organization, the Arab Muslim Association, founded in Edmonton (Alberta) in the 1920s by Lebanese immigrants, was responsible for the construction of the country's first mosque in 1938.

New Muslim organizations were established in London (Ontario) and Windsor (Ontario) in 1954, Toronto (Ontario) in 1955 and Lac la Bichel (Alberta) in 1957. By 1973 there were 28 organized Muslim communities within the country, and by the mid-1980s this figure had grown to around 50, with more than half of these situated in Ontario, and the others spread fairly evenly among the other provinces.

The need to provide some overall co-ordination for these local groups led to the establishment in 1972 of the **Council of Muslim Communities of Canada** (CMCC).

Although Islam is not accorded the same official status as Christianity and Judaism, many local Muslim organizations receive some assistance from local authorities. There are, however, few Muslims in government at either federal or provincial level, and none in the upper echelons. Furthermore, the influence of the Muslim population of Canada has been undermined by the diverse national and linguistic nature of the groups from which it is constituted.

The driving force of Islam in Canada has remained very much in the hands of immigrants. Inevitably, therefore, almost all Muslim religious leaders, who are often clerics (*imams*), have been born outside the country, reinforcing existing perceptions of Islam as essentially foreign to the mainstream native culture of Canada.

SL

Islamic organizations

Council of Muslim Communities of Canada (CMCC)

Established in 1972 to co-ordinate the numerous local Muslim groups which had grown since the 1950s.

Leader. Mir Iqbal Ali.

Structure. The CMCC's work is largely directed through its six committees: finance; youth; women's; public relations; publications; education.

Aims. Co-ordination of local Muslim organizations; improvement in relations between Muslim and non-Muslim populations of Canada; maintenance of Islamic traditions among second and third generation Muslim immigrants.

Publications. Canada-Islam.

Caribbean

Bahamas

A former British colony, the Bahamas has a tiny Muslim population of no more than 1,000 people, most of whom are converts. Over the last few years a new interest in Islamic concerns has been noticed, probably due to the spread of ideas generated by the black Muslim community of North America.

There is one mosque in the Bahamas.

The only Muslim organization, the *Jamiat-al-Islam* (Islamic Association) was formed in 1977.

Barbados

Barbados has a Muslim population of about 2,000, out of a total population of around 255,000 (1989). Roughly one-third of all Muslims in the Barbados are descendants of 19th-century Indian immigrants. Muslims enjoy the facilities of four mosques.

Bermuda

There are believed to be about 500 Muslims in the former British colony of Bermuda. At least one mosque exists.

MCB

Chad

Between 45 and 55 per cent of the population of Chad, estimated in 1989 to total 5,537,000, are Muslims. They are concentrated mainly in the northern provinces of Borkou, Ennedi and Tibesti and follow the Maliki rite of Sunni Islam. About six per cent of non-Muslim Chadians are Christian and the remainder follow animist religions or belong to communities with mixed Christian and animist traditions.

French became the official language at independence in 1960, and most literate Chadians (estimated at under 30 per cent of the population) are literate in this language rather than in Arabic.

A majority of the Muslim population, and 25-30 per cent of the overall population of Chad, are of partly Arab descent who use Arabic as a main language and follow Arab customs. Many live in the country's central provinces while others are nomads and some live in settlements in Salamat province in the south-east. Other distinct ethnic groups who follow Islam are the Hadjerai, who live in the central Guera highlands, and the Zaghawa, who live on both sides of the Chad-Sudan border in the north-east.

Muslim merchants from the Maghreb first brought Islam to the area of present-day Chad in the early 12th century and by the end of the 17th century Sufi-influenced Islam, with a strong admixture of animist practices, had become the dominant religion in Chad.

In the second half of the 19th century the Sanusi (*Sanussiyyah*) brotherhood, preaching a mixture of Sufism and Wahhabi fundamentalism, became an important political force in Libya and its influence was also felt in the north of Chad, especially in the desert areas and the oasis town of Tibesti.

The Darqawi order, founded in the early 19th century and preaching a conservative version of Maliki Sunnism, is also influential among Muslims concerned to preserve the purity of official Maliki Islam against what they regard as the incursions of African paganism and European modernism.

Islam and the state: developments since independence

The only political party to have a base in the specifically Muslim population of Chad in the period immediately prior to independence was the *Mouvement Socialiste Africain*, led by Ahmed Koulamallah, which was in power for just 12 days in 1959.

Following Chad's independence from France in 1960, the issue of religion has intermittently accentuated tribal divisions, although it rarely appears to have been a strong unifying factor between different tribal groups professing Islam. Political tension between the Muslim north and the Christian south, which has characterized the country's recent history, has rarely been expressed in religious terms. The politicization of Chad's Muslims, which began under the one-party regime of President François Tombalbaye, a southern Christian, had more to do with their political alienation from the centres of state power than with any commitment to an Islamic agenda. Nevertheless the outbreak of violent clashes between Muslims and non-Muslims in the capital, N'Djamena, in 1963 contributed significantly to animosity between the two communities.

In 1965 the north was convulsed by a full-scale Muslim rebellion which was only finally suppressed in 1968 with French military intervention. During this period Muslim grievances were voiced primarily by the *Front de libération nationale du Tchad* (Frolinat), founded in Sudan in 1966 by some northern leaders opposed to the Toumbalbaye regime. In the mid-1970s Frolinat split into rival factions led by Goukouni Oueddi and Hissène Habré, both from northern Muslim backgrounds.

In 1978 Frolinat defeated the southern-dominated government of President Félix Malloum with military assistance from Libya. The regime that emerged was the first not to be dominated by the mainly Christian Sara-speaking people of the south, many of whom had had access to a European-style education brought by Christian missionaries in the colonial period. Soon after Frolinat had gained control of the state administration, however, in-fighting within the organisation intensified.

Meanwhile political tension increased after reports in February and March 1979 of atrocities against the economically privileged Muslim minority in the south by sections of the Christian and Animist majority. Up to 10,000 people, nearly all them Muslim, were reported to have been killed during the massacres around the towns of Sarh, Moundou and N'Djamena.

Habré, with French support, finally seized power in 1982. Meanwhile in the north Oueddi's faction established an independent power-base with Libyan support until an agreement in 1984 led to the withdrawal of Libyan and French forces.

International efforts to secure a reconciliation between rival factions of Frolinat resulted in a ceasefire in September 1987. However, in November Habré's forces were reported to have clashed with what was described as an "Islamic Legion" supported by Libya near the Sudanese border.

By early 1989 Habré faced fresh opposition, this time from groups which eventually coalesced in the Patriotic Salvation Movement, founded in Libya in March 1990 and led by Idriss Déby, a Muslim from the Zaghawa group in the north-east, who seized power in November 1990.

In October 1991 the government banned the formation of organizations on an ethnic, religious or regional basis.

Recent reports have indicated that the political weakness of the Deby government has encouraged renewed Libyan and Sudanese involvement in Chad's internal politics, contributing to an upsurge in religious fundamentalism. Increasing numbers of Chadians are said to have been exposed to the strict Islamic teaching prevalent in Sudan through the activities of Sudan's fundamentalist National Islamic Front (NIF) whose members visited the country in early 1992. Meanwhile Libya is reported to have channelled funds during 1991 to Muslim associations in Chad through the Tripoli-based Islamic Call Society (*Jamiyat ad-Da'wa al-Islamiya*). These activities have prompted the **Islamic Affairs Committee of Chad**, which administers the country's mosques, to press for a mosque-building drive in the south.

The head of the Muslim community in Chad, a member of the Islamic Conference Organization (ICO), is Imam Moussa Ibrahim.

EB

Islamic organizations

Islamic Affairs Committee of Chad
Comité Islamique du Tchad
Based in the capital, N'Djamena.

Chile

The Republic of Chile has a Muslim population of about 1,500, most of whom live in or near Santiago. Two-thirds of these are of Syrian or Palestinian origin whose ancestors arrived in the late 19th and early 20th centuries.

In 1984 the most prominent organization representing Muslims in Chile was the *Sociedade Mussulmana de Chile* (Muslim Society of Chile) headed by a member of the Syrian community who is also responsible for administering an Islamic Centre.

MCB

China

The People's Republic of China was established in October 1949 following the victory of communist guerrilla forces led by Mao Zedong. Since Mao's victory real political power has been in the hands of the Chinese Communist Party (CCP). The party permeates the entire political structure, including the National People's Congress, the State Council and the People's Liberation Army.

Almost 95 per cent of the country's total population are ethnic Han Chinese. The heartland of the Han Chinese has commonly been regarded as the territory bounded in the north and north-west by the Great Wall. The 5 per cent or so of the population comprising ethnic minorities chiefly inhabit areas close to China's borders.

Estimates of the numbers of Chinese Muslims vary from 10 million in some official sources to close to 50 million according to Muslim sources. Objective accounts set the total number of Muslims at around 20 million in 1990, mainly among the Wei Wuer (Uygur and Hui peoples. There are no mosque registers in China, making precise figures impossible. Of the 55 national minorities listed in the 1982 national census, 10 are Muslim. They include six Turkic-speaking groups (the Uygur, Kazakh, Kirghiz, Salar, Tartar and Uzbek) who live primarily in Xinjiang Uygur, the large Autonomous Region in the north-west, and the Hui, Tajik, Dongxiang and Baoan. The Shia Tajik, people of Iranian stock who have absorbed many Turkic words into their Shignanai Tajik dialect, adhere to the Ismaili sect, while the remaining groups are Sunnis. By far the largest group in the Turkic/Tajik category are the Uygur, who according to the 1982 census number close to six million. The other groups total just over a million.

The Hui, the Baoan and the Dongxiang are all Sunni and the last two are of Mongolian origin. The Hui, numbering over seven million according to the 1982 census, constitute the largest Muslim group in China. They are distributed throughout the country but are found mainly in the north-west provinces of Qinghai, Gansu and Ningxia and the south-western province of Yunnan. The Baoan and the Dongxiang, who total less than 300,000, are found mainly in Gansu province.

Of the 10 Muslim groups the Hui are by far the most acculturated to the majority Han Chinese. They are descended from Arab merchants and mercenaries who settled inside the borders of present-day China as early as the T'ang dynasty, probably during the eighth century. They arrived in China by way of sea routes, crossing the Indian Ocean to the south-eastern ports, or via the Silk Road, through Central Asia and into the Central Plains of China. Small Muslim communities developed which became increasingly Sinified in their dress, customs and language but which maintained their Muslim traditions, continuing to use Arabic for prayer, marrying within their own community and observing Muslim dietary laws.

The history of the Turkic-speaking Muslims differs from that of the Hui. Islam took root in

Central Asia in the 10th century and slowly gained ground throughout the region, spreading into present-day Xinjiang. The Tartar were converted in the 10th century, the Uzbek in the 13th and 14th, the Uygur in the 15th and the Kazakh in the 16th and 17th until eventually, by the early 20th century, Xinjiang was almost completely Muslim. Unlike the Hui, Turkic Muslims, situated on China's periphery, did not seek to adopt the language or culture of the majority Han.

Tension between Muslims and the Han Chinese increased considerably in the north-west and south-west during the 18th and 19th centuries. In the absence of credible central rule local Han and Muslim militias competed for power in the regions. This period of social instability coincided with the rise of the militant "New Sect" (also "New Teaching"), spearheaded by members of the Naqshbandiyyah Sufi order in the Moslem regions. A mixture of Islamic revivalism and mystic sectarianism, the "New Sect" fanned Islamic revolts in the regions and promoted the idea of a separate Islamic identity.

Turkic Muslims launched a series of revolts in Xinjiang during the 19th century and in the south-west an independent Islamic political entity (Pingnan Guo, ruled by Sultan Suleiman), survived from 1856 to 1873. However, there was little attempt at united action by the Turkic and Hui Moslems. Nationalism had only slight appeal for the Hui and the group's lack of nationalist aspiration only served to accentuate the divisions between them and the Turkic Muslims. The failure of the Hui and Turkic communities to form a united front was one of the prime reasons for the failure of Muslim uprisings in the Republican era (1911-49), which culminated in the establishment of the first Eastern Turkestan Republic in Kashgar in 1933-34 and a second in the Ili region of Xinjiang in 1944-45.

Islam under Communist rule

Historically the CCP has been hostile to all forms of religion. However, since the 1970s it has permitted a limited degree of freedom of worship and belief while at the same time maintaining strict control over all religious organizations. As is the case with other religions, Islam is officially represented by national associations, the most important of which are the **China Islamic Association (CIA)** and the **Beijing Islamic Association (BIA)**. Policy on religion is decided by the CCP's United Front Work Department and implemented by the Religious Affairs Bureau of the State Council.

Throughout the 1950s Muslim-inhabited areas of the country were designated as autonomous regions, prefectures and counties, in line with the party's policy of granting a measure of self-determination to minorities. However, the areas were autonomous in name only; Muslim inhabitants had symbolic representation in local government and party organs but their political influence was negligible.

The party adopted an increasingly uncompromising attitude towards Islam and other religions in the period following the "Hundred Flowers" campaign of 1957. In 1963 the Muslim pilgrimage to Mecca (*hajj*) was halted, effectively isolating China's Muslim community from the rest of the Islamic world. Religion was subjected to an even fiercer assault during the Cultural Revolution of the mid-1960s when communist Red Guards conducted a ferocious campaign against mosques, temples and churches. A large number of mosques and Islamic schools were destroyed at the behest of the Revolutionary Group for the Abolition of Islam.

Demonstrations of Muslim resistance were reported to have taken place during the Cultural Revolution and many Muslims were said to have crossed from Xinjiang into Soviet Central Asia where some of them were reported to have founded the **Uygurstan Liberation Front**.

The party's official policy on religion was relaxed in the aftermath of the Cultural Revolution. Apart from other considerations, a desire for better relations with Islamic countries in the Middle East and Africa encouraged at least limited toleration, and as a result the 1982 Constitution specifically guaranteed religious freedom. In 1982 an Arabic-based script was reintroduced for Turkic-speaking Muslims while greater religious freedom resulted in a proliferation of mosques (by 1984 14,000 had been opened in Xinjiang), in improved training for almost 15,000 *imams* (clerics), and in the printing of almost 150,000 copies of the Quran. The first institute of Islamic theology opened at Yinchuan in Ningxia in 1985, and another in June 1987 in Urumqi in Xinjiang. Private pilgrimages to Mecca have been resumed and 2,000 Muslims are said to have performed *hajj* in 1985.

Nevertheless, Islam, with its significant international connections, continued to be closely monitored by the authorities. In Xinjiang Islam remained an extremely sensitive issue, with the outbreak of numerous violent protests against Beijing during the 1980s. Many of the protests were directed against the influx of Han Chinese into the region and against the government's policy of conducting nuclear tests in the region. However, in 1990 a Muslim nationalist group, the Islamic Party of East Turkistan, planned an uprising in six cities for the 17th day of Ramadan (April 13). The group, which reportedly aimed to establish a separatist Islamic republic and to proclaim a holy war (*jihad*) to "eliminate heathens" from Xinjiang, was forced into premature action by a demonstration in Kizislu Kirghiz Autonomous Prefecture near Kashgar on April 5 in which 22 people died. Disturbances continued during May, resulting in the closure of Xinjiang's border with the rest of China. Later in the year it was announced that 50 mosques would be closed and permission for the construction of a further 100 withdrawn. The Chinese authorities appeared to be particularly concerned that ethnic and Muslim irredentism in the collapsing Soviet Union might spread across the border and encourage the revival of separatist movements in Xinjiang.

DS

Islamic organizations

Beijing Islamic Association (BIA)

Founded in 1979 with a number of regional bureaux to co-ordinate aspects of religious life in China and interpret Muslim religious texts in a manner consistent with government policy. The BIA has produced the Quran, the *Hadith* (sayings of the Prophet Muhammad) and a biography of the Prophet in local languages.

Leader. Imam al-Hadji Salah an Shiwei (chair).

China Islamic Association (CIA)

Founded in 1953, closed in the late 1950s and revived in 1969. Co-ordinates aspects of Islamic religious life throughout the country and produces standard Islamic works in indigenous languages.

Leader. Al-Hodji Ilyas Shen Xiaxi (president); Ma Xian (secretary-general).

Uygurstan Liberation Front

Exiled organization based in the central Asian republic of Kazakhstan representing the Turkic-speaking Uygur of Xinjiang.

Leader. Ashir Vakhidov.

Aims. To re-establish the East Turkestan Republic, founded in 1933-34 and revived in 1944-45 but formally dissolved by the Chinese communist government in 1949.

Colombia

Over 70 per cent of the population of Colombia, estimated to total 33,000,000 in 1990, is of mixed Spanish and Indian origin (*mestizo*), with roughly 22 per cent being of European descent. Ninety-five per cent are Christian Roman Catholics. The total number of Muslims is believed to be around 2,000.

The virtual decimation of the indigenous Indian population by Spanish settlers in the 15th and 16th encouraged the import of African slaves, many of whom were Muslims.

Muslim numbers were swelled by the arrival from the 1890s onwards of Arabs from Syria, Palestine and Lebanon. However, of these Arab immigrants (presently believed to total about 16,000), only a small minority (about 20 per cent) are Muslims who are settled around the capital, Bogota.

There are no registered mosques in Colombia although Islamic centres have been established in Bogotá, Maco and Bona Vintura.

MCB

Commonwealth of Independent States

(See also the individual entries for Azerbaijan, Kazakhstan, Kirgizstan, Turkmenistan and Uzbekistan)

Almost one-fifth of the population of the Commonwealth of Independent States (CIS—the former Soviet Union), established in December 1991, belongs to Islamic nationalities. The number of Muslims is about 54,800,000, a figure based on the 1989 census, although a report in May 1991 from the Spiritual Directorate of Muslims of the Soviet Union put the Muslim population at around 75,000,000 (an exaggerated figure, calculated from the total populations of regions with majority Muslim populations).

Muslims are, however, the fastest growing segment of the population of the CIS: they accounted for 49.4 per cent of the total increase in population in the intercensal period of 1979-89. The Muslim nationalities in the same period grew by 27.0 per cent while the non-Muslim population grew by only 5.5 per cent.

Predominantly Sunni Muslim populations are concentrated in the five Central Asian republics of Kazakhstan, Kirgizstan, Tajikistan, Turkmenistan, and Uzbekistan; in the Transcaucasian republic of Azerbaijan; and in autonomous republics within the Russian Federation: Daghestan, Chechen-Ingushetia, Kabardino-Balkaria, Tatarstan and Bashkortostan. Shi'ism is widespread only in Azerbaijan and parts of Tajikistan. Most speak Turkic languages, except the Tajiks who speak a form of Persian. Substantial Muslim communities are resident in major cities, including Moscow, where they are estimated to number between 500,000 and 800,000, St Petersburg, Nizhny-Novgorod and Astrakhan.

Four Sufi brotherhoods are known to be active in the territory of the CIS: Naqshbandiyyah (the most widespread), Qadariyyah, Yasawiyyah and Kubrawiyyah. The strongholds of Sufism are the Ferghana valley, Daghestan, northern Azerbaijan, Chechnia, Karakalpak and parts of Turkmenia. There is little evidence of Sufism in Tatarstan, Bashkortostan, and Transcaucasia. It is impossible to be sure of the number of adepts, but experts basing their estimates on the 1979 census, calculate a minimum of 500,000 followers.

The paucity of officially registered clerics strengthened unofficial Islam (Sufism). Attacks on Sufism appeared in the Soviet press from the late 1960s, and especially after the invasion of Afghanistan in 1978. The Soviet regime, which regarded Sufism as a cultural and social phenomenon beyond its control, increased the pressure on what it called "parallel Islam", especially after the death of President Leonid Brezhnev in November 1982.

Sufism's history of opposition to Russian domination contributed substantially to its popularity. Attendance at the shrines of Sufi mystics grew during the 1980s despite rulings (*fatwas*) from religious officials (*muftis*), notably the Mufti of Tashkent, Shamsuddinkhan

Babakhan, urging Muslims not to do so. Sufism's growing appeal among sections of the Soviet official hierarchy, including their membership of Sufi brotherhoods and their employment as Sufi clerics after working hours, was confirmed in 1986 after President Mikhail Gorbachev, during a speech in Tashkent, criticised Party members who observed Islamic rituals.

Muslim religious activity in the Soviet era

Muslim regions were brought under Soviet control in the early years after the 1917 Revolution following stiff resistance, including the Basmachi nationalist revolt in Central Asia which was only finally crushed in 1933.

In 1918 Joseph Stalin established the Central Muslim Commissariat under the Tatar leader, Sultan Galiev, who advocated a synthesis of Islam and Bolshevism. By 1922 a purge of Muslim intellectuals including Galiev dashed hopes for Islamic independence. The Steppe tribes were forcibly settled; Islamic customs including the pilgrimage to Mecca (*hajj*) and payment of alms (*zakat*) suspended, and Islamic courts abolished between 1924 and 1934. Muslim religious leaders were among those persecuted during the purges of the 1930s.

The Tsarist territory of Turkestan (now claimed by some Islamic groups as the basis of an Islamic state) was divided into republics beginning in 1924, on grounds largely of nationality, although the borders did not always coincide with the boundaries of nationality populations. The Soviet policy of territorial division, like its language policy, exemplified the policy of divide and rule. For example, the Tatars, regarded as a leading Islamic nation in scholarship and commerce having spear-headed the reform (*jadid*) movement in the late 19th century, became an Autonomous Republic within the Russian Federation, a less important territorial designation than the Union Republics of the Muslims of Central Asia.

In 1941, after a period of intense religious persecution, four spiritual directorates (*dukhov-noye upravleniye* or *muftiyats*) were established by Stalin allowing a limited amount of religious activity. The *muftiyats*, which are still operational, included:

(1) Central Asia and Kazakhstan; official language Uzbek, headquarters Tashkent.

(2) Muslims of European Russia, the Volga and Siberia (reviving the *muftiyat* established in 1788 by Catherine II); official language Tatar; headquarters Ufa.

Both these *muftiyats* serve Muslims belonging to the Hanafi school.

(3) Transcaucasia and Shias throughout the Soviet Union, many of whom belong to the Jafari school (although it also serves Sunnis belonging to the Hanafi school); official language Azeri; headquarters Baku.

(4) The Northern Caucasus and Daghestan; official language Arabic; based in Makhachkala, serving the Hanafi and Shafi Sunni rites.

In the 1970s attempts by sections of the Soviet hierarchy to extend contacts with Islam abroad revived official interest in state-sponsored religious activity. However, popular Muslim religious observance continued to be severely curtailed and was only officially accepted after the beginning of *glasnost*.

Only two religious seminaries (*madrassahs*), those administered by the Tashkent *muftiyat*, were permitted to operate under Soviet rule. By early 1992, however, the Tashkent *muftiyat* was reported to be administering up to 12 seminaries. The Tashkent *muftiyat* was also allowed to print Islamic material, including six editions of the Quran between 1941 and 1989. The 1989 edition was the first since 1968, and had a print run of 25,000.

Nationalism has caused the *muftiyats* to splinter into nationally-based religious administrative divisions. At the same time, the *muftiyats'* long association with Soviet-sponsored Islam have led many Muslims in the CIS to regard them with suspicion.

Language policy and the Muslim republics under Soviet rule

The language policies of the Soviet government at the same time encouraged and repressed nationalism. While national awareness was heightened by the virtual eradication of illiteracy and the creation of scripts for non-literate peoples, including most of Turkestan, a 1926 decree by the First All-Union Turkological Congress effectively separated Muslim nationalities from their Arabic cultural heritage by approving the adoption of the Latin script for all Turkic languages. In 1938 the study of Russian was made compulsory.

In Central Asia, the switch from the Latin to the Cyrillic alphabet was completed in the 1940s. Nevertheless, the Soviet goal of native-language/Russian bilingualism was far from comprehensively attained in the Muslim republics. In Central Asia the percentage of a nationality claiming proficiency in Russian as a second language ranged from 52.3 per cent in Kazakhstan to 25.4 per cent in Turkmenistan (1979 figures).

The Muslim intelligentsia concerned about the arrested development of their native languages have sought unilaterally, under the newly restructured CIS, to bestow greater importance to their titular language. Uzbekistan, Kazakhstan, Kirgizstan and Tajikistan passed language laws in 1989 specifying the titular language as the official republican language; in December 1991 Tajikistan replaced the Cyrillic by the Persian alphabet with help from Iran, and in November 1991 Azerbaijan announced that it was reintroducing the Latin alphabet in order to become culturally closer to Turkey.

Muslim politics in the Soviet era

The relaxation of control heralded by *glasnost* led also to the politicization of Islam. Political parties, legalized in the Soviet Union in October 1990, required them to be registered with the USSR or Republican Ministry of Justice (in fact, many parties were already operating).

In June 1990 the **Islamic Renaissance Party** (IRP) (*Nazdate Islamiye*) was established in Astrakhan, Russia, largely on Tatar initiative, by 400 delegates from Russia, Tajikistan and Azerbaijan. Among its aims were to help Soviet Muslims live in accordance with Islamic law; to bring working practices in line with the observance of Islamic rituals, including Ramadan and daily prayers; and to obtain religiously permitted (*halal*) food.

The IRP has also expressed support for Uzbekistan's Islamic movement, the **Unity Popular Front** (*Birlik*) which envisages the creation of an Islamic state of Turkestan in Central Asia by constitutional means. The IRP, whose leader is Ahmad Qadi Akhtayev, has its headquarters in Moscow. Individual states are setting up autonomous Islamic Renaissance Parties.

Since the creation of the CIS the leaders of the Central Asian Muslim states, most of them former Communists, and therefore ostensibly atheists, have sought to employ a political language based on Islam in quest of popular support and a distinct national identity, supposedly patterned on the Turkish model of development. Plans to co-ordinate policies aimed at creating a Central Asian Commonwealth, made in August 1990 at a meeting in Tashkent, have, however, produced few tangible results so far.

Relations with other Muslim states and international Islamic organizations

Soviet Muslims were kept as far as possible in isolation from contact with their co-religionists, especially after the Iranian revolution of 1979, for fear of triggering an Islamic movement.

An officially sponsored conference on "Islam and Politics" in Dushanbe in May 1988 which addressed the problem of Islamic propaganda from neighbouring countries, recognized its destabilizing potential, particularly in Soviet border areas.

The 10-year war in Afghanistan reinforced the perceived danger. Soviet Muslims, who initally formed the backbone of military and technical support for the Afghan government in 1979, were rapidly replaced by ethnic Slavs. Official concern was heightened after uncon-firmed reports that Soviet Muslims had refused to fire on Afghan Muslims. Elsewhere it emerged that Soviet Turkmen and Tajik areas had been subjected to Islamic propaganda from bases in Peshawar relaying programmes in Russian, thus appearing to confirm fears that the object was religious not ethnic solidarity. Afghan *mujaheddin* were also reported to have penetrated the Tajik border on several occasions.

During the formation of the CIS, Afghanistan, Iran, Pakistan and Turkey all vyed for influence in the area. The Iranian Foreign Minister, Ali Akbar Vellayati, made a 10-day visit to the Islamic states in November-December 1991; shortly afterwards, Pakistan and Afghan-istan recognised the independence of all former Soviet Islamic states. Economic aid has been promised by all these states, including help in constructing transport and communications links.

The Islamic states of the CIS are also beginning to join the world Islamic community. Azerbaijan and Kazakhstan sent delegations to the sixth summit of the Islamic Conference Organization (ICO) held in Dakar on Dec. 9-11, 1991; Azerbaijan was subsequently elected a member of the ICO. Reports that Kirgizstan would also be joining were denied by Kirgiz officials. According to a report in *Izvestiya* of Dec. 2, 1991, all the Muslim states of the former Soviet Union had been invited to attend.

On Jan. 12, 1992, the Islamic Development Bank (IDB) approved grants worth US\$1,414,000 to finance educational and other facilities for Muslims in Russia, including three Islamic schools, two colleges and six centres for Quranic learning, in Moscow, Tatarstan and Bashkortorstan. The grants were also intended to promote the increased use of the Arabic script for national languages.

In February 1992 the five Central Asian Muslim republics of Azerbaijan, Kirgizstan, Uzbekistan, Tajikistan and Turkmenistan were admitted as members of the Economic Con-ference Organization (ECO) to join Iran, Pakistan and Turkey.

WS

Comoros

The Comoros was proclaimed a Federal Islamic Republic in 1975 after the archipelago's four largest islands unilaterally declared their independence from France (the island of Mayotte remains a French *département*). After a brief secular interlude prompted by a Maoist-led coup in 1975, the Islamic Republic was restored by President Ahmad Abdullah in 1978.

Almost the entire population, estimated in 1989 to total 459,000, are Sunni Muslims who observe Shafi rites in matters of marriage and divorce; a few Muslims of Indian origin belonging to the Shia Ismaili sect have their own mosque on the island of Moroni.

Sufi brotherhoods are also important, the most well-established being the Shadhiliyya order whose spread in the Comoros in the early part of the 20th century is attributed to Shaikh Sayyid Muhammad ibn-Shaikh.

Prior to the arrival of the French, Islam was the dominant cultural force. The ruling clans spoke and wrote Arabic, made pilgrimages to Mecca and through their overseas family and business ties maintained contact with developments in the rest of the Islamic world. French colonial rule left many Muslim customs and practices intact while seeking, as far as possible, to ensure continued adherence to Quranic law.

Islam continues to be rigorously observed in both urban and rural areas as reflected by the growing number of mosques, estimated presently to total around 780.

There are no specifically Islamic political organizations, although the importance of Islam is officially endorsed and promoted by a Ministry of Islamic and Arab Affairs. The judicial system, enforcing Islamic law (*sharia*), is administered by a Supreme Court which can, however, be overruled by the President.

TJ

Côte d'Ivoire

The Republic of Côte d'Ivoire became fully independent from France in August 1960. According to unofficial estimates, about 3,000,000 people (35 per cent of the total population estimated in 1989 to number 11,713,000) are Sunni Muslims of the Maliki school.

Among ethnic groups the Dyula are all Muslims and significant numbers are present among the Fulbe, the Kulango and the Mande. The Muslim population is concentrated in the north-west of the country, although internal migration has led to the establishment of smaller Muslim settlements in the predominantly Christian south.

Almost the entire Muslim population belongs to one of three Sufi brotherhoods: the Qadiriyyah being the most dominant, followed by the Tijaniyyah, with the Sanusiyyah claiming far fewer numbers. Some Muslims also belong to the heterodox sect known as the Ahmadiyyah, whose numbers in Africa as a whole are believed to approximate 500,000.

Islam and the state: developments since independence

Attempts to organize the Muslim community began in 1957 with the foundation of the Muslim Cultural Union, which opened branches in Bouake and Abidjan. The Union has played an important role in Islamic teaching and welfare. It has also been influential in the establishment of Islamic primary and secondary schools which work with Qur'anic schools in the hundreds of mosques throughout the country.

Since mid-1987, when the Arab League called for the severance of links with the country following its establishment of diplomatic ties with Israel, there has been little contact with the Islamic world.

A de facto one-party state since independence, Côte d'Ivoire's political organizations have been in operation only since May 1990. No reports have emerged, as of early 1992, indicating the formation of specifically Islamic political organizations.

TJ

Islamic organizations

Muslim Cultural Union
Cultural organization founded in 1957 with branches in Abidjan and Bouake.

Aims. Promotion of Islamic teaching.

Cyprus

The Muslim population of the island of Cyprus is estimated to be about 24.4 per cent, or some 155,000, of a total population of some 695,000 in mid-1989. Most are Turkish Cypriots who are Sunnis adhering to the Hanafi school of law.

Ottoman rule over Cyprus continued until 1878 and between 1878 and 1914 Britain ruled Cyprus on trust for Turkey. In the late 19th century Turkish-Cypriot emigration prompted a fall in the Turkish-Cypriot population to about 18 per cent of the population (some 20,000 people). Meanwhile Greek-Cypriots, who soon came to account for about 80 per cent of the population, launched a vigorous campaign in the last two decades of the 19th century aimed at *Enosis* (union [with Greece]). After Britain formally annexed the island as a Crown Colony in 1914, it resisted Greek-Cypriot claims principally on account of the strategic importance of Cyprus.

Representatives of the Turkish-Cypriot minority were also making known their opposition to any change in the status of the island. From 1935 to 1939 many Turkish-Cypriots emigrated to Turkey and Britain in response to worsening economic conditions.

By the 1950s the Greek-Cypriot dominated National Organization of Cyprus Fighters (EOKA) had intensified its attacks against British targets in order to achieve *Enosis*, while the government of Turkey advocated partition. According to an agreement which came into effect in August 1960, Cyprus was to be an independent state with a House of Representatives composed of two communal chambers, one Greek and one Turkish. A Greek-Cypriot president was to be assisted by a Turkish-Cypriot vice-president. As communal violence escalated in the early 1960s, 20,000 Muslim Turkish-Cypriots fled their villages in the south.

The Turkish invasion of Cyprus in 1974, which followed a Greek-Cypriot military coup, resulted in the effective partitioning of the island, with about 36 per cent of the territory under Turkish control. In 1983 the north declared itself the independent "Turkish Republic of Northern Cyprus" (the south continuing as the Republic of Cyprus) but it failed to achieve international recognition from any country other than Turkey. In total about 60,000 Turkish-Cypriots left their homes in the south to migrate north while about 120,000 Greek-Cypriots left the north for the south. In the 1970s and 1980s immigrants from mainland Turkey were encouraged to settle in the north.

Although religious ideology had not been used to mobilize the Turkish-Cypriot population, in the late 1970s the government in the Turkish-annexed territory under President Rauf Denktash, in an effort to attract support from the Arab world invoked Islam in support of its arguments, and in 1979 discussed the idea of declaring northern Cyprus an Islamic state. In the late 1980s Islamic fundamentalist groups in Turkey also favoured recognition of a sovereign Turkish-Cypriot Islamic state.

In 1991-92 international efforts under the auspices of the United Nations continued in search of a solution to the Cyprus problem. A federal plan proposed by the United Nations was opposed by the Denktash government which demanded the recognition of northern Cyprus as a sovereign state. Meanwhile foreign ministers of the Islamic Conference Organization (ICO), meeting in Istanbul in August 1991, examined a request by the "Turkish Republic of Northern Cyprus" for full membership of the ICO and decided "to strengthen the participation of the Turkish Cypriot Muslim community in all . . . ICO organs" while agreeing to keep open the question of full membership.

EB

Islamic Organizations

Association of the Turkish Minority in Cyprus (KATAK)

Opposed *Enosis* in the 1930s. The organization maintained that Turkish-Cypriots were discriminated against in religious and educational affairs and in the early 1940s campaigned for freedom of speech, the press and assembly.

Islamic Trust

Evkaf (derived from the Arabic *awqaf*)
Under Ottoman rule this was the authority responsible for the adminstration of lands held as Islamic trusts. The *Evkaf*, together with the Turkish military and right-wing Turkish parties, was reported to have resisted a negotiated settlement to the Cyprus dispute.

Djibouti

The great majority of the population of the Republic of Djibouti, estimated to total about 420,000, are Sunni Muslims who follow the Shafi school of law. A small minority belong to the moderate Zaydi (Fiver) branch of Shi'ism.

Djibouti's principal ethnic groups are the Afars of the north, who are part of a wider group of Afars in Ethiopia, specifically Eritrea, and the Issas of the south, also present across the border in Somalia and Ethiopia. Other groups are the Gadabursis, Somalis, Issaqs and Arabs. Arabic, French and various Cushitic languages are spoken.

As with Ethiopia and Somalia, Islam arrived in the region of Djibouti in the seventh century with settlers who brought their religion from the Arabian peninsula.

Djibouti achieved independence from France in 1977. Since independence the office of President has been occupied by President Hassan Gouled Aptidon, who in 1991 responded to international pressures by relaxing one-party rule by the *Rassemblement populaire du progrès* (RPP) and undertaking to hold multi-party presidential elections in 1993.

Political and military opposition to the single-party rule of Aptidon increased in 1991-92 although there was no evidence of political organizations with a specifically Islamic agenda. President Aptidon has habitually attempted to draw support from "elders and religious leaders", and in March 1992 he appealed for national unity during the Muslim holy month of fasting (*ramadan*) in the face of a renewed anti-government offensive by militant Afar groups in the north.

Islamic law (*sharia*) forms the basis of Djibouti's legal system. The Minister of Justice and Religious Affairs is Ougoure Hassan Ibrahim and the *Qadi* (judge) of Djibouti, who acts as the spiritual head of Djibouti's Muslims, is Mogue Hassan Dirir.

Djibouti is a member of the Islamic Conference Organization (ICO).

EB

Egypt

Egypt, a former British protectorate, became independent in 1922. In 1952 King Farouk was deposed and a Republic was proclaimed in June 1953, led first by Gen. Mohammad Neguib, then by Col. Gamal Abdel Nasser. In 1971 the country changed its name to the Arab Republic of Egypt.

At least 90 per cent of Egypt's population, officially estimated to total 53,153,000 in mid-1990, is of Hamito-Semitic origin. Its ethnic homogeneity is closely matched by its religious homogeneity; 94 per cent of the population are Sunni Muslims, the majority adhering to the Hanafi and Shafi schools, although followers of the Maliki rite predominate in the south. Other communities include Christian Copts and a small number of Jews.

Sufism has wide appeal throughout Egypt. According to the Supreme Council of Sufi Orders (SCSO) (*al Majlis al-Aala Lilturuk al Sufiyya*), the number of such registered orders grew from 21 in 1960 to 60 in 1985. It is believed that there may be a number of minor orders in existence that are not registered. Although Sufi orders have sometimes acted as havens for social activists (the founder of the Muslim Brotherhood (*Ikhwan al muslimun*), Hassan al Banna being a case in point), they have traditionally tended to be apolitical and have refrained from taking sides on socio-political issues.

Despite Egypt's long association with Islam, dating back to AD 632, it remains notable for being among the first Arab countries to experience the full impact of European conquest. The Napoleonic invasion and the modernizing regime of Muhammad Ali (1805-49) ensured that Egypt remained close to western political and cultural developments.

The continuing mixture of influences is shown in contemporary Egypt; it has a government and parliament, but also an Islamic consultative council (*shura*) with advisory powers. The system of law is a complex amalgam of English common law, the French Napoleonic code law and Islamic law.

The Islamic movement in Egypt is commonly understood to operate at three distinct levels: "establishment Islam"; mainstream Islamic fundamentalism, notably the Muslim Brotherhood; and militant neo-fundamentalist groups whose operations are largely clandestine. Underlying these different though inter-related phenomena is a generally marked increase in grassroots religiosity dating back to the 1967 defeat of Arab forces by Israel.

Establishment Islam

"Establishment" or official Islam is embodied variously in Al-Azhar (venerated as the Muslim world's foremost centre of religious learning), the Ministry of Religious Endowments (*awqaf*), and to a lesser extent by the Supreme Council of Islamic Affairs (SCIA). While the "establishment" Islam embodied in the ideology of Al Azhar is regarded increasingly, especially by young Egyptians, to be an instrument of government, there are signs of a more critical stance. This is illustrated by one of its leading figures, Shaikh Hafiz Salama, the organizer of several anti-government protests who has called for the immediate application of Islamic law (*sharia*) and a holy war (*jihad*) against Israel.

The government in turn has attempted to accommodate changes in trends within "establishment" Islam by appearing to endorse programmes such as those advocated on state-controlled television by Shaikh Mutawalli al-Sharawi which favour the introduction of a more Islamically-oriented financial system in opposition to socialism.

Despite its links with organs of government, "establishment" Islam still commands considerable respect among ordinary Egyptians. With its control over an estimated 10,000 mosques, hundreds of educational institutions and provincial branches of Al Azhar University, "establishment" Islam has seen a huge increase in its activities between 1970 and 1985, prompted in part by the growth of grass-roots religiosity and a government campaign to control the spread of fundamentalist Islamic activity.

"Establishment" Islam is formally embodied in the Higher Council for the Islamic Call, chaired by the Grand Shaikh of Al Azhar, Shaikh Jad al Haq Ali Jad al Haq, and includes the Minister of Religious Endowments (*awqaf*). Views associated with official Islam are promoted through the weekly *al Liwa al Islami* ("Islamic Standard").

Mainstream Islam

Mainstream Islam in Egypt is best, and most paradoxically, represented by the **Muslim Brotherhood**. Founded in 1928 by Hassan al-Banna, the Muslim Brotherhood gained notoriety in the 1940s as a vehement advocate of an Islamic state and one of the bitterest critics of Egypt's secular politics.

In its most violent phase (1945-65) the Brotherhood developed its own armed secret apparatus and was widely associated with political assassinations, including that of former Prime Minister M. F. al Nuqrashi in 1949. Although initially in favour of the 1952 coup d'état staged by the Free Officers Movement, the Brotherhood was rapidly alienated by Nasser's brand of secular Arab nationalism.

In 1954 the Brotherhood was banned following an assassination attempt on Nasser; thousands of its members were arrested and tortured and its leading figures executed, including Abdel Quader in 1955 and Sayyid Qutb in 1965.

The gradual rehabilitation of the Brotherhood under President Anwar Sadat was symbolized by permission to circulate the organization's broadsheet, *al Dawa* ("The Call"). For its part, the Brotherhood under the leadership of Omar al Telmassani sought during the Sadat era to cultivate a violence-free record which, in turn, contributed substantially to increased membership and improved relations with other political parties.

Although still technically banned, the Brotherhood has enjoyed de facto recognition since entering into coalition politics under President Hosni Mubarak. In 1984 it allied with the secular Wafd Party (WP) to contest parliamentary elections; the coalition served as the major opposition in the People's Assembly for three years.

In 1987 the Brotherhood (still bound by a law restricting the participation of religious parties) allied with two smaller parties—the Socialist Labour Party (SLP) and the Liberal Party

(LP)—to form the Islamic Alliance (*al-Tahaluf Al-Islami*). The Alliance came second to the ruling National Democratic Party, capturing a total of 36 seats, two of which went to Seif al Islam Hassan al Banna (son of Hassan al Banna) and the party's secretary-general, Mamoun al Hudaiby. Included in the coalition's manifesto was a demand for the implementation of Islamic law *Sharia*.

Although the Brotherhood, in co-operation with the country's other main political parties, boycotted the parliamentary elections in November and December 1990, the organization's political re-orientation in the last decade appears to have been successful in ending its alienation from secular political forces in Egypt.

Meanwhile, there are signs of the Brotherhood's continuing influence within the parallel economy and welfare system consisting of a network of "Islamic" schools, medical and welfare centres operating independently of the state sector. The origins of this informal sector lie in President Sadat's open-door economic policy (*intifatah*) of the 1970's which encouraged the return of Brotherhood supporters (forced to flee Egypt during Nasser's ban on the movement). They established a host of "Islamic" companies (estimated in 1991 to control capital worth £E12,000 million) with profits amassed in neighbouring oil-rich Arab states.

Allegations in 1987 that Islamic money utilization companies (MUC) (*sharikat tawzif al-amwal*—roughly equivalent to an Islamic bank) had funded the political campaign of Islamist candidates in the 1987 elections prompted the government to seek closer regulation of enterprises operating under an Islamic logo in the informal sector. Evidence of the links between the Brotherhood and sections of the parallel economy was revived in March 1992 after reports that members of a computer company had been involved in a fundamentalist plot to overthrow the government.

The growing influence of groups sympathetic to the Brotherhood and its programme of Islamization is also apparent in the informal social services sector. A commonly regarded index is the proliferation of private (*ahli*) mosques, which between 1962 and 1982 grew from 14,000 to around 40,000, compared with an increase from 3,000 to 6,000 government-controlled mosques in the same period. Many private mosques have the backing of voluntary, ostensibly non-political, Islamic societies which are known to be unfriendly to the government, including the *Khulafah al Rashidun* in Cairo, the *Dawa al Islamiya* in Bani Suaif, the *Ansar al Sunna al Muhammadiyya* in Port Said and Suhag, the *Fajr al Islam* in Suez, the *al Jamiyya al Islamiyya li al Dawa* in Asyut and the *al Ihya al Islami* in Fayoum.

Neo-fundamentalist Islam

The number of clandestine neo-fundamentalist splinter groups (collectively known as the *jammat al Islamiyya*) presently in operation is estimated by the Egyptian authorities to be around 20 with a fluid and interchangeable membership.

Among these groups, many of which rose to prominence in the 1970s and 1980s as off-shoots of the youth movement of the Muslim Brotherhood, the most notorious is **Holy War** (*al Jihad*) which claimed responsibility for the assassination in October 1981 of President Sadat. First uncovered by the government in 1978, the group, supposedly led by Muhammad Abdel Salam Faraj, was also involved in a series of bloody confrontations with security forces culminating in the storming of police headquarters in Asyut in October 1981. Although members of *al Jihad* have been subjected to numerous rounds of arrests and preventive detentions culminating in prison sentences in 1982 and 1984, it has continued to be linked with a number of terrorist incidents as well as outbreaks of communal violence between Muslims and Christians in Upper Egyptian towns, notably Asyut, Suhag, Minya and Bani Suaif.

Other militant organizations active in the 1970s included the Islamic Liberation Organization, also known as the Technical Military Academy Group (TMA), which in April 1974 stormed the Technical Military Academy in Cairo (in co-operation with some of its own members inside who were cadets) as part of a plan to found the Islamic Republic of Egypt.

Lesser known groups active under the regime of President Mubarak include the *Samawiyyah* organization whose members were tried in 1986 on charges of arson attacks on several night-clubs, video shops and alcohol stores, and the Saved from Inferno group (*al Najun min al Nar*) which in 1987 was linked with assassination attempts on two former Ministers of the Interior and a liberal journalist.

In July 1987 the government arrested 85 members of a pro-Islamic organization, the Islamic Vanguard. Fierce clashes in December 1988 between rival Islamic groups are believed to have prompted the formation of a new group called Reformation of the Jihad Organization.

In May 1990 members of a group called the **New Islamic Jihad** were involved in bloody clashes with police following Muslim-Christian riots in the Fayoum region, 80 kilometres south-west of Cairo, during which their leader, Shawky Risq al Shaikh, was killed.

More recently the group known as **Excommunication and Emigration** (also known as Repentance and Flight—*al Tafkir wa al Hijra*—responsible for the killing in 1977 of the ex-Minister for Religious Affairs, Sheikh al-Dahabi) has gained prominence as a leading exponent of militant Islam in Egypt. Acknowledged by the government in 1973, the group is thought to date back to around 1965 when it emerged as one of the offshoots of the Muslim Brotherhood and its more extreme contemporary, Muhammad's Youth (*Shabab Muhammad*).

The group is believed originally to have encompassed two trends, the first opting for a gradualist approach to the creation of an Islamic state, the second, calling itself the "community of believers" (*jammat al muminun*), preferring immediate action and open confrontation. This latter offshoot which came eventually to dominate the group, was led by Shukri Mustafa, a former agriculture student born in Asyut in Upper Egypt.

Although there is little evidence that the Excommunication and Emigration organization still exists (its leader Shukri Mustafa being among those sentenced to death in 1977 on charges of kidnapping and murder—see above), its sympathizers are thought to have been absorbed into new groups such as the Saved from Inferno (*al Najun min al Nar*) and the Pause and Reveal Group (also known as Repose and Meditation (*al Tawaqqufwa al Tabayyun*).

Other groups still believed to be in operation include the *al Qutbiyyun*, an offshoot of the Muslim Brotherhood, influenced by the teachings of its leading theoretician, Sayyid Qutb (sentenced to death in 1965), and a little known exclusive group, the *al Firmawiyya*.

In October 1990 an Islamic group calling itself the Al-Aqsa Martyrs of the World Islamic Front for Liberation claimed responsibility for the assassination of the Speaker of the National Assembly, Rif'at al-Mahjub.

The Gulf War gave additional stimulus to Islamic fundamentalism in Egypt. The electoral victory of Algeria's Islamic Salvation Front (FIS) has also boosted the morale of Egypt's Muslim Brotherhood, while its suspension has been recently denounced by the Brotherhood as an undemocratic attack on Islam.

In May 1992 savage attacks by Muslim extremists against Christian communities in Upper Egypt were reported to have been organized by members of the *Gammat-i-Islami* (Islamic

Society), reportedly an offshoot of *al-Jihad*, whose local leader (*emir*) was named as Gamal Farghaly Haridi. Although representatives of the organization denied that Christians had specifically been targeted, they maintained that the actions of their group were necessary "to preserve society from moral degradation regardless of the religion of those who perpetrate it".

EW

Major Islamic organizations

Excommunication and Emigration also known as Repentance and Flight
al Takfir wa al Hijra

Strictly fundamentalist and anti-traditional organization discovered by the government in 1973, the group is believed to date back to 1965. It is not known whether the group still operates under this name. The organization derived its name from the notion of takfir, a term applied to judge infidels (a reference to Egypt's rulers), and *hijra* the strategy of retreat adopted by the Prophet Muhammad in preparation for ultimate victory.

Leader. Unknown; its supposed founder, Shukri Mustafa, a former Agriculture student born in Asyut and executed in 1977, was believed to have aspired to a messianic role reminiscent of the *Mahdi* (lit. "the guided one").

Structure. The group is believed to have been organized around tightly-structured, specialized cells (*majmuat*), as well as missionary units (*dawa*); survival and catering units (*isha*) and arms training and intelligence wings. The organization was reputed to be based on personal allegiance (*baya*) to the leader and was rumoured to have included a relatively large number of women.

Aims. The creation of an Islamic state by violent revolution, founded on a return to the letter of the Koran.

Holy War
al Jihad

Clandestine organization uncovered in 1978; claimed responsibility in October 1981 for the assassination of President Sadat. In March 1982 five alleged members, including Khalid al Islambuli were sentenced to death on charges of being directly responsible for the assassination. In 1984 more than 300 of the organization's alleged members were convicted, and some subsequently executed, after being charged with the murder of security forces in Asyut. Since 1986 the group has been associated with a variety of terrorist incidents and most recently, with the outbreak of riots between Muslims and Christians in parts of Upper Egypt.

Leader. There seems to be no dominant personalized leadership although the party's leading ideologue, Muhammad Abdel Salam Faraj is often mentioned as a key figure. Others believed to occupy prominent positions include Abbud al Zummur, a young army officer favouring an Iranian-style Islamic revolution, and Dr Umar Abdul Rahman (arrested in 1989 following clashes in al-Fayoum), a blind professor at the Theological College in Asyut, alleged to have authorized the assassination of Sadat, and who is said by the authorities to have issued religious decrees (*fatwas*) supporting the theft of money by Muslims from Christians. Rahman is reported to be living in New York where he is alleged to be directing the activities of the *Gammat-i-Islami* which has claimed responsibility for recent attacks against Coptic Christians in Upper Egypt. Rahman's reported marriage to a US Muslim convert in the US has so far enabled him to avoid deportation to Egypt to stand trial for a number of terrorist crimes.

Structure. The organization aspires to a form of "democratic centralism" based on a system of commissars (*masuli tanzim*). It is said to have a governing "scholars" council and a "consultation" council as well as three commissions for armaments, finance and preaching. Lower levels are believed to consist of revolutionary committees and mosque units, as well as armed student and worker militias.

Membership. Unknown. Support for the movement is said to be particularly strong in the Greater Metropolis (Cairo, Giza and a few small Delta towns) and parts of Upper Egypt concentrated in the provinces of Minya, Asyut and Sohag.

Aims. The immediate application of Islamic law (*sharia*) by force if necessary, and the creation of an Islamic state. The group's objectives, outlined in a booklet attributed to Faraj entitled *al Faridha al Ghaiba* (The Absent Commandment), are based on the notion that all good Muslims must fight their ungodly rulers' goals.

Publications. The most well-known being a clandestine anonymous monograph entitled *al Muhakamat al nizam al siyasi al misri* (A Trial of the Egyptian Political System).

Muslim Brotherhood
Ikhwan al Muslimun

The most prominent fundamentalist movement currently in Sunni Islam; founded 1928, banned in 1954 and still officially illegal. The Brotherhood has declared that it has no interest in forming a political party of its own until society has opted for the Islamic way of life as propounded by its members.

Leader. Hamid Abu al Nasr (Supreme Guide); Mamoun al Hudaiby (secretary-general).

Aims. The creation of an Islamic state and the adoption of Islamic law (*Sharia*) as the sole basis of Egyptian law.

Publications. al Dawa (The Call) published monthly. Between 1974 and 1981 the organization issued the monthly publications *al Iitisam* and *al Mukhtar.*

National Party
Umma Party

Founded in 1983 as an off-shoot of the Khartoum-based Islamic party of the same name. Although the party contested the 1990 elections, it has no members in the People's Assembly. It is the only opposition party represented in the upper house of the Consultative Council (Shura).

Leader. Ahmed Al Sabahi Awadallah.

Membership. Estimated to total 50,000 members in 1991; this figure may be exaggerated as the party remains politically marginalized.

Aims. The creation of an Islamic state which, in contradistinction to the Muslim Brotherhood, it claims will be founded on the political rather the doctrinal principles of Islam. It favours the introduction of Islamic legal punishment (*hudud*) and is presently campaigning for the total legalization of religious parties.

New Islamic Jihad

First emerged in May 1990, possibly as an offshoot of *al-Jihad*, during Muslim-Christian riots in the al Fayoum region, south-west of Cairo.

Leader. Unknown; the group's supposed founder (killed in May 1990) was Shawky Risq al Shaikh.

Ethiopia

Muslims in Ethiopia are estimated to constitute between 45 and 50 per cent of the population, out of a total population of over 48,000,000. All Muslims in Ethiopia are Sunnis who follow the Shafi school, common throughout east and southern Africa.

The ethnic, linguistic and religious diversity of the approximately 100 groups found in Ethiopia was played down by both Emperor Haile Selassie (who ruled for most of the period 1930-1974), and by Mengistu Haile Mariam (who headed a secular, Marxist regime from 1977 to 1991). No precise statistics on the balance of religions today are therefore available. The Amharic-speaking groups, historically identified with Ethiopian Christianity, continued to dominate government positions under the Selassie and Mengistu regimes, although after 1974 Islam and animist religions were accorded formal equality with Christianity. Religious allegiances in this diverse empire did not, however, necessarily correspond to ethnic or linguistic divisions.

Among the Gurage group in the Sidamo region of southern Ethiopia, for example, Christians, Muslims and followers of traditional religions live alongside each other. This is also the case among the Oromo, one of the largest communities in Ethiopia, who speak a common language and are found in 11 of Ethiopia's 14 provinces. Some members of the Oromo group follow traditional religions, some are Muslims, and some converted from Islam to Christianity as they underwent a process of Amharization in the 19th century. The inhabitants of Tigray province are estimated to be about 70 per cent Christian and 30 per cent Muslim. The Afar groups found in the north-east are superficially Muslim, as are the nomadic Somali people of south-west Ethiopia. Groups found on both sides of the Sudanese-Ethiopian border are in the north predominantly Muslim and followers of traditional religions in the south. At least half of the population of Eritrea, whose integration into Ethiopia has been fiercely resisted since 1962, are Muslims.

Despite its secular orientation the Mengistu regime was keen not to alienate organized religion. In 1986 it appointed a constitutional commission representing leaders of the country's established religions including Muslim clerics and removed a prohibition on polygamy in the original draft of the Constitution in deference to Muslim sentiment. However, Muslims continue to be under-represented in government and resistance to the central government has therefore stemmed mainly from Muslim groups, including the Somalis in the south-east and movements claiming to represent the Afar of the Red Sea plain and the southern Oromo.

The Ethiopian People's Democratic Revolutionary Front (EPRDF), which overthrew the Mengistu regime in May 1991 after several years of guerrilla warfare, had the support of other ethnically-based organizations, notably the five Oromo groups, including the **Islamic Front for the Liberation of Oromo** (IFLO), and the two major Eritrean parties, including the predominantly Muslim **Eritrean Liberation Front** (ELF). The new administration was, however, dominated by Tigrayans.

In its programme of early 1991 the new EPRDF government pledged "to remove all inequalities of rights based on religion", to separate education from religion, and not to recognize any religion as the state religion. In the immediate aftermath of the overthrow of Mengistu various political organizations emphasised religious tolerance in order to overcome tensions and rivalries between different groups.

In Eritrea the Muslim-dominated resistance movement, the ELF, which had been militarily defeated by the pro-Marxist, mainly Christian, Eritrean People's Liberation Front (EPLF) in the 1970s, was reactivated following the overthrow of the Mengistu regime. By early 1992, however, the ELF had split into two factions after some of its leadership rejected co-operation with the new EPLF administration in Asmara in anticipation of possible Eritrean independence.

In 1990 the secretary-general of the EPLF, Issaias Afewerki, consulted with Christian and Muslim leaders, including representatives of the Roman Catholic church, in Eritrea, in an attempt to solve problems of local administration and food distribution.

In November and December 1991 there were reports of the destruction of mosques and churches in clashes between Muslim Oromos and Christian Amharas near Dire Dawa in the east of central Ethiopia. Up to 60 people were killed in violence that took on a religious colouring, although it had originally been triggered by other issues. In an attempt to calm the situation, in October 1991 members of the local hierarchy of the Christian church met representatives of the IFLO in the town of Harar. The IFLO secretary-general, Shaikh Jara Aba Gada, stressed the importance of co-existence and called for an end to "divisions between the people on the basis of belongings and beliefs".

There are Muslim institutes in Asmara, Musawa, Addis Ababa and Harar, and mosques and Islamic schools in all areas of Ethiopia with sizeable Muslim populations.

EB

Major Islamic organizations

Ethiopian Islamic Democratic Movement (EIDM)
Founded in Washington in 1982 by Ethiopian exiles "motivated by the desire to redress the injustices committed against Ethiopian Muslims in the past". In July 1991 it had observer-status at the conference in Addis Ababa which established a transitional administration. In March 1992 the EIDM held its own conference in the capital to celebrate the anniversary of its foundation.
Leader. Ahmed Nur Mohammed (chair).
Aims. "To struggle side by side with all Ethiopians—irrespective of religious, ethnic or political affiliation, sex or profession—to advance the causes of equality, freedom, justice and self determination . . . To support the free political association of all nations and nationality groups . . . [and] universal suffrage leading to the establishment of a popularly elected government."

Eritrean Liberation Front
Muslim-dominated and supported organization founded in 1958 in Cairo, Egypt. It commenced an armed struggle against the government in 1961 and has been split into factions since early 1992.

Leader. Abdullah Mohammad (chair).

Aims. The creation of an independent Eritrea.

Islamic Front for the Liberation of Oromia (IFLO)

One of the armed groups asserting a separate Oromo identity in 1991-92 in the Harar region (east of Addis Ababa). Its leadership maintained that the group would respect the rights of Christian and animist minorities among the Oromo. Unlike its left-wing rival, the Oromo Liberation Front (OLF), it had no representation on the transitional Council of Representatives elected in Addis Ababa in July 1991.

Leader. Shaikh Jara Aba Gada (secretary-general).

Aims. To win "respect for Oromo values without violating the beliefs of other peoples. To struggle for democratic rights and peace for the sons of one united Ethiopia."

Muslim League of Eritrea

This organization gave evidence at the 1950 UN inquiry into the Eritrean question and claimed then that about half of all Ethiopians were Muslims.

France

Islam is the second most important religion in France after Roman Catholicism. It has an estimated 2,500,000 to 3,500,000 adherents, both citizens and immigrants, of whom more than 750,000 live in the area around the southern city of Marseille.

The majority of French Muslims are of Maghrebian origin, that is, they or their families came originally from Algeria (some 800,000 people in total including the "Harkis"), Morocco (450,000) or Tunisia (250,000). Since the 1970s, however, an increasing number of French Muslims have come from regions other than the Maghreb, including Turkey, north-west Africa (mainly Senegal and Mali, numbering around 70,000), Pakistan, Indonesia, Iran and around 16,000 from Yugoslavia, contributing to sectarian diversity. There is a consequent proliferation of Islamic schools of law. There are said to be also some 30,000 French converts to Islam.

Immigration from North Africa, primarily of migrant labourers from Algeria, began in the 1870s. Until 1905 most immigrants settled in Marseilles, with some movement north towards factories in Paris and Lens in the period between 1916 and 1919. Some 175,000 Algerians and Moroccans arrived during the First World War, many of them to join the French army. The French state, technically a secular state, in wartime encouraged North African Muslim clerics (*imams*) and members of religious brotherhoods to minister to the needs of these migrants and a mosque was built on army land near Nogent-sur-Marne, although it was recorded that the soldiers preferred to pray in the open air.

With the end of the war in 1918, the number of Muslims in France fell to some 10,000 but it rose again in the 1920s following immigration from north Africa. In the 1920s and 1930s most mosques, such as that in the Bois du Boulogne, were constructed at the initiative of French employers as Muslims in France tended not to be rigidly observant.

Islam and the state: post-war developments

The steady flow of migrants after the Second World War was mainly of single young men. By the early 1970s there was a sizeable community of second-generation immigrants with families. With the mechanization of agricultural labour, seasonal workers became less important while the introduction of stricter immigration laws in 1974 discouraged migrants from returning to the Maghreb to be replaced by other family members. At the same time the growing resident population of foreign workers gave rise to instances of overt racism.

On October 17 1961, at the height of the Algerian war of independence, clashes between police and Algerian demonstrators in Paris resulted in the deaths of an estimated 200 demonstrators. Another 400 went missing, in circumstances that have never been fully clarified.

Racism became technically illegal in France in 1972. In 1973 there was racist violence against Algerians over several months in Marseilles. In 1980 the Bonnet law gave the authorities wide powers of deportation although legislation introduced in 1981 by the government of President François Mitterrand curbed the worst excesses which resulted from this law.

Revived interest in religious observance in the 1970s and 1980s among first and second-generation Muslim immigrants has been regarded in part as a response to the strident racism of organizations of the extreme right, notably the National Front, led by Jean-Marie Le Pen. Fears that anti-Muslim sentiment might have pervaded established state institutions were compounded by the Barreau affair in November 1991: Jean-Claude Barreau was dismissed as president of the Office des Migrations Internationales (the main official department concerned with immigration) after writing *De l'islam en général et du monde moderne en particulier* ("On Islam in general and on the modern world in particular") which argued that the integration of Muslim immigrants into French society could be achieved only through their renunciation of the "archaic" religious practices of Islam.

In 1989 a controversy over the right of Muslim schoolgirls to wear headscarves was dubbed "la guerre des foulards" (the war of the headscarves) by the French media. The then Minister of National Education, Lionel Jospin, ruled that the girls should be allowed to wear headscarves to school on the grounds of "the right to be different".

Meanwhile pressure grew for Islam and its adherents to be accorded recognition on a par with other religions. A 1939 law prohibiting foreign nationals from forming associations was repealed by the government in 1981. Following this legal change it became common for small Muslim neighbourhood groups to negotiate with local authorities on issues ranging from the construction of mosques to permission to register as cultural organizations. In Marseilles one such organization, the Er-Ramaniyya, which in the 1970s had obtained permission for a prayer site and for the construction of a Quranic school, was subsequently regarded by the local authorities as a representative Muslim association.

Muslim organizations have also successfully lobbied for a change in education laws to allow Muslims the right to control their own schools, a right hitherto restricted to the Christian and Jewish communities.

Somewhat isolated from the rest of the Muslim community of north African origin are the "Harkis", Algerians who had fought in the French army during the Algerian war of independence and their children. The first Harki migrants were some 100,000 former soldiers, who were later joined by their families. They generally came from rural areas and brought with them a popularized Islam. Subsequent generations, better-educated and more articulate, who are concentrated around Lyon and Narbonne, were the first group of immigrants to emphasize Islam as the basis of their communal identity.

More recently, issues internal to French Muslims have also helped radicalize Muslim opinion. A recent example was the controversy about the appointment of the rector and chief cleric (*imam*) of the Paris Mosque, an appointment traditionally the privilege of the Algerian government which has been concerned to direct and monitor the sympathies of the large Algerian community. By the early 1990s growing numbers of Algerian Muslims had come to resent Algerian government control over the management of the Mosque which also controlled 30 of the 150 mosques in the Paris region. When in January 1992 the Mosque's rector, Shaikh Tedjini Haddam, accepted an invitation to become a member of Algeria's recently constituted

High Committee of State (HCS), Algerian-dominated organizations were quick to challenge the legitimacy of Haddam's rectorship and to call for the Paris Mosque to be made independent of Algerian government control.

There are estimated to be over 250 Muslim organizations in France, most of them local. They range from organizations established primarily to raise funds for small local mosques to groups influenced by fundamentalist thinking and with an emphasis on religious and social work. The French government has shown itself in favour of the emergence of a nationwide representative Muslim body.

EB

Major Islamic organizations

Association of Muslim Students in France
Association des étudiants islamiques de France (AEIF)
Seeking to promote Islamic consciousness among Muslim students, this organization is strong in Paris, Strasbourg and other cities with sizeable Muslim populations.

Council for the Study of French Islam
Conseil de réflexion sur l'Islam de France (CORIF)
Created in March 1990 at the instigation of the Interior Minister, Pierre Joxe, its members were intended to be representative of all geographical regions and of all currents within French Islam. In 1990-91 the CORIF Council included Jacques-Yacoub Roty, Tedjini Haddam and Hocine Chabaga from Lyon, Mohand Alili of the Marseille Mosque and Khalil Merroun from the Ile-de-France. In February 1992 CORIF was outspoken in its criticism of Algerian government control over the appointment of the rector of the Paris mosque.
Aims. To provide the government information relevant to the handling of sensitive issues and to prepare for the creation of a representative institution for Muslims in France.

European Institute for Human Sciences (EIHS)
Founded in January 1992 at Saint-Léger-de-Fougeret in Burgundy, reportedly with financial assistance from the UOIF, it claims to be the first pan-European Islamic institute. It has 13 students and offers a four-year course covering Islamic prayer, the study of Arabic and western religious thought. The Institute is reported to have received funding from Saudi Arabia and Kuwait.
Leader. Zohir Mahmoud (director, of Iraqi origin).
Aims. To produce clerics (*imams*) and community leaders with a progressive, rather than fundamentalist, outlook.

French Islamic Association
Groupement islamique en France (GIF)
Founded in 1979 in Valenciennes by a Tunisian student, it moved its headquarters to Paris in November 1981.
Aims. It seeks the re-education of the Muslim masses in line with the ideologies of the Egyptian Muslim Brotherhood and the *Jamaat-i-Islami Pakistan* (Islamic Society of Pakistan.

Islamic Order
Le rang islamique
Created in Amiens in 1983 with an influence throughout the region of Picardy, it follows the ideology of the Egyptian-inspired Muslim Brotherhood (Ikhwan al-muslimun. Members are said to pursue a five-year training course to

become preachers and open meetings are held to make contact with ordinary Muslims.

Muslim Institute of the Paris Mosque
Founded in 1923.
Leader. Shaikh Tedjini Haddam (director and rector of the Paris Mosque).

National Federation of French Muslims
Fédération nationale des musulmans de France (FNMF)
Founded in 1985 by a French convert to Islam [see below] as a follow-up to an earlier nationwide association established in 1983 to regulate the sale of ritually slaughtered (*halal*) meat which failed to obtain official recognition as a regulatory body. The first FNMF congress, at the Palais des Congrès, Paris, was attended by representatives of 108 Islamic organizations although the Federation is presently said to represent no more than 20 associations. The FNMF has been at the centre of developments such as the controversy over the selection of the rector of the Paris Mosque and it has opposed Algerian government control over the administration of the Mosque. The organization is reported to have had financial assistance from the government of Saudi Arabia and the Mecca-based Islamic World League.
Leader. Daniel-Youssof Leclerq (president and founder). In November 1985 Jacques-Yacoub Roty, the organization's first president, was elected head of its "bureau", or policy-making body, but was subsequently replaced by another convert to Islam, André Wormser.

Regional Federation of French Muslims
Fédération regionale des musulmans de France (FRMF)
Formed in June 1988, it includes 147 Islamic associations from Provence and the Côte d'Azur and about 20 from Marseilles.
Aim. The representation of the Muslim community of the region in its relations with the local authorities over community matters.

Union of Islamic Organizations in France
Union des organizations islamiques en France (UOIF)
This organization tends to engage less in public debate than the FNMF. It is based in Paris and in the early 1990s was made up of some 20-30 Islamic organizations from all regions of France.

The Gambia

The Gambia became an independent state within the Commonwealth in February 1965, and a republic in April 1970. The Gambia forms a narrow strip of land along both sides of the river Gambia within the present Republic of Senegal—the whole area being designated Senegambia. The country's physical proximity to Senegal has meant that The Gambia has always been influenced by developments there.

Like its neighbour, The Gambia is characterized by relative religious homogeneity despite ethnic diversity. About 85 per cent of the population (estimated in 1989 to total 848,000) are Muslim, the remainder professing Christianity and a tiny proportion (about 1 per cent), mostly from the Jola and Karoninka ethnic groups, being animists.

The majority of Muslims are Sunnis of the Maliki school who include in their midst sizeable numbers who are followers of the influential Qadiriyyah and Tijaniyyah brotherhoods. Until recently, attempts by the heterodox Muslim sect, the Ahmadiyya, to establish itself have met with a hostile response from the Sunni establishment.

Islam dates from about the 10th century when Arab and Berber merchants from the Mahgreb, developing trans-Saharan trading routes, made converts among the area's relatively settled population. Until the colonial period, Islam and its practices were limited to court circles and elite merchants. However, the Marabout Wars of the mid-19th century played a vital role in facilitating the spread of Islam to the lower orders.

Tension between Muslim and Christian communities, common to other parts of West Africa where the Muslim population was proportionally smaller, was rare in the colonial period. Where tension arose, it was principally as a result of educational disparities. Although Muslim schools were allowed to operate freely, recruitment into the colonial administration was biased in favour of those who had received a Western-style education from Christian missionaries.

These disadvantages were, nevertheless, outweighed by the numerical superiority of the Muslims, which enabled them to play a significant role in the political evolution of the country. Of note in this respect was the formation in 1952 of the Muslim Congress Party (MCP), which subsequently influenced the direction of colonial policy. However, the MCP failed to win sustained support and in 1960 it merged with the Democratic Party, which itself amalgamated with the People's Progressive Party (PPP) in 1965. Sir Dawda Kaibara Jawara (Prime Minister in 1965-70), a Muslim, was re-elected President with an overwhelming majority in 1987.

Islam and the state: developments since independence

The demise of the MCP is an indicator of the effective separation of religion from politics in

The Gambia. Commentators have attributed this to three main factors. First, the personal popularity of political leaders has outweighed not just their religious backgrounds but, to a certain extent, their political backgrounds. Secondly, the prevailing social system, which places importance on the extended family, has meant that political leaders can change their religious views without jeopardizing the support of kinship groups. Finally, compared with other West African Muslims, the Islamic community in The Gambia, despite The Gambia's membership of the Islamic Conference Organization (ICO), is relatively isolated from external Muslim developments, and appears to be untouched by the Islamic movement elsewhere.

Since independence, Islamic law has been recognized under the judicial system. Courts administering Islamic law (*sharia*) have jurisdiction in matters between, or exclusively affecting, Muslims in civil disputes relating to marriage and inheritance.

The Imam of Banjul, Al Haji Abdoulie Jobe, has overall responsibility for Muslim affairs.

TJ

Islamic organizations

Gambian Muslim Association
Committed to the promotion and teaching of Arabic.

Germany

Muslims in Germany were estimated in 1991 to number around 1,700,000 or 2.1 per cent of the total population, making it the third-largest religious group in the country after Lutherans and Catholics. The overwhelming majority are Turkish Sunnis who, along with Turkish Kurds, total about 1,660,000.

The rest, a few thousand, are Muslims from Afghanistan, Morocco, Pakistan, Tunisia, Yugoslavia, and other Arab states. There is a small Shia community drawn mainly from Iran whose members tend, on the whole, to belong either to the academic or business classes, giving them a disproportionate degree of influence. There are also a number of Muslim refugees from the former Soviet Union, Sunnis from Jordan and between 1,000 and 2,000 German-born converts to Islam.

The majority of Muslims are concentrated in the federal states of North Rhine-Westphalia and Baden-Württemberg, and in the city of Berlin. They are generally unskilled and semi-skilled workers with only a minority engaged in business and the liberal professions.

The Muslim presence in Germany grew out of contact with the Ottoman Empire. In 1683, following the second seige of Vienna, the retreating Ottoman army left behind stragglers and prisoners in southern German states. A century later the Prussian army was recruiting Muslim units.

During the 19th century trading and political relations developed, culminating in a formal alignment between the Ottoman Sultan and Germany during World War I. After the war some Turkish prisoners freed by the Allied Powers settled in Berlin to form the nucleus of a Muslim community which expanded gradually with the inclusion of Afghans and Iranians.

German relations with Turkey were revived in the post-war era when Turkish migration to the Federal Republic of Germany was formally encouraged under the terms of a 1961 treaty sanctioning the supply of Turkish industrial labour to Germany. Similar treaties furthering Muslim migration were concluded between Germany and Morocco in 1969, and later between Germany and Tunisia. By the 1970s Germany's need for expatriate labour had ceased owing to the economic recession that had gripped Western economies in the wake of rising oil prices. However, the flow of migrants continued, prompted by the desire of an increasing number of families to be reunited.

Doctrinally Muslim Turks have tended to favour Sunni revivalist trends indigenous to Turkey, the most important of which are the Suleymanci sect founded by Suleyman Hilmi Tunahan (1888-1959), and the Nurcu, a clandestine group pioneered by Sayyid Nursi (1873-1960). Both are fiercely opposed to the secular state established by Kemal Ataturk and favour a return to Islamic law (*sharia*).

The Egyptian Muslim Brotherhood (*Ikhwan al muslimun*) is active among some sections of the Arab and non-Turk population, while Shia activists are known to be influential among Iranians and other Shia-related groups, such as the Alawi.

The heterodox Ahmediyyah movement, which originated in the Indian sub-continent in the 1880s, is favoured by German-born converts, many of whom have been drawn to the sect's evangelical orientation. The movement played an important role in the construction of mosques in Hamburg, Frankfurt and elsewhere in West Germany in the 1950s.

There are almost a thousand mosques of various Muslim denominations spread across the country, but by the early 1980s the majority were associated with a variety of Turkish sects and their corresponding organizations.

Organizational developments in the Muslim community

A number of factors have contributed to the political marginalization of Germany's Muslim minorities. The single most important factor has been the government's policy towards ethnic minorities in general and towards Muslims in particular. The majority of Muslims are foreign nationals and have no political rights, which partly accounts for their low profile on the political scene. This in turn is a consequence of the government's policy of regarding migrant labourers as "guest workers" rather than as immigrants or settlers. A corollary of this policy has been the number of restrictions placed on immigrants wishing to acquire citizenship. Thus, despite the fact that 40 per cent of Germany's Turkish minority were born in Germany, only a small number have applied for citizenship.

Another issue of direct concern to Muslims has been the question of Islamic religious education, to which Muslims are entitled by law, although Islam is not recognized by the state as a statutory organization with specific civil rights. Unlike the Christian and Jewish communities, Muslims do not benefit from a voluntary "church tax" aimed at meeting the needs of particular religious groups. The result has been the dependence of Muslims on a loose interpretation of existing legislation by state governments to obtain funding for Islamic instruction in schools for Muslim children. The debate on the question of religious instruction has been complicated further by the lack of any clear consensus among Muslims as to how such education is to be provided.

The attitude of Turkey has been a crucial factor in shaping the response of Turkish Muslims in Germany. Turkey's close relationship with Germany, aided by Turkish membership of the North Atlantic Treaty Organization (NATO), has helped ensure that the Turkish minority retains links with Turkey and thereby, the continuous flow of foreign remittances. These links have, however, inclined German Turks to regard themselves more as Turks abroad than as one of Germany's ethnic and religious minorities with corresponding rights.

Flowing from Turkey's involvement has been the reproduction of Turkish politics within the Turkish community in Germany. The lack of democracy in Turkey in the 1980s forced political organizations, especially those of the religious right, to become active in Germany. The Turkish government was particularly alarmed by reports that Muslim extremist groups had begun to wield increasing control over mosques and religious institutions through their involvement in the organization of Quranic classes for Turkish children.

In the early 1980s the Turkish government's Directorate for Religious Affairs Abroad, established in 1972, took determined steps to curb the influence among Muslim Turks of

Turkish fundamentalist groups, some with links to Turkish political parties, by seeking to control the provision of religious instruction that more closely reflected the norms of establishment Islam in Turkey.

By the end of the decade it was reported that the **Association of Turkish Islamic Affairs** (ATIA or DITIB), an offshoot of the Directorate of Religious Affairs Abroad, had succeeded in gaining managerial control over the majority of mosques catering to the religious needs of the Turkish Muslim community in Germany.

However, fears that the revivalist current that swept Turkey in the mid-1980s had reached Germany appeared to be confirmed after it was reported in 1992 that a group within the DITIB had broken away to rally behind Cemalettin Kaplan, former Mufti of Adana who was living in voluntary exile in Germany. Kaplan (who substituted his "animal" name meaning tiger, to the Muslim "Hojaöglu"), is a former protegé of Necmettin Erbakan, leader of the Islamist Welfare Party in Turkey, with whom he had severed links after coming out in support of an Islamic state based on the ideas of Ayatollah Khomeini.

Other groups opposed to the Turkish government include the **Nationalist View Association** (NVA, also known as the **Organization of National Vision**), which has denounced the Turkish government's involvement in the religious education of Turks abroad on grounds that it was designed to protect the secular state. The NVA is allegedly linked to Turkey's National Salvation Party, founded in 1972 and subsequently banned for advocating an Islamic state.

The **Islamic Cultural Centre** (*Avrüpa Kültur Merkezleri Birligi*), reportedly controlled by members of the Suleymanci group and associated with the outlawed Turkish Justice Party, is also opposed to the activities of the DITIB. The less influential Nurcu sect has tended generally to eschew politics, preferring to concentrate on activities related to religious proselytization.

Non-Turkish associations active among the Muslim population include local branches of the Mecca-based World Muslim League and the Egyptian Muslim Brotherhood.

YS

Major Islamic organizations

Association of Turkish Islamic Affairs (sometimes referred to as the Turkish Islamic Union)

Diyanet Isleri Türk-Islam Birligi (DITIB)
Türkisch Islamische Union der Anstalt für Religion

Sponsored by the Turkish government, reportedly with the encouragement of the German government, the association became active in the early 1980s as a counter-weight to revivalist currents among the Turkish community in Germany. With headquarters in Cologne, the DITIB maintains numerous branches throughout Germany concerned with increasing control over mosques and Quranic classes for the Turkish community.

Leader. Osman Nuri Gursoy.

Membership. In the late 1980s the association claimed to be the largest Muslim federation in the country.

Aims. To promote Islamic instruction among the Turkish community in Germany. The organization has reportedly sought also to depoliticize mosques and Islamic teaching among the Turkish community and to propagate a version of establishment Islam opposed by Muslim militant organizations, many of which are currently proscribed in Turkey.

Islamic Association of German-speaking Muslims

Islamische Gemeinschaft deutsch sprachiger Muslimei

Leader. Hartmul Mohammad Herzog.

Islamic Cultural Centre

Avrüpa Kültur Merkezleri Birligi

Based in Cologne with alleged links to the banned Turkish Justice Party (JP); it is reportedly backed by the fundamentalist Suleymanci sect, an orthodox Naqshbandi offshoot, founded by the anti-Kemalist reformer, Suleyman Hilmi Tunahan (1888-1959).

Membership. In 1982 it had 210 local centres, but its influence has reportedly been sharply curbed by the success of the DITIB.

Aims. Critical of the Turkish regime which it wants replaced by an Islamic state. In Germany it organizes Koranic classes for children.

Nationalist View Association (also known as the Organization of National Vision)

Avrupa Milli Görüs Teskilati

Right-wing organization said to be linked to the Turkish National Salvation Party (NSP), recast in 1983 as the Welfare Party under Necmettin Erbakan. Claims of tacit co-operation between the NVA and the Turkish government-sponsored DITIB emerged after reports of the NVA's sympathetic posture vis-à-vis Turkish President Turgut Ozal, a former member of the NSP.

Membership. Although predominantly Turkish, the organization claims also to represent non-Turkish Muslims.

Aims. It calls for the implementation of an Islamic state in Turkey and runs Quranic classes in Germany.

Publication. *Milli Gazette* and the weekly journal *Hicret*.

Greece

The Muslim population of Greece is made up principally of a group of Turkish-speaking Muslims in Western Thrace, the area in the north-east bordering Turkey and Bulgaria. The group numbers possibly as many as 120,000 people. There are some 40,000 Bulgarian-speaking Muslims, known as Pomaks, in the villages just south of the Bulgarian border as well as smaller numbers of Macedonian Muslims, the remnants of a population that in 1912 constituted 39 per cent of the population of south Macedonia. Rhodes and Chios have between them about 15,000 Muslims and there are an estimated 35,000 Muslims in Athens. Greece also has small numbers of Muslim gypsies and recent Muslim refugees from Albania.

Muslims make up less than 2 per cent of the total population. About 97 per cent of Greeks are members of the Greek Orthodox Church, which is recognized in the Constitution as the national religion of the Greek people, although the state itself is decreed to be secular.

In recent decades the Turkish Muslim community in Western Thrace, which traces its origins back to 12th-century migrations from central Anatolia, has been subjected to social and economic discrimination, resulting in a steady trickle of emigration to Turkey. Figures for Turkish-speaking Muslims are disputed: Greek government statistics of 1981 cite 60,000 Turkish-speaking Muslims in Greece, but other sources claim that there may be between 100,000 and 120,000 Turkish-speaking Muslims in Western Thrace.

In the late 1980s 200 primary schools, four secondary schools and about 300 mosques served this community. There are claims of discrimination by local government in the provision of basic services such as roads as well as in the granting of permission to buy land or buy and build houses, and in public-sector employment. Greek law continues to be used to refuse re-entry to Greek citizens of Muslim Turkish origin who travel abroad. In 1988 Turkish-speakers in the town of Komotini in Western Thrace demonstrated against what they deemed official discrimination. The demonstration was followed by bomb explosions in the central mosque and in a Muslim cemetery.

In the general election of April 1990, which finally broke the deadlock produced by the two inconclusive general elections of 1989, two seats were won by representatives of the Turkish-speaking Muslims of Thrace. One of them, Sadik Ahmet, had already been elected in the June 1989 election, but had then served two months of an 18-month prison sentence for using the word "Turkish" to describe his Muslim constituents. (The usage had been banned by the Greek High Court in 1988 as a danger to public order and the term "Greek Muslims" was the only one acceptable to the authorities.) Ahmet had previously, in 1986, been sentenced to a longer prison sentence (never imposed) for charges in connection with the organization of a petition to the United Nations and the Council of Europe which claimed that the Greek authorities were pressurizing Turkish-speakers to emigrate. Since 1990 a new electoral law has made the election of such independent members of parliament less likely, as it stipulates a threshold of 3 per cent of the national vote for a party to qualify for seats in parliament.

The annual human rights report produced by the United States State Department in February 1991 referred to "a pattern of economic and social discrimination against the Muslim minority in western Thrace". This provoked protests from the Greek government, especially as the report also recognized the existence of a Macedonian minority in northern Greece which is not recognized by the Greek government.

The dissolution of the Soviet Union in 1991 brought to the surface tensions surrounding the issue of the Turkish-speaking minority. In August 1991 members of the Bulgarian Turks Association in Turkey, led by Ibrahim Efendioglu, demonstrated outside the Greek embassy in Ankara, Turkey, claiming harsh treatment of the Turkish-Muslim minority by the Greek authorities. They cited in particular incidents that had taken place in the Greek town of Xanthi in August that year when Muslims had been involved in violent protests against the appointment by the government of a new local *mufti* (Muslim religious leader). The Greek government had responded by saying that it was usual even in Muslim countries for the chief Mufti to be appointed by the government rather than be elected by the local community.

Meanwhile there was renewed interest in Turkey in the condition of the Turkish-Muslim minority in Western Thrace, especially among nationalist and Islamic fundamentalist sympathizers. This led to the creation of an Association for Solidarity with the Turks of West Thrace in 1991. In November 1991 the treatment of Muslim Turks in Western Thrace was described by the new Turkish Prime Minister, Suleyman Demirel, as "inhuman" and in need of urgent international attention.

EB

Islamic Organizations

Islamic Union
Created in 1932 to promote the interests of the Muslims of northern Greece and to make representations to the authorities on provisions for education and religious worship.

Turkish Teachers' Association
Active in the early 1980s opposing what it claimed were discriminatory measures against Turkish-language education in Western Thrace. It was closed by order of the Komotini court in March 1986, a decision upheld by the Athens High Court in July 1987.

Guinea

The Republic of Guinea achieved full independence from France in October 1958. Post-independence history was dominated by the country's first President, Ahmed Sékou Touré. Touré also headed the sole legal party, the Democratic Party of Guinea (PDG), which pursued a policy of revolutionary socialism. Following his death in 1984, the military seized power and banned the PDG.

A country of just over 5,500,000 people, Guinea is predominantly Muslim (around 95 per cent); a substantial minority adheres to traditional African religions while the remainder follow Christianity. Guinea is the only African Muslim state where almost the entire Muslim population is of indigenous rather than of Arab or Berber descent.

The Muslim community is overwhelmingly Sunni, adhering to the Maliki school of law. Recent indications suggest that the actual hold of Islam may be more tenuous than is acknowledged, with many Guineans being only nominally Muslim while continuing to adhere to animism. Unlike neighbouring Mali and Mauritania, the influence of Islam on daily life in minimal. Far more important are ethnic divisions.

Islam and the state: developments since independence

Successive governments have tended on the whole to regard Islam as a conservative force and a potentially competing focus of loyalty.

Although the PDG relied in the pre-independence period on the backing of Islamic leaders and Muslim merchants, once in power it rapidly sought to develop a policy of control. Under Touré the party's rigid policy of Marxism, which dominated Guinean society until at least 1978, resulted in severe curbs on the influence of Muslim clerics (*imams*) who were removed from positions of secular authority within the community and denied permission to collect alms (*zakat*) as a source of livelihood.

Imams were, on occasion, also required to preach their Friday sermons on topics provided by the government. Permission to interrupt the working day was restricted, with the number of permitted breaks reduced from five times to twice daily, apparently to avoid disruption. The number of people performing the Muslim pilgrimage to Mecca (*hajj*) has also been curtailed.

At the same time the government has been careful not to alienate Muslim sentiment by denouncing Islamic beliefs. It has made some conciliatory gestures, including the free supply of electricity to the country's mosques since 1971. Muslims are represented in government by the secretary-general of the **National Islamic League**.

TJ

Islamic organizations

National Islamic League (NIL)
Government body created in October 1988 to replace the Ministry of Religious Affairs; responsible for all Muslim affairs.
Leader. Al Haji Ahmed Tidiane Traore (secretary-general (with rank of Cabinet Minister)).

Union Culturelle Musulmane (UCM)
Social and cultural organization founded in 1953; suppressed by the government and later reorganized with a government-appointed leadership.

Guinea-Bissau

The Republic of Guinea-Bissau gained independence from Portugal in 1974. Until the introduction of a multiparty system in 1991, the sole legal political party was the *Partido Africano da Independência da Guiné e Cabo Verde* (PAIGC).

Of a population estimated in 1989 to total 960,000, the majority (about 65 per cent) adhere to traditional religions; about 30 per cent follow Sunni Islam or profess syncretic beliefs derived from a fusion of Islamic and indigenous religious practices, and the remainder (8 per cent) are Christian Roman Catholics.

Islam was brought to the country following the Fula *jihads* (holy wars) in the early 19th century. The Muslim population is now concentrated in the interior of the country among the cattle-raising people. In recent years, however, there has been a slow but steady spread towards the coastal region. Ethnically, the Fula, Mandinga, Beafada, Susu and several other smaller groups follow Islam.

Islam and the state: developments since independence

The socialist PAIGC government has been tolerant of the country's religious diversity and unlike in some other African countries, no single religious group dominates in terms of political, economic or social power.

A broad range of religious opinion is given space in the national media, including state radio. The newspapers often give substantial coverage to Islamic tradition, culture and practices. There are several mosques and Islamic schools which operate unhindered. There are no major Islamic organizations and of the many political parties to emerge from mid-1991, none was specifically Muslim in outlook.

Muslims in Guinea-Bissau maintain links with their co-religionists abroad through Guinea-Bissau's membership of the Islamic Conference Organization (ICO).

TJ

Guyana

The Co-operative Republic of Guyana a former British colony and the only English-speaking country in South America, gained independence in 1966 and has remained a member of the Commonwealth.

The first Muslims to enter the country were of African origin, brought in as slaves during the 18th and early 19th centuries.

As in other countries in the region, the abolition of slavery resulted in the import of indentured labour, including many Muslims from the Indian subcontinent. In 1834 some 60,000 Indians were brought from the Indian states of Bihar and West United Provinces and by 1917 254,500 Indians had arrived.

Enticed by offers of land, only one-third of these people returned to Asia. Muslims make up about 13 per cent, or 130,000, of Guyana's total population, estimated in the 1980 census at 811,000 (of which 50 per cent are East Indian). About 125,000 Muslims are of Indian origin and the rest are of African descent. The majority of Guyanese Muslims are Sunni.

Islam and the state

Although until at least the mid-19th century many Muslims were subject to religious prejudice, many subsequently came to play a prominent part in national politics. In 1974 there were four Muslim government ministers out of a total of 24, and 10 Muslim MPs out of a total of 83.

The Muslim community has in recent times been divided, with a debate in the 1970s as to whether the community should support the African-dominated People's National Congress (PNC) or the People's Progressive Party (PPP), identified with the Indian community. The debate ultimately led to a split within one of the country's leading Muslim organizations, the **Guyana United Sad'r Islamic Anjuman** (GUSIA). More recently, Muslims have formed their own national political organization, the **al Mujaheddin Party**.

Guyana has 130 mosques and Quranic schools receive government subsidies. Islamic education does not feature in the country's state education.

MCB

Islamic Organizations

al Mujaheddin Party
Political organization representing Guyanese

Muslim opinion.
Leader. Hoosain Ganie.

General Congress of Islamic Brotherhood

Formed in 1973, this organization was formed along with the Muslim Youth League and the Islamic Centre on a neutral platform as a reaction to the split within the USIA [see below].

Guyana United Sad'r Islamic Anjuman (GUSIA)

Formed in 1936 to give Muslims a national voice, this organization split in 1972, with the dominant right-wing faction identifying with the ruling PNC and a breakaway group supporting the opposition PPP. In the 1980s it had 120 branches.

Leader. Haji Abdool Rahman (president); Haji S.M. Yaseen (secretary).

Membership. 120,000.

Hungary

There are estimated to be around 3,000 Muslims in the Republic of Hungary, whose total population stood at 10,600,000 in 1990.

Muslim religious affairs are administered by the Hungarian Islamic Community (*Magyar Iszlam Kozosseg*) headed by Balazs Mihalfy.

GR

India

India was established as a democratic and secular state on its independence from Britain in August 1947. Although many Muslims left India for Pakistan, some 35 million chose to remain in post-partition India and they still constitute the country's largest minority. According to the 1981 census there were 75,400,000 Muslims in India (11 per cent of the population), making India the fourth most populous Muslim nation in the world after Indonesia, Bangladesh and Pakistan.

Most Indian Muslims are Sunnis who adhere to the Hanafi school of law. The rest are Shias, the majority of whom belong to the Twelver (*ithna ashariyya*) sect, with a small but influential group of Ismailis. Sufi brotherhoods have traditionally been important and the most well-established orders are the Naqshbandiyyah, Chishtiyyah, Shattariyyah and Suhrawardiyyah.

Indian Muslims are a heterogenous and culturally varied community. From the point of view of language and custom, for instance, there are significant differences between the Urdu-speakers of North India and Andhra Pradesh, the Malayalee-speaking Mappillas of Kerala, and the Tamil-speaking Labbais of Tamil Nadu. Indian Muslims are also divided on religious and political issues, and they range from Islamic fundamentalists to secular communists.

Islam and the state: developments since independence

The dominant trend since 1947 has been for Indian Muslims to support political parties with avowedly secular goals. However, the increasingly communal nature of Indian politics in recent years has resulted in a growing feeling among sections of the Indian Muslim community that they need to adopt a more assertive stance in order to protect their rights as Muslims. The vast majority of Muslims continue to live in depressed rural areas, though urban middle-class Muslims have come to enjoy increased prosperity, due in large part to opportunities for employment in the Gulf states. Communal tension has therefore been fed by economic competition and resentment which deepens Muslim feelings of vulnerability and fuels Islamic revivalism.

In the years following independence, Indian Muslims on the whole appeared to reject overtly Muslim political alternatives and opted for low political visibility. With the virtual collapse in India of the main pre-independence Muslim political organization, the All-India Muslim League (ALML), many Muslims turned to the Society of Indian Scholars (*Jamiat-ul-Ulama Hind*—JUH) for political guidance. The JUH, dominated by the reformist current associated with the theological seminary at Deoband, had supported the nationalist campaign launched by the Indian National Congress Party (henceforth Congress) which promoted a vision of a free and multi-religious India in which Muslim communities would live their personal lives according to Islamic law (*sharia*) and in harmony with non-Muslim communities. In December 1948 the JUH convened an all-India conference in the northern Indian town of Lucknow. This resulted in a consensus to favour a non-communal approach to politics to which the JUH responded by formally resolving to eschew electoral politics: though its members were permitted to join non-communal parties, as an organization it decided to concentrate on social and religious reform and it subsequently welcomed the secular constitution of the Republic of India.

In the first three general elections, in 1952, 1957 and 1962, Muslims overwhelmingly supported Congress which under the leadership of Jawaharlal Nehru retained its image as the country's leading secular party; JUH leaders often stood as Congress candidates. The Muslim Convention, revived in June 1961 by Maulana Hifzur Rahman, acted within the Congress framework and appealed to Muslims to co-operate with non-Muslims within secular political and social organizations. Attempts in 1959 to revive the ALML proved futile, with the renamed **Indian Union Muslim League** (IUML) managing to send only one representative to the *Lok Sabha* (lower house of Parliament) in 1957 and two in 1962. Regional Muslim organizations such as the *Ittehadul Muslimeen* (Muslim Unity) made some headway in state elections but the electoral appeal of this party remained limited in places such as Hyderabad in Andhra Pradesh.

Growing Muslim disenchantment with Congress was reflected in the 1967 elections results in which Muslims deserted the party in large numbers, particularly in Uttar Pradesh, Bihar and Bengal. The establishment of the *Muslim Majlis-i Mushawarat* (Muslim Consultative Committee) in August 1964 highlighted this changing political response. Intended to articulate Muslim grievances and to seek ways of alleviating them through party and electoral politics, the *Muslim Majlis* was a loose confederation of diverse socio-political interests variously associated with former leaders of the ALML, IUML, **Indian Islamic Society** (*Jamaat-i Islami Hind*—JIH), Khilafat Party, Progressive Muslim League, Anjuman-i Tameer-i Millat (National Reconstruction Body), and some Muslim members of Congress supported by the JUH. The *Muslim Majlis*'s "People's Manifesto" of 1967 summarised Muslim demands: the introduction of proportional representation, the protection of Muslim personal law, and the recognition of Urdu as a second official language in north Indian states. But although its campaign helped influence electoral results in Uttar Pradesh and Bihar, the erosion of Muslim support for Congress derived more from anti-Congress sentiment in general than from the emergence of Muslim communal politics.

Disillusionment within the Uttar Pradesh *Muslim Majlis* with Muslim legislators revived interest in an all-India Muslim political party able to endorse Muslim candidates nationwide. However, the all-India *Muslim Majlis* was not in a position to convert itself into a political party since one of its component units, the JIH, was opposed to such a move and so the Uttar Pradesh *Muslim Majlis* decided in 1968 to convert itself into a political party. It failed, however, to make any headway in state and national mid-term elections in 1969 and subsequent attempts to revive the party proved unsuccessful.

The 1960s witnessed an upsurge in communal conflict, in large part due to increased levels of Hindu communal activity linked to the resurgence of nationalist feeling after the Indo-Chinese war of 1962 and the Indo-Pakistan war of 1965. Proposals to "Indianize" Muslims in order to purge them of disloyal tendencies caused apprehension among many Muslims, as did the electoral advances of the Hindu fundamentalist *Bharatiya Jana Sangh* during the decade.

Muslim perceptions of Congress's inability or unwillingness to defend Muslim interests alienated much of the party's traditional Muslim constituency although at the same time Muslims continued to support Congress's secular ideal as the only real guarantee of their welfare as a religious minority. Even the JIH, after years of diffidence on the matter, declared in 1970 that "in the present circumstances, the *Jamaat-i Islami Hind* wishes that, in contrast to other totalitarian and fascist modes of government, the . . . secular democratic mode of government in India should endure".

India's victory in the war with Pakistan over Bangladesh in 1970-71 was followed by Prime Minister Indira Gandhi's cultivation of a more conspicuously Hindu image in order to strengthen her popularity. In a reversal of earlier secular traditions, the apparent state patronage of Hindu religious fervour further undermined Muslim support for Congress and during the 1970s there was a slow but steady Muslim drift away from Congress and towards regionally based political organizations such as the Jammu and Kashmir National Conference, the *Lok Dal* in Uttar Pradesh and Bihar, and those constituting the coalition left-wing government in Bengal. The imposition of a state of emergency in 1975-77, which included a ban on the JIH, further undermined Muslim support.

The gradual weakening of Muslim support for the Indira Gandhi faction of Congress (henceforth Congress (I)) enabled Muslim organizations to broaden their support by emphasizing Congress's failure to guarantee the welfare of India's ethnic and religious minorities, and it resulted in improved positions for the *Ittehadul Muslimeen* in Hyderabad and the JIH in Kashmir. With the departure of north Indian Muslims to Pakistan, what remained of the ALML (renamed the IUML—see above) had been almost entirely transformed into a regionally based south Indian party. In the June 1991 elections the IUML acquired substantial strength in Kerala, winning 19 seats in the State Assembly to become the second most important component of the Congress (I)-led United Democratic Front government, and sending two representatives to the *Lok Sabha*. Its main objectives were the protection of the Muslim community through non-religious demands, including the preservation of the Urdu language (and Arabic in Kerala) and fixed Muslim quotas in education, government and employment in general, and in parliament and the state assemblies.

The basic aim of Muslim organizations in India (with the exception of those in Kashmir—see below) has been the preservation of Muslim cultural and religious identity. In particular, they have opposed the demand for a uniform civil code, an issue that helped unite otherwise diverse Muslim organizations such as the JUH, the JIH, the **Missionary Society** (*Tablighi Jamaat*) and the **Assembly of Religious Scholars** (*Nadwah t-al-Ulama*). These bodies regarded any change in the Muslim personal law on marriage, divorce, inheritance and adoption as a threat to Muslim culture in India and an infringement of India's composite nationalism. Following a convention in December 1974, representatives of leading Islamic organizations established the All-India Muslim Personal Law Board (AIMPLB) to monitor and actively resist any changes to the Muslim personal law.

In the mid-1980s the AIMPLB spearheaded opposition to a Supreme Court judgement in April 1986 which appeared to overrule Islamic law by granting maintenance rights to a divorced Muslim woman, Begum Shah Bano. The Supreme Court's verdict on the Shah Bano case, as it came to be known, was perceived by many, though not all, Indian Muslims as an assault on the *sharia* and as the thin end of the wedge, substituting Muslim personal law with a common civil code. One hundred thousand Muslims marched in Bombay in protest against the ruling, prompting Muslim organizations to petition the government to pass legislation exempting divorced Muslim women from the sections of the Indian Criminal Procedure Code which entitle them to claim maintenance from their former husbands. Street protests, combined with electoral results in which the Muslim vote tipped the balance in favour of opposition parties, in May 1986 led the Congress government under Rajiv Gandhi to pass the Muslim Women (Protection of Rights on Divorce) Bill, allowing Muslim women to appeal to the Muslim religious endowment (*waqf*) for compensation equal to the sum that Hindu women in such circumstances would receive. Congress likewise acted in October 1988 to safeguard its support among Muslim voters by making India the first country to ban the novel *The Satanic Verses* by the UK-born Indian writer Salman Rushdie.

In the mid-1980s Islamic organizations were involved in another major and long-standing controversy centring on a disputed mosque, the Babri Masjid at Ayodhya in Uttar Pradesh, claimed by Hindu fundamentalists as the birthplace of the Hindu god, Rama, and therefore a site of Hindu worship. In December 1986 representatives from leading Islamic organizations formed the All-India Babri Masjid Action Conference under the leadership of Syed Shabuddin, aimed at co-ordinating Muslim responses to prevent Hindu fundamentalist organizations from reclaiming the mosque to construct a Hindu temple. In August 1990, apparently in response to calls from Muslims for a national party to represent the interests of minority groups, Syed Shahabuddin, a *Lok Sabha* member of the Janata Dal (JD), formed the *Insaf* (Justice) Party with himself as its sole MP.

More recently, the rise and electoral success of the Hindu-oriented *Bharatiya Janata* Party (BJP) has led to reports of similarly organized Muslim militant groups. In Kerala the formation in early 1992 of the *Islamic Seva Sangh* (ISS) is believed to have been a response to the Hindu fundamentalist organization, the *Rashtriya Swayamsevak Sangh* (RSS). Meanwhile the national leadership of the IUML is reported to have endorsed the creation of a militant youth wing, the White Guards, with the aim of combatting the BJP and the RSS.

The deterioration in relations between Hindus and Muslims in the late 1980s, triggering the worst communal rioting since independence, and the corresponding Muslim disillusionment with Congress, have been reflected most acutely in recent developments in the Muslim-majority state of Jammu and Kashmir where a movement for political autonomy rapidly developed into a Muslim religious cause. By 1989 opposition by Kashmiri separatist organizations to the ruling alliance of the Jammu and Kashmir National Conference (Farooq group) and Congress (I) had degenerated into a bloody civil war, with factions led by self-appointed Muslim *mujaheddin* (holy warriors). In April 1990 Indian troops were sent into Kashmir to supervise an indefinite curfew which culminated in a ban on eight leading Muslim political organizations, including the Pakistan-based para-military Jammu and Kashmir Liberation Front (JKLF), the principal secessionist group headed by Amanullah Khan whose military wing is under the command of Javed Ahmed Mir and its affiliated organization, the Jammu and Kashmir Student Liberation Front (JKSLF); the People's League (PL) led by Shabir Shah; the Students' Islamic Movement of India (SIMI); the *Ikhwan al-Muslimeen*; the *Hizbul Mujaheddin* (Muslim Crusade Force—MCP, also known as *Hizbul Muslimeen*), one of the largest guerrilla groups in Kashmir; the pro-Pakistan *Hezbullah*; and the *Jamaat-i Islami Jammu and Kashmir* (JIJK), headed by Sayyed Ali Shah Gilani.

The main Muslim missionary organization in India is the *Tablighi Jamaat* which carries out missionary work among Muslims throughout the country. Although not directly involved in political issues it, like the JIH, took an active stand in Assam where ethnic conflict between local Assamese and Bengali Muslim settlers in the 1970s and 1980s acquired a communal character. The question of conversion has periodically activated Muslim missionary organizations which are believed to have contacts with Islamic fundamentalist groups in the Middle East and Gulf and to receive financial assistance from pan-Islamic sources.

SA

Major Islamic Organizations

Assembly of Religious Scholars
Nadwah t-al-Ulama
Orthodox organization representing Muslim religious scholars, founded in 1893 with its headquarters in Lucknow. It concentrates on educational reform but played a leading role in the 1986 Muslim campaign against the Supreme Court's ruling on the Shah Bano case. It is reported to have had close links with Saudi Arabia's ruling family since the 1960s and is a member of the Muslim World League.
Leader. Abul Hasan Ali Nadwi (also President of the All-India Muslim Personal Law Board).

Indian Islamic Society
Jamaat-i Islami Hind (JIH)
Fundamentalist religio-political organization with restricted membership, formed after independence from what remained of the Jamaat-i Islami founded by Maulana Abul Ala Maududi in 1941. In recent years the organization has been most active in Kashmir where, under the leadership of Sayyed Ali Shah Gilani, it has helped transform a secessionist movement into a Muslim religious crusade.
Membership. In 1981 this was officially put at 2,831 with 36,243 "sympathisers".
Aims. Its Constitution, adopted in April 1956, aims at safeguarding the religious and cultural identity of Indian Muslims. Special emphasis is laid on a programme of religious education and a common struggle in defence of Muslim personal law, religious endowments, the Urdu language and Muslim educational institutions.

Structure. The organization functions through 13 zonal branches and has its headquarters in Delhi.
Affiliated organizations. Students' Islamic Movement (SIM).

Indian Union Muslim League (IUML)
Offshoot of the original pre-independence All-India Muslim League associated with the campaign for Pakistan, but with a distinct programme which supports cultural rather than political autonomy for Indian Muslims. After a series of attempts to revive it as a national party in the late 1970s, the organization succeeded in establishing a firm regional base in the state of Kerala where its candidates won 19 seats in the June 1991 state elections, forming the second most important component in the Congress (I)-led state government, and two seats in the lower house of Parliament *Lok Sabha*.
Leader. Ibrahim Suleiman Sait (all-India president); Panakkad Mohammad Ali Shihab Thangal (president of Kerala Muslim League).
Affiliated organizations. Muslim Youth League; White Guards.

Justice Party
Insaf Party
Founded in August 1990.
Leader. Syed Shahabuddin (member of the *Lok Sabha*).
Aims. To represent the interests of Indian Muslims.

Missionary Society

Tablighi Jamaat

Leader. Inam ul Hasan.

Ostensibly non-political orthodox missionary organization established by Maulana Muhammad Ilyas in the 1920s with the aim of uniting all sections of the Indian Muslim community and striving for Islamic revival without overt involvement in politics. Since independence it has extended its activities from Uttar Pradesh and the Punjab to other parts of the subcontinent, most notably in Assam where it was involved in fuelling religious tension between Hindu Assamese and Bengali Muslim settlers in the 1970s and early 1980s. The organization has a wide and extensive network abroad, especially in Muslim communities in western Europe.

Structure. The national headquarters are in the Nizamuddin suburb of south Delhi.

Society of Indian Scholars

Jamiat ul-Ulama Hind (JUH)

Orthodox religio-political organization founded in 1919 to encourage the participation of Muslim religious scholars (*ulama*) in the independence movement. It rejected a party-political role but has been a consistent supporter of Congress for much of the period since independence. Perhaps less intolerant of social and educational modernization than other religio-political groups, it remains vigorously opposed to any review of Muslim personal law. In 1983 it called on the Indian government not simply to refrain from any amendment of the Muslim personal law "as long as the Muslims do not want it", but to take steps to delete Article 44 of the Indian Constitution which stipulates that "the State shall endeavour to secure for the citizens a uniform civil code".

Leader. Maulana Easied Madani (president).

Indonesia

Indonesia, a former Dutch colony, was granted independence in 1949. Indonesian society is composed of a mixture of races and peoples belonging to over 300 different ethnic groups and speaking over 250 languages and dialects. The main ethnic minority is the Chinese, who number approximately 3,500,000. Other groups include the Javanese and Sundanese on Java, the Acehnese, Batak and Minangkabau on Sumatra, the Dayaks of the Kalimantan interior, the Irianese of Irian Java, the Makasarese, Buginese, Toraja and Menadonese of Sulawesi, the Ambonese of the Maluku islands, and the Balinese of Bali.

Though not an Islamic state in the constitutional sense, Indonesia has the world's largest Islamic population, numbering between 150 and 160 million. All Indonesian citizens are required by law to state their religion and in 1985 an official survey indicated that 86.9 per cent were Muslim, while 9.6 per cent were Christian, 1.9 per cent Hindu, 1 per cent Buddhist and 0.6 per cent professed adherence to tribal religions.

The overwhelming majority (80-90 per cent) of all Indonesian Muslims are Sunni who follow the Shafi school of law. Sufi brotherhoods are important, the most influential being the various branches of the Shadhiliyyah, Qadiriyyah and Khalwatiyyah orders.

According to the relatively scant historical data, Islam was brought to Sumatra by Arab traders in the seventh and eighth centuries. The first substantive evidence that Islam had emerged as an active force was provided by Marco Polo who visited Sumatra on his way back to Venice from China in the late 13th century. After the introduction of Islam into the archipelago, its dispersion was a slow and peaceful process over many centuries. The religion originally flourished among the less Indianized communities dotted along the trading routes. Muslim traders from Gujarat in western India played an important part in the propagation of the faith, as did Indonesians themselves.

In the early 16th century the first Islamic state emerged on the island's northern coast in Java, Demak. In the course of the century other coastal regions of Java adopted the faith and the process of Islamization began to accelerate, possibly as a result of the competition of Christian missionary activity. By the time of the arrival of the European powers, Islam was well entrenched in the region, with Aceh in northern Sumatra recognized as a centre of Islamic culture and learning.

While Islam was readily and peacefully accepted in Java, the faith never completely displaced existing indigenous religions or the Hindu-Buddhist traditions of the old Javanese kingdoms. Islam was in effect absorbed by the prevailing ideology and in the process lost much of its characteristic rigidness. In the 19th century, however, the relationship between Islam and indigenous Javanese ideology was transformed from one of tolerance and assimilation into one of intolerance and divergence. The introduction by the Dutch colonialists of the highly exploitative *Culturstelsel* (under which Javanese peasants were compelled to cultivate export crops to aid the Dutch economy) coincided with the rise to prominence of a new type of Javanese Muslim who in the course of the pilgrimage to Mecca (*hajj*) was exposed to new currents, embodied in the puritanical Arabian-based Wahhabi movement and in Egyptian Muslim modernism.

A rift developed between the returning pilgrims (*hajjis*) and their traditional religious teachers who were still under non-Islamic spiritual influences. Two distinct categories of Javanese Muslims emerged, the *santri*, or the devout Muslim, and the *abangan*, or nominal Muslim. The *santri* were entirely orientated towards the orthodox Islam of the Middle East, while the majority *abangan* continued to adhere to an amalgam of Islamic elements and Hindu-Buddhist mysticism.

By the early 20th century Islam had become the focus for Indonesian political organization. The first mass-based national movement against the Dutch was the **Islamic Union** (*Serekat Islam*), established in 1912. In the same year Muslim religious scholars (*ulama*) in Java established the **Followers of the Prophet Muhammad** (*Muhammadiyah*), a modernist, *santri*-based socio-religious organization which aimed to "purify" Indonesian Islam through educational reform. The establishment of the traditionalist **Council of Religious Scholars** (*Nahdatul Ulama*—NU) by Kyai Hasyim Asyari in 1926 was a direct response to the *Muhammadiyah*'s brand of Islamic modernism. The NU was particularly concerned to protect the traditional, village-based Muslim schools (*pesantrens*) against the reforms of the urban-based *Muhammadiyah*.

Neither the NU nor the *Muhammadiyah* was an overtly political organization and both openly co-operated with the Dutch, whereas *Serekat Islam* was divided over the issue of co-operation with the Dutch. In the late 1920s one faction, the *Serekat Merajh* (Red Union), joined with communist insurgents and launched a series of unsuccessful anti-Dutch uprisings in West Java and West Sumatra.

After the Dutch suppressed these uprisings the *Serekat Islam* went into decline, eventually transforming itself into the *Partai Serekat Islam Indonesia* (PSII) (Indonesian Islamic Association Party) in the 1930s.

Islam and the state: developments since independence

The post-independence regimes of President Sukarno and General Suharto have regarded Islam with considerable apprehension and caution. While nominally professing an Islamic outlook, both leaders sought to maintain Indonesia as a secular state in which the political activities of religious groups are strictly regulated.

During the first decade after independence the state's fragile unity was threatened by Islamic radicals who waged a guerrilla war against Jakarta. The so-called **Abode of Islam** (*Darul Islam*), which first appeared in western Java in 1948, was committed to the establishment of an Islamic state. The movement continued to be implicated in regional revolts in the region until its leader, Sekar Madji Kartosuwiryo, was captured and executed in 1962. It was also active in Aceh and in southern Kalimantan and southern Sulawesi. The revolts were generally unco-ordinated and regional in character and hence failed to pose a significant security threat. Nevertheless, the Darul Islam rebellions did serve as a signal to the armed forces, warning the military of the potential dangers of politicized Islam.

During the immediate post-independence period legitimate Islamic organizations were consolidated in the Council of Indonesian Muslim Associations (*Masyumi*), a party founded during the Japanese occupation of the early 1940s. By the early 1950s the strongest faction within *Masyumi* was led by Mohammed Natsir, a modernist and a proponent of "religious socialism". Natsir's liberal orientation alienated some of the more orthodox Muslims and in 1952 the traditionalists of the NU (until then a member of the *Masyumi*) withdrew to form a separate party.

The *Masyumi*-NU division highlighted the main predicament of organized political Islam in post-independence Indonesia, the movement's failure to form a credible united front to oppose secular nationalists and communists. Nevertheless, although *Masyumi* failed to win a majority in the first post-independence elections in 1955, it emerged as the only party with a national following. Its main opponents, the Communist Party of Indonesia (PKI), the Sukarnoist Nationalist Party of Indonesia (PNI) and the NU were popular chiefly among the Javanese, the dominant ethnic group. Following the election, Sukarno introduced his authoritarian "Guided Democracy" system. *Masyumi*'s influence waned, its leadership became increasingly associated with the *Darul Islam* revolts, and in 1960 it was formally proscribed.

Sukarno's exceptional political acumen allowed him to balance and play against each other the two great contending power factions, the Army and the PKI, for over a decade, but by 1965 he had evidently lost control. In that year the Army moved against its communist rivals and within a matter of months as many as 500,000 communists, leftists and supporters of the "old order" had been killed during violent protests in Java, Bali and Sumatra.

The NU youth movement, *Ansor*, was in the vanguard of the Army's extermination programme, organizing a bloody "holy war" against the PKI at village level. Both the NU and the *Muhammadiyah* expected to be rewarded by the Army for their support during the upheaval of 1965-66 but instead the political influence of Islam waned under Suharto's "New Order", and with the defeat of the PKI the Army began to regard organized Islam as the major threat to state security.

The military permitted the *Masyumi* to reform itself as the **Muslim Party of Indonesia** (*Partai Muslimin Indonesia*—Parmusi) in the late 1960s, but it was subjected to such rigorous state control that it posed little threat to Suharto's New Order regime. Meanwhile all other existing Muslim groups complied fully with the regime's requirements in order to ensure their own survival.

In 1970 the regime called on all political parties to contest the forthcoming legislative elections on the basis of a three-way alignment. The first grouping was to be associated with the supposedly neutral and non-political functional groups (*golongan karya*), commonly known as Golkar, in reality pro-government and dominated by the military and civil service. The second grouping, described as "spiritual", would comprise Muslim parties while the third grouping, identified as nationalist, was to represent the remaining parties. In the elections, held in mid-1971, Golkar won a clear majority and in early 1973 legislation was passed obliging the four Islamic parties (the NU, *Parmusi* and the smaller Indonesian Islamic Association Party and Islamic Education Party) to officially amalgamate as the **Development Unity Party** (*Partai Persatuan Pembangunan*—PPP).

The compulsory merger was intended to diminish the popularity of political Islam but the PPP went on to win more seats in the 1977 elections than its four constituent units had in 1971.

During the early 1970s the military had become increasingly concerned with Islamic muscle-flexing as when in 1974, for example, Muslim groups had organized unprecedented, and ultimately successful, demonstrations in Jakarta against the government's draft legislation aimed at reforming Muslim marriages. The same groups went on to play a leading role in the student protest movements of 1974 and 1978. The military responded by launching its own scheme to attract Muslims into the ranks of Golkar. Just prior to the 1977 election Golkar established its Federation for the Advancement of Islamic Education (GUPPI), intended to compete directly with the PPP.

Despite the PPP's impressive showing in the 1977 elections, it was not regarded as a serious threat by the Army partly because of the PPP's acquiescent leadership. John Naro, the party leader, had close links with the Army and in 1984 he engineered the party's transformation from an overtly Muslim grouping into what was at least nominally a secular organization. Naro managed the transformation at the party's first conference in 1984, persuading delegates to accept as their sole doctrine the doctrine of *pancasila* ("five pillars"), which posited a secular state ideology. At the conference the NU decided to pull out of PPP and formal state politics and return to its roots as a socio-religious organization. The party went on to sustain heavy losses in the 1987 general election.

While the government and the Army were able to fully control Islam at the level of organized political organizations, they were initially less successful in confronting the new wave of Muslim radicalism that emerged in the villages in the 1970s. Lay preachers (*muballigh*)) had managed to build up a village-based network (*usroh*)) during the 1970s, and by the early 1980s they were in a position to articulate grassroots dissatisfaction on a number of issues, including unemployment, landlessness and the government's birth-control programme, as well as specifically religious issues such as the ban on the wearing of head-scarves at school. A number of mosques organized youth groups (*remaja mesjid*) and mass religious rallies (*pengajian*) emerged as important political platforms.

Military concern over potential widespread Islamic unrest was increasingly evident in the early 1980s. Eventually, in 1984, the Army acted, initially targeting a *muballigh* network based on the Rawabadak mosque in the Jakarta dockland area of Tanjung Priok. When the police moved into the area to make a number of arrests fighting erupted and in the ensuing mayhem well over 60 people were killed. The Tanjung Priok massacre marked the beginning of a widespread military campaign against Muslim activism. High-ranking opponents of the New Order, including Muhammad Sanusi and General H. R. Dharsono, were arrested as well as ordinary *muballigh*. In the resulting trials the military linked the accused with a host of other incidents, including a series of bombing incidents and an assassination plot against Suharto in the early 1980s. The courts, armed with severe anti-subversion legislation, handed out long prison sentences. The trials continued into the early 1990s, with many of the alleged Muslim extremists accused of involvement in a nationwide conspiracy forcibly to undermine *pancasila*.

Opponents of the government claimed that the trials were often designed to legitimize Army offensives against Muslim activists, such as the attack on villages in Lampung province, southern Sumatra, in February 1989 in which an unspecified number of villagers were reported killed. In the early 1990s the Army concentrated its efforts against Islamic separatist rebels in Aceh. Hundreds of people were reported killed and hundreds more missing as a result of serious fighting between the armed forces and rebels in the region.

While the Army continued to carry out military and intelligence operations against Muslim groups in the early 1990s, Suharto himself seemed to adopt a more positive attitude towards Islam. In late 1990 he personally sanctioned the creation of an **Indonesian Muslim Intellectuals' Association** (ICMI) and in mid-1991 he provided funds for the establishment of Indonesia's first Islamic Bank, the Bank Muamalat Islam Indonesia. In April members of Indonesia's leading religious, cultural and intellectual communities had been permitted to create a **Democracy Forum** with the aim of promoting political dialogue.

There was intense speculation that Suharto was preparing to use Islam as a vehicle to ensure his re-election as president in 1993. However, some commentators regarded Suharto's new-found support for Islam as little more than a government attempt to co-opt the Muslim intelligentsia and silence any fledgling Muslim opposition. Nevertheless the Army leadership, who had long regarded the polarization of politics along religious lines as a threat to stability, observed Suharto's new line with some trepidation.

DS

Major Islamic organizations

Abode of Islam
Darul Islam
Proscribed political and guerrilla movement committed to the establishment of a Moslem theocracy. Appeared in western Java in 1948 and continued to be implicated in regional revolts on Java and other islands until 1962.

Council of Indonesian Muslim Associations
Masyumi
Sumatra-based organization formed in 1943 with the encouragement of the occupying Japanese forces. A pan-Islamic organization which brought together modernist and orthodox groups, it developed in the immediate post-independence period into one of the strongest parties. *Masyumi*'s position was weakened by the withdrawal of the *Nahdatul Ulama* in 1952. The party was eventually banned in 1960 for refusing to endorse Sukarno's "Guided Democracy" but in 1968 the Suharto regime allowed it to resume its activity under the name *Parmusi*.

Council of Religious Scholars
Nahdatul Ulama (NU).
Traditionalist socio-religious organization founded in 1926 by Kyai Hasyim Asyari to safeguard the village-based Islamic education system. The NU joined the *Masyumi* during the Japanese occupation, but left in 1952 to create a separate political party. It was the largest component of the PPP formed in 1973, but 11 years later removed itself from the PPP and party politics, a move which appeared to enhance its influence. In the early 1990s the government-sponsored Golkar courted the NU as the politically acceptable face of organized Islam.
Leader. Abdurrahman Wahid.
Membership. With 20,000,000 members it is the largest Muslim organization.
Affiliated organizations. Ansor, the party's youth wing which played a prominent part in the Army's campaign against the PKI in 1964.

Democracy Forum
Created in 1991 by leading religious and academic figures.
Leader. Abdurrahman Wahid (also leader of the Council of Religious Scholars).

Development Unity Party
Partai Persatuan Pembangunan (PPP)
State-approved party formed in 1973 after the

merger of four Islamic parties including *Nahdatul Ulama, Parmusi,* the Indonesian Islamic Association Party and the Islamic Education Party

Leader. Ismael Hassan Metareum (chair); Mardinsyah (secretary-general).

Aims. To campaign for Islamic social and political reform.

Followers of the Prophet Muhammad
Muhammadiyah

Socio-religious group reflecting the influence of Egyptian Muslim modernism, formed in 1912 in Yokyakarta. The movement has built up an extensive network of schools, colleges, hospitals and orphanages.

Aims. To Arabize Indonesian Islam through educational reform.

Free Aceh Movement (FAM)
Clandestine guerrilla organization.

Aim. The creation of an independent Islamic state in Aceh, the extreme north-western province of Sumatra. Islamic Union

Islamic Union
Serekat Islam

Formed in 1912 under the leadership of Umar Said Tjokroaminoto, it rapidly developed into the first national anti-colonial movement but split in the 1920s over the issue of co-operation with the Dutch authorities. One faction joined with the communists and remnants formed the Indonesian Islamic Association Party (*Partai Serekat Islam Indonesia* (PSII) in the 1930s.

Aims. These included the promotion of Islamic teaching.

Indonesian Muslim Intellectuals' Association (ICMI)
Broad-based Muslim organization formed in late 1990 and endorsed by President Suharto.

Leader. Emil Salim.

Indonesia Ulama (religious scholars) Council (MUI)
Officially sponsored central Muslim organization.

Leader. Hassan Basri.

Komando Jihad
In the 1970s and 1980s the government alleged that this organization, which it claimed was composed of terrorists seeking to establish an Islamic state, was responsible for a number of terrorist acts.

Muslim Party of Indonesia
Partai Muslimin Indonesia (Parmusi)

Islamic political party created in 1968 as the successor to *Masyumi*. One of four parties which formed the PPP in 1973.

Iran

The Islamic Republic of Iran, proclaimed in April 1979, had hitherto been a monarchy ruled by a Shah (Emperor), the last of whom, Muhammad Reza Shah Pahlavi, was forced to flee the country amid widespread popular opposition in January 1979.

Overall authority is exercised by the country's supreme spiritual leader (*walih faqih*), a position occupied from 1979 until his death in June 1989 by Ayatollah Khomeini, and since then by Ayatollah Sayed Ali Khamenei. An 83-member elected Council of Experts, created in December 1982, is charged with the responsibility of electing the country's supreme leader. An elected President exercises executive authority while legislative functions are performed by an Islamic Consultative Assembly (*Majlis-i-Shura*) elected every four years. A 12-member Council of Guardians, established in 1980, ensures that all legislation conforms to the Islamic Constitution and has powers to veto candidates for high office.

An arbitrating Committee to Determine the Expediency of the Islamic Order, established in February 1988, has powers to adjudicate in the event of a dispute between the *Majlis* and the Council of Guardians, in matters relating to Islamic law. A National Security Council, created in July 1989, routinely reviews defence and national security policies.

There are technically no political parties in Iran, although it was reported in June 1990 that the government was reviewing existing laws relating to the formation of political parties. Since May 1988 all candidates for legislative and presidential elections have been recommended by informal political groups and approved by local screening committees.

The overwhelming majority of the population of Iran, estimated in January 1991 at 56,825,000, are Muslims. More than 90 per cent of all Muslims are Shia belonging to the Twelvers (*ithna ashariyya* sect of Shi'ism) who are concentrated among the Persian and Azeri ethnic groups; an Ismaili Shia community which owes allegiance to the Aga Khan inhabits the northern mountainous region bordering the Caspian Sea. Sunnis, who constitute about 8 per cent of the total Muslim population, are dispersed among the Kurds, Baluchi, Turkmen and Arabs.

The Constitution approved by a popular referendum in December 1979 declares Islam of the Ja'fari school of Shia jurisprudence to be the official religion of the state and reserves the posts of President and Prime Minister for Shias. Other Islamic sects and schools of law, including the Zaydi Shias (Fivers) and the four dominant Sunni Muslim schools of law (Hanafi, Hanbali, Maliki and Shafi) are also deemed to be valid. Jews, Zoroastrians and Christians (estimated at less than 1 per cent of the population) are also officially recognized, although none of their members is entitled to hold political office.

A notable omission in the category of legally recognized religions is the Bahai faith, representing a schismatic break from Shi'ism, whose precepts are regarded as heretical by both Shias and Sunnis. In 1983 the government banned all Bahai institutions, and it is believed that since 1979 almost 10,000 of Iran's estimated 300,000 Bahais have fled the country to escape persecution. The latest in a series of officially sanctioned measures against the community was reported in April 1992 following the execution in March (the first since December 1988) of Bahman Samandari, a 52-year-old economist.

The country's judicial system is based entirely on Islamic law. Islamic punishments (*hudud*; sing. *hadd*), introduced in 1983, are meted out for offences ranging from fornication to violations of the Islamic dress code for women.

In June 1987 the first clerical courts were established to try members of the clergy opposed to the government. Allegations of the abuse of "revolutionary justice" led to the appointment in January 1983 of investigative teams charged with ensuring the limits of judicial authority.

Islamic opposition under the monarchy

Organized political activity among sections of Iran's Shia religious establishment was a well-established tradition. One of the earliest organizations, the **Devotees of Islam** (*Fedayeen-i-Islam*), established shortly after World War II and led by the young cleric Nawab Safawi was formed with the aim of expressing the growing discontent with the modernizing reforms of Reza Shah. Initially founded as a forum of clerical opposition against the relegation of Islamic law, the *Fedayeen* succeeded in capitalizing on popular discontent among *bazaar* (market) merchants and sections of the urban poor who failed to benefit from the social and economic reforms initiated by the Shah's "White Revolution". In the 1950s and 1960s the *Fedayeen*, allegedly responsible for the assassination of key government officials, including Prime Minister Hassan Ali Mansour (killed in 1965), attracted members of the radical clergy, most notably Ayatollah Sadeq Khakhali, later to be dubbed the "hanging judge" of the Islamic revolution.

Senior Shia divines committed to the creation of a republican Islamic order were also engaged in political organization. The early 1950s and 1960s saw the emergence of the Warriors of Islam (*Mujaheddin-i-Islam*) led by Ayatollah Abul Qasim Kashani, the underground National Resistance Movement (*Nihzat-Muqavamat-i Milli*) led by Ayatollah Taleghani and the Combatant Clergy (*Ruhaniyat-i-Mobarez*) headed by Ayatollah Beheshti, later to found the Islamic Republican Party (IRP). In 1963 street protests led by Ayatollah Khomeini led to his imprisonment and exile in Iraq from where he laid the groundwork for a formidable Islamic network which successfully evaded the Shah's secret police (SAVAK).

In the early 1970s commitment to a republican Islamic order founded on more progressive interpretations of Islamic law also grew, largely among young Muslim intellectuals grouped around the eminent sociologist Ali Shariati. The group's organizational identity was later embodied in the **Holy Warriors of the People** (*Mujaheddin-i-Khalq*) led by Massoud Rajavi.

The rapid modernization of the Iranian economy between 1965 and 1977, paralleled by increasing Westernization, intensified Shia religious opposition. Its most prominent spokesman, Ayatollah Khomeini, who had arrived in France in October 1978 after 14 years of exile in Iraq, consistently demanded the restoration of Islamic principles. Religious and political protest which rose to crisis levels during 1977 and 1978, culminated in early 1979 with the departure of the Shah and the formal assumption of power in February by Ayatollah Khomeini and a 15-member Islamic Revolutionary Council.

Islam and the state: developments under the Islamic Republic

The new Islamic Republic was almost immediately engulfed in a fierce power struggle between rival Islamic factions representing "moderates" and "extremists". Mehdi Bazargan, appointed Prime Minister in February 1979, was forced to resign in November after failing to resolve the growing polarization between laymen pressing for a "Western-style" democracy and clerics committed to an Islamic theocracy.

Presidential elections held in January 1980 which resulted in a win for Abolhasan Bani-Sadr, representing the liberal faction, were followed by the consolidation of the recently established IRP whose extremist wing dominated the 270-seat *Majlis* inaugurated in May 1980. Mounting tension between Bani-Sadr and radical deputies from the IRP led in June 1980 to Bani-Sadr's dismissal and departure for France. The grip of the extremist wing on foreign and domestic policy was demonstrated by its endorsement of the seizure by militant students in November 1979 of 63 US hostages, and its obstruction of key economic reforms aimed at nationalization and land reform.

Extra-parliamentary forces, including the pro-Khomeini Revolutionary Guard (*Pasdaran*) and a band of urban guerrillas dubbed Followers of the Party of God (*Hezbollahi*), were vigorously employed to help maintain revolutionary fervour. Promotion of the official ideology of Twelver Shi'ism was entrusted to the Islamic Propagation Organization, formed in 1979, and presently headed by Ayatollah Ahmed Jannati and Hojatoleslam Mahmud Muhammadi Araki.

Meanwhile, bloody fighting erupted between Revolutionary Guards and "Islamic Marxists" belonging to the *Mujaheddin-i-Khalq*. Between 1979 and 1981 thousands of *Mujaheddin* members were purged and hundreds arrested, tortured and summarily executed. In October 1981 Bani-Sadr and Massoud Rajavi, leader of the *Mujaheddin*, formed the National Council of Resistance in Paris which included 15 opposition groups; in June 1987 Rajavi announced the formation of the National Liberation Army (NLA) as the military wing of the *Mujaheddin-i-Khalq*.

Bitter confrontation between "moderates" and "extremists", clerics and laymen, culminated in spectacular displays of violence the worst of which were bomb attacks in June and August 1981 which resulted in the deaths, among others, of Ayatollah Beheshti, leader of the IRP, and Muhammad Ali Rajai, elected President in July 1981. By the early 1980s ethnic minorities, notably Azerbaijanis and Kurds, had joined the opposition against the regime's hard-line policies endorsed by Khomeini.

In December 1979 thousands of Turkic-speaking Azeris responded to a call by the **Muslim People's Republican Party** (MPRP) to boycott the referendum on the Constitution on grounds that it had failed to guarantee Azeri autonomy. Attempts by the senior Azeri cleric, Ayatollah Shariatmadari to mediate in the dispute between the government and the MPRP failed after the government took action to disbanding MPRP, executing more than 50 of its leading members and placing Shariatmadari under house arrest in Qom. The government's drive to impose Shia hegemony was also resisted by Sunni Kurds who regarded as discriminatory constitutional provisions reserving high office for Shias.

Criticism of the government's hard-line stance grew in the late 1980s after senior clerics in the holy city of Mashad voiced their opposition to Khomeini's version of the Islamic republic. In November 1987 the distinguished religious leader, Ayatollah Qomi, issued a ruling (*fatwa*) denouncing the regime's policies as "un-Islamic". In May 1988 other religious notables, among them Ayatollah Reza Golpayegani and Ayatollah Shahebbedin Marashi-Najf, endorsed a petition from the Society of Qom Theological Teachers calling on the government to end the "un-Islamic excesses" of the revolution.

Factional strife within the government, allegations of the widespread abuse of human rights and the outbreak of the Iran-Iraq war, fuelled popular opposition to the government which resulted in demonstrations in a number of Iranian cities in 1985. Meanwhile, elections held in April and May 1984 to the second *Majlis*, which were boycotted by the only officially recognized party, the **Liberation Movement of Iran** (*Nehzat-i-Azadi Iran*) led by Mehdi Bazargan, resulted in another clear win for the IRP. In August 1985 the conservative, clerical-oriented Council of Guardians vetoed Bazargan's candidacy for President, a post subsequently assumed by Ayatollah Khamenei.

Reports that the power struggle between rival factions had assumed critical proportions gained ground after Ayatollah Khomeini in February 1989 issued a ruling (*fatwa*) sentencing the Indian-born British writer Salman Rushdie to death for the allegedly anti-Islamic tenor of his novel *The Satanic Verses*. The ruling, which came amid growing divisions between "radicals" and "pragmatists" compounded by Iran's acceptance of a ceasefire with Iraq in July 1988, was believed to have strengthened substantially the radical faction which had opposed the ceasefire and stood against any rapprochement with the West. Reports also indicated that Khomeini's ruling had been timed to undermine the presidential candidacy of Hojatoleslam Hashemi Ali Akbar Rafsanjani, a leading "pragmatist" and proponent of closer links with the West.

Khomeini's death in June 1989 did not immediately alter the prevailing balance of power. Rafsanjani's election to the post of President in July 1989 was partially neutralized by the election as Speaker of the *Majlis* of Ayatollah Mahdi Karrubi, a prominent figure in the "radical" faction. By the end of 1990, however, there emerged a noticeable shift tilting the balance in favour of the "pragmatists". A crucial factor was the supposedly tacit agreement between Rafsanjani and Khamenei, newly elected as supreme religious leader, to prevent the election in October 1990 of leading "radicals" to the influential Council of Experts.

The steady consolidation of power by "pragmatists" during 1991 was challenged by "radicals" who succeeded in mobilizing popular resistance to Rafsanjani's programme of economic reform, his rapprochement with conservative Arab regimes, notably Saudi Arabia (with which relations had been severed in 1987), and his active involvement in securing the release of Western hostages held by pro-Iranian groups in Lebanon. Rafsanjani retaliated by stressing his determination to resist all attempts to "sabotage" his government, and in May 1991 ordered formal charges to be brought against Ayatollah Khalkhali, a leading hardliner and former head of the Islamic revolutionary courts. Reports of a "radical" backlash resurfaced in late 1991 after reports indicated that riots in the city of Qom calling for the removal of Khamenei as supreme leader (*walih faqih*) on grounds that he did not possess the requisite qualifications, had been orchestrated by dissidents opposed to the government's pragmatic and allegedly anti-Islamic orientation. Anti-government groups had reportedly rallied around the Grand Ayatollah Hussein Ali Montazeri, who had resigned his post as successor to Khomeini in 1988, and who was known for his interest in exporting the Iranian revolution.

Elections to the *Majlis* held in April and May 1992 confirmed the dominance of the "pragmatist" faction whose supporters, represented by the **Society of Combatant Clergy** (*Jameh-i-Ruhaniyat-i Mobarez*), gained almost 70 per cent of the total seats. The "radical" faction, referred to as the **Association of Combatant Clergy** (*Majma-i-Ruhanyun-e Mou-*

barez), suffered defeat compounded by the failure of its leading spokesmen, former Interior Minister Ali Akbar Mohtashemi and Mehdi Karrubi, to secure re-election. The defeat of the "radicals" had apparently been ensured by a screening process adopted by the Council of Guardians which eliminated those deemed to be financially, morally or politically "corrupt".

Control by diverging factions over the course of the Islamic revolution has been reflected in the fortunes of state-sponsored organizations used to export the revolution. Overall responsibility for the propagation of Iran's Islamic revolutionary message continues to be concentrated in the Ministry of Culture and Islamic Guidance, presently headed by Hojatoleslam Sayed Muhammad Khatami. The Ministry's activities are wide ranging and include the dissemination of religio-political publications sometimes through the cultural section of Iranian embassies abroad, and the holding of conferences, the latest of which, the Conference on Islamic Thought, was held in Tehran in January 1992.

A less well-known bureaucratic institution, the Bureau of World Liberation Movements, alleged to be responsible for the formation of radical Shia groups in Bahrain, Lebanon and Kuwait, is reported to have been disbanded following the execution in October 1987 of its director, Mehdi Hashemi, who worked under the general supervision of Ayatollah Montazeri. The government is also known to provide official backing, both material and moral, to exiled Iraqi Shia groups, the most prominent of which are grouped under the Tehran-based Supreme Assembly of the Islamic Revolution in Iraq (SAIRI).

Recent reports have indicated, however, that the Rafsanjani government intends to re-orient its policy towards radical Shia groups in the Middle East and Asia. Clandestine fundamentalist groups who reportedly held a secret summit in Tehran in early June 1992, convened by Javed Larijani, a "pragmatist" close to President Rafsanjani, were believed to have been advised to pursue moderate policies especially in other Muslim countries. Meanwhile, Iran has continued to resist calls for the lifting of the death sentence on Salman Rushdie; in February 1992 the Iranian 15th Khordad Foundation which had offered a US$1,000,000 reward in 1989 for the assassination of Rushdie, raised its offer to "upwards of US$1,000,000 . . . to ensure [he] is executed".

FS

Major Islamic Organizations

Association of Combatant Clergy
Majme-i-Ruhaniyun-i-Mobarez
Informal cleric-dominated grouping, reportedly an offshoot of a similarly named clandestine organization founded in the 1960s by the late Ayatollah Beheshti. The group is said to represent "radicals" closely associated with the revolutionary politics of the late Ayatollah Khomeini. Candidates endorsed by the group contested legislative elections in April and May 1992 although successful candidates failed to form a majority in the *Majlis*, reportedly because

of strict vetting by the Council of Guardians which disqualified many of the group's supporters.

Leader. No one individual is identified as leader; the group's most prominent spokesmen are Ali Akbar Mohtashemi, former Interior Minister, Mehdi Karrubi, former Speaker of the *Majlis*, and Moussavi Khoeiniha, leader of the militant students who seized 63 US hostages in 1979.

Aims. The group tends to employ the rhetoric of the immediate post-revolutionary era, emphasising opposition to the USA, the struggle against "Zionism", the export of the Islamic revolution, centralized control of the economy and consumer subsidies to protect the poorer classes.

Holy Warriors of the People
Mujaheddin-i-Khalq

Lay guerrilla organization representing radical left-wing Muslim opinion founded in the early 1970s; proscribed under the Islamic Republic. The group was engaged in a bloody confrontation with pro-Khomeini Islamic Revolutionary Guards in the late 1970s and 1980s and has alleged the arrest, torture and summary execution of thousands of its members. In 1981 the group became a founding member of the National Council of Resistance (NCR) dedicated to overthrowing the Islamic Republic of Iran. The party headquarters established in Paris in 1981 were moved to Iraq in June 1986, where its bases have been subjected to repeated aerial bombardment by the Iranian air force.

Leader. Massoud Rajavi and Maryam Rajavi.

Affiliated organizations. National Liberation Army (NLA), formed in June 1987, with forces estimated to total between 10,000-15,000.

Islamic Republican Party (IRP)

Party of clerics founded as the vanguard of the Islamic revolution in 1978, reportedly by the late Ayatollah Beheshti. The IRP formed the ruling party until its official disbandment by Ayatollah Khomeini in June 1987 on grounds that it had become "an excuse for discord and factionalism". In legislative elections held in 1980 and 1984 the IRP emerged with a clear majority of seats in the *Majlis.*

Liberation Movement of Iran (LMI)
Nehzat-i-Azadi Iran

Lay Muslim organization representing moderate forces founded in 1961; it enjoyed official recognition under the Islamic Republic until 1988 when the activities of all political parties were suspended. The party boycotted legislative elections in April and May 1984 alleging undemocratic practices.

Leader. Mehdi Bazargan (general secretary; Prime Minister from February to November 1979).

Aims. The party emphasises basic human rights as defined by Islam.

Muslim People's Republican Party (MPRP)

Azeri organization based in Tabriz, Iranian Azerbaijan; proscribed under the Islamic Republic. The party was subjected to a violent purge by the government in December 1979 following its campaign, backed by the senior cleric Ayatollah Shariatmadari, for greater autonomy for Azerbaijan.

Leader. Hossein Farshi (secretary-general).

Membership. 3,500,000 (2,500,000 in Azerbaijan).

Society of Combatant Clergy
Jameh-i-Ruhaniyat Mobarez

Informal cleric-dominated grouping representing "pragmatist" faction allied with the government of President Rafsanjani. Candidates endorsed by the group claim to have won more than 70 per cent of the seats in the fourth *Majlis* elected in April and May 1992.

Leader. The group's most prominent supporter is said to be President Hojatoleslam Ali Akbar Rafsanjani. Prominent legislative candidates backed by the group included Alinaqi Khamoushi, head of the Chamber of Commerce and Industry, Javed Larijani, former Deputy Minister of Foreign Affairs, and Ali Akbar Hossaini, a popular cleric who hosts the television programme *Islam and the Family.*

Iraq

Since its subjection by Islamic armies in the seventh century, Iraq has been predominantly Muslim and has a special claim to the "golden age" of Arab-Islamic civilization under the Abbasid caliphate (740-1258) which ruled the eastern empire from its capital, Baghdad.

More than 90 per cent of the population of Iraq, estimated in 1989 to total 18,271,000, are Muslims. The rest belong to a variety of Christian and Sabean sects prevalent among small groups of Assyrians, Armenians and Persians.

Around 60 per cent of Iraqis are Twelver (*ithna ashariyya*) Shias, the largest branch of Shi'ism, although a small number are also known to belong to the Ismaili and the more moderate Zaydi ("Fiver") division of Shi'ism.

Sunni followers of the Hanafi school account for roughly 30 per cent of Muslims. Of these, the overwhelming majority are Kurds, some of whom also adhere to an obscure dualistic sect, the Yazidi. Sunnis also prevail among the tiny Turkoman minority.

Sectarian friction, notably between Shias and Sunnis, has been a characteristic of modern Iraq. The dominant position of the Sunni minority had its origins in the Ottoman empire whose institutions in Iraq and elsewhere were predominantly manned by Sunnis. The decline in Shia influence was compounded by the reluctance of most middle and upper-class urban Shias to benefit from the modern educational facilities offered by the Ottomans.

By the time Britain established its mandate (1920-32), few Shias were deemed to possess the qualifications necessary for public office, opening the way for disproportionate Sunni Arab representation in government.

Although measures to reverse the decline in Shia educational and material standards were encouraged under the monarchy (1932-58), many Shias continued to be numbered among the poorest of the country. Increased Shia political integration, symbolised in the appointment in 1947 of the country's first Shia Prime Minister, Salih Jabr, was effectively neutralized by Shia under-representation in the upper echelons of the army; following the Ba'athist coup of 1968 this contributed substantially to Shia political alienation.

The estrangement of Shias from the Ba'ath Party, despite their contribution to its early history, was aggravated by the ousting from the party in 1964 of the prominent Shia Ba'athist, Ali Salih al-Sadi, after a period of protracted factional in-fighting. Declining Shia participation was demonstrated in the fact that out of the 53 members of the top command of the [Ba'ath] party from November 1963 to 1970, 84 per cent had been Sunni Arabs (who constituted 38.5 per cent of the population overall in the period up to November 1963), 5.7 per cent Shia Arabs (53.8 per cent of the population) and 7.5 per cent Kurds (7.7 per cent).

Charges of the "Sunnization" of the decision-making process grew between 1968 and September 1978, by which time the ruling Revolutionary Command Council (RCC) did not

111

include a single Shia member. More recently, President Saddam Hussein appears to have encouraged Shia participation in government with the appointment of two Shias, Saadoun Hammadi and Hamza al-Zubaydi, as Prime Ministers in 1991 and 1992, and the inclusion of al-Zubaydi and Mizban Khader Hadi, also a Shia, as members of the present RCC. These gestures are, however, regarded by Saddam Hussein's critics as token measures aimed at defusing the impact of the government's brutal suppression of the Shia uprising in March 1991.

There is little evidence of any broad Sunni revivalist movement in Iraq although a small group of Muslim Brothers (*Ikhwan al-muslimun*) was reportedly active during the 1950s and 1960s. Sunni discontent threatened to resurface in the 1970s after the assassination, allegedly ordered by the Ba'ath Party, of the respected Sunni cleric, Shaikh Abdul Aziz al-Badri. In March 1991 a Jordan-based Sunni dissident, Kayreddin Hasib, who attended a meeting of Iraqi opposition groups in Beirut, was described by Middle East observers as "one of the few possible political leaders who could win support in the Iraqi Sunni heartland".

Evidence of religious organization among Sunni Kurds emerged in January 1992 when the official Iranian media reported a statement attributed to Adham Barzani, leader of a group calling itself the **Kurdish Revolutionary Hezbollah of Iraq** (*Hezbollah-e-Inquilab-e-Kurd-e-Iraq*).

In July 1991 the **Turkoman Islamic Union** (of the tiny Turkoman Sunni minority) announced its participation in the opposition to the regime of Saddam Hussein.

Shia opposition since independence

There was evidence of burgeoning Islamic opposition, spearheaded by Shia clerics (*imams*), long before its more recent bloody confrontation with the politics and ideology of the ruling Ba'ath Party. In the years immediately preceding the overthrow of the monarchy, some Shia clerics sought to reassert their authority by challenging the inroads then being made by the Iraqi Communist Party (ICP), especially among the Shia urban poor around the holy cities of Najaf and Karbala. Sections of more affluent urban Shia communities were also known to have responded to the appeal of the ICP.

In 1958 leading Najaf-based religious scholars (*ulama*) formed the *Jamaat al-Ulama fi Najaf al-Ashraf* (Association of Najaf *ulama*), a political organization ostensibly devoted to combating atheism among Shias. In 1960 it backed an edict (*fatwa*) by a senior Shia cleric (*marja*), Ayatollah Muhsin al-Hakim al-Tabataba'i, calling on Shias to reject communism as atheistic.

Meanwhile the emergence of Arab nationalism in the form of the increasingly influential Iraqi Ba'ath Party posed a fresh challenge to Shias, the majority of whom regarded it as an extension of Sunni domination. In the first Ba'ath coup of February 1963, all the districts which offered resistance to the Ba'athists were said "without exception" to be Shia.

By the late 1960s the uncompromising secularism of the Ba'athist regime (notwithstanding its constitutional recognition of Islam as the religion of the state) and its intrusion into areas of public life traditionally reserved for the *ulama* prompted some clerics to urge active political resistance. Their most influential spokesman was the young cleric, Muhammad Baqer as-Sadr, believed by some to be the principal figure responsible for the formation of the clandestine group, **Party of the Islamic Call** (*al-Da'wa al-Islamiya*), in 1968. As-Sadr's most notable contribution was his attempt to extend the ideological basis of the movement by infusing it with a universalist Islamic message that reached beyond Shias to encompass Iraqi Sunnis, both Arabs and Kurds.

In 1969 prominent Shia *ulama*, including Ayatollah Muhsin al-Hakim, led demonstrators in Najaf who chanted slogans against the Ba'ath Party, accusing its leaders of being infidels. In 1972 as-Sadr was arrested for the first time, and in 1974 political protests coinciding with *Ashura* (celebrations marking the Islamic month of *Muharram*) ended in arrests and in the execution in December 1974 of five *ulama* alleged to have organized the demonstrations. In February 1977 government troops shot and killed Shia demonstrators and arrested a further 2,000 during marches in Karbala and Najaf commemorating *Ashura*. A special court appointed to inquire into the disturbances ordered the execution in March of eight *ulama* and the sentencing of another 15 to life imprisonment.

The outbreak of the Iranian revolution in 1979 had a decisive impact on the course of Shia opposition and the regime's response to growing Islamic unrest. The modus vivendi between the government and *al-Dawa* since 1977 broke down as militant Shia clerics led by as-Sadr sought openly to engage the regime in conflict by staging attacks on Ba'ath Party offices and by publicly supporting the Iranian revolution. Evidence of the growing involvement of women in the protest movement emerged when as-Sadr's sister Amina, known as Bint al-Huda, organized demonstrations in Najaf following as-Sadr's arrest in June 1979.

The intensification of Shia opposition led the regime to adopt a two-pronged policy: the systematic elimination of militant clerics and the promotion of a greater regard for popular Shia religious sentiment. In April 1980 as-Sadr and his sister were executed after being implicated in a bomb attack to commemorate victims of an earlier assault aimed at Tariq Aziz, a high-ranking Ba'athist who was later to become Foreign Minister. In 1983 six members of the al-Hakim family, including three brothers of Muhammad Baqer al-Hakim, were executed. According to opposition sources, 5,000-10,000 people were executed in the wave of repression organised by the government in 1979-83 while the disappearance and torture of hundreds of Shia activists in 1979-82 were recorded by the human rights organization, Amnesty International.

Clerical dissent was controlled by the introduction of measures, embodied in a government decree of 1981, granting the Ministry of (Religious) Endowments (*awqaf*) and Religious Affairs responsibility for the promulgation of laws governing places of worship, the right to appoint Shia clergy (henceforth put on the government payroll), and the authority to permit or refuse participation by *ulama* in religious councils. These initiatives reportedly had the backing of Najaf-based pro-Ba'athist Shia *ulama*, led by Ali Kashif al-Ghata, who were said to have regarded as-Sadr's activist stance as an attempt to undermine their local following.

The politicization of the Shia community as a whole was substantially weakened by the deportation, under the Iraqi Nationality Law, of several thousand Iraqi Shias to Iran in the early 1980s, ostensibly on the grounds of their Iranian origins.

Meanwhile, conciliatory gestures aimed at appeasing popular Shia religious sentiment led in 1978-79 to the approval of substantial government grants for religious purposes as well as the official endorsement of holidays marking Shia religious festivals and the identification of the regime's leaders with revered Shia figures in Islamic history. Expansion in the communitarian basis of government was reflected in the composition of the RCC in which Shias formed a majority for the first time in 1982. The composition of the National Assembly elected in 1980 was 40 per cent Shia, including the Speaker, and the Assembly elected in 1984 was also presided over by a Shia.

Evidence that the government's policies had failed to win popular Shia support emerged with reports of renewed Shia opposition following the outbreak of the Iran-Iraq war in September 1980. After a series of still-born organizations, including the Council of *Ulama* for the Islamic Revolution in Iraq, the Islamic Revolutionary Army for the Liberation of Iraq, the Group of the Fighting *Ulama* in Iraq and the Bureau of the Islamic Revolution in Iraq, it was finally announced in November 1982 that *ulama* loyal to Muhammad Baqer al-Hakim, son of Ayatollah Muhsin al-Hakim, had formed the Supreme Council of the Islamic Revolution in Iraq (SCIRI), which was subsequently referred to as the **Supreme Assembly of the Islamic Revolution in Iraq(SAIRI)**.

Meanwhile a group led by the brothers Hadi al-Mudarrissi and Muhammad Taqi al-Mudar-rissi formed the **Organization of Islamic Action** (*al-Amal al-Islami*) which in 1985 claimed responsibility for a number of bomb attacks on Iraqi institutions inside and outside the country.

Reports in September 1989 indicated possible links between the Islamic opposition in exile and sections of the Iraqi army allegedly involved in a series of unsuccessful coup attempts against Saddam Hussein during 1989. In January 1990 the Organization of Human Rights in Iraq claimed that the Iraqi army had launched attacks against the Shia-dominated cities of Basra, Nasiriya and Amara, killing 10,000 people.

The Gulf crisis lent new momentum to the Shia opposition movement, partly as a result of its closer co-operation with groups hitherto estranged from it, notably Kurdish and Communist parties. Although SAIRI remained opposed in principle to western involvement in the Gulf, its leaders refused to back Saddam Hussein's call for a *jihad* (holy war) against the western alliance. (A group of unidentified *ulama* was quoted by the government-controlled Iraqi News Agency (INA) on October 1 as having supported the government's call to *jihad*.) In November 1990 SAIRI claimed that more than 4,000 religious militants, mostly students, had been arrested in Baghdad after distributing pamphlets calling for the overthrow of the regime.

In March 1991 Shia demonstrators in Basra, Nasiriya, Karbala and Najaf staged a massive rebellion backed by SAIRI and calling for the establishment of an Islamic government in Iraq to be headed by Baqer al-Hakim. Shia suburbs around the capital, Baghdad, were also reported to have seen widespread unrest. By late March the Shia uprising was effectively suppressed amid claims by SAIRI that more than 30,000 people had died during the fighting. Between 500,000 and 900,000 Shia refugees were reported in May to be still trapped in the marshes of southern Iraq surrounded by 10,000 Iraqi troops, some in airborne units.

In December 1991 opposition groups met in Damascus to consider plans initiated by SAIRI which called for a popular uprising against Saddam Hussein involving elements in the army. In mid-April 1992 Shia opposition leaders accused the government of stepping up its campaign against Shia strongholds in the country's southern marshes.

FS

Major Islamic organizations

Islamic Alliance
Sunni organization based in Saudi Arabia; a member of JACIO.

Leader. Abu Yasser al-Alousi.

Kurdish Revolutionary Hezbollah of

Iraq

Hezbollah-e-Inquilab-e-Kurd-e-Iraq

Founded in January 1992 as "an extension and inseparable part of the Islamic movement in Iraq".

Leader. Adham Barzani.

Aims To overthrow Saddam Hussein in co-operation with Iraqi Shias and Muslims from other parts of the country.

Kurdish Party of God

Kurdish Hezbollah

Founded in 1985 as a breakaway group from the Democratic Party of Kurdistan (DPK); a member of SAIRI.

Leader. Muhammad Khaled.

Party of the Islamic Call

al-Dawa al-Islamiya

Clandestine organization reportedly established in 1968 under the spiritual leadership of Ayatollah Muhammad Baqer as-Sadr. Its nucleus lay in the *Jama'at al Ulama fi Najaf al-Ashraf* (the Association of Najaf Ulama), formed in the late 1950s at the instigation of Ayatollah Muhsin al-Hakim.

Leader. Reported to be Shaikh al-Assefi, who represents the organization in the Supreme Assembly of the Islamic Revolution in Iraq (SAIRI).

Membership. Precise figures are unavailable. Enquiries by Amnesty International indicated that of people arrested between 1979-82 whose whereabouts were still unknown, 11 were communists and one a member of *al-Dawa*, while seven of a list of 16 people who died under torture while in custody during the same period were reportedly *al-Dawa* members. In March 1991 *al-Dawa* was listed as a constituent group of the Supreme Assembly of the Islamic Revolution in Iraq (SAIRI) which formed part of the Joint Action Committee of the Iraqi Opposition (JACIO), established in December 1990.

Aims The creation of an Islamic order in Iraq.

Publications. *Sawt al-Dawa*, reportedly a follow-up to the Islamic journal *ad-Adwa* (Lights) published in the early 1960s with backing from as-Sadr and a group of militant *ulama*.

Supreme Assembly of the Islamic Revolution in Iraq (SAIRI)

The most important Islamic opposition coalition, formally established on November 17, 1982, with headquarters currently in Tehran.

Leader. Ayatollah Sayyid Muhammad Baqer al-Hakim; Mahmud al-Hashimi (chief spokesman and president until 1986).

Structure. An advisory committee restricted to *ulama* and an unspecified number of military units, some of which were reported during the Iran-Iraq war to have gained control over part of the Hajj Omran border area.

Membership. Unknown, although the front encompasses a number of well-established Islamic groups representing several hundred thousand Iraqi Shia exiles based in Iran, Syria and Lebanon. These include:Movement of the Iraqi *mujaheddin*, leaders Sayyid Muhammad al-Haideri and Ayatollah Muhammad Baqer al-Hakim; Islamic Movement in Iraq, Tehran-based, leader Shaikh Muhammad Mahdi al-Kalisi; *al-Dawa al-Islamiya* (Party of the Islamic Call), leader Shaikh al-Assefi; Soldiers of the Imam (*Jund al-Imam*), leader Abu Zaid; Organization of Islamic Action (*Al-Amal al-Islami*), Tehran-based, leader Shaikh Taqi Mudarrissi; and Islamic Scholars Organization, leader Shaikh al-Nasseri.

Aim. The creation of an Islamic republic modelled along Iranian lines.

Publications. SAIRI has been associated with a range of publications including *al-Jihad* (Holy War), *Liwa as-Sadr* (Battalion of *as-Sadr*), *ash-Shahid* (The Martyr), *Rah-e-Inquilab* (Way of the Revolution) (published in Persian) and *Kayhan al-Arabi*. Periodicals propagating SAIRI's ideology include *Dirasat wa Buhuth* (Studies and Investigations), *al-Adwa* (Lights, named after an earlier publication—see above), *Sorush* and *at-Tawahid* (Unity), the last two published also in English and Persian.

Affiliated organizations. Mostly Tehran-based and including the Institution of the Martyr as-Sadr, the Centre for Contemporary Islamic Studies and several women's organizations committed to the work of as-Sadr's sister, Bint al-Huda.

Turkoman Islamic Union

Anti-government organization reportedly formed in July 1991 and representing the predominantly Sunni Turkoman community.

Israel

Israel's Muslim population, numbering 677,700 at end-1990, are almost equally divided between the four main Sunni schools of law. Overall, Muslims form approximately 14.6 per cent of Israel's total population, which was estimated to be around 4,821,700 at end-1990.

Although evidence of Islamic revivalism within Israel's Arab Muslim population has been a relatively recent phenomenon, fundamentalist groups have been active since the early 1930s when a rural-based Islamic uprising in what was then northern Palestine sought through *jihad* (holy war), to oust British power and curb Jewish immigration.

In 1946 the Muslim Brotherhood was launched in Jerusalem with branches in Jaffa, Lydda and Haifa.

Although Arab Muslim opinion until the mid-1960s was traditionally expressed through the Arab section of the dominant Mapai party, the country's last two general elections in 1984 and 1988 indicated a marked preference for specifically Arab parties committed to Israeli withdrawal from the occupied territories and the establishment of a Palestinian state. More significantly, municipal elections in Arab towns and villages in February 1989 revealed a sharp increase in support for Islamic fundamentalist candidates at the expense of the hitherto more popular Israeli Communist Party.

Evidence of a revivalist trend among young Israeli Muslims coincided with the formation in 1980 of the Young Muslims association, inspired by the Iranian revolution of 1979 and reportedly funded by the Iranian government. The group, whose leadership and organizational base remain unclear, is known to profess its opposition on religious grounds to Israel, Arab nationalism and communism.

Attacks by members of militant Islamic factions have grown in recent years, culminating in May 1989 with the stabbing to death of two elderly Israelis in West (Israeli) Jerusalem.

Increasing numbers of Israeli Arabs have been drawn to the legally established **Israeli Islamic Movement** (IIM) headed by Shaikh Abdallah Nimr Darwish. Although the group claimed as recently as March 1992 not to have links with radical Islamic groups active in the West Bank and the Gaza Strip, sections of the Israeli government are concerned about its growing influence among young Arab Muslims and its alleged involvement in terrorist crimes against security forces, and have called for the organization to be suspended.

Muslim religious courts have exclusive jurisdiction over matters of marriage and divorce of Muslims who are not foreigners, or who are foreigners who are subject by their national law to jurisdiction of Muslim religious courts. In all other matters of personal status they have concurrent jurisdiction with the district courts.

FS

Islamic organizations

Israeli Islamic Movement (IIM)

Legal Muslim movement established in 1984.

Leader. Shaikh Abdallah Nimr Darwish.

Structure. According to information based on official Israeli sources, the IIM has major centres in Kafr Kanna, Umm al-Fahm, Kafr Qasim and Rahat. There are some 70 additional active cells in other locations. Municipal elections held in 1992 in some Arab-dominated areas, including Umm al Fahm, were successfully contested by the movement.

Membership. Unknown.

Aims. Recognition of Israel and the creation of an independent Palestinian state founded on Islamic principles.

West Bank and Gaza Strip (Israeli-occupied territories)

A clearly discernible Islamic political trend in the West Bank and the Gaza Strip became evident in the early 1950s with the emergence of fundamentalist parties including the **Muslim Brotherhood** and the **Islamic Liberation Party** (*Hizb al-Tahrir al-Islami*).

However, the dominant force of pan-Arab nationalism during the 1950s and 1960s, coupled with the latent hostility of both Jordan and Egypt which at that time administered the West Bank and Gaza respectively, ensured that the Islamic movement remained powerless to mobilize popular opinion.

The defeat of Arab forces and the occupation of the West Bank and Gaza by Israel in 1967, widely regarded as a blow to Muslim self-esteem, did not immediately trigger a rise in Muslim militancy. The Muslim Brotherhood in the West Bank and Gaza played little part in the armed resistance movement against Israel, with only a few of its members reportedly doing so in an individual capacity. Meanwhile, the political vacuum in the occupied territories was filled by the essentially secular Palestine Liberation Organization (PLO), which steadily won mass support as the sole legitimate representative of the Palestinian people.

A second Arab defeat in 1973 and the failure of political initiatives to end Israeli occupation of the West Bank and Gaza fuelled popular disillusionment with the policies advocated by the PLO. The Islamic revolution in Iran and the assassination of Egypt's President Anwar Sadat by a militant Islamic group opposed to a peace agreement with Israel contributed to a noticeably pro-Islamic trend, especially among young Arab Muslims in the occupied territories.

Evidence of the growing influence of pro-Islamic groups appeared to be confirmed after Palestinian nationalists agreed between 1979 and 1981 to form a tactical alliance with these groups to win control of the hitherto communist-dominated student councils of the universities of Bir Zeit and an-Najah.

By 1984 a non-official survey of religious and social change undertaken in the West Bank and Gaza since 1978 clearly established the existence of an Islamic revivalist trend with increased support for the Muslim Brotherhood and other Islamic organizations. While the survey found some regional variations in degrees of religiosity with those residing in Gaza scoring higher (57.8 per cent) than those in the West Bank (48.4 per cent), there was a uniform trend across the region indicating a rise in Islamic revivalism among college-educated young people.

The Islamic youth movement in the Occupied Territories in the period preceding the Palestinian *intifada* of December 1987 was broadly divided into five groupings consisting of the Muslim Brotherhood, the Islamic Liberation Party, followers of the late Ayatollah Khomeini of Iran, pro-PLO Muslims and the non-political missionary movement *al-Da'wa wal Tabligh*. Of the remaining groups, only the Muslim Brotherhood and the *Tahrir* party are relatively well-defined. However, pro-Iranian Islamic factions are expected to win favour among young Arabs willing to ignore Sunni-Shia divisions in the interests of armed resistance against Israel and Western governments.

The influence of pro-PLO Islamists in the occupied territories is limited, with support drawn mostly from sections of the traditional Islamic leadership and professional communities. These groups believe that the PLO's brand of nationalism is a necessary phase in the evolution towards an Islamic state.

The propagation of Islamic politics in the late 1970s tended, as traditionally, to be concentrated in the northern and southern parts of the West Bank and in refugee camps in the Gaza Strip. Islamists maintained their own clubhouses in the major towns of the West Bank and the Gaza Strip, including the Young Men's Muslim Association in Jerusalem and the Islamic Center in Gaza. The Gaza Islamic University was established in 1979 reportedly with backing from the Israeli government, in an attempt to counteract the influence of the PLO among Gaza's student population. The growing number of mosques in the region also acted as rallying sites for followers of the Islamic movement.

The outbreak of the Palestinian *intifada* in December 1987 provided Islamic revivalist groups the opportunity to tap the sources of widespread political alienation among young Arabs in the West Bank and the Gaza Strip. The depth of support for radical Islamic groups, most notably the hitherto unknown **Islamic Resistance Movement** or *Hamas* (derived from its Arabic acronym), was most clearly demonstrated in August 1988 after West Bank Arabs responded massively to a strike called by the organization. Although outlawed by the Israeli authorities, *Hamas* succeeded in mobilizing further mass demonstrations in Gaza in April 1989. In May Israel announced that it had arrested more than 250 alleged members of *Hamas*, including a cell responsible for eliminating Palestinians accused of collaborating with the Israeli authorities. Despite this, increasing frustration among young Palestinians in the Occupied Territories was reported by late 1989 to have fuelled fresh support for *Hamas*.

In January 1990 the trial opened in Gaza of the leader of *Hamas*, Shaikh Ahmed Yassein, who was arrested in May 1989 and charged with 15 offenses including the murder of two Israeli soldiers. In December 1990 a further 600 alleged members of *Hamas* were arrested following a concentrated Israeli campaign against Muslim militants. Yassein was sentenced to life imprisonment plus 15 years by an Israeli military court in Gaza in October 1991 after he confessed to charges ranging from founding and directing a hostile organization; homicide; and the killing of Palestinians suspected of co-operating with the Israeli authorities. (As of end-April 1992, around 500 Palestinians suspected of collaboration were estimated to have been killed by other Palestinians since the *intifada* began.)

The Gulf War led to a temporary alliance between the secular forces of the PLO and Islamic militants belonging to *Hamas*, both of which openly supported Iraq against the Western allies. By June 1991 simmering tension between the two groups led to an outbreak of armed violence in the West Bank city of Nablus. Renewed attempts by the PLO in September to secure the co-operation of Hamas failed after *Hamas* refused an invitation to participate in the 20th session of the Palestine National Council (PNC) held in Algiers.

In October 1991 a group calling itself *Hezbollah Palestine*, which claimed to be an offshoot of *Hamas*, said it was responsible for an attack near Ariel on a bus carrying Israeli settlers from the West Bank. One of the first reported bomb attacks on an Israeli settlement in the Gaza strip in February 1992 was claimed by *Hamas*.

Meanwhile, an extremist group calling itself **Holy War for Jerusalem** (*Jihad bayt al-muqaddas*) claimed responsibility in February 1990 for a grenade attack on a bus carrying Israeli tourists near Ismailiya in Egypt. In May the same group claimed responsibility for a bomb explosion in West Jerusalem which it said was in retaliation for the killing near Tel Aviv of a group of labourers from Gaza. In late October the organization was declared illegal by the Israeli authorities.

In January 1991 the spiritual leader of *Jihad bayt al-muqaddas*, Shaikh Asad Bayyud al-Tamimi, called for suicide attacks on Western and allied interests in retaliation for their war against Iraq.

Meanwhile, the organization **Islamic Jihad** (*Al-jihad al-Islami*) claimed responsibility for an attack on three Jews in east Jerusalem in May.

Both *Hamas* and Islamic Jihad have expressed opposition to the round of peace talks which began in Madrid in November 1991. In October *Hamas* and PLO supporters clashed in Gaza City following a strike call by *Hamas* in the Occupied Territories, which led to armed clashes between *Hamas* supporters and those of the PLO-mainstream *Fatah* organization. However, a setback to Islamic candidates who won only three of the 16 seats to the Gaza Chamber of Commerce in November prompted *Hamas* to seek what was reported as a "quiet dialogue" with the PLO to avoid further clashes between their respective supporters.

In recent elections to Gaza's professional organizations *Hamas* modestly improved its performance, although its candidates fared worse than the PLO which won five out the nine seats on Gaza Strip Engineers Association in January 1992. In February *Hamas* was defeated again after nationalists won nine out of 11 seats in elections for the Gaza Strip Medical Association. Both losses were deemed significant by *Hamas*, which had enjoyed wide support among sections of the professional classes. By March *Hamas* appeared to have regained its influence after ten of the 11 seats on the Ramallah and al-Bira Chambers of Commerce went to Islamic candidates backed by the militant movement.

FS

Major Islamic organizations

Holy War for Jerusalem
Jihad bayt al-muqaddas
Clandestine Sunni Muslim organization which gained prominence in February 1991 and was reportedly patterned along lines of similarly named groups in Egypt and Lebanon.
Leader. Shaikh Asad Bayyud al-Tamimi, sometimes described as the Mufti of the Palestine Liberation Army.
Membership. Unknown.
Aims. To wage a holy war (*jihad*) against Israel

and liberate Islamic Holy Places in Saudi Arabia.

Islamic Jihad
Al-jihad al-Islami
Clandestine Sunni organization, representing a split from the Muslim Brotherhood in Egypt in the mid-1960s, which emerged in the Occupied Territories in 1979. Although ostensibly independent it is believed to retain links with Islamic Jihad in Egypt.
Leader. Little is known about its leadership and

organizational structure; in 1987 the Israeli authorities issued a deportation order against Abdel-Aziz Odeh, a lecturer at Gaza's Islamic University, who was presumed to be a leader of the organization.

Membership. Unknown.

Aims. Advocates armed resistance against Israel in the West Bank and Gaza; critical of most Arab regimes, but strongly supportive of Iran. The organization is opposed to what it deems the reformist ideology of the Muslim Brotherhood. Despite strong political and ideological differences it has backed the PLO as the most important liberation movement in the region. The organization's uneasy relation with the PLO was reflected in its decision to allow some members to attend, in a strictly individual capacity, the 20th session of the PNC held in September 1991.

Islamic Liberation Party

Hizb al-Tahrir al-Islami

Founded in 1951 by a Palestinian jurist, Shaikh Ahmed Taqi ad-Din al-Nabhani and based principally in Jordan.

Membership. The party suffered a loss of mass support after a decision in the late 1970s to resume activities in the occupied territories which had been suspended in 1967. Although the party's influence in the Islamic movement remains marginal, it has pockets of support among university students in Jerusalem, Hebron and the Gaza strip.

Aims. The organization's manifesto advocates revolution (*inqilabiya*) and favours the use of military force against Israel. It is committed to the creation of an orthodox Islamic state in Palestine, including the territories constituting the state of Israel and the occupied territories. Its opposition to the Muslim Brotherhood is believed to stem less from ideological differences than from political rivalry.

Islamic Resistance Movement

Hamas

Outlawed Sunni Muslim organization that traces its origins to the Egyptian Muslim Brotherhood. Although the precise date of its foundation is unclear, Hamas rose to prominence during the Palestinian *intifada* in Gaza in August 1988.

Leader. Shaikh Ahmed Yassein (imprisoned October 1991); official spokesman, Ibrahim Ghawshaw.

Membership. Although Gaza-based, the movement is known to have extensive support among young Muslims in the West Bank and Israel. Reports in October 1991 indicated that *Hamas* claimed that over half of Gaza's estimated 750,000 people (less than 1 per cent of whom are Christians) supported the group. Israeli army estimates indicate that while the PLO was still the most popular organization in the West Bank, support in the region for *Hamas* could be as high as 30 per cent. The dean of the medical faculty at Gaza's Islamic University and a prominent Islamic figure, Mahmoud al Zahar, was quoted in April 1992 as saying that "at least 50 per cent of people in the occupied lands now support the Islamic movement".

Aims. The *Hamas Covenant* of 1988 calls on all Palestinian Muslims to wage holy war (*jihad*) against Israel. It advocates the creation of an Islamic state in Gaza and eventually in all territories presently under Israeli control. It commands opposition to the PLO until it accepts Islam as its principle ideology. *Hamas* also opposes the Middle East peace process, which its supporters habitually describe as "treachery".

Funding. The movement is reportedly a recipient of financial aid from Saudi Arabia; in 1990 Kuwait acknowledged that it had paid US$60,000,000 to *Hamas* in the preceding year.

Muslim Brotherhood

Ikhwan al-Muslimun

Sunni Muslim group established in Jerusalem in 1946 as an off-shoot of similarly named organization launched in Egypt in 1928. The movement's more active Gaza-based section, which advocated armed struggle against Israel, ceased to exist by the mid-1960s following a crackdown by the Egyptian authorities against Muslim militants. The Brotherhood's West Bank section, which formed part of the Muslim Brotherhood of Jordan and refrained from advocating violence against Israel, was recognized as a legal organization by the Jordanian authorities. Since 1967 both sections of the Brotherhood have operated as clandestine organizations.

Leader. There is reportedly no single leader.

Membership. Estimates based on surveys conducted in the West Bank in late 1987 indicated that active membership did not exceed several thousand, although the number of participating and supporting members may be several times larger. The Brotherhood is known to have wide support among students at universities throughout the West Bank and Gaza.

Aims. Although the Brotherhood has a broad social and cultural programme, its political objectives include the establishment of an Islamic state in Palestine, including the boundaries of present-day Israel and all lands occupied in 1967.

Funding. The Brotherhood is supported by membership dues and local tithe (*zakat*) committees. Financial support is reported also to come from Saudi Arabia through the Mecca-based Muslim World League and its off-shoot, the World Council of Mosques, as well as the Riyad-based World Assembly of Muslim Youth.

Italy

There are estimated to be about 150,000 Muslims in Italy, the bulk of whom are immigrants from eastern Europe, North Africa and Somalia, and concentrated in the cities of Milan and Rome and in Sicily.

A *Concordat* approved by the Italian parliament in 1929 made Roman Catholicism, the religion of some 90 per cent of Italians, the official religion. In June 1985 the approval of a new *Concordat* led to the end of Roman Catholicism as the state religion and to the abolition of compulsory religious instruction in schools.

In the first half of the 20th century Italy ruled as a colonial power over substantial Muslim populations in Libya, Ethiopia and Somalia. The Fascist government in the 1930s attempted to present itself as a natural ally of Islam, hoping thus to gain an advantage over rival colonial powers.

In the 1970s Italy became an importer of foreign labour, having previously been a country from which large numbers of people emigrated each year. From 1970 to 1985 most of the non-Europeans who entered the country were Africans from former Italian colonies and Iranian refugees, along with some Moroccans and Tunisians who settled in Sicily. After 1986 further immigrants arrived from Senegal, Tunisia and Ghana, most of them relatively well-educated single young men. In the 1980s there were sporadic incidents of violence against immigrants and in the autumn of 1990 North Africans were attacked in Bologna and Africans in Naples.

The "Martelli law", approved by Parliament in February 1990, ruled that from June 1990 it would not be possible for illegal immigrants to regularize their residency. It also envisaged stricter immigration controls, in anticipation of the abolition of border controls within the European Communities (EC) under the terms of the Schengen agreement, signed by Italy in October 1990.

In the general election of April 1992 an Egyptian-born Muslim candidate, Mohammed Ashmawi, unsuccessfully contested a seat in a Rome constituency. In contrast to France, immigration was not a major election issue; although regionalist parties such as the *Lega Nord* were generally opposed to immigration, the issue was not an explicit issue in their election campaigns.

EB

Islamic Organizations

Islamic Cultural Centre of Italy
Centro Islamico Culturale d'Italia
Established in Rome with funding from Muslim countries, its projects have included the building in 1991-92 of a large mosque near the Villa Ada in Rome.
Leader. Abdul Ghassem Amini (secretary-general).

Aims. To promote knowledge of the Islamic faith.

Union of the Muslims of the West
Created as a cultural and religious organization by Muslim refugees from eastern Europe in the period after the Second World War but later eclipsed by the Islamic Cultural Centre of Italy.

Japan

A constitutional monarchy, Japan has an emperor as its head of state, while the Prime Minister is head of government and is responsible to the parliament.

The majority of Japan's estimated 123,611,541 population are followers of one of the country's two established religions, Shintoism and Buddhism. There is a small Christian community (1,081,387 in 1988) and a number of more recently founded syncretist religious cults.

There is a small native Japanese and foreign Muslim community, some of whose activities date back to the late 19th century. In recent years the immigration of Muslims from Pakistan and Bangladesh has contributed to the emergence of a more active community. About 30,000 Muslims are reported to be members of the Islamic Centre in Tokyo; the community also maintains a mosque at Kobe.

In recent years there have been signs of increasing militancy among Japan's growing number of foreign Muslim resident workers, prompted mainly by the publication and translation into Japanese of the *The Satanic Verses* by the Indian-born British writer, Salman Rushdie. In 1989 the Islamic Centre in Tokyo issued a formal request to Japanese publishers, newspapers and radio stations not to translate or reproduce the novel which it described as "anti-Islamic".

The decision not to accede to Muslim demands met with protests from Muslim demonstrators amid reports that some Muslim militants had issued death threats against the book's Japanese publishers, *Shinseisha*. In February 1990 a Pakistani national attending a press conference at the Foreign Correspondents' Club in Tokyo was arrested after attacking Gianna Palma, the Italian publisher of the Japanese translation of the *The Satanic Verses*.

In July 1991 the Japanese translator of *The Satanic Verses*, Professor Hitoshi Igarishi, was found stabbed at the campus of Tsukaba University in Mito, outside Tokyo. Although some reports suggested that the killing had the backing of the Iranian government, a spokesman for the Pakistan Association of Japan, who claimed that his organization had supported the murder, said that "because it is a non-Muslim country, [the murder] is against the law in Japan, but according to the law of Islam it's quite alright".

DS

Islamic organizations

Pakistan Association of Japan
Leader. Raees Siddiqui (president).

Jordan

The Hashemite Kingdom of Transjordan (renamed Jordan in 1949) attained full independence in 1946, having hitherto been administered by the United Kingdom under a League of Nations mandate. The country's constitutional monarch, King Hussein ibn Tallal, who appoints the Prime Minister, has played an active role in Jordanian politics since succeeding his father in 1952. All political parties have been technically banned since July 1963; however, in June 1991 King Hussein endorsed a National Charter lifting the ban, and in April 1992 formally abolished all martial law provisions in force since the 1967 Arab-Israeli war.

The overwhelming majority (between 80 and 90 per cent) of Jordan's population—estimated in 1990 to total 4,009,000—are Sunnis adhering to the Hanafi school of law. A small community of Christians is concentrated mainly in urban centres, with an even smaller number of Shias. Recent evidence of the existence of the heterodox Ahmadiyyah sect emerged after the Islamic Higher Court of Appeal in February 1991 overruled a lower Islamic court in the town of Naour which had pronounced an alleged Ahmadiyyah follower, Ibrahim Abu Nab, a "repentant Muslim" and ordered him to be forcibly divorced from his wife so as to be remarried under Islamic law.

Although Jordan's Constitution recognizes Islam as the official religion, the regime has been careful to maintain the distinction between this provision and those normally governing an Islamic state. Nevertheless, the emphasis placed on the ancestry of the ruling Hashemite family as directly descended from the Prophet Muhammad has been an important factor in maintaining the legitimacy of the monarchy. King Hussein's active involvement in the country's extensive mosque building programme and his support for religious programmes on radio and television, also suggest his willingness to be identified with the Islamic faith. Officially sponsored moves aimed at bridging the divide between Sunnis and Shias were confirmed in March 1992 after reports that the Ministry of *Awqaf* (Religious Endowments) and Islamic Affairs was considering proposals for a Chair of Shia Studies at Amman University.

Islamic courts applying rules derived from the Quran and Hadith (Precepts of the Prophet Muhammad) operate alongside secular courts applying a system mainly derived from English common law. There is a Minister of Religious Affairs, and the Ministry of *Awqaf* and Islamic Affairs sponsors a monthly publication, *Huda al-Islam* ("The Right Way of Islam"), founded in 1956.

Islam and the state: developments since independence

Since independence the monarchy has followed a policy of co-operation with the Muslim religious establishment, which is dominated by Muslim religious scholars (*ulama*). Official sponsorship of Islamic affairs has been pursued through the Ministry of *Awqaf* and Islamic Affairs, the Higher Council of Islamic Affairs and the Supreme Muslim Secular Council. Religious dissent has been controlled by the increasing bureaucratization of the clerical hierarchy whose members are almost entirely dependent for their livelihood on state stipends.

The incorporation of the Muslim religious establishment into the state administrative and financial system has not, however, succeeded in neutralizing the country's Islamist lobby or its most prominent representative, the **Muslim Brotherhood** (*Ikhwan al muslimun*). Established in 1953 as an offshoot of the Society of the Muslim Brothers of Palestine (founded in 1945-46), the Muslim Brotherhood enjoyed a degree of official tolerance in its early years owing primarily to its shared hostility to the pan-Arab and socialist ideals of Nasserism and Ba'athism. Under the leadership of Abd al Rahman al Khalifah, the Muslim Brotherhood rose steadily in the 1960s and 1970s to become an essential component of the Hashemite regime. In legislative by-elections held in March 1984 two Muslim Brotherhood sympathisers, Ahmed Kufani and Abdullah al Akailah, successfully contested seats to the reconvened House of Representatives.

The reformist orientation of the Muslim Brotherhood which had, in part, contributed to its political respectability, contrasted sharply with the activist stance of its rivals in the **Islamic Liberation Party** (ILP—*Hizb al-Tahrir al Islami*), founded in Jerusalem in 1953. Committed to the establishment of a unitary Islamic caliphate through a strategy of holy war (*jihad*), the ILP proclaimed itself as a "political party whose principle is Islam and whose activity is politics". The ILP, which remains proscribed, was implicated in a series of take-over attempts directed against the Jordanian government in 1968 and the early 1970s, is also believed to have an active network extending beyond Jordan. A former ILP member, Salih Sairiyya of Palestinian-Jordanian descent, was reported to have led the assault on the Cairo Technical Military Academy in 1974, while another sympathiser, Salim al Rahhal, was allegedly responsible for the organization of the *al Jihad* group which was accused of the assassination in October 1981 of Egyptian President Anwar Sadat. The Jordanian regime's hostility to the ILP and other militant Islamic offshoots, including factions of **Islamic Jihad** and the Prophet Muhammad Army, intensified after Islamist groups were blamed for a series of disturbances on university campuses in 1986, countrywide price riots in April 1989 and a planned bombing and assassination campaign in mid-1991.

Meanwhile, the regime's growing rapprochement with the Muslim Brotherhood, prompted in part by its attempts to counter the growing influence of the Palestine Liberation Organization (PLO) on the Israeli-occupied West Bank, led to the emergence of the Brotherhood as the only legal and well-organized opposition group on the eve of the November 1989 legislative elections. (The group had circumvented the ban on political parties by winning recognition as a charity). Campaigning on a programme dedicated to the introduction of Islamic law (*sharia*), the reform of education along Islamic lines and a total and immediate ban on the sale of alcohol, the Muslim Brotherhood won 20 of the 80 seats in the House of Representatives; a further 12-14 seats were won by other Islamist candidates sympathetic to the Muslim Brotherhood. The leading Muslim Brotherhood candidate, Abdul Munim Abu Zant, won the highest number of votes—19,373—from the economically deprived district of Amman-2.

A new government appointed in December 1989 included three independent Muslim deputies (the Muslim Brotherhood having declined to participate after its request for allocation of the Education portfolio was denied). A Cabinet reshuffle in January 1991, prompted by divisions over the government's Gulf war policy, led to the inclusion of five members of the Muslim Brotherhood who received the Health, Justice, Religious Affairs, Social Development and Education portfolios.

By mid-1991 there were reports of growing strains between King Hussein and the Muslim Brotherhood. A Cabinet reshuffle in June, allegedly at the instigation of the King, who had disapproved of Prime Minister Mudar Badran's sympathy for the Muslim Brotherhood, resulted in its exclusion. Opposition from the Muslim Brotherhood and other Islamist deputies intensified after King Hussein resisted calls to boycott the Middle East Peace Conference which opened in Madrid on October 30, 1991. In November the Muslim Brotherhood, as part of the recently formed Parliamentary Arab Islamic Coalition Front (PAICF), was at the forefront of a no confidence move against the government which led to the resignation of Prime Minister Taher al-Masri.

A new government appointed in late November failed to include representatives of the Muslim Brotherhood. However, the government's need to win broad-based support for its economic policies, outlined in its 1992 budget, was reportedly behind its unwillingness to challenge the re-election in December 1991 of the Muslim Brotherhood deputy, Abdel-Latif Arabiyat, as Speaker of the House of Representatives.

The regime's conciliatory policy towards the Muslim Brotherhood came under renewed pressure in early 1992 following fears of an impending government crackdown against Islamists along lines similar to those witnessed in Algeria in recent months. In March tension between the government and the Muslim Brotherhood re-surfaced after the Muslim Brotherhood helped initiate a resolution in the House of Representatives, passed by 34 votes to 20, recommending a ban on the consumption, sale and manufacture of alcohol.

FS

Major Islamic organizations

Islamic Jihad al-Aqsa
Reported to be an underground militant offshoot of the Muslim Brotherhood, founded by Shaikh Ibrahim Sirbil who was arrested by Jordanian security forces in March 1991. The group was allegedly responsible for the infiltration into Israel from Jordan of a six-member fighter group on March 11, 1991.

Islamic Liberation Party
Hizb al Tahrir al Islami
Militant Islamic party proscribed by the government; established in Jerusalem in 1953 by a Palestinian lawyer, Taqi al din al-Nabhani (died 1977). Influenced by the ideas of Sayyid Qutb

who led a radical offshoot of the Egyptian Muslim Brotherhood, the group is reported to have a wide network extending across the Israeli-occupied West Bank and across Egypt, where its sympathisers were allegedly involved in the attempted takeover of the Cairo Technical Military Academy in 1974 and in the assassination of President Sadat in October 1981. Sympathisers of the group have also been implicated in a number of violent political acts in Iraq and Tunisia. In 1968 the ILP was reportedly involved in an attempted coup against the Jordanian government.

Aims. A 1985 pamphlet released by the organization lists its political aim to be the creation of a unitary Islamic caliphate, its economic aim to be the "distribution of wealth, not the production of wealth", and its international aim to be a strategy of holy war (*jihad*).

Muslim Brotherhood

Ikhwan al Muslimun

Founded in 1953 as an offshoot of the Muslim Brothers of Palestine (proclaimed in 1945-46 as an extension of the Egyptian Muslim Brotherhood), it has enjoyed a degree of official tolerance denied its counterparts in Egypt and Syria. The organization's political respectability, coupled with its recognition as a registered charity permitting the circumvention of the 1963 law banning political parties, has allowed it successfully to contest seats in legislative elections. In 1989 the organization made substantial gains after it won 20 out 80 seats in the House of Representatives. In January 1991 the Muslim Brotherhood joined the government, being allocated five portfolios, including the sensitive Education portfolio which had been denied it earlier, causing it to withhold co-operation. However, growing disagreements centring on the regime's Middle East policy resulted in the organization's exclusion from government in June 1991. In October 1991 Muslim Brotherhood deputies joined with other opposition parties to form the Parliamentary Arab Islamic Coalition Front (PAICF) which, in November, helped secure the election of the Muslim Brotherhood deputy, Abdel-Latif Arabiyat, as Speaker of the House of Representatives.

Membership. The organization's main recruitment ground is believed to be centred among young Jordanians and Palestinians in urban centres and refugee camps as well as among middle-class students, teachers and officials.

Aims. Although officially reformist in outlook, the organization is believed to have undergone a process of radicalization following the Gulf war and the recent crackdown on fundamentalist organizations in Egypt and Algeria.

Kazakhstan

(For a broad survey of Islam in the former Soviet Union see separate entry for the Commonwealth of Independent States)

Kazakhstan gained the status of a Union Republic in 1936. Territorially the second-largest republic in the Commonwealth of Independent States (CIS), it has a population of only 16,500,000, of which only 40 per cent are of the titular nationality. Much of the remaining population is European—38 per cent Russians, 5 per cent Ukrainians, 5 per cent Germans.

The conversion to Islam of the native nomad population of Kazakhstan in the 19th century was originally encouraged by the Russian government in the hope that it would unify and civilize the different tribes of the region. There are about 40,000 Kazakhs in Mongolia, and between 600,000 and 700,000 in China, as well as 3,000 in Afghanistan.

The undercurrent of Kazakh nationalism provoked one of the earliest nationalist demonstrations against the Soviet administration of Mikhail Gorbachev when, in December 1986, up to 3,000 people protested in Alma Ata against the replacement of the admittedly corrupt, but Kazakh, Communist Party First-Secretary, Dinmukhamed Kunayev, by an ethnic Russian, Gennady Kolbin (who was subsequently replaced by the Kazakh Nursultan Nazarbayev in 1990).

In August 1991 Kazakh nationalism was once again inflamed by remarks made by the Russian President Boris Yeltsin, who suggested that Russia had a valid claim to the northern area of Kazakhstan where there is a concentration of ethnic Russians.

The republic's independence from official Islam was underlined in early 1990 when the Mufti of Kazakhstan, Ratbek Nysanbayev, established an independent *muftiyat* in Alma Ata after accusing the Mufti of Tashkent, Mufti Sadik, of corruption. Despite his action, however, Nysanbayev underlined his opposition to an Islamic party in Kazakhstan, claiming it was "a sin for politicians to want to use Islam to achieve their narrow ambitions".

In December 1991, Nysanbayev was physically attacked by members of the clandestine **Alash Party**, who broke up Friday prayers at the Alma Ata mosque apparently in protest against the Nysanbayev's religious moderation.

Kazakhstan's first religious seminary (*madrassah*) was inaugurated on Sept. 1, 1990, with 25 pupils. Clerics from Turkey have been particularly active in rendering assistance to their Kazakh counterparts; in April 1992 a group of visiting Turkish clerics (*imams*) led by one of Turkey's senior *imams*, Halif Altay, confirmed that "the number of Muslim communities and mosques [in the region] has lately increased".

WS

Islamic organizations

Alash Party

Clandestine organization named after the mythical ancestors of the Kazakhs, which traces its origins to the hitherto underground Kazakh Islamic Panturkist Group. Its founding congress, held in April 1990, claimed to resurrect the *Alash-Orda* (Camp of Alash), a party which existed between 1905-20.

Leader. Aron Atabek. (The party's first chairman was removed on grounds of insufficient religious devotion.)

Membership. Active membership is estimated to be no more than 100. There are said to be related groups in Tashkent, Baku and Yakutsk.

Aims. To organize protest meetings and hunger strikes. Its self-professed aim is the creation of a united Islamic Turkestan "from Vladivostok to Istanbul".

Publication. *Khak* (Truth), a Russian language newspaper published for the first time in Moscow in November 1991 with a circulation of 100,000 (for the whole Islamic region of the CIS). The origin of the organization's broadsheet lies in the party's early history when, after being denied permission to register as a political party in Kazakhstan, it registered itself as a business under the name *Khak* in Moscow.

League of Muslim Women in Kazakhstan

The movement held an extraordinary congress in March 1992.

Leader. Roza Buglanova (president); Sara Nazarbayeva, wife of Kazakhstan's President Nazarbayev, (honorary president).

Aims. To promote the greater influence of women in public life.

The **Islamic Renaissance Party** (IRP—see Commonwealth of Independent States entry) has a small branch in the Chimkent region, active since April 1991.

Kenya

The Republic of Kenya was proclaimed in December 1964, having achieved independence within the Commonwealth the previous year. Until the introduction of a multiparty system in December 1991 political life was dominated by the ruling Kenya African National Union (KANU).

The majority of the population hold traditional beliefs and 25 per cent profess Christianity. About 10 per cent, concentrated in the coastal, north-east and eastern provinces, follow Islam.

Islam arrived in present-day Kenya in the seventh century when the coastal population encountered Arab traders developing commercial routes. At the beginning of the 19th century the coastal area was incorporated into the Muslim state of Oman and later came under the control of the United Kingdom. Islam, which until then had been largely confined to the coastal region, subsequently extended its influence inland to both the urban and rural populations.

Arabic and Swahili-speaking Muslims constitute the bulk of the Islamic population and are Sunni followers of the Shafi school of law. There are also significant numbers of Muslims of Sudanese origin concentrated around Nairobi who follow the Maliki school, as well as a sizeable group of Muslims of Asian origin who adhere to the Hanafi school.

Specially constituted *Kadhi* (Arabic *qadi*—judge) courts have jurisdiction within districts to determine questions of Islamic law.

Islam and the state: developments since independence

Muslims have exerted little political influence in recent years and there are no significant Islamic political organizations. As in other parts of Africa, the existence of Christian mission schools has affected Muslims. Fearing conversion as the price for education, many Muslims were reluctant to send their children to missionary-run schools, with the result that at independence there were few educated Muslims able to participate in the government, which remains dominated by Christians.

The teaching of Islam is administered exclusively by Quranic schools which receive support from the Muslim **Kenya Welfare Society**. There are over 120 non-political Islamic associations, most of which are concerned with maintaining mosques.

With the legalization of political activity in December 1991 there was some evidence of Muslim organization. In February 1992 a senior official cautioned the Muslim community against holding political meetings in mosques, claiming that prayer meetings were frequently being transformed into political gatherings.

The formation of the **Islamic Party of Kenya** (IPK) was reported in March 1992. According to subsequent reports the IPK was responsible for organizing a series of riots in the country's predominantly Muslim coastal region after the government banned religious parties from contesting Kenya's first multiparty elections scheduled to take place before April 1993. A prominent Muslim leader, Abdullahai Kiptonui, criticized the IPK as a group representing "self-seekers and power-hungry people who are not known to many Muslims". He called on Muslims to reject the new party and to continue to support the KANU government.

TJ

Islamic organizations

Islamic Foundation
Muslim educational organization concerned with publications on Islam in local languages and dialects; supports Islamic schools in Isiolo and Machakos.

Islamic Party of Kenya (IPK)
Reportedly founded in March 1992; it was subsequently involved in a series of riots in Mombasa, Voi and other coastal towns after a decision by the government banning religious parties from contesting multi-party elections.
Leader. Khalid Salim Ahmed Balala.
Membership. The IPK is based in Kenya's predominantly Muslim coastal region.

Kenya Welfare Society
Muslim educational and social organization.
Aims. The provision of support for Islamic schools, improvement of health education, and provision for Muslim children.

Supreme Council of Kenya Muslims (Supkem)
Founded as a federation of over 100 Muslim organizations in 1976.
Leader. Ahmed Khalif (secretary-general).

Kirgizstan

(For a broad survey of Islam in the former Soviet Union see separate entry for the Commonwealth of Independent States.)

Kirgizstan became a Union Republic in 1936, having previously been an autonomous administrative region (*oblast*) within the Russian Federation.

The population of 4,300,000 is only 52 per cent Kirgiz; sizeable minorities include Russians (22 per cent) and Uzbeks (12 per cent). Other minorities include Ukrainians, Tatars and Kazakhs. The Kirgiz were originally nomads, converted to Islam from the mid-17th century, mainly by Sufi missionaries.

The Kirgiz are Sunni Muslims of the Hanafi school. There are about 25,000 Kirgiz in Afghanistan and 80,000 in China, with which Kirgizstan shares a border which has frequently witnessed the migration of Muslim minorities from China.

The republic has experienced ethnic tension. In June 1990 riots in Osh between Uzbeks and Kirgiz, sparked by a dispute over the use of land for housing, left 200 people dead. Osh remains closed to journalists.

The republic's government is perceived as moderate and reformist. Its President, Askar Akayev, prominent in his opposition to the attempted August 1991 coup, went on to promote economic reforms, including private land and property ownership.

President Akayev has declared himself against Islamic fundamentalism, but in an interview in December 1991 he said that he favoured "the revival and strengthening of religion, in the hope that it will allow us to consolidate morality in our society and assist in the moral upbringing of our young people".

WS

Islamic organizations

There are no overtly Islamic organizations, although the Islamic Renaissance Party (IRP—see Commonwealth of Independent States entry) is known to have a small active group of Uzbeks in the Osh region.

135

Kuwait

The State of Kuwait, a former British protectorate, gained independence in 1961. Only about 40 per cent of the population, assessed in mid-1990 at 2,014,135, are native Kuwaitis. Thirty-nine per cent of the remainder is of Arab origin, with the rest predominantly South Asian and Iranian.

The majority, about 85 per cent, are Muslim. Of these, roughly 45 per cent, including the ruling royal family, are Sunni and follow the Maliki school of law, while a much small number adheres to Shafi rites. A sizeable minority (about 35 per cent) are Twelver Shias (*ithna ashaariyya*), and many of them form the country's commercial oligarchy.

Of all the Gulf states Kuwait, with international trading links which predate the discovery of oil, has had the longest exposure to Western influences. The discovery of oil and a dizzying pace of modernization did not immediately fuel religious protest, despite their dislocating effects. Demographic conditions in Kuwait, with a large expatriate workforce of different ethnic origins (as elsewhere in the Gulf), has inhibited a broadly based Islamic revivalist movement, while the presence of Shia families in the country's commercial oligarchy has effectively precluded the threat of a Shia uprising on the Iranian model, although the economic backwardness of Kuwait's Shia population may have heightened Shia discontent.

In the early 1970s Kuwait's most prominent Sunni Islamic organizations were the relatively non-militant Guidance Society (*Jamiyyat al Irshad*), divided into a "pro-establishment" faction led by Abdul Aziz al-Ali al Mutawa, and a "youth" faction headed by Muhammad al-Adsani.

Early signs of a revivalist trend, introduced by the growing Pakistani and Egyptian populations, emerged with the gradual re-orientation of two other organizations, the Social Reform Group and the Social Educational Group. Both groups were influenced by the ideas of the Egyptian Muslim Brotherhood (*Ikhwan al Muslimun*) and rose to prominence in late 1971 campaigning in support of separate higher education for male and female students.

The first serious manifestation of Shia discontent occurred in September 1979 after the government deported a leading Shia cleric (and brother-in-law of Iran's Ayatollah Khomeini), Hojateleslam Sayyid Abbas Muhri, for his involvement in a series of demonstrations in the capital, Kuwait City. In October 1983 militant Sunnis attacked Shia workers after claims by a group of Shia intellectuals that the government had removed Shia officers from commanding positions in the army and the police forces.

Indications of links between radical Kuwaiti Shias and militant Shia organizations abroad were confirmed in December 1983 when members of the underground Iraqi Shia movement *ad-Dawa al Islamiya* (The Call of Islam) infiltrated Kuwait and claimed responsibility for a series of explosions at Western and Kuwaiti targets, including embassies and industrial depots. The arrest of some of those involved, who included both Kuwaitis and Iraqis, provoked further incidents including the hijacking of a Kuwaiti airliner to Tehran by a Shia group which demanded the release of the prisoners. In May 1985 Shias belonging to a group calling itself the **Call of Islam** *(ad -Dawa al Islamiya)* claimed responsibility for an assassination attempt on the Amir, Shaikh Jaber al-Ahmed al Jabir and in July Shia militants belonging to the Black Brigades attacked a café on the waterfront. In January 1987 members of a Shia revolutionary organization, **Forces of the Prophet Muhammad**, were arrested on charges of attempting to plant bombs at oil facilities with the intention of disrupting a summit meeting of the Islamic Conference Organization.

The spread of Kuwaiti Shia militancy abroad was highlighted by a bomb attack in the holy city of Mecca in July 1989. Sixteen Kuwaiti Shias found guilty of the bombing were publicly beheaded in Saudi Arabia. The executions triggered Shia protests in Kuwait and led to the arrest of senior Shia clerics and the disbanding of the Shia Social Culture Society. In February 1990 the government arrested a group of Shias for involvement with the Mecca attack.

Meanwhile growing criticism by Islamic fundamentalist groups of the government's educational and financial policies influenced the Amir's decision to dissolve the popularly elected National Assembly *(Majlis al Umma)* in July 1986.

While political parties were illegal in Kuwait, the National Assembly had provided a forum for opposition groups, including religious factions. In elections held in 1981 and 1985 several seats were won by Sunni and Shia revivalists, the most prominent of whom were Khaled al-Sultan of the **Islamic Heritage Revival Society** (elected in 1981, ousted in 1985), Isa Majid al-Shaheen of the **Muslim Brotherhood** (elected in 1981, ousted in 1985), Salih Fadlallah (elected 1981), Abdullah al Nafisi (elected 1981) and Abdul Aziz al Mutawa of the Social Reform Group (elected 1985). Of 50 members elected to the Assembly in 1981, four were Shias (a drop from the ten in the previous Assembly, dissolved in August 1976).

As part of the pro-democracy National Constitutional Front (formed in 1990), Islamic Sunni and Shia parties have joined with other groups to press for the restoration of the National Assembly, the separation of the government from the ruling as-Sabah family (presently headed by the Amir of Kuwait, Shaikh Jaber al-Ahmad as-Sabah), the legalization of political parties, and an independent judiciary.

The end of the Gulf War and the liberation of the country from Iraqi occupation in February 1991 brought the ruling family under increasing pressure from pro-democracy campaigners including Islamists from the Muslim Brotherhood *(Ikhwan al-muslimun)* who demanded the immediate restoration of parliamentary and press freedom. More radical elements in the movement also demanded the resignation of the as-Sabah family from all important positions in the government and the establishment of a constitutional monarchy.

In July 1991 the Amir sought to meet opposition demands by reconvening the country's nominated body, the National Council, to act as a forum for opinion until elections, scheduled for October 1992, had been held. Meanwhile a combination of royal decrees, Islamic law *(sharia)* and civil codes continues to be the base for most existing legislation.

Reports quoting the Interior Minister, Shaikh Ahmed Al Hammoud as-Sabah, in February 1992 indicated that the government was seeking to ban women from voting in the planned legislative elections. According to other reports appearing simultaneously, opposition parties including the Muslim Brotherhood but excluding the fundamentalist **Islamic Alliance**, were pressing for the enfranchisement of women.

EW

Major Islamic organizations

Call of Islam
ad-Dawa al Islamiya
Clandestine Shia organization about which little is known. It came to light in May 1985 following an attempt to assassinate the Amir of Kuwait.

Forces of the Prophet Muhammed
Clandestine Shia organization which rose to prominence after it claimed responsibility for a series of attacks in 1987 on Kuwaiti oil installations.
Aims. The implementation of an Islamic state, by violent means if necessary.

Islamic Alliance
Fundamentalist Muslim organization founded in 1991.
Leader. Ahmed Baqar.

Islamic Constitutional Movement (ICM)
Sunni Muslim organization founded in 1991 as an offshoot of the Social Reform Group, closely allied to the Muslim Brotherhood. Following Kuwait's liberation from Iraqi forces, the ICM reportedly fell out with the Brotherhood over what it termed its "negative attitudes" towards the plight of Kuwaitis under Iraqi occupation.
Leader. Ismail al-Shatti.
Membership. Its main constituency lies with young Kuwaitis from professional or academic backgrounds.
Aims. The ICM aims to introduce Islamic reform by concentrating on changing educational and social practices. Its ultimate goal is the creation of an Islamic republic by non-violent means.
Publication. The party organ is *al-Mujtama*

(Society).

Islamic Heritage Revival Society (IHRS)
Salafiyyin
Conservative Sunni Muslim organization founded in the 1980s.
Leader. Khaled al-Sultan.
Aims. The IHRS favours a literalist interpretation of the Quran and campaigns for an Islamic republic to be achieved through non-violent means. It has called for free elections and a return to parliamentary democracy.

Kuwaiti Hezbollah
A hitherto unknown Shia group which came to light in 1988 after it announced that it intended to commence a holy war (*jihad*) against Kuwait's ruling family.

Muslim Brotherhood
Ikhwan al muslimun
Leader. Isa Majid al-Shaheen.

National Islamic Coalition (NIC)
Shia Muslim group founded in 1991 with the aim of unofficially fielding candidates in elections scheduled for October 1992.

Repentance and Flight
Al-Takfir wa'l Hijra
Clandestine Sunni fundamentalist group inspired by a similarly named organization in Egypt. It is believed to have been introduced to the Gulf in the early 1970s by Egyptian expatriate workers.
Membership. It is thought to have support mainly among young Kuwaitis.

Lebanon

The Republic of Lebanon, formerly part of Syria, was mandated to France in 1920 and established as a semi-autonomous Republic in 1926 with a French-drafted constitution. In November 1941 Lebanese leaders, both Muslim and Christian, declared independence. Full independence from France was eventually granted in 1944.

Lebanon's ethnic composition is relatively homogeneous, with the vast majority of the population of Arab origin (93 per cent according to 1990 estimates); the remainder is composed of Armenians, Kurds, Assyrians, Turks and Greeks.

Seventy-five per cent of Lebanon's population, estimated in 1990 to total 3,300,000, are Muslims. They are divided along sectarian lines and include Shias, Sunnis, Alawis (a heterodox Shia group), Nusayris (an offshoot of the Alawi), Druzes (a Shia Ismaili sub-group) and Ismailis (a Shi'ite branch). The remaining 25 per cent of the population are divided between various Christian denominations.

Islam came to Lebanon following the Arab conquest of 635. Maronite Christians, secure in their central mountain strongholds, retained their faith; in 1932, according to a census, they comprised the majority, 55 per cent, of the population although in recent years they have lost their majority status. (Estimates in 1983 suggested that the number of Maronite Christians had fallen to around 900,000.)

Lebanon's confessional democracy was based on the 1943 "National Covenant" under which institutional power was allocated to various religious groups on the basis of their numerical strength. By convention the President was always a Maronite Christian, the Prime Minister a Sunni Muslim, the Speaker of the National Assembly a Shia Muslim, and the Chief of Staff of the Armed Forces a Druze.

However, members of the majority Maronite Christian community soon became the most powerful figures in post-independence Lebanon. Their dominant role during the dramatic rise in the Muslim population in the 1970s was to be a major catalyst in the outbreak of the country's bloody civil war.

Islam and the state: developments in the post-independence period

Muslim-Christian discord quickly emerged after the formation of the new republic, owing to the Christian-dominated government's pro-Western stance and its acceptance of economic and military aid from the United States in 1957. The government's refusal to join the newly formed Egyptian-Syrian United Arab Republic (UAR) also alienated large sections of the Muslim population, leading in 1958 to an insurrection in which Muslims attacked Christians.

The Muslim community came increasingly to perceive the Lebanese Army, equipped and trained by the USA, as an instrument directed against them by a Christian President aided by a Christian militia, the Phalanges Libanaises (also known as *al Kaateb*). Years of factional fighting resulted in 1984 in the de facto division of Beirut along the so-called "green line", separating Christian East from Muslim West Beirut.

The Christian-Muslim divide has been exacerbated by the rapid growth and subsequent radicalization of the Shia community, which has grown from 18 per cent of the population in 1968 to 30 per cent (between 2,500,000-3,000,000) and now forms the largest community in Lebanon. The influx into southern Lebanon of Palestinian refugees, many of them Muslims, in the 1970s also disturbed the traditional balance between religious communities. Meanwhile the Christian-dominated government continued to resist a more equitable distribution of power which would reflect the changes in Lebanese society.

Compared with the Sunni Muslim and Maronite Christian communities, the Shia community was politically, economically and educationally disadvantaged. In the 1970s discontent was harnessed by the Shia religious leadership which employed an Islamic rhetoric and succeeded in enlisting popular support for a campaign for greater Shia representation in government.

The turning-point in the radicalization of the Shia community came in 1975, when a group of left-wing Muslims led by Kamal Jumblatt allied itself with Palestinian Liberation Organisation (PLO) groups to press for constitutional and economic reforms aimed at redressing the Christian-Muslim imbalance and giving Muslims a dominant role in government. In April 1976 the government called on Syrian military assistance to help combat the spiralling trend towards all-out civil war.

The influence of the 1979 Iranian Revolution and the disappearance in 1978 of Imam Sayyed Musa Sadr, spiritual head of the Lebanese Shia community and founder of **Amal** also helped to intensify Shia religious and political sentiment. Shia discontent was further aggravated by the 1982 Israeli invasion of Lebanon, which saw Shias caught in the crossfire between Israeli forces and guerrillas loyal to the PLO.

Both factors contributed substantially to the consolidation of Lebanon's two most prominent Shia Muslim religio-political movements, the pro-Syrian *Amal* movement and the Iranian-backed **Party of God** (*Hezbollah*).

Lebanon's Sunni community has been relatively unsuccessful in its quest for a share of political power. Unlike the Shias and Christian Maronites, the Sunnis lacked a powerful militia of their own, allying themselves instead to the PLO. As the fortunes of the PLO have waned in Lebanon, so have those of the Sunni community.

Notable Sunni militias include the small and relatively ineffectual **Defenders of the Islamic Frontier** (*Murabitoun*) whose leader, Ibrahim Qulayat, lives in Paris, and the **Popular Liberation Army**, led by Mustafa Saad. Sunni Muslim political organizations include the **Islamic Unity Movement** (*Tawhid-i-Islami*), led by Shaikh Sayyed Shaban.

In recent years there have signs of moves to enlist Sunnis in populist religious movements extolling Sunnism over Shi'ism. Among these organizations, which tend to be neighbourhood-based, the most important is the Islamic Military Council (IMC), orientated to asserting an independent Sunni identity.

The 1980s were marked not only by the Christian-Muslim division but also by a struggle for power in the Shia Muslim community between forces loyal to the pro-Syrian *Amal* movement and those loyal to the Iranian-backed *Hezbollah*.

While *Amal* and *Hezbollah* co-operated in the February 1984 takeover of West Beirut, rivalry between the two groups intensified as *Hezbollah* gained ground in large parts of West Beirut and southern Lebanon. *Amal*'s leader, Nabih Berri fled to Damascus from where he supervized the running of the organization between 1986 and February 1987, after which Syrian troops were deployed to counter *Hezbollah* influence.

Internal Shia conflict reached a head in 1988 when *Hezbollah* kidnapped a member of the UN peacekeeping force, Marine Lt.-Col. William Higgins, in protest against the presence of these forces. Berri, however, publicly endorsed the UN presence. The ensuing struggle between *Hezbollah* and *Amal*, marked by vicious fighting by both sides, was temporarily curbed by a Syrian-Iranian brokered accord.

Continuing Shia Muslim opposition to the Christian-dominated government reached a head in 1988 when the failure to elect a successor to President Amin Gemayel, whose term of office was due to expire in September 1988, led to the appointment of an interim military government under a Maronite Christian, Gen. Michel Aoun. The acting government under Sunni Prime Minister Selim al-Hoss refused to recognize Aoun's government and the country was plunged into a constitutional crisis with two governments, a predominantly Christian one in east Beirut and a predominantly Muslim one in west Beirut.

December 1990 was a turning-point in the Muslim drive for increased representation in the Lebanese government: under the auspices of a Tripartite Committee of the Arab League the Lebanese National Assembly endorsed constitutional changes which included the equal division of institutional posts between Muslims and Christians (as opposed to the old 5:6 ratio in favour of Christian deputies) and a new government of national reconciliation under Prime Minister Omar Karame. In January 1991 the National Assembly approved a motion of confidence in the new government, although its impact was dampened by the resignation almost immediately afterwards of the Druze leader, Walid Jumblatt

Meanwhile Israeli attacks on Palestinian bases in southern Lebanon thwarted plans to disarm the country's militias, including many Muslim factions which claimed to be involved in resistance to the Israeli-backed South Lebanese Army (SLA). Shia resentment of Israel had intensified following the kidnapping by Israel of the Shia cleric and leading member of *Hezbollah*, Shaikh Obeid in July 1989.

Mounting tension between Israel and Shia Muslim militias in southern Lebanon escalated dramatically after the assassination in February 1992 of Shaikh Abbas Musavi, appointed secretary-general of *Hezbollah* in May 1991, who died when an Israeli helicopter gunship attacked his motorcade travelling from the village of Jibshit, a *Hezbollah* stronghold.

The release of the majority of Western hostages during 1991 by pro-Iranian Shia groups was regarded as an indication of Iran's growing influence in curbing the groups' fierce anti-Western rhetoric in the interests of its rapprochement with the USA and its Western allies.

EW

Major Islamic organizations

Amal

Acronym (also meaning "hope") for *Afwaj al-Muqawama al-Lubnaniyya* (Groups of the Lebanese Resistance)

Pro-Syrian Shia politico-military organization founded in 1974 as an extension of the Supreme

Islamic Council of the Shia Community of Lebanon (SICSCL) by the SICSCL's president and the spiritual leader of Lebanese Muslims, Imam Musa as-Sadr who disappeared while on a visit to Libya in August 1978. (An earlier incarnation of *Amal*, also led by Sadr, had been launched in the late 1960s as "The Movement for the Disinherited".)

Leader. Nabih Berri (presently Minister of State in the Lebanese government); Shaikh Muhammad Mahdi Shamsaddin (Principal Controller of Command Council and Deputy President of the SICSCL); Sadr ad din as Sadr (chair).

Aims. Originally directed at weakening the traditional leadership of feudal land-owners in southern Lebanon, the organization developed as a militant Shia nationalist group pursuing the redress of Shia grievances under the leadership of the militia chief Nabih Berri (first elected in 1980). Among its professed goals are greater equality for Shias in government (to reflect the demographic changes in Lebanese society) and a more equitable distribution of wealth and educational opportunities. Although influenced by clerical views (the most important cleric currently a member is the leading Shia *mufti*, Shaikh Abd al Amir Qabalan), the organization's programme makes no mention of any need to ensure Shia dominance or an Islamic state.

Structure. There is a decentralised organizational structure reflecting the fragmented Shia community which is dispersed over three areas: the south, the northern Bekaa, and Beirut. Nabih Berri's influence reportedly does not extend beyond Beirut and certain regions of southern Lebanon, leaving regional warlords with a considerable degree of power.

Publication. al Haqiqa (Truth).

Defenders of the Islamic Frontier

Murabitoun

Sunni Muslim militia which rose to prominence in 1984.

Leader. Ibrahim Qulayat.

Islamic Amal

Founded in 1982 as a breakaway group from *Amal* and rejecting the organization's alleged secular nationalist objectives. Based in Baalbek, it is reported to function as the military arm of *Hezbollah*.

Leader. Hussein al-Musawi.

Aim. The creation of an Islamic state.

Islamic Holy War

Islamic Jihad

Pro-Iranian faction believed to be an underground offshoot of *Hezbollah*, it gained notoriety when it claimed responsibility for two suicide truck bombings in Beirut which killed 300 American and French servicemen in 1983 and for the kidnapping of British hostages John McCarthy and Terry Waite and US hostages Terry Anderson, and Thomas Sutherland. Observers are divided as to whether it is an independent organization or merely the codename for *Hezbollah* terrorist activity.

Leader. Imaad Mougnieh.

Aims. It professes the same ideology as *Hezbollah*, including a commitment to an Islamic state and opposition to western powers and pro-western Muslim governments including Saudi Arabia, Kuwait and the Lebanese government. It believes in its duty to eradicate the "enemies of God".

Islamic Unity Movement

Tawhid-i-Islami

Sunni fundamentalist group founded in Tripoli 1982, reportedly with close links to Iran from which it receives financial support. The Islamic Liberation Organization, responsible for the kidnapping in 1985 of four Soviet diplomats, is reportedly linked to the organization.

Leader. Shaikh Sayyed Shaban.

Aims. The establishment of an Islamic state in Lebanon along the lines of the Sunni Caliphate and, more immediately, the expulsion of all Christian groups from the Lebanese government.

Party of God

Hezbollah

Pro-Iranian militant Islamic group founded in the summer of 1982 as a response to the Israeli invasion on the initiative of Ali Akbar Mohtashemi, Iran's former Interior Minister, who also headed the Iranian Islamic Revolutionary Guards. The group, which has been engaged in a bitter power struggle with the rival *Amal* movement led by Nabih Berri, rose to prominence in the mid-1980s as a result of its involvement in the kidnapping of scores of Western hostages. By the mid-1980s the group had become a broad umbrella organization spawning a number of more or less independent cells some of which, notably Islamic Jihad and the Revolutionary Justice Organization (RJO), claimed responsibility for the kidnapping of Western hostages. Other groups known to have links with the *Hezbollah* include the Islamic Resistance Movement, *Jund Allah* (God's Army), the Hussein Suicide Squad, the Lebanese branch of *al Dawa* (The Call), Holy Warriors for Freedom, Organization of the Oppressed of the Earth and *Islamic Amal*.

Leader. Shaikh Muhammad Hussain Fadlallah (spiritual leader); Shaikh Hassan Nasrallah, (appointed secretary-general in March 1992 following the assassination in February of his predecessor, Shaikh Abbas Musavi).

Aims. The organization advocates political and social reform along the lines of the Iranian revolution. It is committed to the creation of an Islamic state through holy war (*jihad*).

Structure. There is a tightly-knit structure consisting of a Consultative Council of 12 members, most of them clerics, with the rest military officers or members engaged in military affairs. Decisions are made by unanimous or majority vote and where this fails representation is made to Iran, the group's main source of military training and financial support. There are also seven specialised committees. The consultative council and the specialised committees are replicated in the three regions which constitute *Hezbollah*'s field of operation: Beirut, its southern suburb, al-Biqa', and the south of the country.

Publication. Al Ahd (The One—a reference to one of the attributes of God).

Popular Liberation Army

Sunni Muslim faction active in southern Lebanon.

Leader. Mustafa Saad.

Revolutionary Justice Organization (RJO)

A pro-Iranian cell believed to be a radical Shia offshoot of *Hezbollah*, it claimed responsibility for the kidnapping of US hostages Edward Tracey and Joseph Cicippio and the British hostage Jackie Mann.

Libya

The majority of the population of Libya, estimated to total about 4,385,000 in 1989, are Sunni Muslims who adhere to the Maliki rite; there are also small groups of Hanafi followers which date back to the country's subjection to Ottoman rule. Since 1971 Islamic law (*sharia*) has been recognized as the basis of the legal system.

Islam reached Libya in AD 647. In 1835 the area of present-day Libya came under Ottoman control for a second period during which the Sanusiyya sect, founded by Mohammed Ben Ali al-Sanusi (1791-1859) became important in the maintenance of order and the provision of basic Quranic education among the nomadic population of the rural areas.

By the close of the 19th century Sanusi lodges (*zawiya*) had grown into a network providing points of contact with the entire tribal system of present-day Libya and beyond. Preaching a purist return to Islamic orthodoxy, the Sanusiyya order slowed the modernizing influence of Salafiyya reformism which had gained ground elsewhere in North Africa.

Islam and the state: developments since independence

King Idris I, who in 1951 led Libya to independence from Italian control, was also regarded as spiritual head of the Sanusi order. During the 1950s and 1960s his Sanusi-dominated government was perceived by younger nationalists as being increasingly subservient to European and North American interests.

Nationalist criticism derived in part from the influence of Salafiyyism and from the ideology of the *Ikwan al-muslimin* (Muslim Brotherhood) in neighbouring Egypt, both of which regarded maraboutic brotherhoods, centring on saints and their veneration, as an aberration from true Islamic practice.

In 1969 a group of young army officers led by Colonel Muammar al-Qaddhafi overthrew the monarchy and pledged to introduce a new regime rooted in local tradition but free from the Sanusi-dominated political system.

The new Constitution of 1969 identified Islam as the national religion, although this was qualified by guarantees of religious freedom similar to those contained in the monarchical Constitution. Under the ruling party, the Socialist Arab Union created in 1971, the new regime set about effectively nationalizing all religious institutions including mosques, educational institutions and religious endowments (*awqaf*).

In a predominantly non-urbanized society with older forms of political culture still strong outside the cities, Islam was used, together with the proclamation of "socialism" and an emphasis on the traditions of the desert, as a unifying factor. It was important for the new regime to have some religious legitimacy, since it had replaced a monarchy backed by the religious prestige of the Sanusi order.

In his populist and "anti-imperialist" rhetoric, therefore, Qaddhafi emphasized Libya's identity as a country practising Islam, albeit an Islam defined by Qaddhafi himself. Inclining towards a reformist rather than a fundamentalist version of Islam, manifested by his rejection in 1978 of the *Sunna* (example set by the Prophet Muhammad) as the work of men and therefore not binding in any way, Qaddhafi is said to be the only head of state of a Muslim country to accept the Quran alone as a basis of religion and law.

Rejecting the right traditionally reserved for religious scholars (*ulama*) to exercise independent reasoning (*ijtihad*) in matters of Islamic exegesis, Qaddhafi stressed that each individual was capable of interpreting the Quran. He also announced that the Islamic punishments (*hudud*) were not intended for literal enforcement; declared that the Muslim piligrimage to Mecca (*hajj*) was no longer compulsory, and that Islamic taxation (*zakat*) could be variable, not fixed according to tradition.

In April 1973 Qaddhafi proclaimed a "popular revolution". In the Green Book, which he published in 1976, Qaddhafi laid new emphasis on the implementation of the "people's will" through locally-based popular committees and a national General Popular Committee. The "third-theory", contained in the Green Book, which propounded a form of pre-capitalist socialism, was deemed to be rooted in Islamic tradition.

Qaddhafi's idiosyncratic interpretation of Islam was fiercely denounced by orthodox religious scholars (*ulama*). In 1975, fearing a backlash from the religious establishment, Qaddhafi decreed that Friday sermons should be restricted to spiritual matters and should refrain from any discussion of worldly issues pertaining to politics. By the late 1970s the government had ensured that most mosques were administered by a compliant religious leader (Iimams).

In 1977 the Grand Mufti of Libya, Sheikh Al-Tahir Ahmad al-Zawi, joined the opposition of religious leaders to the government's new property laws on grounds that they affected religious endowments (*awqaf*), traditionally a preserve of the clergy. Increasing dissatisfaction led to Zawi's resignation (subsequently withdrawn) in January 1984; later that year (in May and June) two well-known religious figures, Shaikh Mohammed al-Khalifi and Shaikh Hamidah al-Hami, were imprisoned without trial.

Opposition to the government came not just from the religious establishment, but also from militant Islamic groups which in the 1970s and 1980s were subject to widespread repression by the regime. Whilst the number of such groups is small in relation to other North African countries, their influence has been sufficiently strong for the regime to accede to some of their demands, including the prohibition of alcoholic drinks and the dismantling of churches. Nevertheless the broad thrust of Qaddhafi's version of Islam remains at odds with Muslim fundamentalist groups who are deeply hostile to key aspects of the government's reforms, including restrictions on private property, deemed by Islamists to be against the strictures of the Quran; the exclusion of religious leaders from the circle of political power; greater freedom for women including a ban on Islamic dress, and the right of each individual to interpret the Quran.

Confrontation between the government and militant Islamic groups intensified during 1988 after an official press campaign denouncing members of Islamic groups as heretics was followed by a police raid on Tripoli University, which reportedly harboured fundamentalist factions.

In December 1988 and January 1989 police raids on mosques in Tripoli and Benghazi at which Islamic activists were said to have been present, triggered disturbances in Tripoli, Benghazi, Ajdabiya and al-Kufrah. The riots came in the midst of further police attacks on students wearing Islamic garb at university campuses in Tripoli and Benghazi.

Detailed information about independent Islamic organizations in Libya is not readily available. (The RCC was dissolved in 1979 and no political parties are permitted in Libya.) Of around 400 people executed at the time of the "popular revolution" of April 1973, some were said to be members of the **Muslim Brotherhood** (*Ikhwan al-Muslimun*) influenced by their counterparts in Egypt, others of the **Islamic Liberation Party** (*Hizb al-Tahrir al-Islami*). The human rights organization Amnesty International claimed that 18 persons arrested and sentenced to prison terms ranging from six years to life imprisonment in Septemeber 1983, were alleged to have been Islamic activists.

In 1984 two students who were hanged at Tripoli's Al-Fatih University were reported to have been members of the Islamic Liberation Front and the Islamic Vanguard.

In September 1986, 26 men arrested were accused of membership of the **Organization of Islamic Holy War** (*Munazzamat Jihad al-Islami*). In February 1987 six civilians and three army officers executed on charges of carrying out the assassination of Soviet military advisers, were accused of being members of the *Munazzamat Jihad al Islami* and the hitherto-unknown *Hizbollah* (Party of God.

A law promulgated by the General People's Congress in June 1991 declared that "religion is a direct relationship with the Creator, without an intermediary. It is prohibited to claim monopoly over religion or to exploit it for any purpose".

EB

Islamic organizations

Islamic Call Society
Jamiyat ad-Dawa al-Islamiya
Established by the government in 1980 as a missionary organization.
Publications. Ad Daawa al Islamiya, weekly.

Islamic Liberation Party
Hizb al-Tahrir al-Islami
Clandestine group inspired by similarly named organization founded in Jordan in the 1950s; it was probably the most important radical Islamist faction operating in the 1970s and 1980s.
Aims. Advocates the creation of an Islamic state; the party is reported to favour the infiltration of the armed forces in pursuit of its objectives.

Muslim Brotherhood
Ikwan al-Muslimun
Clandestine Muslim militant organization influenced by Egyptian counterpart; subject to repression in 1970s.
Aims. Establishment of an Islamic state and reintroduction of the Caliphate through the unity of all Islamic states.

Organization of Islamic Holy War
Munazzamat al-Jihad al-Islami
Clandestine group active in the early 1970s; outlawed in 1973. It appears to have re-surfaced in the mid-1980s following the trial of 26 of its alleged members in September 1986. Some civilians and army officers executed in February 1987 were charged with belonging to it.
Aims. Unknown.

Madagascar

The Democratic Republic of Madagascar achieved independence from France in 1960. In March 1990 the lifting of restrictions on the formation of political parties by the ruling *Front National pour la défence de la révolution* (FNDR) was followed in 1991 by a burst of anti-government protest. Transition towards a third republic began in November 1991.

About 50 per cent of the population of 12,000,000 follow animist beliefs; 43 per cent are Christians; while the remainder, about 7 per cent, are Muslims.

Islam arrived in the 13th century, brought by traders from the Persian Gulf as well as from east Africa, and was embraced by the Antaimoro people in the south-east corner of the island. A later wave of immigration which began in the 19th century brought Muslims from the Indian sub-continent as well as from the neighbouring Comoros archipelago. Mainly traders, they settled along the west coast.

The Muslim community is free to practise its faith and there are believed to be over 100 mosques and Quranic schools in the country. However, the Muslim community tends to view the Socialist and predominantly Christian government range with at best suspicion, and at worse hostility.

There are no significant Islamic organizations.

TJ

Malaysia

The Federation of Malaysia was established in 1963 through the union of the independent Federation of Malaya, the internally self-governing state of Singapore, and the former British colonies of Sarawak and North Borneo (Sabah). Singapore was removed from the Federation in 1965, reducing the number of Malaysia's component states from 14 to 13.

Malaysia's complex racial and religious composition, a product of British colonial policies, has been at the root of many of the country's most sensitive political and economic issues. According to the 1980 census Malays constituted around 47 per cent of the population, Chinese 33 per cent, Indians 9 per cent and the indigenous races of Sarawak and Sabah 9 per cent.

Almost all Malays are Muslims, representing some 53 per cent of the total population in 1985. The rest of the population consists mostly of ethnic Chinese and Indians who follow Buddhism, Confucianism, Daoism, Sikhism and Christianity and there are small communities of animists in eastern Malaysia.

The majority of Muslims of indigenous Malay stock follow the Shafi school of law, with a minority, mostly of Indian origin, who adhere to Hanafi rites. The most important Sufi brotherhoods are the Qadiriyyah, the Shadhiliyyah and the Naqshbaniyyah orders.

The *Yang di-Pertuan Agong* (Supreme Head of State), elected every five years, is the head of the Islamic religion in the nine states of peninsular Malaysia with a hereditary Malay ruler. Muslim religious matters are under the jurisdiction of each state and differ from state to state. Freedom of religious practice is guaranteed under the constitution but proselytizing Islam is not permitted.

The establishment of the Islamic Sultanate of Malaka (Malacca) in the 15th century is conventionally regarded as the first major event in the modern history of Malaysia. The importance of Malaka in the political and economic development of Malaysia, and south-east Asia generally, cannot be overestimated. Situated on the western seaboard of the Malay peninsula, the Sultanate controlled the waters separating the peninsula from Sumatra and linking the whole Indonesian archipelago with the eastern Indian Ocean. Inevitably Malaka emerged as the most important commercial centre in the region, steadily replacing rival Sumatran ports as the hub of the transmission of Islam throughout south-east Asia.

Apart from Malaka and Johore in the south (which developed under the Dutch administration), up to the 18th century the Malay states evolved outside the political influence of the European colonial nations. However, British colonization of the Malay peninsula between the late 18th and early 20th centuries radically transformed the Malay states. The development and expansion of tin extraction and rubber production prompted the large-scale immigration of Chinese and Indian workers, the origins of Malaysia's modern pluralist society in which racial divisions have been reinforced by religious differences.

Islam and the state: developments since independence

Post-independence politics in Malaysia have been largely defined by the country's ethnic-religious composition. Since independence the country has been ruled by a multi-racial coalition, the National Front (*Barisan Nasional*, BN), headed by a Malay-Muslim party, the United Malay National Organization (UMNO). UMNO's major opponents have been the primarily Chinese left-wing Democratic Action Party (DAP) and the Malay Muslim right-wing conservative **Pan-Malaysian Islamic Party** (*Parti Islam SaMalaysia*—PAS) .

The principal political objective of all post-independence governments has been to satisfactorily accommodate the interests and ambitions of the Malay, Chinese and Indian communities. The period has been marked by the political domination of the Malays, generally expressed through UMNO, although since the 1970s the PAS has competed with UMNO for the support of Malay-Muslim voters.

The pluralist nature of Malay society has posed a dilemma for UMNO—on the one hand the party has had to accommodate the multi-racial aspirations of the BN while on the other it has consistently needed to demonstrate its commitment to Islam in order to maintain the support of Malay-Muslims. Local UMNO politicians and leaders have tended to emphasize their loyalty to Malay and Islamic expectations whereas national leaders have tended to adopt a more balanced approach. The dilemma has allowed PAS, with its forthright commitment to Islam, to denounce UMNO as too lenient in conceding the demands of its non-Malay, non-Islamic, partners in the BN.

While the Malays have been the politically dominant group in post-independence Malaysia, the Chinese and Indian communities have been more powerful in the economic sphere. At independence there was an unwritten understanding that Malays would eventually secure a greater economic stake in the country and that the Chinese and Indians would accept increasing political responsibility. However, the prospects for such an accommodation were demolished by the events of May 1969 when hundreds of people were killed in serious inter-communal rioting in the capital, Kuala Lumpur. The unrest forced the government to remove a number of sensitive issues, including the status of Islam in Malaysia, from public discussion.

The government's recognition of Islam as a sensitive issue was timely. Shortly after the riots Malay political assertiveness merged with the emergence of Islamic revivalism, activated in the early 1970s by a renewal of interest in Islam among young urban Malays, many of whom had been educated in the Western secular tradition. A leading role in the propagation of Islam was at this time assumed by the semi-official missionary *Dakwa* organisation, the Islamic Welfare and Missionary Association (PERKIN), which played an important role in the proselytising campaign among the Chinese community and tribal peoples. Also active was the Indian-inspired *Jamaat-i-Tabligh* (Missionary Movement) which began by winning support among Indian Muslim communities in Penang, Kuala Lumpur and Singapore and eventually succeeded in extending its reach to Malay communities in rural areas.

By the late 1970s the Islamic revival in Malaysia had gained momentum not only from the Iranian revolution of 1979 but also from a realignment of internal political forces.

Between 1973 and 1977 PAS was a partner in the BN coalition, leaving a political vacuum for rival Islamic organizations, notably the *Darul Arqam* (Abode of the Companions [of the Prophet Muhammad]), established in 1968 under the leadership of Ashaari Mohammad. By the early 1980s, however, the *Arqam*'s growing rapprochement with the government had led to the dilution of its anti-establishment stance and by mid-1987 there were indications that it had effectively been absorbed into UMNO.

Meanwhile PAS had been expelled from the BN coalition in 1978 and had entered into a tacit alliance with the powerful **Malaysian Islamic Youth Movement** (*Ankatan Belia Islam Malaysia*—ABIM). PAS failed to capitalize on the Islamic revival: in the 1986 election the party secured only one seat in the federal legislature and only two seats in the state assemblies.

During the early 1980s UMNO finally responded to the Islamic resurgence by launching its own Islamization drive. Symptomatic of this development was the defection to UMNO of the ABIM leader, Anwar Ibrahim. Anwar, an Islamic scholar of international repute and a leading critic of government policies from a liberal-Islamic standpoint, had been elected president of the UMNO youth movement in 1982 and entered the Cabinet the following year. By the early 1990s he had risen to become Finance Minister and was widely tipped to succeed Prime Minister Mahathir Mohamad.

The rise of Anwar exemplified the manner in which Islamic revivalism had altered the political and social landscape. At the level of international relations, the Mahathir government (which came to power in 1981) has overtly increased its involvement in international Islamic organizations, including the Islamic Conference Organization (ICO). In the mid-1980s leading UMNO politicians engaged in vehement anti-Zionist rhetoric and organized demonstrations to protest against the visit to Singapore of the Israeli President.

Other developments indicating the government's awareness of the importance of the Islamic revival include the establishment of a State-sponsored Islamic Bank, increased efforts to enlarge the role of Islamic law (*sharia*), the acceptance of Islamic dress for Malay women, and pressure to control gambling and the sale of alcohol.

Almost inevitably, the Islamic revival of the 1970s and 1980s has created fresh ethnic and religious tensions. The impact of the revival on the political process and its potential impact on almost all spheres of everyday life has caused disquiet amongst Malaysia's non-Muslims. Fear of an Islamic resurgence is commonly regarded to lie behind the refusal of a majority of Malay-Chinese to vote against the BN in the 1986 general election.

In the aftermath of the 1990 general election attention was focused on the state of Kelantan where PAS, in coalition with UMNO-renegades within the breakaway **Spirit of '46** (*Semangat '46*), had won control of the state legislature to form a government under Chief Minister Nik Abdul Aziz Nik Mat, formerly a religious teacher.

PAS had ruled Kelantan, which is 93 per cent Malay and Muslim, for almost 20 years from 1959 to 1978. Although the party had made little impact in the national polls, its latest state victory provided a new opportunity to implement radical Islamic policies although it soon became clear that PAS's commitment to Islamic reform had been tempered by the influence of its more pragmatically oriented members.

Soon after coming to power PAS adopted a more tolerant approach to the state's non-Muslim minority. This was reported to be an attempt to wrong-foot the central authorities which, soon after the Kelantan victory, had launched a media campaign against PAS leading to a cut in State subsidies. A planned visit by Nik Aziz to China in mid-1992, allegedly to extend its support among non-Muslim voters in two other northern Muslim-majority states, Kedah and Trengganu, was heavily publicized by PAS.

In April 1992 western press reports indicated that PAS may be reverting to a pro-Islamic stance after Nik Aziz was quoted as saying that the PAS government intended to reform

Kelantan's penal code in line with Islamic punishment (*hadd*) so as to permit stoning, whipping and the amputation of hands.

DS

Major Islamic organizations

Angkatan Democratic Liberal Sabah (Adil)

Based in Sabah; intended to attract Malay Muslims.

Islamic Front of Malaysia (IFM)

Parti Hisbul Muslimin Malaysia (Hamin)

Founded in 1983 as an alternative to the *Parti Islam Sa- Malaysia* (PAS) but has had little electoral success.

Leader. Datuk Asri Muda (president).

Front Malaysian Islamic Council (FMIC)

Barisan Jam'aah Islamiah Sa-Malaysia (Berjasa)

Founded in 1977 with its headquarters in Kelantan.

Leader. Dato' haji Wan hashim bib Haji Wan Achmed (president); Mahmud Zudi bin Haji Abdul Majid (secretary-general).

Membership. 50,000.

Aim. Advocates pro-Islamic reform.

Kongres Indian Muslim Malaysia (KIMM)

Founded in 1977.

Leader. Ahamed Elias (president); Mohammad Ali bin Haji Naina Mohammad (secretary-general).

Membership. 25,000.

Aims. To unite Muslims of Indian origin politically.

Malaysian Islamic Youth Movement (MIYM)

Angkatan Belia Islam Malaysia (ABIM)

Founded in 1971 by students of the National Association of Malaysian Islamic Students, it draws support mainly from universities and other institutions of higher education and reportedly maintains close links with Muslim fundamentalist movements elsewhere, including the *Jamaat-i-Islami* in Pakistan and the *Ikhwan al-muslimun* (Muslim Brotherhood in Egypt.

Aims. Seeks to re-define the constitutional status of Malaysia as an Islamic state and to introduce economic reforms based on Islamic law (*sharia*), including the abolition of bank interest.

Muslim Unity Movement

Angkatan Perpaduan Ummah (APU)

Founded in 1989 as an opposition coalition representing four Muslim parties (FMIC, IFM, PMIP (PAS) and *Semangat '46*).

Pan Malaysian Islamic Party

Parti Islam Sa-Malaysia (PAS)

Founded in Penang in 1951 as an offshoot of the United Malays National Organization (UMNO—Baru), the party presently controls the state government of Kelantan.

Leader. Fadzil Nor (president).

Membership. 300,000. Support for the party is greatest in the northern Malay states of Kelantan, Trengganu, Perak, Kedah and Perlis.

Aims. Although it is best known for its commitment to the establishment of an Islamic state, the party has also favoured the promotion of Malay nationalism.

Spirit of 1946

Semangat '46

Founded in 1989 as a breakaway group from UMNO after its de-registration in 1988.

Leader. Tunku Razaleigh.

Maldives

The archipelago of the Maldives formed an independent kingdom early in the Christian era. It now constitutes the third largest Muslim country of South Asia (after Bangladesh and Pakistan).

The majority of the population, estimated in 1990 at 214,139, are Sunnis belonging to the Shafi school of law. The population of the Maldives was probably Buddhist until large-scale conversion to Islam from the mid-12th century.

In 1887 the Maldives became a British protectorate and in 1932 the Sultan was compelled to accept a Constitution. The country was later converted from a monarchy into a presidential republic for a brief period in 1953 and, more permanently, with the inauguration of a second republic in 1968, a consequence of independence in 1965.

The Constitution of 1968, as amended in 1970 and 1975, proclaims the Maldives to be an Islamic republic with an executive president elected by direct popular vote every five years. Islam is the state religion and Muslim law the dominant legal system. Islam is promoted officially through the government's Department of Religious Affairs and religious publications are issued by the President's Office, namely *Dheenuge Magu* (Path of Religion). Maldivian citizenship is confined to Muslims, although non-Muslims may be given permits to reside there permanently and to do business in the Maldives.

There are no political parties or organizations, although in recent years there have been indications of a more questioning attitude among younger, less traditionalist members of the *majlis* (Citizens' Council).

In early 1990 there were 713 mosques. There is a strong tradition of Quranic scholarship at all levels, with Quranic schools (*maktabs*) forming the backbone of the Maldivian education system and providing the only formal education which most Maldivian children receive. Quranic schools are also largely responsible for the very high level (82 per cent) of adult literacy in the Maldives which is fairly uniform across age groups and sexes.

SA

Mali

After a short-lived federation with Senegal in (the Federation of Mali), the Republic of Mali, formerly French Sudan, came into being in September 1960. The country was ruled by a Military Committee for National Liberation from 1968 until 1991, the last 12 years of which were as a one-party state under the United People's Democratic Union (UDPM). This regime was overthrown in a military coup in March 1991; a transitional government which eventually took power has promised to hand over power to a civilian adminstration.

Between 80 and 90 per cent of the population are Muslim, the overwhelming proportion of whom follow the Maliki school of law. There are also small numbers of nomadic Ibadites. The remainder follow traditional African beliefs; Christians make up less than 2 per cent. In ethnic terms, the Sarakolé, Maure, Tuareg, Songhay, Dioula and Toucouleur are all Muslim, as are significant proportions of the Fulbe (Peul, Fulani), Bozo and Somono. The extent and strength of the conversion to Islam varies between ethnic groups and regions; syncretic practices incorporating both Islamic and indigenous rituals are common.

Islam was introduced to Mali in the 11th century by merchants from the Mahgreb following desert trading routes. Until the mass conversions of the mid-18th century, Islam was the exclusive preserve of the ruling elite who acted as patrons of the faith and helped to establish Djenna and Timbuktu as centres of Islamic learning.

The Tijaniyyah and Qadiriyyah Sufi orders are long established in Mali but their influence is relatively modest. Also of note is the influence of the Hamallist sect which has its strongholds in Nioro and Yélimané. The founding of the sect in Mali caused great concern among Tijaniyya clerics and even led to violent unrest in Nioro on at least two occasions before the 1940s.

Today Malian *marabouts* (saints or venerated descendants of saints) reportedly exercise influence as informal advisers to the country's political leaders; President Moussa Traore is said to defer to the advice of the Sherif of Niora, Muhammadu Ould Chiekna.

The most important fundamentalist current is expressed by the Saudi-inspired Wahhabi movement, a strict anti-Sufi crusade which arrived in Mali in the 1930s but became firmly established only in the 1950s. In May 1957 followers of the movement were involved in violent anti-Wahhabi riots in the capital, Bamako (where the most important mosque, the Bagadadji Mosque, is sited). However, since the movement was particularly popular among wealthy traders, economic considerations may have been a contributory factor.

Islam and the state: developments since independence

Despite the fact that Mali has always had a secular constitution, Islam has played a significant role in the development of the country since independence and serves as an important unifying force, providing common institutions and practices. Moreover, as the largest religious group, Muslims have not had to compete to the same extent with mission-educated Christians as they have in countries where they form a smaller proportion of the population. As a result, tension between the two groups, common elsewhere in Africa, is slight.

Although Islam has a great influence on the everyday lives of its followers, Islamic organizations have had only a limited role in the political development of the country. In the period of the one-party state, any such role was positively discouraged by the regime which also repressed any form of opposition. Religious groups did, however, take part in the demonstrations that preceded and encouraged the military coup in March 1991. Since then there has been little evidence of activity by Islamic groups and no party with a specifically Islamic agenda featured in the local and legislative elections which had taken place by March 1992.

TJ

Mauritania

The Islamic Republic of Mauritania (proclaimed in 1980) won independence from France in 1960. The Constitution stipulates that Islam is the official religion and that the office of President can only be held by a Muslim. Since 1980 Islamic law (*sharia*) has been recognized as the basis of the legal system.

The population, estimated at just over 2,000,000, is ethnically diverse. One half are Arab and Berber whites while the other half is made up of members of various black groups including the Sarakoll, Fulani, and Wolof, the last also found in Senegal. Arabic (of the Hasaniyyah dialect) and French are the dominant languages, with French the common medium among blacks, who have 14 different languages.

Sunni Islam of the Maliki school of law (the religion of almost the entire population) is the principal factor uniting the nomadic Berbers of the north with the settled pastoral Blacks of the south. Chinguetti, in the district of Adrar, is the seventh holy place of Islam and a centre of pilgrimage.

Many Mauritanians are informally associated with a number of Sufi brotherhoods. The two most important are the Tijaniyyah and the Qadiriyyah orders, the latter presently under the leadership of Ould Shaikh Sidya.

Mauritania was Islamicized under the rule of the Almoravid dynasty (1056-1147) which established its base near the city of Attar. In the 17th century Mauritania was one of the regions affected by the religious fervour that swept the Maghreb in the form of the "*Jihad* (holy war) Movement".

During the French occupation (which began in 1850), Islamic institutions were exempted from the provisions of a law passed in 1905 decreeing the strict separation of church and state. In 1914 a *medersa* (religious seminary, or *madrassah*) was established under French sponsorship at Boutlimit in western Mauritania and in 1936 another *medersa*, devoted to the teaching of classical Arab culture, was opened in Attar, in north-western Mauritania.

In 1946 French West Africa was given direct representation through elected deputies in Paris. In 1951 the *Union Progressiste Mauritanienne* (UPM) sent a deputy to the French parliament and had one religious figure among its leadership. In 1958 Mauritania became a self-governing member of the French Community, and from 1960 to 1991 it was a one-party state under various regimes dominated by the Bidan Moors (or "white Moors").

Islam and the state: developments since independence

Since independence the Arabization of education and the emphasis on Mauritania's Arab cultural identity have been controversial issues which have alienated the Black population for whom Arabic is a sacred, rather than a commonly employed, language.

In 1966 a decision by the authorities to make the use of Arabic compulsory in secondary schools led to strikes by Black students and civil servants, culminating in inter-ethnic riots in Nouakchott. In 1968 Arabic became a second official language alongside French.Mauritania's military involvement in the disputed territory of the Western Sahara from 1975 to 1978 was also unpopular among southerners, many of whom would have preferred an alignment with Black Africa.

From 1961 to 1978 Mauritania's Arab and Muslim identity was actively promoted by President Moktar Ould Daddah. In 1978 a coup led by the Black Hausas (the so-called "Black Moors", ethnically Negro but culturally Moorish), overthrew the Daddah regime and sought support among the Bidan Moors. The Mauritanian branch of the Muslim Brotherhood (*Ikhwan al-muslimun*) offered its co-operation in return for a systematic programme of Islamization.

The full implementation of the *sharia* was announced in 1980, apparently in response to continued Muslim Brotherhood support for the regime, and in September 1980 the first public hand amputations for theft took place. Slavery was abolished and many Black Moors freed.

The Afro-Mauritanian population remains the object of intermittent repression. Since the mid-1980s an armed group, the *Forces de libération africaine de Mauritanie* (FLAM), operating from Dakar, Senegal, has emerg d as the principal opposition to the Bidan-dominated regime and its alleged policy of discrimination against Afro-Mauritanian groups.

Presidential elections held in January 1992 returned Colonel Mohammed Ould Taya as President, but opposition parties boycotted legislative elections in March, leaving the ruling Social Democratic Republican Party (PRDS) in control of all but 12 of the seats in the National Assembly.

In November 1991 the authorities were reported by Algerian Radio to have withheld recognition from an Islamic group that had applied for the status of a political party (possibly a reference to the **National Party** (*Umma* Party)), on the grounds that the Constitution prohibited parties based on religious programmes.

EB

Major Islamic organizations

Mauritanian Muslim Socialist Union (MMSU)

Formed in 1961, later joined with two other parties to form the Parti du Peuple Mauritanien (PPM) which was subsequently banned in 1978 and most of its leaders exiled in Paris. Like the other parties, however, the MMSU had no real popular base beyond religious or ethnic affiliations and virtually all leaders came from leading tribal families.

National Party
Umma Party

Reportedly formed in November 1991, the party had yet to secure legalization in January 1992 when it backed the candidacy of Ahmed Ould Daddah in the presidential elections that month. The party is said to be affiliated to the Muslim Brotherhood.

Leader. Ould Siddi Yayia (head of the Supreme Council).

Membership. The party's support base is among city market traders in the capital, Nouackchott.

Mauritius

A former British colony, Mauritius became an independent state in 1968. Executive power was formally vested in the British sovereign until March 1992 when the island was declared a republic within the Commonwealth.

Ethnically, Mauritius has a particularly diverse population. The Muslim community comprises about 16 per cent of the total population, estimated in 1990 at 100,100,000. Most are the descendants of Urdu and Gujarati-speaking Indians who arrived in the 19th century and they tend to live and work in the rural areas.

Three weekly newspapers cater for the Muslim community: *La Voix de l'Islam* (founded in 1951), *Le Progrès Islamique* (founded in 1948) and *Le Croissant* (founded in 1979).

Islam and the state: developments since independence

There are various Islamic welfare and social organizations and the main political organization is the **Muslim Action Committee** (*Comité d'Action Musulman*—CAM), dating from the pre-independence period and on the right of the political spectrum. The CAM was in electoral alliance with the ruling Labour Party between 1952 and 1982; from 1967 the alliance was known as the Independence Party.

Support for the CAM began to wane in the mid-1970s and in the 1976 election the party won only two seats in the National Assembly. Muslims turned instead to the Militant Mauritian Movement, *Mouvement Militant Mauricien* which successfully fielded seven Muslim candidates that year. Since that time a merger with the Labour Party has been proposed on several occasions but has been resisted by the CAM. The CAM has not been represented in the National Assembly since 1982.

In spite of the recent electoral failure of the CAM, a system of "best losers" ensures that Muslims are represented in the legislature: eight seats are apportioned between unreturned electoral candidates according to ethnic affiliation, with two each for the Muslim, Hindu and Chinese communities and the "general population".

In recent months there has been increasing pressure on the government to reintroduce Muslim personal law. In early 1992 a group of Muslim community leaders members of the Privy Council of Queen Elizabeth II, reportedly to press the issue, and they declared their intention of holding another meeting with the Privy Council in June 1992. However, since Mauritius became a republic in March 1992, it was not clear what status a decision of the Privy Council would have. Muslim leaders have made clear that they were not calling for the complete adoption of Islamic law (*sharia*) but only for its partial implementation, in particular of the provisions relating to marriage.

TJ

Islamic organizations

Muslim Action Committee
Comité d'Action Musulman (CAM)
Muslim political party founded in 1958 by Adbool Razack Mohammed.
Leader. Youssuf Mohammed (president).
Membership. 4,000.

Aim. The protection of constitutional and other rights of the Muslim community.

Mauritius Islamic Mission
State-sponsored Muslim body.
Leader. Imam S. M. Beeharry.

Mongolia

Muslims form roughly 4 per cent of the total population of the People's Republic of Mongolia, estimated in 1989 to stand at around 2,200,000. Most are nominally Sunnis, concentrated among the Kazakhs settled in western Mongolia.

During the 1930s the Communist-led government of the Mongolian People's Revolutionary Party (MPRP) waged a campaign against the practice of religion, destroying hundreds of religious centres, including mosques. The party's anti-religious bias was formally endorsed by the Constitution of 1960, which not only upheld the separation of religion from the State, but also permitted citizens to carry out anti-religious propaganda.

The end of years of economic and military dependence on the former Soviet Union (now the Commonwealth of Independent States—CIS) led in July 1990 to the country's first democratic, multiparty elections which succeeded finally in breaking the monopoly of the MPRP.

Changes in attitudes towards Soviet Communism were reflected in a revival of interest in indigenous Mongol culture, including religion. In December 1990 the new all-party government decreed the removal of religious affairs from government jurisdiction and promised help with the restoration of religious buildings which had fallen into disuse during the years of Communist rule.

FS

Islamic organizations

Muslim Society
Founded in 1990.
Leader. Haji Hadiryn Sayraan (chair of Central Council).

Morocco

An estimated 99 per cent of the population of Morocco, which totals approximately 24,000,000, are Sunni Muslims observing Maliki rites. Some nomadic tribes are known to adhere to Ibadite beliefs.

A number of Sufi orders are active, particularly the Shadhiliyyah brotherhood (sometimes known as the Alawiyyah) and its associated branches, the Darqawiyyah, Kettaniyyah, Isawiyyah and Ouezzzaniyyah.

Islam was brought to the non-Arab Berber population in the late ninth century. It is estimated that at least 40 per cent of the population continue to employ one of the three main Berber dialects as their first language rather than Arabic.

Islam and the monarchy have been deeply fused in the political culture of Morocco. Under the French protectorate the country's religious institutions and the authority of its traditional Muslim scholars (*ulama*) were left virtually intact. The nationalist movement led by the *Istiqlal* (Independence) party, which stressed a reformist Islam consistent with democracy, also upheld the religious legitimacy of the monarch. In 1955 *Istiqlal* was at the forefront of demands for the return from exile of King Mohammad I.

Islam and the state: developments since independence

Morocco became independent in 1956. Under the rule of King Mohammad I and his son King Hassan II, the country's present ruler, Islam has been used to strengthen the political legitimacy of the country's monarchical dynasty whose members claim direct descent from the Prophet Muhammad.

In the period immediately following independence King Mohammad I sought to curb the influence of some Sufi brotherhoods considered not to owe unquestioning loyalty to the ruling dynasty by ordering the confiscation of their land and properties. In the early 1960s the Ministry of Islamic Affairs (subsequently the Ministry of Religious Endowments and Islamic Affairs) antagonized sections of the religious establishment by accusing them of collaborating with the colonial authorities after some religious scholars (*ulama*) refused to co-operate in the administration of Islamic law under state supervision.

Meanwhile the monarchy built up its own network of trained religious leaders, supporting the Karawiyine University in Fez and the Ben Youssef University in Marrakesh where religious judges, lawyers and preachers were encouraged to lend support to the monarchy. In 1961 King Mohammad I backed the creation of the state-sponsored **League of Religious Scholars** (*Rabitat al-Ulama*).

In February 1961 King Hassan II succeeded his father King Mohammed V. A new constitution, adopted in 1962, declared Islam to be the state religion and reaffirmed the legitimacy of the hereditary monarchy. A mixed legal system was introduced, based partly on Maliki *sharia* law and partly on French civil codes.

1963 saw the first public demonstration of religious opposition to the monarchy when in December Shaikh al-Islam Moulay al-Arbi al-Alawi of the *Union Nationale des Forces Populaires* (UNFP) issued a ruling (*fatwa*) which implicitly questioned monarchical authority by stressing the Islamic system of consultation (*shura*).

The move came amid signs of a concerted attempt to revive the status of the King as Caliph (in addition to his formal title of "Commander of the Faithful" (*amir al-Muminin*), used by early Muslim leaders who combined religious and political authority). The religious prestige of the monarch was underlined by annual ritual ceremonies of allegiance (*baya*) and by official decrees proclaiming the personal grace (*baraka*) of the king.

A revised Constitution adopted in 1972 retained a clause from the earlier constitution forbidding any "questioning of the monarchical regime or the Muslim religion". During the 1980s left-wing opposition parties which spearheaded anti-government protests were suppressed on the grounds that they were incompatible with Islam. (In February 1960 an Appeal Court in Rabat had dissolved the Moroccan Communist Party (MCP), judging it un-Islamic.)

Until the mid-1980s Islamic fundamentalist movements had marginal influence and little popular support. The most prominent Islamist critic of the regime to emerge in this period was the writer Abdessalam Yassin, a moderate fundamentalist and leader of the subsequently banned **Justice and Virtue** (*Adl wal Ihsan*) organization. Periodically imprisoned since 1974, Yassin now lives under house arrest in Sale, near Rabat.

The spread of Islamic radicalism in the wake of the Iranian revolution of 1979 renewed fears of an Islamic opposition and prompted fresh government measures aimed at controlling the use of religion for political subversion. In February 1980 a royal decree established Regional Councils of *Ulama* and a new High Council of *Ulama*, under the presidency of the King, to monitor religious appointments, define religious orthodoxy and authorize the construction of mosques. Earlier, in August 1979, King Hassan II had persuaded pro-government *ulama* to issue a ruling (*fatwa*) denouncing the views of Ayatollah Khomeini as inconsistent with Islamic orthodoxy.

Reports of a burgeoning Islamic opposition were confirmed in 1983-84 with the arrest and trial of Islamic activists alleged to be members of the banned **Association of Islamic Youth** (*Jamiyat al-Shabiba al-Islamiya*) on charges of "plotting against the monarchy and planning to establish an Islamic state". There were further trials involving Islamic activists in 1985.

The only apparently tolerated, though not officially registered, Muslim fundamentalist group presently operating in Morocco is the **Movement for Reform and Renewal** (MRR—formerly the Islamic Association), which has renounced violence and decided to join legal politics.

Muslim militant activity resurfaced in October and November 1991 after Muslim activist students clashed with left-wing students on university campuses in Oujda, Fez, Meknes and Kenitra. Reports indicated that the Muslim militants belonged to the banned Justice and Virtue organization.

EB

Major Islamic organizations

Association of Islamic Youth (AIY)
Jamiyat al-Shabiba al-Islamiya
Clandestine organization founded in 1972 and considered one of the most radical fundamentalist opposition groups. In December 1975 it was responsible for the assassination of Omar Benjelloun, one of the leaders of the Union Socialiste des Forces Populaires (USFP). In September 1980 two of its members received death sentences, prompting protest demonstrations, and in 1984 71 of its members were tried and a further 3 death sentences announced.
Leader. Abd al Karim Mouti (a former civil servant in the Ministry of Education).
Membership. Most members are drawn from secondary schools and universities.
Structure. The organization is said to be composed of five major groups.
Aim. The replacement of the monarchy by a republican Islamic state.

Islamic League (IL)
Affiliated to the pro-government Mouvement Populaire Constitutionnel et Démocratique (MPCD) (founded in 1967).
Leader. Abd al Karim Khatib.

Justice and Virtue (JV)
Adl wal Ihsan
Banned clandestine group reportedly formed in the 1970s to represent moderate fundamentalists. Its members were said to have been involved in a spate of disturbances at university campuses in Oujda, Fez, Meknes and Kenitra.
Leader. Abdessalam Yassine.
Aims. Reform of the monarchy along Islamic lines.

League of Religious scholars
Rabitat al-Ulama
State-sponsored missionary body created in Tangiers in 1961 with the aim of promoting the revival of Islam in Morocco and its propagation in other African states. The League works in close co-operation with the Ministry of Religious Endowments (*awqaf*) and Islamic Affairs. During the 1970s it was used to support the official supervision of Islam in Morocco.
Publications. The League acts as a consultant for the monthly publications *Da'ouat al-Haqq* (Call of the Truth), founded in 1957, and *al Irschad* (Spiritual Guidance), founded in 1967 and issued by the Ministry of Religious Endowments (*awqaf*) and Islamic Affairs.

Movement for Reform and Renewal (MRR)
Founded in 1983 as the Islamic Association, the organization adopted its new name in 1986. Although not officially registered, the party is one of the few militant Muslim fundamentalist groups tolerated by the regime.
Leader. Abdellilah Benkiran, a physicist by training and a former member of the AIY which he left in 1981 to form the Islamic Association.
Aims. The movement supports the monarchy but demands strict adherence to Islamic law including the abolition of bank interest, a prohibition on women working and a tax levy (*zakat*) on the rich. The party is opposed to violence and has opted to join legal politics.

Movement of Holy Warriors (MHW)
Mouvement des Moujahidine
Secret Muslim militant organization some of whose alleged members were arrested in June 1985.
Leader. Abdelaziz Naamani.

Movement of Islamic Moroccan Youth (MIMY)
Mouvement de la Jeunesse Islamique Marocain (MJIM)
Twenty-six members of this group went on trial in Casablanca in August 1985.

Mozambique

Mozambique won independence from Portugal in 1975. Until the introduction in 1990 of a new Constitution providing for a multiparty system, the sole legal political party was the Marxist-Leninist Front for the Liberation of Mozambique (Frelimo), founded in 1962, which led the struggle for independence. The effects of a civil war since independence, together with drought and famine, have combined to make Mozambique one of the poorest countries in the world.

Of a population estimated in 1989 to total 15,326,000, roughly 4,000,000 were classified as Muslims, mainly of the Shafi school.

The majority of Muslims live in the four northern provinces of the country: Nampula, Zambézia, Cabo Delgado and Niassa.

The Makua, the largest ethnic group of about 4,000,000 people, are predominantly Muslim, as are the Yao and the Angoni.

Islam in the area now known as Mozambique has a history of over 1,000 years. From the ninth century a string of Muslim city-states was established along the coast forming a vital link in Arab trading routes, with Sofala (near the present-day Beira) being the most important. These Muslim states eventually extended up the Zambezi river.

The Muslim population was historically opposed to colonial rule and often victim of harsh Portuguese efforts to crush resistance. At the beginning of the 20th century several thousand Muslims fled to neighbouring Malawi and Tanzania after being subjected to atrocities committed by the colonial authorities. Restrictions on Muslims under colonial rule included granting permission to Muslim children to attend Christian missionary schools only on condition that they accepted conversion.

Islam and the state: developments since independence

Although Muslims played an important role in the formation and development of Frelimo, most of its leadership had Christian backgrounds. Many Muslims in Mozambique now regard Frelimo as hostile to their faith, pointing to the very small number of Muslims in the government.

There is no government support for Quranic teaching, which is imparted in mosques by poorly paid teachers. There are virtually no Muslim social, welfare or political organizations. Those which do exist command a small membership as well as very little in the way of financial resources.

Recently, however, the government has taken steps to regain the support of alienated

Muslims. In August 1991 Mozambique was granted observer status at the Islamic Conference Organization (ICO) and began negotiations aimed at establishing diplomatic relations with Saudi Arabia, Brunei and the United Arab Emirates (UAE). These efforts have been coupled with greater government assistance to Muslims wishing to undertake the pilgrimage to Mecca (*hajj*).

TJ

Islamic organizations

Islamic Congress of Mozambique
Anwar-ul-Islamo
Representing Sunni Muslims.
Leader. Hassan Makdá.

Islamic Council of Mozambique
Leader. Shaikh Aboobacar Ismael Mangira.

Myanma

Myanma (Burma until June 1989) was a British colony until it became an independent parliamentary democracy, outside the Commonwealth, in 1948. Following a military coup in 1962, the country became a one-party state committed to self-reliant "socialist" development under the State Law and Order Restoration Council (SLORC). Despite elections in May 1990 which promised a return to democracy, the military failed to relinquish control.

Predominantly Buddhist, Myanma has a sizeable Muslim minority and Muslim personal laws are in force. Burmese Muslims are divided into two main ethnic groups. The first consists of urban Muslims of Indo-Pakistani origin who speak Urdu and Tamil. The second are of Burmese origin.

The majority of Muslims, descended from Arab, Moor, Bengali and Indo-Mongoloid stock, and known as Rohingyas, reside in Arakan province (known in ancient times as Rohang). Located in the north-west of the country, Arakan province was the centre of a Muslim state until 1784 when it was conquered by the Buddhist south and subsequently incorporated as part of Burma at independence.

Arakan's population is divided into two main religious communities: the Muslim Rohingyas, estimated in 1982 to number 1,460,000 or 56 per cent of the province's population, and the Buddhist Moghs. By 1992, Arakan's Muslim majority had risen to about 70 per cent of the province's estimated 4,000,000 people.

More than 2,000,000 Muslims live elsewhere, bringing the total number of Muslims to about 4,800,000 or over 12 per cent of the total population of Myanma, estimated in 1988 to be around 39,350,000. Muslim communities outside Arakan are concentrated mainly in the Rangoon region and the north-east, forming a majority in the towns of Moulmein, Moulmeingyn, Pyinmana, Kyaukse and Shwebo.

Despite an unsuccessful attempt in 1942 to restore an Islamic republic in Arakan, Muslims were relatively well-integrated into Burmese society prior to the military take-over in 1962. While the majority of Muslims were farmers, others were traders and members of the professional classes who occupied posts in the government and bureaucracy.

By the early 1960s there were signs that the military regime was prepared to adopt a more systematic policy, restricting the language and culture of the country's religious and ethnic minorities which were regarded as a threat to Buddhist Burman nationalism. The Rohingyas formed an easy target, many being designated illegal immigrants, owing to the absence in 1948 of a representative Rohingya component in the Union of Burma. Mounting Muslim resentment prompted the formation in the early 1960s of the United Islamic Organization, Burma, which advocated armed struggle to safeguard Muslim rights.

Thousands of Muslims are believed to have died in bloody ethnic riots involving Buddhists and Muslims in 1958, 1962 and 1974; thousands more became refugees in neighbouring East Pakistan, later Bangladesh. Several hundred thousand Rohingyas left the Arakan region to settle abroad, initially in India and Pakistan and then in the Middle East. It is estimated that successive regimes have carried out at least 13 armed operations against Rohingya Muslims since independence, the worst being in 1978.

That year more than 300,000 Muslims fled to neighbouring Bangladesh after the government ordered a military crack-down against demonstrators protesting against a decision in February 1978 which denied Rohingyas the right to national identity cards and thus forced them to register as foreigners. In August 1978 the government bowed to pressure from Bangladesh and accepted the return of all Rohingya refugees.

The introduction of the 1982 Citizenship Law, which precluded members of non-indigenous races from claiming automatic Burmese nationality or from holding important positions, triggered widespread resentment among Rohingya Muslims, many of whom were effectively disenfranchised under the new rules.

In late 1991, a renewed government campaign against Rohingya Muslims prompted a fresh exodus to Bangladesh involving an estimated 145,000 refugees at the rate of some 4,000 a day. World Muslim leaders issued appeals to the United Nations to end the "persecution" and "extermination" of the Rohingya community. The Mecca-based Muslim World League (*Rabita al-Alam-i-Islam*) which was reported to have been actively engaged in missionary work along the Burmese-Bangladesh border since 1978, was among international Muslim bodies calling for a halt to the government's anti-Muslim campaign.

Meanwhile, the government's military presence in the Muslim-dominated towns of Maungdaw and Buthidaung in north-western Arakan increased from an estimated 10,000 troops in mid-1991 to 25,000-30,000 troops in early 1992; a programme of the systematic destruction of mosques, religious seminaries (*madrassahs*), and Muslim graveyards was also reported to have been officially endorsed. Hundreds of Rohingya Muslims were reported by international relief agencies in February 1992 to be in danger of starvation, and human rights organizations claimed that the government had subjected thousands of Muslim rebels to long periods of detention without trial, frequently accompanied by torture.

In April 1992 the government signed an agreement with Bangladesh which provided for the repatriation of an estimated 200,000 Rohingya Muslims. The agreement was described by the two main Rohingya groups, the **Arakan Rohingya Islamic Front** (ARIF) and the **Rohingya Solidarity Organization** (RSO) as unacceptable on grounds that any permanent solution would have to contain United Nation guarantees on the safety of returning refugees.

SA

Islamic organizations

Arakan Rohingya Islamic Front (ARIF)
"Moderate" Rohingya Muslim guerrilla group.
Leader. Muhammad Nurul Islam (president).
Membership. Estimated to be about 2000.

Muslim Liberation Organization of Burma (MLOB)
Muslim organization which, along with the All-Burmese Muslim Organization (ABMO), forms a part of the Democratic Alliance of Burma

(DAB), an umbrella organization of 21 opposition parties which contested the 1990 general election.

Leader. Mustafa Kamal (also known as Kyaw La).

Rohingya Solidarity Organization (RSO)

Militant Rohingya Muslim guerilla group which claims to receive extensive financial support from Pakistan and some Middle Eastern countries where there are substantial Rohingya Muslim communities, and from sections of the Afghan *mujaheddin.*

Leader. Muhammad Yunus (president).

National United Front of Arakan (NUFA)

Organization representing Rohingya Muslims; a component of the National League for Democracy (NLD) led by Daw Aung San Suun Kyi which won elections in May 1990, but was subsequently prevented from taking power by the military.

Smaller Muslim militant groups, whose popular following and armed strength are difficult to determine, include the **Rohingya Liberation Army(RLA)**, the **Rohingya Patriotic Front (RPF)**, the **Arakan People's Freedom Party (APFP)**, and the **Harkate Jihadul Islam (HJI)**.

Other lesser-known Muslim organizations known to be operating in various parts of Myanma are the **Jamiat Ulama-i-Islam (JUI)** and the **Islamic Religious Affairs Council (IRAC)**.

Nepal

Nepal is a constitutional monarchy where almost 90 per cent of the population profess Hinduism, which is also the state religion. According to the 1981 census, Muslims formed 2.7 per cent of the population of the country. By 1982 the percentage of Muslims had risen to 3.2 per cent, numbering an estimated 500,000.

The majority of Nepali Muslims are Sunnis who belong to the Hanafi school of law. There is a small Shia community concentrated in Eastern Nepal.

Nepali Muslims are concentrated in the Tarai region bordering India, where they form more than 10 per cent of the population of these districts. Ethnically, some Nepali Muslims claim foreign descent from non-Indian groups, including Arabs, Afghans and Turks. The majority, however, are descendants of Nepali converts.

Muslims in the capital, Kathmandu, are known as Kashmiri Muslims on account of their professed links with Kashmir. The Muslim community as a whole has strong links with India from where the first Muslim settlers arrived in the 14th and 15th centuries.

The connection with India is reflected in the use of Urdu, the language of North Indian Muslims, as the main Muslim language of culture in Nepal. Nepali Muslims also speak a variety of other languages: in the capital and in Western Nepal, they speak Urdu together with Nepali and Newari; in Bara and Parsa districts it is Bhojpuri; and in Eastern Nepal, Maithali.

Historically, Muslims were handicapped by living in an overwhelmingly non-Muslim state. Until 1963, an effective caste system, known as the *Muluki Ain* code, distinguished between foreign and native Muslims, and, although subsequently abolished, it continues to operate socially. But while the state has never officially recognized Islam or permitted Muslim personal law to operate, Nepali Muslims have generally been free to practise their religion.

In recent decades Muslims have become increasingly integrated into wider Nepali society. Until the 1960s, for instance, Muslim children were not permitted to attend Hindu-administered schools on grounds of their presumed religious impurity, nor allowed to open separate Muslim schools. Today, Muslims attend state schools in increasing numbers and there is a noticeable proliferation of Islamic schools.

Most Muslim clerics (*imams*) are trained in India. Kathmandu has two major mosques, the Nepali Jama Masjid and the Kashmiri Mosque.

A new Constitution adopted in November 1990 granted the right to the country's religious groups, including Muslims, to practise their religion, and manage and protect their religious places and trusts.

Muslim organizations known to be active include the All-Nepal *Anjuman Islah Samiti*, the Muslim *Seva Samiti*, the *Bajme Adab*, and the All-Nepal Muslim *Sudhar Samiti*.

SA

Netherlands

The Muslim population of the Netherlands, which forms the fourth largest Muslim community in Western Europe after France, Germany and the United Kingdom, numbers around 350,000 or just over 2 per cent of the total population, estimated in 1990 to be around 14,943,486.

The overwhelming majority are immigrants originating from Turkey, Morocco and the former Dutch colony of Surinam. In 1984 the Muslim population, then totalling 285,000, was dominated by Turks (155,000), followed by Moroccans (106,400) and Surinamese (23,600). Although the arrival of Muslim groups from Indonesia, Pakistan and Iran and elsewhere in the Middle East has contributed to the steady enlargement of the Muslim population, Turks continue to form the largest Muslim sub-group.

The majority of Muslims are Sunni adhering to the Hanafi and Maliki schools of law; recent immigration from Iran has swelled the numbers of Shia Muslims. The heterodox Ahmadiyyah sect has a well-established following among Surinamese Muslims, dating back to the 1950s. The Lahore Ahmadiyyah *Anjuman Ish'aat Islam*, whose membership is Surinamese, has branches in Amsterdam, The Hague, Rotterdam and Utrecht.

While Islam is not accorded the same legal status as other religions, Muslims are entitled to equal treatment under constitutional provisions, formally adopted in 1983, recognizing the Netherlands as a plural society. The formal separation of state and religion has meant that the appointment and emoluments of religious functionaries, including Muslim clerics (*imams*), are considered to be the internal affairs of religious associations. However, government involvement in religious affairs has periodically occurred as for instance from 1976-1983 when provisions for an "investment subsidy" from the Ministry of Welfare, Health and Cultural Affairs were used to cover the cost of social and cultural activities organized by immigrant communities, including the renting or purchase of Muslim prayer halls. In the 1980s the government was drawn into religious controversy after it resisted calls from Muslim groups demanding the recognition of polygamous Muslim marriages.

The exact number of mosques and prayer halls for Muslims in the Netherlands remains imprecise, as many are unregistered. (Under Dutch law only an association or foundation can form the legal basis of a mosque or prayer hall.) It is estimated, however, that there may be up to 200 prayer-halls for the Muslim population as a whole. Most *imams* associated with mosques and prayer halls tend to be recruited from abroad especially from Turkey and Morocco; in 1986 the total number of *imams* was estimated to be around 120, including 70 Turkish, 40 Moroccan and 10 Surinamese (including Ahmadiyyah *imams*). During Muslim religious festivals, such as *ramadan* (the month of fasting), an increase in the number of visiting *imams* may add to the total number of resident *imams*.

An estimated 60 per cent of all Muslim children in the Netherlands receive Quranic instruction. Much of it is in the form of private education by *imams*. Although some Muslim children attend confessional schools supported by state subsidies, religious instruction in such schools is predominantly Christian; a number of local Muslim organizations are reported to have lobbied the government to set aside special hours for Islamic instruction.

One of the first mosques in the Netherlands was built in Balk (Gaasterland, Frisland) in 1956 with a government subsidy for Muslim Moluccans from Ambon. The Ahmadiyyah mission to the Netherlands opened its Mobarak Mosque, the centre of the Rabwah Ahmadiyyah community in the Netherlands, in The Hague in 1955. However, the first systematic mosque-building programme in the Netherlands was initiated in the late 1960s by Surinamese Muslims, followed in the 1970s by Turkish and Moroccan immigrants.

In 1973 the Ministry of Welfare, Health and Cultural Affairs allocated funds towards the building of a mosque in Almelo for Turkish workers under the provisions of a law permitting grants for the construction of churches enacted in 1962 and abrogated in 1975. More recently, international Islamic bodies including the Muslim World League (*Rabitat al-Alam al-Islami*) and the London-based Islamic Council of Europe have been known to provide material support and advice for the construction of mosques and prayer halls. Additional financial assistance for mosques and prayer halls is also reported to have come from Kuwait, Libya and Saudi Arabia.

Organizational developments in the Muslim community

Until recently linguistic and cultural differences of Muslim immigrants in the Netherlands had prevented the formation of broadbased umbrella organizations. Surinamese Muslims were in the mid-1960s among the first to establish social and cultural organizations located in and around large cities including Amsterdam and The Hague. Their success was due primarily to the fact that as cultural bodies they were entitled to public subsidies from the Ministry of Welfare, Health and Cultural Affairs.

Attempts to establish a representative Muslim body able to bridge differences between Muslims from different national and ethnic groups led in 1974 to the creation of the Federation of Muslim Organizations in the Netherlands (FMON). Founded on the initiative of Dutch converts to Islam, the FMON formed the most important Muslim organization between 1975 and 1981. The objectives of the FMON (dissolved in 1981) were pursued through the efforts of its former members who re-grouped under the **Muslim Information Centre** in The Hague, which also took over the publication of FMON's mouthpiece, *Qiblah*.

As in Belgium and Germany, the governments of the native states of Muslim immigrants in the Netherlands have played an active role in directing the religious and political allegiances of their erstwhile citizens. Both the Turkish and Moroccan authorities are reported to have increased their participation in the administration of mosques and prayer-halls in the Netherlands.

The Turkish government's Directorate of Religious Affairs (*Diyanet Baskanligi Isleri*), which has been sending *imams* (with the status of civil servants in Turkey) to the Netherlands since the early 1980s, co-operates closely with the **Federation of Turkish Islamic and Cultural Associations** (FTICA). Since 1980 the Turkish government has contributed initially a part and subsequently the whole of the salary of Turkish *imams* operating in the Netherlands.

(According to some reports Turkey's military government led by Gen. Kenan Evren sanctioned the MWL to pay the salaries of Turkish *imams* sent to Europe in order to ensure that Turkish workers abroad would not be exposed to "foreign ideologies".)

An alternative Turkish organization opposed to the activities and ideology of the *Diyanet* is the **Islamic Centre Foundation** which reportedly maintains links with Muslim fundamentalist groups in Turkey.

Locally based Moroccan Muslim organizations are grouped under the little-known **Union of Moroccan Muslim Organizations in the Netherlands** (UMMON). Attempts by the Moroccan regime to influence the political orientation of Moroccan Muslims in the Netherlands was demonstrated in March 1986 when King Hassan of Morocco issued specific guidelines advising Moroccans on how to vote in local elections in which they and other immigrant minorities had been permitted to participate. Only about 15 per cent of the Moroccan electorate were reported to have departed from the King's guidelines.

Surinamese Muslims who between 1973 and 1982 were represented by the Netherlands Islamic Society, are presently said increasingly to favour the Foundation for the Welfare of Muslims in the Netherlands which tends to advocate a rigid and orthodox interpretation of Islamic law and practice.

FS

Islamic organizations

Federation of Turkish Islamic and Cultural Associations (FTICA)

Founded in January 1979 as the Turkish Islamic Cultural Foundation. It brings together about 80 local Turkish organizations and co-operates closely with the Turkish government's Religious Affairs Department (*Diyanet Baskanligi Isleri*) in the supervision and training of Turkish *imams* sent to the Netherlands.

Foundation for the Welfare of Muslims in the Netherlands (FWMN)

Surinamese Muslim organization founded in the early 1980s to supplant the Netherlands Islamic Society (also predominantly Surinamese); support for the FWMN is believed to come mainly from local Surinamese Muslim organizations professing a rigid and orthodox interpretation of Islam.

Islamic Association of the Netherlands (IAM)

Organization representing Turkish Muslims;

based in The Hague.
Leader. F. Demir.
Membership. 63,000 members; the IAM claims also to have the support of up to 87 local Turkish organizations.
Aims. To promote the social, cultural and religious activities of the Turkish Muslim community in the Netherlands.
Publication. Arayis ve Islam.

Islamic Centre Foundation (ICF)

Turkish umbrella organization inspired by the fundamentalist Suleymançi movement in Turkey, it is opposed to the activities of the *Diyanet Baskanligi Isleri*. The ICF, which is not officially recognized by the Turkish government, claims to represent up to 17 local Turkish Muslim organizations in the Netherlands.

Union of Moroccan Muslim Organizations in the Netherlands (UMMON)

Little-known umbrella organization founded in

1978 to represent Moroccan Muslims; UMMON claims to represent about 40 local Moroccan Muslim organizations in the Netherlands.

Muslim Information Centre

Founded in 1981 with headquarters in The Hague, it superseded the Federation of Muslim Organizations in the Netherlands (FMON) which had been established in 1974 on the initiative of Dutch Muslim converts.

Aims. To provide for the welfare of Muslims and work for the promotion of Islam in the Netherlands.

Publication. Qiblah ("The direction of Mecca"), published quarterly; formerly the organ of the FMON.

Niger

The Republic of Niger became independent from France in 1960. Following a coup in 1974 all political parties were banned and the country was ruled by a military regime until 1989 when steps were taken to restore democracy. In November 1991 a transitional government was named whose term of office is due to expire on January 31, 1993.

Almost the entire population (85-95 per cent) is Muslim. The remainder follow traditional beliefs and there are a few thousand Christians.

All Nigerian Muslims follow the Maliki branch of Sunni Islam. Most of them belong to one of four Sufi brotherhoods: the Tijaniyyah, the Qadiriyyah, the Sanusiyyah and the Hamallis.

The Tijaniyya is the most influential of the brotherhoods. It is strongest among the Beri, the Djerma and the Songhay groups and its most important strongholds are in Tahoua, Niamey, Gouré and N'guigmi. The Qadiriyyah, historically the most important of the brotherhoods, lost ground to the Tijaniyya in the 1920s but still has a significant following, particularly among the Tuaregs and the Arab Kunta clans. The authority of the Sanusiyyah is largely restricted to the Tuaregs and the Toubou; it has a number of lodges in Kaouar. The influence of the Hamallis is minimal.

Apart from the differences between the brotherhoods, there are also variations in practices and values. Large numbers of people are relatively recent converts and have retained many of their pre-Islamic practices. There is some evidence that many Muslims practise syncretic forms of the religion, drawing on both Islamic and indigenous African rituals.

Islam and the state: developments since independence

Since independence Islam has been an important unifying force, creating a foundation for homogeneity based on shared institutions, beliefs and cultural practices. It has provided a framework of law which is applied at a local level and which has played an important part in legitimizing the authority of the state.

At the same time, Islam has been a source of discord as a result of differences between the brotherhoods. Different brotherhoods frequently claim followers within single communities, thus fostering divisions. There has also been friction between communities where one community has been identified with a specific brotherhood, alienating it from surrounding villages and towns. By limiting the power of the brotherhoods by various means the government has been able partially to stem the conflict.

Although the brotherhoods have great authority among their followers, Islamic organizations play a limited part in the political and social life of the country. Islamic leaders and teachers are, however, accorded a special role in the functioning of the state and in the 1980s Islamic leaders, identified as part of the "socio-professional" group, participated in a series of advisory bodies which brought together "three pillars of society" (youth, farmers and "socio-professionals").

In 1991 Islamic leaders participated in a national conference on the political future of the country which drew up plans for the transition to democracy. Niger is an active member of the Islamic Conference Organization (ICO).

TJ

Nigeria

Nigeria, which won independence from Britain in 1960, has the largest Muslim community in sub-Saharan Africa. Muslims represent about 50 per cent of the total population, estimated in 1989 to be around 113,665,000. (The last census, recorded in 1963, indicated that almost 48 per cent of the population were Muslim.) About 40 per cent are Christian with the remainder following traditional African religions. There are over 600 ethnic groups, of which five (Hausa, Yoruba, Ibo, Bini/Ishan and Effik/Ibibio) are the most numerous.

The majority of Muslims live in the north of the country where they form the majority; in the western states Muslims form about one-third of the population, and there are relatively small, but significant, Muslim communities in the south. Overall, Muslims form a majority in 11 of the country's 31 states.

Ethnically, Islamic groups include the Hausa; the Fulani (Peul); the Kanemis; the Kanuris; the Bagirimis and the Wadayans. Islam has also been embraced by about 40 per cent of the Yoruba people of south-west Nigeria.

The spread of Islam in Nigeria began in the 14th century, gaining impetus during the Hausa-Fulbe struggles at the beginning of the 19th century and leading finally to the establishment of the Sokoto Caliphate under Usuman dan Fodio (1754-1817). Today, the Muslim population, under the spiritual leadership of the Sultan of Sokoto, is predominantly Sunni of the Maliki school.

Most of the Islamic community belong to one of the main Sufi brotherhoods—the Qadiriyyah; the Tijaniyyah and the Shadhiliyyah. There is also a well-established Ahmadiyya community and small groups of Mahdists. Followers of heretical groups such as the *Yan Tatsine* have also emerged in recent years.

Islam and the state: developments since independence

The period since independence has witnessed the growing unity of the Muslim population, prompted in part by the temporary loss of Muslim power at the centre in 1966. However, even before then traditional Muslim values were being actively promoted by the country's first Fulani-Muslim Prime Minister, Abubaker Tafawa Balewa (1912-66). Under Ahmedu Bello, differences between northern and southern Muslims created by conflicting loyalties to distinct Sufi brotherhoods, especially the Tijaniyyah and the Qadiriyyah, were steadily eroded through a programme of mass conversion and the efforts of reformist organizations, including the **Society for the Victory of Islam** (*Jamaatu Nasril Islam*) founded in 1961 and the Council of *Mallams* (Quranic schoolteachers) set up in 1963.

The establishment of national Islamic organizations, namely the Islamic Council of Nigeria set up in 1973, and the Supreme Council for Islamic Affairs created in 1977 under the chairmanship of the Sultan of Sokoto, also helped promote Muslim consciousness. Improved communications, leading to the publication in 1951 of a Muslim paper, *Truth*, still circulated weekly in Lagos, along with the spread of Islamic education in the second half of the 1970s, provided a firm base for the future development of Islam.

Muslim demands for the creation of federal Islamic *sharia* courts, which dominated constitutional negotiations in 1977-78, contributed substantially to political solidarity between northern and southern Muslims.

As elsewhere, heightened Muslim consciousness and the results of social dislocation prompted by Nigeria's oil boom, encouraged a Muslim revivalist trend represented by the loosely organized **Those who reject innovation** (*Bida Yan Izala*); the **Muslim Students Society** (MSS); the **Young Muslim Association of Nigeria** (YMAN), and influential Muslim spokesmen, including Alhaji Ibrahim Sulaiman and Shaikh Abubaker Mahmud Gumi, former Grand Judge (*qadi*) of the old northern region of Nigeria) and founder of the Kaduna-based *Bida Yan Izala* sect.

In the late 1970s and early 1980s Muslim fundamentalist sects intent on exposing the alleged moral corruption of some Sufi brotherhoods, fomented religious unrest in Kano, Maidugari, Gombe and Yola. The most potentially significant of these sects was the Kano-centred, anti-materialist *Yan Tatsine* movement, brutally suppressed by the government in December 1980. Led by Mallam Muhammadu Marwa (dubbed Mallam Maitatsine—Hausa for "he with powers of *tatsine* or cursing"), the movement professed adherence to Quranic principles, although its members were said to regard the Prophet Muhammad with derision. Mallam, who assumed the prophetic mantle, was killed along with 4,000 of his followers by the Nigerian army in Kano in December 1980. Maitatsine riots erupted again in 1982 and 1984, and despite constant surveillance by the authorities, followers of the sect are said still to be active in parts of northern Nigeria.

Fears of religious unrest, fanned by millenarian movements reminiscent of the *Yan Tatsine*, prompted some states to adopt restrictive measures including the ban by Gongola in January 1988 on open-air religious preaching, and by Bauchi and Kwara curbing the activities of the pro-Iranian Muslim sect, *Kungiyar yan Shia*.

More recently there have been indications of a trend towards Islamization in the otherwise more tolerant south-west of the country where reformers such as Alhaji Adham al Iluri have campaigned for closer co-operation among Nigerian Muslims; the introduction of *sharia* courts; improvement in Islamic education and the adoption of Muslim indigenous names.

Moves towards closer unity among Muslims in the post-independence period coincided with a marked increase in tension between Muslims and Christians. In 1966 tensions led to the outbreak of political, though ostensibly anti-Christian, demonstrations initiated by Muslim activists in the north.

Political differences between Muslims and Christians have been sharply exacerbated by the Muslim demand for federal *sharia* courts, first aired by Ahmedu Bello in the early 1960s. The issue, which almost split the country in 1977-78, has rekindled fresh demands from Muslim representatives debating a new constitution, for a Federal *sharia* Court of Appeal, and the creation of *sharia* courts in those states where they do not already exist. (Under the 1979 Constitution *sharia* courts of appeal could be set up at the request of individual states.) Muslim representatives have also demanded wider powers for existing *sharia* courts whose jurisdiction is presently restricted to personal law. Muslim demands are opposed by Christian advocates of a secular constitution who want the complete exclusion of federal *Sharia* courts, believing that their introduction would herald political control by proponents of an intolerant and inflexible brand of Islam.

Christian-Muslim tension erupted in March 1987 after Muslim student activists in the northern state of Kaduna led anti-Christian protesters in Kafanchan, Zaria and Kaduna city, organized the burning of an estimated 145 churches and contributed to the deaths of up to 19 people belonging to both communities. Despite the intervention of President Major-General Ibrahim Babangida (who assumed power in 1985), reaffirming that Nigeria would remain a secular state, the debate continues.

Meanwhile attempts by moderate Muslim organizations, notably the Muslim Association of Nigeria (MAN), to bring about a reconciliation between Muslims and Christians led in June 1987 to the formation of Muslim-Christian "Committee of Elders" aimed at monitoring and defusing communal tension.

These attempts appeared to fail after Muslim demonstrators calling for the introduction of the *sharia* triggered riots between Muslims and Christians in April 1991, resulting in the deaths of over 250 people (both Muslims and Christians) in Bauchi and other northern states.

In October 1991 clashes between Muslims and Christians prompted the authorities to impose a dusk-to-dawn curfew and ban all religious gatherings following the outbreak of communal rioting in Kano, a principal Muslim centre. The trouble began when 10,000 Muslims marched to the town centre, protesting that permission had been granted to hold a five-day Christian revivalist rally when some weeks before permission to invite a South African Muslim cleric to Kano had been refused. As tension rose, mobs of Muslim and Christian youths, chanting religious slogans, engaged in street battles. Over 100 people were reported to have been killed.

Renewed clashes between Muslims and Christians in May 1992 led to the deaths of up to 800 people (including three Christian priests) in Kaduna state, and the destruction of four churches and one Muslim centre. Reports indicated that the riots had been been triggered by growing resentment among Christians who opposed decisions by Hausa-dominated councils in localities, such as Zangon-Kataf, where Christians predominated.

Successive governments have responded to Nigeria's underlying religious tension by seeking actively to depoliticize areas vulnerable to political manipulation by religious groups. In May 1992 the government banned all organizations that drew support from selected states or interest groups.

Earlier, in a significant departure from common practice, the nationwide census conducted in November 1991 specifically omitted questions relating to religious affiliation in order to neutralize demands for greater representation by religious groups claiming numerical superiority.

However, these attempts to engineer Nigeria's religio-political equilibrium have themselves contributed to conflict. When President Ibrahim Babangida, a Muslim, attempted in 1986 to transform Nigeria's observer status to full membership of the Islamic Conference Organization (ICO), Nigerian Christians regarded it as a deliberate ploy to inititiate a programme of Islamization. Christian pressure forced Babangida in August 1991 to announce the suspension of the country's membership, which had never officially been confirmed (and, indeed, formally denied on at least one occasion).

Charges of blatant government intervention to manoeuvre the country's religio-political balance resurfaced in November 1988 after violent demonstrations by thousands of Muslim protesters demanding the removal of a government-backed candidate, Alhaji Ibrahim Dasuki, a successful businessman and Secretary-General of the Supreme Council of Islamic Affairs, who had been nominated to succeed the Sultan of Sokoto.

As Nigeria approaches a return to civilian government and with multiparty elections scheduled for end-1992, there has been renewed debate on Muslim voting habits. Although the results of the 1979 election suggested that Nigerians voted on regional and ethnic lines, these often coincided with religious affiliation.

Meanwhile, reports of moves to secure Muslim power at the centre grew in November 1991 after Alhaji Abubakar Alhaji, the Finance and Economic Planning Minister, was named Sardauna of Sokoto (captain of the guard of the Sultan of Sokoto)—an appointment widely regarded as strengthening Alhaji's presidential prospects.

Since the mid-1970s Nigeria has sought closer relations, both formal and informal, with Muslims elsewhere. The influx of doctors and teachers from other Muslim states including Egypt, Pakistan, Saudi Arabia and Syria, and growing numbers of Nigerian Muslims performing the Muslim pilgrimage to Mecca (*hajj*) every year (106,000 in 1977, a rise of over 60,000 in less than five years), have brought Nigerian Muslims closer to their co-religionists in Asia, Africa and the Middle East. Meanwhile, increasing numbers of Nigerian Muslims who have trained at Islamic institutions of higher education, including the Al Azhar University at Cairo, are regularly recruited to serve in the country's diplomatic and civil services as well as in the armed forces.

TJ

Major Islamic organizations

Islam in Africa Organization
Regional organization with headquarters in Abuja, formed in July 1991 to provide a forum for Muslims in Africa to address themselves to the issues facing Islam in the continent.
Structure. The highest policy-making body of the organization, the General Council, has 70 members.
Aims. To reunite and strengthen Muslim co-operation; to combine resources to tackle the problems of the continent, particularly in regard to Muslim refugees; and to promote peace and religious understanding.

Islamic Education Trust (IET)
Educational and missionary organization founded in 1976.

Aims. To promote educational and missionary literature and provide field instructors who preach Islam.

Muslim Association of Nigeria (MAN)
Moderate national organization whose main function is to support and act as a pressure group for the Supreme Council for Islamic Affairs; mobilizes Muslim youth outside universities, especially those still at secondary school.
Aims. The formation of a Muslim youth movement to "learn and teach about Islam and thereby influence the older and younger generations".

Muslim Students Society (MSS)
Fundamentalist national student body founded in

Lagos 1954 largely on the initiative of the Ahmadiyyah; from 1956, based in Ibadan. The organization radically extended its support base between 1966 and 1976 claiming up to 400 branches in 1970.

Aims. To bridge regional differences between Nigerian Muslims and establish an Islamic state modelled along Iranian lines.

Society for the Victory of Islam
Jama'atu Nasril Islam

Fundamentalist educational and missionary organization founded in 1961; took on a more national character after the end of the Nigerian civil war (1967-70) when it established branches outside the north.

Membership. The group claims that every Nigerian Muslim is either "an active member or a sleeping member".

Aims. The training and despatch of missionaries throughout Nigeria; the running of schools and colleges, and the erosion of differences between Muslims loyal to diverse Sufi brotherhoods.

Society of Overflowing Islam

Youth organization, founded in Kano in 1963 as the Youth of Islam, later changed its name to Society of Young Muslims in Nigeria before taking present title; unaffiliated to any of the brotherhoods.

Aims. The training of leaders for the Islamic community and the extension and reform of Islamic education and society.

Supreme Council for Islamic Affairs

The most important officially sponsored Muslim organization, founded in 1977.

Leader. Alhaji Ibrahim Dasuki, Sultan of Sokoto (president).

Structure. The Council's governing body is made up of representatives from each state.

Aims. To act as a forum for debate for all Nigerian Muslims; to unify Muslim opinion on issues relating to legal and educational developments in the country.

Those who reject innovation
Izalatul-Bid'a wa Iqamat al Sunna (Bida Yan Izala)

A loosely integrated fundamentalist organization with headquarters in Kaduna.

Leader. Abubakar Mahmud Gumi.

Aims. The eradication of innovation (*bida*) and the preservation of an Islam based solely on the Quran and the Sunna.

Young Muslim Association of Nigeria (YMAN)

Fundamentalist youth organization.

Oman

The Sultanate of Oman gained independence from the United Kingdom in 1951. The population, estimated in 1989 at 1,422,000, is predominantly of Arab origin, with small Baluchi, Zanzibari, Iranian and Pakistani groups of expatriate workers. (No census has ever been held in Oman and estimates of the country's population, including its expatriate workforce, are based on conjecture.)

Since the eighth century the people of Oman have owed allegiance to the Ibadiyyah sect (Ibadites), the only surviving branch of the Khariji movement which became the earliest schismatic grouping in Islam. Up to 75 per cent of the population adhere to the strict and puritanical version of Islam espoused by the Ibadi, with the rest, roughly one-quarter, following Sunni rites.

Until the 17th century Oman was dominated by the forces of Ibadi conservatism which favoured a special combination of religious and political leadership in the form of the *imamate*. Following the expulsion of the Portuguese in 1648, and the expansion of Oman's political and economic influence throughout the Gulf, the *imamate* became increasingly concerned with secular matters, causing a rift between conservatives and moderates.

By the end of the 18th century the ruling Al Bu Sa'id clan had become secular rulers whose territorial control was based in the coastal region, leaving the interior to religious conservatives who in the 19th century attempted to establish a theocratic state founded on Saudi Wahhabism.

In the early 1950s Said Ibn Taymur finally succeeded in uniting the coastal are, controlled by the Sultan, with the hinterland, controlled by the *imam*. However, the coastal region remains more cosmopolitan and ethnically diverse than the conservative interior.

Under its present ruler, Sultan Qaboos bin Said, Oman has entered a period of rapid socio-economic development and modernization based on its new oil wealth. Until the inauguration of the first session of a Consultative Council in January 1992, the Sultan had absolute power. There is no formal Constitution, Islamic law (*sharia*) and royal decree being the only source of law. There are no political parties.

There is no recent evidence of an Islamic opposition to the regime; organizational activities in the country have centred on the sharp sectarian divisions between the Ibadite majority and minority Sunni groups in the southern province of Dhofar, who in the mid-1960s and 1970s attempted to promote a secessionist movement which was fiercely suppressed by the government.

Since then there has been official backing for a non-sectarian version of Islam, with the promotion of government-supported mosques and the steady implementation of *sharia*. All jurisdiction is exercised by *sharia* courts which operate in conjunction with the Ministry of *Awqaf* (Religious Endowments) and Islamic Affairs.

More recently there have been attempts by groups such as the Omani Women's Society to persuade religious leaders to consider reforming aspects of traditional Islamic law, particularly those relating to the practice of polygamy.

EW

Pacific Islands

The presence of Islam in the Pacific predates that of Christianity. However, although much of the western Pacific was traversed by Muslim traders en route from Arabia to China, it was not colonized in the way that many of the Indonesian islands were settled. Nevertheless, Muslims from Indonesia did make regular visits to New Guinea, the north coast of Australia, and some of the nearby Pacific islands.

In 1982 it was estimated that there were some 158,000 Muslims in the Pacific (excluding Indonesia, the Philippines, Australia and New Zealand), constituting roughly 3 per cent of a total population of 5,330,000.

The greatest concentrations are in Fiji, where there were estimated to be around 50,000 Muslims in 1982 representing 7.7 per cent of the total population; in 1990 the percentage of Muslims had risen to 10 per cent out of an estimated total population of 800,000. Muslims in New Caledonia numbered around 14,000 (about 10 per cent) of a total population of 140,000 in 1982.

In the second half of the 19th century the French authorities deported anti-colonialist fighters from Algeria to New Caledonia, part of which had been designated a penal colony. Later their number was boosted by deportees from other North African territories conquered by the French. In the early 20th century there was an influx of Muslim immigrants from Indonesia, and there were further waves in the period after 1945.

The Muslims of New Caledonia first organized themselves in 1970, establishing the Association of Arabs and Friends of the Arabs of New Caledonia and Dependencies (*Association des Arabes et Amis des Arabes de Nouvelle Caledonie et Dependances*). This was superseded in 1975 by the **New Caledonia Muslim Association** (*Association des Musulmans de Nouvelle Caledonie*).

The British also shipped Muslims, mainly from the Indian sub-continent, as indentured labourers who were used to work the sugar cane plantations of Fiji. Between 1879 and 1917 some 63,000 Indians were transported to Fiji, of whom about 15 per cent were Muslims. About two-thirds of the indentured labourers chose to settle in Fiji after the expiration of their contracts, although the percentage of Muslims who exercised this option was somewhat lower, with some 4,350 choosing to stay. By 1921 the Muslim population had expanded to 6,435 (4.1 per cent of the total), and by 1970 this proportion had risen to almost 8 per cent.

Muslims in Fiji began organizing themselves in the early 20th century through local associations; attempts to establish a national co-ordinating structure were unsuccessful. In 1926 a broad Muslim umbrella organization, the **Fiji Muslim League** (FML), was finally created. By 1944 the FML had established itself as the single most representative national Muslim organization.

Although the FML was successful in improving the position of the Muslim community in Fiji, some of its achievements were reversed by the two military coups in 1987. The coups ensured that political power remained in the hands of the native Melanesian population, the majority of whom were Christian. Widespread anti-Indian discrimination and outbreaks of communal violence following the coups stimulated increased emigration by the Indian community, including both Muslims and Hindus. By the end of the 1980s the Melanesian population had re-established itself as the single largest racial group within the country, although the economic cost of the loss of so many members of the Indian community has yet to be fully reckoned.

Papua New Guinea, which shares a long border with Muslim Indonesia, also has a small Muslim population. There are small but largely unorganized Muslim communities in Belau, Guam, the Marshall Islands, the Federated States of Micronesia, French Polynesia, the Solomon Islands, Tonga, Western Samoa, and Vanuatu.

SL

Islamic organizations

Fiji Muslim League (FML)
Created in 1926.
Aims. Provision of Islamic education for Muslim children; securing financial stability for Islamic activities and ensuring the availability of *imams*.
Publication. The Muslim Voice.

Islamic Council of the South Pacific (ICSP)
Created in 1984 as a result of mutual consultation and contact between representatives of the Muslim communities of Australia, New Zealand, Papua New Guinea, Fiji, New Caledonia and Tonga; its headquarters are in Suva, Fiji.

Islamic Society of Papua New Guinea (Ispang)
Established in 1978, Ispang followed the examples of Muslims in Fiji and New Caledonia by seeking to organize the 500 or so Muslims in Papua New Guinea.

Aims. Improvement in welfare of Muslims; provision of Islamic education for Muslim children.

New Caledonia Muslim Association (NCMA)
Association des Musulmans de Nouvelle Caledonie
Established in 1975.
Aims. To encourage the observance of Muslim religious practices; liaise between New Caledonian Muslims and Muslim populations of other countries; and provide Islamic education for Muslim children.

Regional Islamic Da'wa Council for South-East Asia and the Pacific (RIDCSEAP)
Founded in 1980 as a regional body with headquarters in Kuala Lumpur, Malaysia.
Publication. al Nahda (Renaissance).

Pakistan

The Islamic Republic of Pakistan was established in August 1947 following the partition of the Indian subcontinent (and included present-day Bangladesh). The first modern state to be founded on explicitly religious principles derived from Islam, its creation was justified as the outcome of the "two-nation" theory which held that Indian Muslims (about one-fifth of the total population of India) formed a distinct nation with a right to separate statehood.

The emergence of the new state was accompanied by the mass emigration, especially from the western part, of non-Muslim communities, particularly Hindus and Sikhs, ensuring a high degree of religious homogeneity. Whereas East Pakistan (which became Bangladesh in 1971) retained a sizeable minority of non-Muslims (some 20 per cent), West Pakistan, which constitutes today's state, became overwhelmingly Muslim.

According to the 1981 census over 96 per cent of Pakistan's population is Muslim, with Christians (about 1.3 per cent), Hindus (1.6 per cent), Parsees, (Zoroastrians) and Buddhists making up very small religious minorities.

Most Pakistani Muslims are Sunnis adhering to the Hanafi school. A Shia minority, estimated to account for about 5 per cent of all Muslims, is divided into sub-sects, representing the Ismailis, the *ithna ashariyya* and the Bohras. Members belonging to the small but influential heterodox Ahmadiyyah sect account for less than one per cent of all Muslims in Pakistan.

In addition there is considerable popular support in rural areas for representatives of Sufi orders, particularly the Suhrawardi, Chishtiyyah, Qadiriyyah and Naqshbandiyyah orders.

Islam and the state: developments since independence

Pakistan's post-independence constitutional development has been marked by tensions within the political system generated by the country's need to reconcile its identity as a homeland for Indian Muslims with its claim to be a self-consciously Islamic state.

The country's first Constitution of 1956 sought to accommodate as many different opinions as possible while basing itself on the 1949 Objectives Resolution which emphasized Islamic values. Declaring Pakistan to be an Islamic republic, the Constitution upheld divine sovereignty, envisaged the reconstruction of a society based on Islamic principles, and affirmed that all new laws were to conform to the Quran and *Sunna* (the example set by the Prophet Muhammad). However, in the absence of any state mechanism to implement them these provisions remained little more than statements of intent.

Pakistan's second Constitution, issued in March 1962, followed the direct intervention of the military in politics in 1958. Unlike the 1956 Constitution it did not, at least initially, refer to Pakistan as an Islamic republic (the adjective had been dropped in 1958 and was not restored until the Amendment of 1965) and did not recognize Islamic law (*sharia*) as the sole source of legislation. It did, however, reaffirm the commitment to ensure the prohibition of any law repugnant to Islam and to establish Islamic councils to advise on these matters.

The country's third Constitution, adopted in April 1973, was influenced primarily by the need to repair the political and economic structure of what remained of Pakistan following the secession of Bangladesh in 1971. In addition, one of its stated aims was to reach a consensus on the role of Islam in politics. While the new Constitution declared Pakistan to be a parliamentary republic, it also broke new ground by proclaiming Islam as the state religion.

However, the programme of "Islamic Socialism" advocated by the ruling Pakistan People's Party (PPP) under Zulfiqar Ali Bhutto ensured that pressure by religious parties to initiate full-scale Islamization was temporarily curbed.

This situation was reversed with the reintroduction of martial law in 1977. General Zia ul-Haq, who proclaimed himself President, firmly believed that Pakistan's political system had to be Islamized in order to forge national unity. Propounding the idea of *Nizam-i-Mustapha* (the system of the Prophet), Zia sought to enlist popular support in order to disarm moral opposition to his regime.

In March 1981, despite the failure of a committee of religious specialists to reach a consensus on recommendations for the structure of an Islamic system of government, Zia promulgated a Provisional Constitutional Order which retained wholly or in part 119 articles of the 1973 Constitution. Its main provisions were the establishment of a Federal Consultative Council (*Majlis-i-Shura*) on the grounds that parliamentary democracy was not compatible with Islam.

While partisan political activity was permitted to gradually resume, parties continued to risk proscription if their manifestos were deemed not to contain Islamic provisions. Following a referendum in December 1983 which apparently endorsed Zia's Islamization programme, elections were held on a non-party basis in February 1984. Zia then moved to implement a series of controversial measures, including the notorious Islamic punishment (*hudud*) ordinances, which were widely criticized by women's groups, human rights activists and members of the Shia minority.

In June 1988, following Zia's dismissal of an elected civilian government on the grounds of "lack of attention to the Muslim faith", a presidential decree formally introduced Islamic law and repealed all existing secular civil laws.

Fresh elections in November 1988, following Zia's death in an air crash in August that year, resulted in a substantial victory for the PPP led by Benazir Bhutto, the first woman to be elected premier of a Muslim state. Bhutto's government did not, however, take decisive steps to reverse the Islamization programme of the previous regime and with the return to power in October 1990 of the **Islamic Democratic Alliance** (IDA—*Islami Jumhuri Ittehad*), the Islamic programme appears once more to have gained momentum.

In May 1991 the newly elected government passed the Shariat Bill, formally designating Pakistan an Islamic state, and in August blasphemy was made punishable by death, bringing the penal code into line with Islamic law. As in the past, the lack of mechanisms to enforce Islamic law has meant that Pakistan has been unable to assess precisely the effect of the changes introduced.

The close relationship between Islam and the State in Pakistan, especially in recent years, has forced ostensibly secular political parties to affirm their Muslim identity by recasting their election manifestos along Islamic lines and by seeking political support from leading religious figures.

Meanwhile religious parties have continued to play an active role in the country's political life although their electoral support has tended to remain limited. Pakistan's main religio-political organizations are the fundamentalist **Islamic Society of Pakistan** (*Jamaat-i Islami Pakistan*—JIP), the **Association of Islamic Clergy** (*Jamiat-i Ulama-i-Islam*—JUI) and the **Association of Pakistani Religious Scholars** (*Jamiat-i Ulama-i-Pakistan*—JUP), the last two of which are led by clerics (*ulama*) who are influenced by the ideas of the Indo-Muslim Barelvi sect and the Deoband reform movement respectively.

As well as their campaign in favour of an Islamic state in Pakistan, religious parties have also been involved in ostensibly sectarian issues with far-reaching political implications, such as the move in the early 1950s to designate as non-Muslims the small but influential Ahmadiyyah sect.

Although religious parties participated in the country's first democratic elections in 1970, they failed to make much impact. The JIP gained only four seats in the National Assembly and four in the Provincial Assemblies. In the Punjab the JIP had only 4.6 per cent of the vote, less than the combined total of the two other religious parties, the JUP and JUI, which both won seven seats. On the whole these successes owed more to alliances with powerful local elites than to the strength of popular religious commitment. The 12 remaining so-called *"Islam Pasand"* (Islam-loving) parties worked mostly at cross-purposes with one another.

In the mid-1970s, however, there was a noticeable shift in favour of religious parties, partly as an expression of protest against the PPP government. The JI and JUP, which had become members of the United Democratic Front (UDF), formed in March 1973, played a key role in formulating the 1973 Constitution.

The revival of the anti-Ahmadiyyah agitation in May 1974 enabled religious parties to seize the political initiative and force the already crippled PPP government to declare the Ahmadiyyah community a non-Muslim minority. The group was officially designated "non-Muslim" in 1980 as part of the government's Islamization programme.

The participation of religious parties in the opposition Pakistan National Alliance (PNA) in 1977 ensured that the Islamization of society and politics returned to the top of the political agenda. President Zia's programme of Islamization received strong backing from religious parties, especially the JIP which did not, however, command sufficient popular support to win public backing for the new reforms.

Gradual disillusionment with the military regime led religious parties, with the exception of the JIP, to side with the opposition Movement for the Restoration of Democracy (MRD), which called for the return of democratic rule and was dominated by non-religious parties.

The controlled non-party elections held in 1985 were boycotted by most of the religious parties, with the exception of the JIP, as well as by their non-religious counterparts. The JIP's political isolation was brought home by its failure to win substantial support in key constituencies despite the absence of serious contenders.

In the November 1988 elections religious parties joined the IDA and opposed the appointment of a woman as the political leader of an Islamic country. In early 1989 a group of Islamic religious leaders, many of whom belonged to the JIP, issued a ruling (*fatwa*) to the PPP to dismiss Bhutto and elect a male Prime Minister.

Following the defeat of the PPP in the October 1990 elections, the IJI formed a coalition government in which the JI was the second most powerful partner. Other religious parties in the coalition included the **Islamic People of the Traditions** (*Islamic Ahle Hadith Party*), **Society of Religious Elders** (*Jamaat ul-Mashaikh*), **Holy War Movement** (*Hizbe Jihad*) and the System of the Prophet (Muhammad) (*Nizam-i-Mustafa*).

The government's increasing vulnerability to religious groups has recently been manifested in a ruling by a federal Islamic court in November 1991 which ordered the elimination of bank interest, prohibited under Islamic law. The tenuousness of the government's hold over its allies in the religious parties was accentuated in May 1992 when the JIP announced its decision to quit the ruling coalition following disagreement over the government's refusal to back the extremist Afghan *mujaheddin* faction led by Gulbuddin Hekmatyar.

Political activity by the Shia minority gained momentum with the Iranian Revolution of 1979 and with Shia opposition to the allegedly Sunni orientation of Zia's Islamization programme. The main organization representing Shias in the immediate post-independence period was the *Tahafuz-i-Haquq-i-Shia* (Protection of Shia Rights), recast in the 1960s as the *Shia Mutalbat Committee* (Shia Demands Committee) under the leadership of Syed Mohammad Dehlavi.

In 1979, stimulated by the Iranian revolution, Mufti Jaffer Hussain founded the **Movement for the Implementation of the Shia Code** (*Tehrik-i-Nifaz-i Fiqah-i-Jafria*—TNFJ) which reflected the emergence of Shia political activism. On Hussain's death in 1984, the organization split into two groups: old-style traditionalists led by Hamid Ali Shah Mousavi and a reformist tendency under Allama Arif Hussain al Hussaini. Both groups regarded themselves as followers of Iran's Ayatollah Khomeini and Hussaini's more militant style was a significant factor in enhancing Shia political consciousness in Pakistan.

Shia political activism heightened sectarian tensions which resulted in fierce Sunni-Shia riots throughout the 1980s and encouraged the birth of parallel Sunni organizations, the People of the Traditions (*Islamic Ahle-i Hadith*) and the **Society for Expansion of the Majority** (*Sawaad-i Azam*). In June 1992 sectarian violence between Shias and militant Sunnis belonging to the puritan Wahhabi sect erupted in northern Pakistan after the assassination of the leader of the little-known Sunni Wahhabi group, the **Force of the Lions of Pakistan** (*Sipah-i-Sabaha-i-Pakistan*—SSP).

In 1990 the TNFJ joined the Pakistan Democratic Alliance (PDA), a loose grouping including the PPP which was formed in response to the IJI alliance of right-wing and Islamic parties. Meanwhile the Shia-dominated *Hizbe Jihad* agreed to join the ruling coalition but was subsequently expelled from the IDA in September 1991, allegedly for having co-operated with opposition parties.

SA

Major Islamic organizations

Association of Islamic Religious Scholars
Jamiat-i-Ulama-i-Islam (JUI)
Religio-political organization founded in 1945 under the leadership of Maulana Shabbir Ahmad

Usmani to win support for the "creation of Pakistan" movement among Indo-Muslim clergy associated with the Deoband reform movement. It was formally revived in Pakistan in 1950.

Leader. Maulana Fazlur Rahman (president).

Aim. Advocates an Islamic state based on a Constitution founded on (Sunni) Islamic teachings.

Association of Pakistani Religious Scholars

Jamiat-i-Ulama-i-Pakistan (JUP)

Religio-political organization founded in 1948. The JUP joined the centre-right Tehrik-i Istiqlal in 1988 to found the Pakistan People's Alliance (PPA) (*Pakistan Awami Ittehad*). The JUP joined the IDA-led ruling coalition in November 1990 and has remained a member of the IJI despite the resignation in March 1991 of its nominee, the Local Government Minister, Maulana Abdus Sattar Niazi, criticized by Prime Minister Sharif for not supporting government policies over the Gulf war. (Niazi was re-appointed as Minister for Religious Affairs in a Cabinet re-shuffle in September 1991.)

Leader. Maulana Shah Ahmad Noorani (president); Maulana Abdus Sattar Khan Niazi (secretary-general).

Aim. Advocates an Islamic state based on the implementation of progressive Sunni Islamic principles.

Force of the Lions of Pakistan

Sipah-i-Sabahah-i-Pakistan (SSP)

Militant Sunni Muslim organization representing followers of the Wahhabi sect.

Leader. Muhammad Ghiassuddin (assassinated on May 31, 1992, in Gilgit, northern Pakistan, reportedly by Shia gunmen).

Holy War

Hizbe Jihad

Shia political group, originally part of ruling IDA coalition; expelled September 1991.

Leader. Murtaza Pooya.

Islamic Democratic Alliance (IDA)

Islamic Jumhoori Ittehad (IJI)

Formed as an electoral alliance in 1988 to represent nine right-wing and Islamic parties and oppose the PPP-led Movement for the Restoration of Democracy (MRD). It is now the dominant partner in the country's ruling coalition; other minor religious parties forming part of the coalition include the *Ahle Hadith* (People of the Traditions), one of whose chief spokesmen is Maulana Moinuddin Lakvi; the *Nizam-i-Mustapha* (System of the Prophet, led by Maulana Abdul Sattar Khan Niazi (also of the JUP); and the *Jamaat-ul Mashaikh* (Society of Religious Elders) under Pir Fazle Haq. The Shia-based Hizb Jihad (Holy War Movement), led by Murtaza Pooya, was expelled from the IDA in September 1991.

Leader. Mian Nawaz Sharif (chair).

Aims. The alliance favours the systematic introduction of Islamic law (*sharia*). In May 1991 it won parliamentary approval for the Shariat Bill and it has succeeded in reforming the penal code to make blasphemy punishable by death. Sections of the alliance representing religious parties have increased pressure on the government to Islamize the economy by abolishing bank interest, prohibited under Islamic law.

Islamic People of the Traditions

Islamic Ahle Hadith

Formed in reaction to Shia activism in the 1970s, its roots are in the conservative Indo-Muslim reformist movement, the *Ahl-i-Hadith* (People of the Traditions) which dates back to the 19th century. The group, which is currently a member of the ruling IJI, is reportedly divided into a number of different factions.

Leader. There is no generally accepted leader although Maulana Moinuddin Lakvi, who is also a member of the National Assembly (MNA), is among the group's better-known spokesmen.

Islamic Society of Pakistan

Jamaat-i-Islami Pakistan (JIP)

Religio-political organization founded in 1941 by Maulana Abu Ala Mawdudi along the lines of the Egyptian *Ikhwan al muslimin* (Muslim Brotherhood). Initially opposed to the creation of Pakistan on the grounds that its creation did not presuppose a theocratic state, it increasingly sought to influence constitutional and political developments by campaigning for increased Islamization. In the 1950s the party was active in the campaign to win support for the movement to declare the Ahmadiyyah minority non-Muslims. The JIP was opposed to the promulgation of the Family Laws Ordinance of 1961 which sought, among other things, to restrict polygamy, and to the Constitution of 1962 which refrained from designating Islamic law as the sole basis for legislation. In the 1965 presidential elections the JIP endorsed Fatima Jinnah to oppose President Field-Marshal Ayub Khan as the candidate of the Combined Opposition Parties (COP), of which it was a member. The JIP endorsed the Islamization programme initiated by President Zia in the late 1970s and subsequently formed part of the ruling coalition led by the IDA. In May 1992 the JIP withdrew from the government following policy differences over support for the Afghan *mujaheddin*.

Leader. Amir Qazir Hussain Ahmed (chair); Mohammad Aslam Saleemi (secretary-general).

Membership. Restricted. The JIP's original base of support in the cities of the Punjab was extended during the 1950s to include migrant, mostly Urdu-speaking communities in the cities of Karachi and Hyderabad in the province of Sind.

Aim. The establishment of a (Sunni) Islamic state.

Publications. The party organ is *Jasarat*.

Affiliated organizations. *Jamaat-i-Tulaba* (Students' Society), the student wing of the JIP, founded in 1947 with the declared objective of constructing human life on the basis of Islam. Other organisations linked with the JIP include the Labour Welfare Committee and the *Jamaat-i-Ittehad ul-Ulama* (Society for the Unity of Clergy).

Movement for Implementation of the Shia Code
Tehrik-i-Nifaz-i-Fiqah-i-Jafria (TNFJ)

Shia pressure group formed in 1979 to oppose the allegedly Sunni bias of President Zia ul-Haq's Islamization programme. The organization was registered as a political party in 1987. The party split in 1984 after a reformist faction led by Arif Hussain al Hussain broke away from the dominant traditionalist faction under Hamid Ali Shah Mousavi. Hussain was assassinated in Peshawar in August 1988.

Leader. Hamid Ali Shah Mousavi.

Aims. To seek the formulation of an Islamic constitution incorporating Shia principles as expounded by Ayatollah Khomeini. Other objectives are to unite the Shia community, protect Shia rights in a Sunni-majority state, and actively involve Shias in the politics of Pakistan.

Pakistan Khaksar Party (PKP)

Militant Muslim organization originally formed during British rule. It was dissolved in 1947 but was subsequently revived.

Leader. Mohammad Ashraf Khan (president).

Aims. Advocates the introduction of Islamic values and universal military training.

Society for the Expansion of the Majority
Sawaad-i Azam

Sectarian Sunni (Hanafi) organization established in the late 1970s to counter growing Shia assertiveness.

Leader. Maulana Azam Asvandyar.

Membership. Active among Urdu-speakers in Karachi.

Aim. Favours a Sunni-based Islamic constitution for Pakistan which would affirm and expand the rights of the Sunni majority against the Shia minority.

Society of Preachers
Tablighi Jamaat

Proselytizing movement founded in Delhi in the

1920s; also known as the *Tehrik-i-Iman* (Faith Movement) and the *Dini Dawat* (Religious Mission).

Leader. Currently none, following the death in May 1992 of its *Amir* (leader), Alhaj Muhammad Bashir.

Aims. To inculcate a missionary spirit, to acquire and transmit Islamic knowledge, and to implement the *sharia* in the realm of personal law. The movement is publicly opposed to mixing politics with preaching and refrains from engaging in religio-political controversy.

Panama

The Republic of Panama has an estimated population of 2,370,000 of which the majority, some 70 per cent, is mixed-race (*mestizo*). Afro-Caribbean and Indian communities constitute roughly 21 per cent of the total population.

The Muslim community numbers about 1,500. Of these, around 1,000 are Arabs, 300 are of Indian descent (mainly from the state of Gujarat), and approximately 200 are native Panamanians. At the turn of the 20th century many Muslims were brought from Bengal to work on the construction of the Panama Canal. Muslims tend to be involved in business and retail activities.

Panama built its first mosque in 1980. The first Muslim organization in Panama, established in 1930, was the Islamic Mission which changed its name in 1967 to the Indo-Pakistan Islamic Association and again, in 1974, to the Panama Islamic Mission.

MCB

Peru

There are approximately 5,000 Muslims in the Republic of Peru. Most are of Palestinian or Syrian origin and live in the capital, Lima. An Islamic Society was established in 1975. There are no reports of the existence of mosques in Peru.

MCB

Philippines

The 7,000 or so islands which comprise the Philippines became a Spanish colony in the 16th century, and were ceded to the USA in 1898. After occupation by Japanese forces during the Pacific War, the territory achieved independence in 1946, although it has retained close economic, military and cultural ties with the USA. The Philippines has a popularly elected President and a bicameral legislature.

Despite the ethnic diversity of the Philippines, one of the most enduring legacies of the long period of Spanish colonial rule is the country's religious homogeny. Of a population estimated in 1990 to total 66,100,000, some 94 per cent of the population is Christian (84 per cent Roman Catholic), and about 5 per cent Muslim.

Twelve ethno-linguistic groups are identified as Muslim, the most important of which are the Maguindanao (the Mindanao), the Maranao (with their close kinsman the Iranun), the Tausaga and the Samals.

Islam was well established in the Philippines prior to Spanish colonisation, having been introduced in the 14th century by Malays and by the Dayaks of Borneo. Although the Spanish conquerors sought to eradicate Islam, often displaying the same degree of ferocious zeal toward the territory's Muslims (called Moros after the Muslim Moors in Spain) as was directed towards the Muslim population of Spain, they failed to subdue the southern regions.

The Muslim community has wielded a degree of influence beyond its numerical proportion because of its long history of independence from Luzon and the geographically concentrated nature of its distribution.

Mindanao (Maguindanao), some of the other southern islands and the Sulu archipelago, constituted separate Muslim Sultanates which resisted with considerable success integration into the colonial regime. This southern homeland, known as Bangsa Moro by Muslims, remained unconquered until 1914, when it finally fell to US forces after a protracted struggle. The last Muslim Sultan was forced to abdicate on March 11, 1915, but the territory was not fully incorporated into the Philippines until the abolition of the last Sultanate in April 1940.

Islam and the state: developments since independence

Following its subjugation in the early 20th century, Bangsa Moro was opened up for immigration and development by the Christian population of the northern islands. Initially this process of de-Islamization was slow, but it accelerated dramatically after the Philippines became independent in 1946. Hundreds of thousands of Muslims were evicted from their land by Christian settlers, and massacres and atrocities were committed by both sides. Whilst it continued to constitute a majority in many parts of the southern provinces, the Muslim population was increasingly marginalised, enduring an inequitable share of social and economic resources, and the partisan application of authority by the Christian-dominated agencies of the state.

At the same time, many Muslims showed signs of heightened awareness of their Islamic identity, encouraged in part by the education of young Muslims at well-established centres of Islamic learning, including the Al Azhar University in Egypt, and the performance by increasing numbers of the annual pilgrimage to Mecca (*hajj*). The 1950s and 1960s also witnesssed the opening of a growing number of Quranic schools (*madrassahs*), a rise in mosque attendance and the emergence of Muslim professional associations.

The Jabidah Massacre of March 1968, which led to the summary execution of an estimated 60 young Muslim soldiers on charges of staging a mutiny, proved a major catalyst in shaping Muslim political consciousness. In May a prominent member of the traditional Muslim leadership (*datu*), Datu Udtug Matalam of Cotabato, launched the Muslim Independence Movement (MIM—which later changed its name to the Mindanao Independence Movement in an effort to win Christian support).

Meanwhile, radical sections among the burgeoning Muslim professional and educated classes found a vehicle of self-expression in the **Moro National Liberation Front** (MNLF). The MNLF and its military arm, the Bangsa Moro Army, rebelled against the government with the avowed aim of achieving independence for the Muslim population of the southern territories through armed struggle. Attempts by the government of the late President Ferdinand Marcos to suppress the rebels served only to stimulate the MNLF's rapid growth.

Moves by Muslim insurgents to seek support from Muslims abroad helped internationalize the issue, encouraging states such as Libya, Malaysia, Kuwait and Morocco to recognise the guerrilla war as a legitimate community response to the threat of genocide against Philippine Muslims by the government. In March 1972 the Islamic Conference Organization (ICO) expressed its grave concern and requested the government to "guarantee the lives and properties" of the Philippine Muslims. In September the Shaikh of Al Azhar University condemned what he called the "genocide" of Philippine Muslims.

Although costly in terms of lives and property (some estimates suggest that up to 50,000 people may have died as a result of the clashes in the 1970s), the government's military campaign against the insurgents was inconclusive.

The military stalemate, together with the MNLF's adoption in 1974 of a position whereby it was willing to consider autonomy rather than outright independence, opened the way for a negotiated settlement. On December 23, 1976, the two sides—negotiating in Tripoli under the auspices of the ICO—reached an agreement which involved the granting of autonomy to the 13 provinces in Mindanao, Palwan and the Sulu archipelago, in return for a ceasefire.

Notwithstanding numerous local infractions the resulting truce held until late 1977. Nevertheless, the Tripoli Agreement was dogged by the issue of whether the three predominantly Christian southern provinces should be included (as demanded by the MNLF), and whether each province should be subject to a referendum prior to its inclusion in the autonomous Muslim region (as demanded by the Marcos government).

On March 25, 1977, Marcos formally declared autonomy for the 13 provinces, but also announced a referendum in the 13 provinces on April 17. Although boycotted by the MNLF, the turnout was said to be 75 per cent, with an overwhelming majority voting against the autonomy plan. The MNLF accused Marcos of bad faith in deviating from the Tripoli Agreement, and of rigging the ballot. Further negotiations proved fruitless, and the ceasefire gradually collapsed in the latter half of 1977, with the MNLF reverting to its former demand for complete independence.

Although the government continued to make cosmetic concessions to Muslim autonomous sentiment, these were repudiated by the MNLF. The war continued, but the organization's energies were increasingly sapped by serious internal divisions. These were accentuated by the ICO's efforts to pressurize the movement into accepting some form of autonomy short of independence.

By late 1982 three distinct groups had emerged: the mainstream MNLF, supported initially by Libya and more recently, by Iran; the **Muslim Islamic Liberation Front** (MILF) sponsored by Egypt; and the smaller **Bangsa Moro National Liberation Front (BMNLF)**—also known as the MNLF-Reformist Group—supported by Saudi Arabia.

The overthrow of Marcos in 1986, and his replacement as President by the more conciliatory Corazon Aquino, opened the way for renewed negotiations. In September 1986 Aquino met with MNLF leader Nur Misuari, and agreed to begin fresh talks.

Although the MILF and the BMNLF—both of which demanded complete secession—did not participate, the MNLF and the Aquino government appeared to have made progress. Aquino's commitment to the concept of autonomy was written into the country's new Constitution (adopted in February 1987) which provided for an autonomous Muslim region in Mindanao. The talks eventually foundered, however, amid accusations that the MNLF was seeking secession rather than autonomy, and that the government was no more sincere about ceding real authority than had been the Marcos regime.

In July 1987 Aquino offered limited autonomy to 10 Muslim provinces designated the "Muslim Mindanao Autonomous Region", subject to approval by Congress and by a plebiscite in the area. MNLF officials rejected the offer because: it applied to only 10 of the 13 provinces which had been covered by the 1976 Tripoli agreement; the composition of the region's proposed governing council was unclear; and the autonomy package was dependent upon a referendum (problematic for Muslims who constituted a majority in only five provinces). In early 1988 the secessionists also rejected an invitation by Aquino to participate in the newly formed Mindanao Regional Consultative Commission.

Nevertheless, the government went ahead with an autonomy referendum in all 13 of the country's southern provinces on Nov. 19, 1989. Once again the Muslim secessionists appealed for people to boycott the poll and there were reports of numerous acts of violence in an attempt to disrupt the voting. The turnout was less than 50 per cent and in only four of the provinces (Lanao del Sur, Maguindanao, Tawi Tawi and Sulu) was there a majority in favour of regional autonomy. These four provinces were formed into an autonomous region, and in February 1990, Zacaria Candao (formerly a legal representative for the MNLF and the favoured candidate of the Aquino government) was elected Governor of the region.

Almost immediately Candao was confronted by serious fighting arising from a dispute between family clans. Nevertheless, the autonomous region assumed somecredibility when, on Oct. 12, Aquino granted limited executive powers to the Candao administration. An official statement said that the functions of the departments of public works, labour and employment, local government, environment and natural resources, tourism, science and technology, and social services had all been transferred to the Autonomous Regional Government.

The MNLF and its associated groups opposed the autonomy arrangement on the grounds that it fell far short of independence, and failed to meet the terms of the 1976 Tripoli Accord. Although the guerrilla war has continued, its scale—both in terms of the numbers participating and the destruction wrought—is much reduced compared with the 1970s.

SL

Major Islamic organizations

Bangsa Moro National Liberation Front (BMNLF) also known as MNLF-Reformist Group

Like the MILF the BMNLF developed within the MNLF in the early 1980s, and by the end of 1982 had a distinct identity. Unlike the MILF, however, it retained close links to the MNLF despite developing a high degree of autonomy. Based in Malaysia, supported by Saudi Arabia, the BMNLF has always been the smallest of the three Muslim secessionist movements. It includes members of the now extinct Bangsa Moro Liberation Organization (BMLO) faction.
Leader. Dimas Pundato.
Membership. Active membership is estimated at 11,000.
Aims. Autonomy or independence for Muslim provinces, and improved level of resources for Muslims in the Philippines.

Moro National Liberation Front (MNLF)

A militant Muslim organization founded in 1968 to co-ordinate armed struggle against the Manila-based government. The MNLF is reported to be backed by Libya and Iran.
Leader. Nur Misuari (chair and president of central committee).
Membership. The armed wing of the MNLF, the Bangsa Moro Army (BMA), is estimated to number up to 15,000.
Aims. The achievement of independence for the traditionally Muslim provinces of the south

through armed struggle. At times, however, it has taken a reformist position by demanding increased resources for the country's Muslim population together with greater autonomy for the southern provinces. In 1977 Misuari defined the MNLF as "a Muslim nationalist movement trying to free a Muslim country from the Philippine colonial yoke".

Muslim Association of the Philippines (MUSAPHIL)

Revived in April 1981 as the moving spirit behind a Muslim conference aimed at re-opening negotiations on the Tripoli Agreement between the government and the MNLF.
Leader. Salipada Pendatun.

Muslim Islamic Liberation Front (MILF)

Developed from within the MNLF in the early 1980s, and by late 1982 had a distinct identity. The organization acquired its present name in 1985. Based in Pakistan, the MILF drew its international support from Egypt. In early 1988 there was heavy fighting between supporters of the MILF and the MNLF.
Leader. Hashim Salamat (chairman).
Membership. The bulk of its membership is concentrated in Lanao del Sur.
Aims. Independence for the Muslim provinces of the south, and improved level of resources for Muslims elsewhere in the Philippines.

Poland

There is a small Muslim minority in Poland which is believed to total between 3,000 and 5,000 people, many claiming to be of Tatar origin dating back to the 14th century.

Muslim communities are settled mainly around the district of Bialystok, north-east of Warsaw, where there are two mosques. Another mosque is nearing completion near Gdansk where the Muslim community has recently become politically active.

GR

Islamic organizations

Islamic Party
Hizbe Islami
Founded April 1992 and initially based in Gdansk.
Leader. The party's main spokesman is Salim Chazbijewicz.
Structure. The party is governed by a six-person political council.
Membership. The organization, which claimed 40 members in April 1992, hoped that "soon 1,000 to 2,000 Muslims from the 5,000 Muslim community in Poland will join our party".
Aims. "To consolidate Muslim circles in Poland and to expand co-operation with other Muslim communities in the world . . . it is to have a right-wing orientation, abstaining from any links with left-wing Muslim parties such as the ones representing Libya or the Palestine Liberation Organization."

Portugal

There were estimated to be 15,000 Muslims in Portugal in 1991, most of whom originated from the former Portuguese colonies of Mozambique, Guinea-Bissau, Macao and Timor. There are also growing numbers of Muslims from north Africa who entered the country as migrant workers.

EB

Islamic organizations

Islamic Community of Lisbon
Comunidade Islamica de Lisboa cil
Based at the Central Mosque, Praca de España, in Lisbon, this is the principal organization aimed at promoting the social, cultural and religious interests of Portugal's Muslim community.
Leader. Abdool-Karim Vakil (secretary).

Portuguese Centre of Islamic Studies
Centro Portugues de Estudos Islamicos
Reportedly formed after a split within the country's Muslim community.
Leader. Suleiman Valy Mamede.

Qatar

Qatar, a former British Protectorate, achieved independence in 1971 and in 1972 the country's present Amir (ruler), Shaikh Khalifa ibn Hamad al-Thani, ousted his cousin in a palace coup.

Qatar is marked by ethnic diversity. Of a population assessed in 1990 at 468,632, 40 per cent are Arab, 18 per cent Pakistani, 18 per cent Indian and 10 per cent Iranian. Indigenous Qataris are estimated to comprise between 20 and 25 per cent of the population.

Qatar's ethnic diversity contrasts sharply with its religious homogeneity. Ninety-five per cent of the population are Sunni Muslim, adhering to the strict Hanbali school of law as interpreted by the fundamentalist Wahhabi sect. A minority (about 16 per cent) are Twelver Shias (*ithna ashaariyya*), many of them immigrants from southern Iran who now constitute the Shaikhdom's merchant oligarchy.

Prior to the production of oil in 1949, Qatar was one of the poorest states bordering the Persian Gulf. The oil wealth and the effects of rapid modernization in the 1970s shattered the delicate political balance between the ruling family and Qatar's tribal community. Fear of political, and possibly sectarian, upheaval led the Amir to insist on the absolute obedience of tribal leaders and on strict adherence to Wahhabism.

The Amir rules as an absolute monarch, advised by a Cabinet which he appoints himself and by a nominated Advisory Council. In January 1992 the Amir received a petition from 50 leading Qataris demanding the establishment of a consultative assembly to check what they regarded as the growing abuse of power in the country.

The ruling family has ensured strict supervision of Wahhabi Islam by working in close co-operation with religious notables and scholars, many of whom exercise influence in judicial and educational matters and advise the Amir as to the legality of official decrees according to a strict reading of the Quran and *Sunnah* (the example of the Prophet Muhammad). In 1988 Qatar became one of the first countries to ban the novel *The Satanic Verses* by the Indian-born British author, Salman Rushdie. The process of consultation and co-operation between the Amir and religious leaders resulted in Cabinet approval in February 1990 of the establishment of the country's second Islamic Bank.

Although based on Islamic law, Qatar's legal system has a hybrid nature. Islamic law (*sharia*) courts adjudicate on all matters relating to Muslim personal law, specific offences where the defendant is Muslim, and civil disputes where the parties elect to have recourse to Islamic law. Non-Muslims are tried by a court operating codified law. The Amir has substantial discretion, only to some extent limited by the development of civil codes.

There are no political parties and no reports of organized religious opposition to the regime.

EW

Romania

Outside the Balkans the only other substantial Islamic community in eastern Europe is to be found in Romania. An estimated 52,000 Muslims of Turkish-Tatar descent live mainly around the Dobrudja region. It is believed that the total number of Muslims in Romania could be as high as 250,000.

The spiritual head of Romania's Muslims is the Grand Mufti of Romania, Yacub Mehmet Septar.

GR

Russian Federation

(For a broad survey of Islam in the former Soviet Union see separate entry for the Commonwealth of Independent States)

The Northern Caucasus region is home to at least 20 nationalities. Its Muslim population is mostly Sunni, of the Shafi school in Daghestan and of the Hanafi school in other areas (Daghestan also has a Shi'ite Azerbaijani community).

It is divided administratively into the Republics of Kabardino-Balkaria, North Ossetia (only partly Islamic), Chechen-Ingushetia, Daghestan, Adyghe and Karachai-Cherkess.

Micro-nations, each with an official language, they demonstrate the policy of divide and rule practised during the Soviet era. Many of these peoples were deported on Stalin's orders to Central Asia and Siberia for "collaboration" with the Nazis in 1943-44; thousands of deportees were reported killed.

Sufism has been a strong influence in the Northern Caucasus: leadership of the resistance against Russian invaders in the 19th century, spearheaded by the Naqshbandiyyah order, was subsequently assumed by the Qadiriyyah movement when Naqshbandi leaders were deported to Siberia and Central Asia where they eventually founded the Basmachi movement.

The disintegration of central power has generated widespread demands for independence and intensified inter-ethnic hostility. At the same time, political demands were underpinned by the revival of distinct religious and cultural identities fomented by cultural organizations based in parts of Northern Caucasus, (eg. Untsuqul and Shamil).

European Russia

Muslims belonging mostly to the Sunni Hanafi school are concentrated along the Volga. There are estimated to be up to fifty distinct ethnic and linguistic groups in the Volga and the North Caucasus areas (not all Muslim). The Mufti of the Russian Federation Sheikh Talgat Tajuddin, was elected in 1980 at the age of 32.

In February 1992 an international forum held at the cathedral mosque in St Petersburg to celebrate the city's Muslim community (many of them Tatars) was marked by a bomb attack.

Bashkortostan

The Bashkirs, like the Tatars, are dispersed among other nationalities and in Bashkortostan, their titular republic, constituted only 21.9 per cent of the population in 1989. Russians and Tatars made up the remainder. As in Tatarstan, there is a substantial degree of russification, with 64.9 per cent claiming a good knowledge of Russian as a second language in 1979. Ufa, the capital, is particularly russianized, despite being the seat of the Spiritual Directorate of Russia.

Islam is, here as elsewhere, on the increase. In 1989 Tatars in Ufa asserted their Islamic heritage by celebrating the 1,100th anniversary of the conversion to Islam of the Volga Bulgars (a tribe wich once inhabited the area). Meanwhile, mosques are reopening rapidly; the number of mosques rose from 90 in 1990 to an estimated 500 in mid-1991).

Chechen-Ingushetia

Signs of Muslim revivalism are also emerging in Chechen-Ingushetia, commonly regarded as one of the most religiously vibrant regions. The traditional hold of Islam in the area may be illustrated by the number of mosques, which in 1917 totalled 806; the number of religious seminaries (*madrassahs*) during the same period was estimated to be around 427. In 1943 all mosques were closed in Chechen-Ingushetia; no reliable figures are available for the number of mosques and other religious institutions in Chechen-Ingushtia today.

Towards the end of 1991 the Chechen-Ingush Autonomous Republic (57.8 per cent Chechen; 12.9 per cent Ingush; 23.1 per cent Russian, at the beginning of 1991) demanded to secede from Russia, following the election as president in October of Dzhokar Dudayev—an election unrecognised by Russia. (Chechnia has also laid claim to part of Ingushetia, which has expressed a wish to remain within the Russian Federation.)

In November Dudayev was sworn in as President of Chechen-Ingushtia during a ceremony marked by his oath-taking on the Quran, amidst charges by the Russian-controlled media of playing the "very strong Islamic trump card". In a move aimed at reaffirming Muslim self-determination, Dudayev called upon autonomous Muslim republics in Russia as well as independent republics, namely Turkmenistan, to stop gas and oil supplies to Russia.

Muslim militancy in Chechen-Ingushtia has been intensified by the Chechen Islamic Way Party (CIWP), led by A. Shishani, which has expressed keen interest in acquiring arms to promote its political objectives. Reportedly founded in November 1991, the party aims to restore Islamic values in the Caucasian republics; to protect them from "infidels" and to wage a "holy jihad" (*holy war*) in all territories occupied by Muslims. According to the organization, its party units presently contain about 30,000 armed militants.

Crimean Tatars

The 1989 census listed Crimean Tatars separately for the first time. (The Crimea has been a part of the Ukraine since 1954, before which it was administratively part of Russia.) Officially, they numbered 268,739—a figure below their own estimate. The Crimean Tatars have waged a long campaign to return to the Crimea, from where they had been deported to Central Asia in 1944 (the year the Crimea had been stripped of its status of Autonomous Republic granted in 1921).

In August 1991 (before the attempted coup), the Soviet and Ukrainian governments passed resolutions allowing the Tatars to return to Crimea, and promising state aid for resettlement. This appears not yet to have been implemented. The First Congress (*Kurultai*)) of Crimean Tatars held in June 1991 in Simferopol elected a 31-member assembly (*majlis*) to act as the basis for local Tatar self-government. Mustafa Dzhemilev, a leader of the Crimean Tatar National Movement (CTNM) founded in the early 1950s, was elected chair. The CTNM demands the state-sponsored return of the Crimean Tatars to their homeland, and restoration of national statehood to Crimea.

Daghestan

In Daghestan, home to 10 nationalities, rioting erupted between Chechen and Avars over allocation of land in September 1991.

Daghestan is also reported to have witnessed violent Muslim demonstrations which are sketchily reported in the Soviet and foreign press. There were reports in 1989-90 of demands, accompanied by religious demonstrations, for the replacement of the Mufti of the Northern Caucasus. (The religious associations of republics other than Daghestan were said to have demanded the right to set up their own religious boards.)

Evidence of growing Muslim consciousness emerged in February 1991 after a newspaper entitled *Put Islama* ("Path of Islam"), founded by the Islamic Renaissance Party of Daghestan (IRPD) went on sale seeking the promotion of the historical and religious knowledge of Islam, and declaring that all profits would be put to the use of the development of Islam in Daghestan. The birth of the IRPD was followed by the creation of the Islamic Democratic Party of Daghestan (IDPD).

Signs of Muslim militancy resurfaced in June 1991 after a state of emergency was introduced following a demonstration by hundreds of Muslims demanding subsidised travel for the Muslim pilgrimage to Mecca (*hajj*). The leader of the IRPD, Ravil Sadykov, claimed that there had been one death and four wounded. The situation in Daghestan was described by *Izvestiya* on December 17, 1991, as "approaching civil war", but added that national movements had agreed to cease political activity during the session of the Supreme Soviet.

Kabardino-Balkaria

In November 1991 Kabardino-Balkaria declared its independence and elected a national council (Kabardino-Balkaria is 48.2 per cent Kabards, 9.4 per cent Balkars who are over-whelmingly Muslim and 32.0 per cent Russians).

Tatarstan

The Tatars form the largest ethnic group without its own Union Republic, numbering an estimated 6,700,000 in 1989. Only 26 per cent live in Tatarstan, the rest being dispersed throughout Central Asia, Siberia, and the lower Volga. By the beginning of 1991, Tatarstan was 48.5 per cent Tatar and 43.3 per cent Russian. More urbanized than other Muslim groups, the Tatars have a lower birthrate than their religious counterparts elsewhere in the CIS (6.5 per cent in 1970-79, equal to that of Russia).

In 1979, 68.9 per cent of Tatars claimed to be fluent in Russian as a second language. The awareness of Islam as fundamental to national identity is strong among the Tatar intelligentsia, noted for being among the few Islamic communities in the CIS who produced *samizdat* literature in the pre-Gorbachev period.

Demands for Tatar autonomy have been strengthened by centuries of cultural and religious awareness which continues to be encouraged by existing cultural organizations in Tatarstan, including the the Tatar Public Centre (TPC), founded in February 1989 and instrumental in planning the March 1992 referendum in favour Tatar sovereignty; the Tatar Islamic Cultural Centre and the Centre for Tatar Studies.

Prominent in the movement to win recognition for Tatarstan as a sovereign state and founding member of the CIS are the TPC and the radical *Ittifak* Party (Unity Party), led by Fawziya Bairomova. Both organizations stress the fundamental role of Islam in the Tatar national movement and have appealed for broader political co-operation among Muslims in the CIS.

Meanwhile, the Russian government has indicated its willingness to make partial concessions towards greater Tatar autonomy. On June 18, 1991 it was announced that a Russian shareholders' Muslim Bank, established by industrial enterprises and by the cathedral mosques of Moscow and Kazan, would specialize in financing an oil processing plant in Tatarstan, hotels and facilities for foreign companies in Moscow, and help organize the Muslim pilgrimage to Mecca (*hajj*). In December 1991 Russia and Tatarstan signed an economic agreement allowing Tatarstan to export oil, concluding discussions initiated by Tatarstan's declaration of independence on Aug. 31, 1990.

WS

Saudi Arabia

Saudi Arabia, where Islam is both indigenous and central, is characterized by ethnic and religious homogeneity; 90 per cent of its population is Arab, the other 10 per cent are of Afro-Asian origin.

Ninety-nine per cent of its population, estimated in 1990 to total 16,108,539, are Muslims, of whom the majority (80 per cent) adhere to Sunni Hanbali rites (the strictest and most conservative of the four Sunni legal schools).

Members of Saudi Arabia's Shia minority are followers mainly of the Twelver (*ithna ashariyya*) sect (15 per cent), with the remainder divided between Zaydis (the Fivers) and Bedouin Kharijites, also known as Ibadites (5 per cent). Twelver Shia communities are concentrated in the eastern oil fields facing Iran, while the Zaydis are resident along the southern border with Yemen.

The origins of the Islamic regime peculiar to Saudi Arabia lie in a religio-political alliance sealed in 1744 between Muhammad ibn Abd al Wahhab (1703-92), leader of the Wahabiyya movement (a revival of orthodox Sunnism), and Muhammad ibn Saud (d. 1765), ruler of Dariyya (close to the modern city of Riyadh). By the beginning of the 19th century, this fusion of military and religious zeal had generated a powerful resistance that successfully challenged Ottoman rule in Central Arabia and eventually helped establish a unified nation-state in 1932.

The process of territorial consolidation was paralleled by the emergence in 1912 of a movement of renewal among the bedouin Wahhabis of Nejd (home of Abdul Wahhab), who called themselves the *Ikhwan* (Brethren or Brotherhood—not to be confused with the Egyptian *Ikhwan al muslimun*). Preaching a return to pristine Islam, the *Ikhwan* established settlements (*hujar*) symbolizing the early Islamic theme of emigration (*hijra*) away from idolatry to faith. In 1916 the new Saudi leader, Abd' al Aziz ibn Saud, appealed to his Bedouin supporters to join forces with the *Ikhwan*, thereby substantially enhancing its political standing, subsequently boosted by its leading role in a series of bold offensives, dubbed holy war (*jihad*), which secured the capture of the holy cities of Mecca and Medina in 1924.

By the late 1920s, however, the fanatical zeal of the *Ikhwan* and the ferocity of their supporting apparatus, particularly the band of "enforcers" (*mutaween*) employed to ensure conformity to the Wahhabi ethic, were regarded by Abd'al Aziz as inimical to the modern state he wished to create. After a series of military campaigns in 1929-30, Abd'al Aziz succeeded in ensuring the dispersal of the *Ikhwan* and severely curtailing the influence of its supporters.

Islam and the state

The defeat of the *Ikwan* did not, however, spell the end of Wahhabism; the state and society which emerged as Saudi Arabia was stamped with the strict scriptural orthodoxy of Wahhabism and remains formally so to the present day. Inspired by the Wahhabi ethic, Saudi Arabia has sought to emulate the ideals of early, uncorrupted Islam. Although ruled by an absolute monarch (who is also Prime Minister and "Custodian of the Holy Places") the country has no written constitution other than the Quran, supplemented by the provisions of Islamic tradition and the rulings of Hanbali law. The country's legal code is based on Islamic law (*sharia*) and a body of state-issued "regulations" which, unlike most other Muslim states, has no independent status but connotes decrees aimed at the proper implementation of the *sharia*. The Islamic law of punishment (*hadd*) is widely and rigorously applied.

Islam permeates almost every aspect of social and economic life in Saudi Arabia. Muslim observances of prayer and fasting are formally obligatory; the rule of the public segregation and veiling of women (*hijab*) is strictly enforced, and business ethics, food, clothing, methods of address and greeting are all governed by Islamic law.

There are no officially recognized political parties or movements. Demands for political reform were met in March 1992 by an announcement from the country's ruler, King Fahd, endorsing the creation, within six months, of a Consultative Council (*majlis ash shura*). However, neither the Council nor its manner of election are expected to conform to prevailing norms of Western democratic practice. It is also believed that any future political reform will reaffirm allegiance to the King and the supremacy of the Quran and *Sunna* (the ways of the Prophet Muhammad) as the basis of the state.

The legitimation of Islam in Saudi Arabia has been ensured through the government-sponsored institutions, notably the Institute of Religious Decrees (*Dar al Ifta*, founded in 1953), the Council of Grand Ulama (founded in 1971), the Organization for the Enforcement of Good and Prevention of Evil (*Hayat al Amr b'il Ma'ruf wa'n nahi an al-Munkar*, established in 1929), and the "morality police" (*mutaween*). In August 1991 the government announced plans to create a Higher Council for the Islamic Call headed by the grand Imam of Al Azhar, Shaikh Jad al Haq Ali Jad al Haq, which would also include the Minister for Religious Endowments (*awqaf*), with a view to draft proposals for all existing Islamic institutions.

The use of education to inculcate religious values is encouraged by the Ministries of Education and Higher Education. However, the number of students in programmes specifically oriented to a religious career has remained low; in 1979 only 380 students were registered at the Islamic University of Medina, founded in 1960 and reputed to have been the alma mater of the leaders of the Meccan revolt, Juhaiman al Utaibi and Muhammad ibn Abdallah al Qahtani [see below].

As the world's first fundamentalist state with a claim to represent the ideals of authentic Sunni Islam, Saudi Arabia has sought also to revive the notion of pan-Islamic unity by initiating international efforts aimed at combating the threats of secularism and radicalism. The Muslim World League (*Rabitat al Alam al Islami*), founded in Mecca in 1962, was followed by the formation in 1971 of the Islamic Conference Organization (ICO) with headquarters in Jeddah. The Saudi Fund for Development (SFD), established by royal decree in September 1974, professes to abide by the Islamic stipulation requiring Muslims to help their neighbours and is actively committed to providing for the needs of Muslims in developing countries.

Throughout its history Saudi Arabia has strongly opposed Israel. It supported the Arab side during the 1973 Arab-Israeli war, and afterwards put pressure on the USA to encourage Israel to withdraw from the occupied territories by cutting oil production and placing an embargo on all exports to the USA. In 1980 it declared an official state of holy war (*jihad*) against Israel and has continued to protest vigorously against Israel's occupation of Jerusalem. It is also known to have extended substantial financial support to the Palestine Liberation Organization (PLO).

The neo-fundamentalist challenge

The process of Islamization, sometimes referred to as the "routinization of Wahhabism", was seriously challenged by the consequences of the oil boom of the 1970s. Tensions emerged as the traditional ethos of Wahhabi puritanism grew increasingly out of step with the encroaching culture of "consumerism" and "materialism".

The depth of the conflict was revealed in November 1979 when members of a messianic sect belonging to a revived *Ikhwan* nucleus (80 per cent of which reportedly consisted of students) laid siege to the Grand Mosque in Mecca. Led by Juhaiman al Utaibi, a former member of the National Guard and resident of an *Ikhwan* settlement on the Riyadh-Mecca route, the rebels held the mosque for 22 days before being forced to surrender following the deaths of 450 of their members and up to 2,700 government troops. Over 60 of the captured rebels, including Juhaiman, were subsequently executed in different cities.

The rebels, several of whom belonged to Nejdi nomadic tribes centred in regions untouched by the oil boom, were said to have espoused an extreme form of Wahhabism directed against the alleged corruption of the al Saud family and the presence of Christian foreigners in Saudi Arabia. Having proclaimed Muhammad Qahtani as their messiah (*mahdi*), the rebels also issued a fierce denunciation against official clerics in the service of the state.

The Mecca revolt revived questions about the legitimacy of the Saudi monarchy (seen by most fundamentalist groups to be incompatible with Islam) and highlighted the regime's vulnerability to charges of political and financial corruption. Reports that religious decrees (*fatwas*) sanctioning the government's action against the rebels had taken several days to be issued, and that some senior clerics had refrained from formally endorsing them, heightened speculation that sections of the religious establishment had been sympathetic to the aims of the Mecca rebels.

1979 also witnessed the first serious outbreak of anti-government Shia riots in the eastern oil producing region, led by the now banned Shia opposition group the **Organization of the Islamic Revolution in the Eastern Peninsula** (OIRAP—*Munadhamat al Thawara al Islamiyya fil Jazira al Arabiyya*) which aims to create an Islamic republic along Iranian lines, based on popular participation, and an independent foreign policy.

In the last decade Shia opposition has been intensified by the reported displacement of entire Shia villages from the eastern oil fields to the more remote and politically less sensitive western provinces. In December 1980 riots erupted in the towns of the al-Qatif Oasis, the heartland of the kingdom's estimated 300,000 Shias. The government responded by clamping down on the rioters while promising to pay greater attention to Shia demands, including a greater share of the Kingdom's oil wealth. Shias from the eastern region figure prominently in recent lists of alleged "political prisoners" circulated by clandestine opposition groups.

Other neo-fundamentalist opposition groups believed to be in operation include a radical branch of the Egyptian Muslim Brotherhood (*Ikhwan al muslimun*) whose Saudi members claim to be engaged in exposing the corruption of the ruling royal family.

The Gulf crisis and the government's Gulf War policy ushered in dramatic changes in relations between the royal family and religious scholars (*ulama*). In a move suggesting the break-down of the traditional modus vivendi that had marked relations between the two parties, religious conservatives led by Saudi Arabia's most senior religious authority, Abdulaziz bin Abdullah bin Baz, backed a petition in May 1991 calling on King Fahd to introduce wider political representation through the creation of a "completely independent" consultative assembly. The petitioners demanded an end to corruption and the abolition of all un-Islamic laws, including the charging of bank interest prohibited by the Quran.

In a veiled attack on King Fahd's Gulf war policy, the petition also called for the creation of a powerful, well-equipped army to defend Saudi Arabia, and a foreign policy untainted by "non-Islamic pacts and treaties". In an unusual breach of customary Saudi discretion in such matters, the petition was later distributed in mosques, schools and street corners; security police questioned some of the signatories, while others were forbidden to leave the country.

Since then there have been fresh indications of a renewed challenge by radical Islamic groups, led by a younger generation of preachers. Reports in February 1992 confirmed the arrest of up to 20 "extremist" clerics believed to be supporters of the Algerian Islamic party, the Islamic Salvation Front (FIS). Other reports spoke of the arrest of around 50 pro-fundamentalist students, illustrating a noticeable trend among university students, particularly in the scientific faculties, towards Islamic revivalist groups.

Meanwhile, in January 1992, the government ordered the removal of Shaikh Abd al Muhsin, president of the main Islamic law (*sharia*) court in Riyadh, reportedly for opposing the presence (because of the Gulf crisis) of US troops in Saudi Arabia. Reports emerging at the same time indicated also that a group of clerics had addressed a letter to the head of the Board of Religious Decree (*Dar al Ifta*) expressing opposition to the Madrid peace conference on grounds that Islam forbade any truce with Zionism.

There have also been reports of attempts by radical clerics to curb the trend in favour of greater freedom for women. In December 1991 the government ordered the public flogging in Riyadh of a preacher who had allegedly denounced the liberal Saudi Women's Renaissance Society (founded after a group of Saudi women defied existing laws by driving their cars down Riyadh's main thoroughfare in December 1990).

EW

Islamic organizations

Organization of the Islamic Revolution in the Arabian Peninsula (OIRAP)

Munadhamat al Thawra al Iskamiyya fil Jazira al Arabiyya

Principal, anti-monarchist Shia opposition group, founded in 1975 and banned by the government. Since its part in organizing Shia protests in the eastern region in 1979, hundreds of its alleged members and sympathizers have been detained without charge or trial.

Leader. Unknown; in March 1992 the human rights organization Amnesty International adopted Ali Hassan al Amrad, detained in July 1991 by the Saudi authorities on charges of sympathizing with a banned organization, as a "prisoner of conscience".

Membership. Unknown.

Aims. The creation of an Iranian-style Islamic republic and an independent foreign policy. The party defines its goals as "educating and enlightening the masses" and securing equal rights for all Saudi Shias who, it claims, are

discriminated against in Saudi Arabia.
According to Amnesty International the party is
not known to have advocated armed resistance.

Senegal

Senegal, a former French colony, in 1959 became part of the Mali Federation, which comprised French Sudan (later Mali), Upper Volta and Dahomey. In August 1960 Senegal opted for secession from the Federation, following disagreements with French Sudan over plans to instal Leopold Sédar Senghor as President of the Federation.

Like other African states, Senegal is characterized by ethnic diversity. Six major groups, the Wolof (who account for more than one third of the total population), Serere, Peul, Toucouleur, Dioula and Manding, make up almost 90 per cent of the population. Until the outbreak of recent civil strife between Casamance separatists and the government of President Abdul Diof there were few reports of serious ethnic strife.

Senegal's ethnic diversity contrasts sharply with its religious homogeneity. According to unofficial estimates more than 95 per cent of the population are Sunni Muslims following the Maliki school of law.

Most Senegalese Muslims belong to one of the three Islamic brotherhoods or *tariqas*, the Tijaniyyah, the Muridiyyah and the Qadiriyyah. Almost 60 per cent of Muslims are reported to belong to the Tijaniyya, about 26 per cent to the Muridiyya and 16 per cent to the Qadiriyyah, with the rest distributed between various smaller brotherhoods such as the Layennes and the Hamallis.

No major doctrinal differences divide the brotherhoods from one another; all adhere to the brand of mystical Islam known as Sufism. Differences in ritual, however, have led some brotherhoods, including the Tijaniyyah, to be more flexible and individualist in approach while encouraging others, like the Muridiyyah, to stress a more rigorous and disciplined organization. These variations have led to differences in support between social classes, with the educated elite and the urban classes preferring the Tijaniyyah and the rural poor and ex-slaves opting for the Muridiyyah.

Islam and the state: developments since independence

Although Senegal has a secular Constitution, its politics and society have been markedly influenced by the activities and political preferences of the brotherhoods and their leaders, the *marabouts* (saints). The importance of *marabouts* as political brokers first emerged during French colonial rule when many were reported to have co-operated with the colonial authorities in destroying powerful local "pagan" aristocracies, most notably those belonging to the Wolof.

Opposition to the brotherhoods in recent years has been greatest among young Muslim intellectuals influenced by north African and Middle Eastern reform movements. Many regard the semi-worship of the *marabouts* as inconsistent with the principles of Islam and resent the political and economic control exercised by the *marabouts* over their disciples.

The importance of brotherhoods during the Second World War was highlighted by the political programmes of the Senegalese national parties which depended on religious leaders to secure the majority of rural votes and the economic resources many *marabouts* were known to control. The victory of Senghor's *Bloc Démocratique Sénégalais* (BDS) over the Senegal branch of the *Section Française de l'Internationale Ouvrière* (SFIO), led by Lamine Gueye, in the Territorial elections of 1952, was attributed to Senghor's success in winning the support of the most powerful *marabouts* of the Muridiyyah brotherhood by promising increased Arabic teaching in schools and the creation of Muslim tribunals in major towns.

While Marxist parties in the 1950s chose not to court the *marabouts*, their efforts to win Muslim votes by supporting the cause of increased Arabic teaching in schools were seen as evidence of the continuing importance of Islamic issues in politics.

The backing of leading *marabouts* for individual politicians was also in evidence during the events leading up to the dissolution of the Mali Federation. Both Senghor and the Sudanese President, Modibo Keita, cultivated links with leading Senegalese *marabouts* who ultimately determined the outcome by siding with Senghor's *Union Progressiste Sénégalaise* (UPS).

The break-up of the Federation coincided with a gradual decline in the political influence of the brotherhoods but they re-emerged as a political force during the 1962 political crisis, precipitated by a power struggle between rival factions loyal to Senghor and the Prime Minister, Mamdou Dia.

Dia's subsequent political defeat was understood to have stemmed from his failure to loosen the alliance between Senghor and the leading *marabout* and Murid caliph, Falilou M'Backe. It was also suggested that Dia's campaign of "agrarian socialism" had alienated a number of *marabouts* who perceived it as a direct threat to their economic interests.

During the late 1970s strains in the relationship of the government and the Murid brotherhood emerged, prompted in part by the reluctance of the new Murid caliph, Adbul Lahat M'Backe, to support the government uncritically. Observers believed that M'Backe's espousal of peasant grievances was instrumental in forcing Senghor to relinquish power to his young successor, Abdou Diouf, in 1981.

Defiance of state power among *marabouts* is rare, although there was an attempt by Abdullah "Khalifa" Niasse to apply the Iranian lesson when he proclaimed Senegal an Islamic republic in Paris in November 1979. However, the standing of his group, the *Hezbollahi* (Party of God), was seriously undermined by allegations that Niasse had been involved in financial corruption. Repudiated by his family and without support, Niasse was arrested in 1981.

The Iranian revolution spawned a host of Muslim religious and cultural associations as well as Islamic broadsheets, the most important of which was *Wal Fadjiri*. It also prompted a shift in the country's awareness of its links with the wider Islamic world, a trend that has become more marked as Diouf, a Tijanni Muslim, cultivates his international image as the Muslim leader of a Muslim nation. In December 1991 Senegal hosted the sixth heads of state summit of the Islamic Conference Organization (ICO).

The "re-Islamization" of Senegalese politics is also expected to benefit from Diouf's close links with the Murids, whose numbers and influence have grown under the leadership of Abdul Lahat M'Backe.

Elsewhere, what religious tension exists is the result less of Islamic revivalism in the Muslim world than of rivalries between the two largest brotherhoods, the Tijaniyyah and the Muridiyyah.

TJ

Major Islamic organizations

Association for Islamic Co-operation
Association pour la coopération islamique
Founded in 1988, based in Dakar.
Leader. Thiernao Ka (president).

Federation of Islamic Associations in Senegal
Fédération des Associations Islamiques du Sénégal (FAIS)
Government-sponsored co-ordinating body.
Aims. The co-ordination of the activities of Islamic groups throughout the country.

Muslim Association for Black African Students
Association Musulmane des Etudiants d'Afrique Noire (AMEAN)
Radical student body founded in 1953.
Aims. The teaching of Arabic in primary and secondary schools and the recognition of private Arabic schools.
Publication. Vers Islam.

National Association of Arab Students—Progressive Union of Senegal
Regroupment National des Etudiants d'Arabe—Union Progressiste Sénégalaise (RNEA-UPS)
Government-sponsored reform group founded in 1966 to counter the FNACMS.
Aims. The promotion of Arabic teaching, employment for *Arabisants* (Arabic-speaking students from Arab universities), and the selection of official delegates to world Muslim meetings.

National Association of Imams
Founded in 1984, based in Dakar.
Leader. El Hadj Maodo Sylla (president and Grand Imam).

National Association of Muslim Cultural Associations in Senegal
Fédération Nationale des Associations Culturelles Musulmanes du Sénégal (FNACMS)
Moderate umbrella organization founded in 1962 by Abdul Sy and Oumer Dieng.
Structure. A 130-member National Council drawn from constitutive groups including the UCM.
Aims. The "amelioration of the moral, social and material conditions of the Muslims", the elimination of the *marabouts* as intermediaries in religious worship, and greater government support for *Arabisants* (Arabic-speaking students from Arab universities).
Publication. L'Afrique Musulmane.

Muslim Cultural Union (MCU)
Union Culturelle Musulmane
Initially radical, later more moderate, movement founded in 1953 by Chiekh Touré and Oumer Dieng with branches across North and West Africa.
Aims. The elucidation of Islamic practices, the publication of educational material on Islam, and the cultural defence of Islam.
Publication. Le Réveil Islamique.

Seychelles

Independent within the Commonwealth since 1979, the Republic of Seychelles was established in 1979 as a one-party state. In December 1991 the government announced that the Constitution would be modified to legalize the activities of opposition parties.

The vast majority (90 per cent) of the islanders are Christian Roman Catholics, with the Muslim population numbering only a few hundred. Mostly migrants from neighbouring islands and East Africa, they are organized under the Seychelles Muslim Organization, which was instrumental in the construction of a mosque in Victoria.

TJ

Sierra Leone

The Republic of Sierra Leone became independent within the Commonwealth in 1961. From 1971 to 1991 the country was a one-party state under the All People's Congress (APC).

Muslims are estimated at between 30 and 40 per cent of the total population of just over 4,000,000; about 60 per cent adhere to traditional African beliefs; the rest are Christian.

The country did not come under Islamic influence until the early 18th century. Although the heterodox Ahmadiyyah sect, which was established in the country in the 1930s, is influential, the majority of Muslims are orthodox Sunnis, many of whom arrived as migrants from Nigeria. The Sufi Tijaniyyah brotherhood also claims to have significant support in the country, having been instrumental in the conversion of large numbers of Christians since World War II.

Islam and the state: developments since independence

Although the political, economic and social life of the country is dominated by a small Christian Creole population (the descendants of freed slaves), Muslims have occupied important positions in the government and the ruling party—both Vice-Presidents are currently Muslims, and in 1989 a religious leader (*imam*) was made a member of the APC's central committee.

A Constitution allowing for multiparty politics was adopted in September 1991; as of June 1992 there were no reports of the emergence of parties with a specifically Islamic agenda. There are several Muslim societies based in Freetown, some of which may be encouraged to organize as political pressure groups.

TJ

Islamic organizations

Ahmadiyyah Muslim Mission
Ahmadiyyah organization based in Freetown.
Leader. Khalil A. Mobashir (Emir and Chief Missionary).

Muslim Brotherhood
Ikhwan al-muslimun
Based in Freetown, reportedly with close links to the Tijaniyyah order.

Muslim Reformation Society
Based in Freetown.

Sierra Leone Muslim Congress
Based in Freetown.
Leader. Alhaji Muhammad Sansusi Mustapha (president).

Sierra Leone Muslim Men and Women's Association

Kankaylay

Founded in 1972; based in Freetown.

Leader. Alhaji Ibrahim Bemba Turay; Haja Isata Kebe (lady president).

Membership. 500,000.

South Africa

A former British colony, South Africa's social and political structure has been based on a policy of racial segregation known as apartheid. The Constitution of 1984 created a tricameral parliament in which the minority white population retained dominance of government and some representation was given to Indians and Coloureds. However, the majority black population remained excluded. In December 1991 the government began substantive negotiations on constitutional change with the African National Congress (ANC), the main liberation movement, and other political parties. A new constitution enfranchising the majority black population is widely expected to be introduced by the end of 1993.

Despite the ethnic and political diversity of the country, there is relative religious homogeneity, with the majority of the population professing Christianity. Although Muslims constitute less than 2 per cent of the total population of South Africa (estimated at 34,925,000 in 1989), there is a significant Muslim population concentrated in parts of the Western Cape and Natal.

The first evidence of a Muslim presence dates from the early days of the Dutch settlement in the area around Cape Town in 1652-62. They came as slaves and political prisoners from Indonesia. The most famous political prisoner was Sheik Yusuf of Macassar who was banished to the Cape in 1694. A respected leader, he inspired the spread of Islam.

The Muslim presence had a significant influence on early white settlers—the first book written in Afrikaans was the Quran. Initially Muslims mixed with the white and indigenous black population masters on an intimate level. It is largely the descendants of this initial integration of the white, African and Asian people that make up the present "Coloured" population, which is still based predominantly in the Western Cape area.

A second wave of Muslims arrived in the late 19th and early 20th centuries. The majority were traders from India, who settled in Durban and Pietermaritzburg in Natal and in the Pretoria/Witwatersrand/Vaal metropolitan area of the Transvaal. In the past decade an increasing number of blacks have converted to Islam (full translations of the Quran are available in Zulu and Xhosa); nevertheless blacks still comprise a small proportion of the total Muslim population.

Although legislation relating to racial ownership and occupation of land was repealed in June 1991, the population effectively remains divided into the racial groups, with Indian Muslims separated from Coloured Muslims. However, religious freedom has been tolerated and Muslims have been free to observe their faith. In the late 1980s the government indicated its willingness to recognize certain aspects of Quranic law (for example, polygamy) in an effort to co-opt the Muslim community in a period of growing political turbulence.

Although Muslim governments abroad have been slow to endorse the Islamic movement in

South Africa, the Saudi Arabia-based Islamic Development Bank (IDB) is known to have sponsored projects, apparently of a missionary nature.

Islam and the state: developments in the era of apartheid

The Muslim community has a long and prominent history of struggle against the government. As early as 1882 Muslims launched protests against health measures which they believed threatened the practice of their religion. However, the involvement of the community in the struggle against white-minority rule, far out of proportion to its size, only dates from the 1948 electoral victory of the National Party and the implementation of its policy of apartheid.

In the late 1950s and early 1960s large numbers of Muslims were forcibly removed from their homes (and consequently their mosques) under the terms of the Group Areas Act. This, as well as the other effects of apartheid, resulted in the increasing politicization of the Muslim community.

From the 1960s the focus of several Islamic organizations expanded to include not only the defence of their faith and culture but also the fight for political rights. However, the development of a united Muslim front in this period was precluded by the competing claims of conservative and progressive organizations. By the mid-1970s student radicalism had ensured a leading role in the struggle against apartheid of a number of prominent youth movements. A Muslim newspaper, *Muslim News*, launched in 1975 (published fortnightly until June 1986), sought to project a radical image of Islam while also promoting the politics of Black Consciousness. In 1980 Muslims affiliated to the Pan African Congress (PAC) launched the country's foremost Muslim political organization, **Direction of Prayer** (*Qiblah*).

Some of these Muslim groups played a leading role in the campaign against the 1984 Constitution, ensuring that the turnout in elections for the Indian and Coloured chambers remained extremely low.

Although basically opposed to white minority rule, differences in ideology have proved a source of tension between Islamic groups; the traditional Islamic scholars (*ulama*), for example, have regularly denounced radical Muslim opposition to apartheid, claiming that "in Islam there is no such thing as Muslim radicalism". At present South African Muslims are divided in their loyalties to the leading Muslim organizations, notably the NDM-affiliated **Call of Islam** and the more radical *Qiblah* and **Muslim Youth Movement** (MYM).

The contribution made to the anti-apartheid movement by the Muslim community was recognized by ANC president Nelson Mandela in 1991. He praised the community for the sacrifices it had made in the struggle against apartheid and pledged that the ANC would defend the rights of Muslims.

Meanwhile, indications that the political weight of South African Muslims was likely to increase in future appeared to be confirmed after South Africa became in November 1989 one of the first countries to ban the novel *The Satanic Verses* by the Indian-born British writer Salman Rushdie.

TJ

Major Islamic organizations

Al-Hidayah Da'wa Movement (AHDM)
Founded in 1982 with headquarters in the Western Cape.

Call of Islam
The most prominent Muslim organization, founded in 1983, but not to be confused with the defunct umbrella organization of the same name launched in Cape Town in May 1961 under the leadership of Imam Abdullah Haroon, to which it is unrelated. A member of the National Democratic Movement (NDM), it looks to South African, rather than external Islamic tendencies. The organization has close links with the MJC, some of whose members played a key role in its formation. It believes that the survival of Islam in a post-apartheid society depends on incorporation within the liberation struggle.
Leader. The movement's most prominent spokesman is Maulana Farid Esack.
Membership. Membership concentrated in the Western Cape.
Aims. The creation of a "non-racial, non-sexist, democratic and just South Africa".
Publications. Call of Islam.

Cape Islamic Federation (CIF)
Youth movement spear-headed by the defunct Claremont Youth Movement, a component of the now extinct Muslim umbrella organization, Call of Islam, established in 1961.

Direction of Prayer
Qiblah
Radical Muslim organization founded in 1980 with headquarters in the Western Cape. Initially intended to be a "mass movement of super-conscious Muslims", it is affiliated to the Pan-Africanist Congress (PAC) with whose militants it is said to have forged links. Several *Qiblah* guerrillas, including their leader, were banned and imprisoned in the late 1980s.
Leader. Ahmed Cassim; *Qiblah* is officially

opposed to the cult of leader, claiming that the South African struggle requires "leadership and not leaders".
Membership. The organization was reported in 1986 to have claimed 2,000 followers.
Aims The promotion of an Islamic revolution in South Africa modelled along Iranian lines.

Holy War
Al-Jihad
A small grouping of Shias active in the Western Cape; part of the NDM. Although inspired by the Iranian revolution, it is primarily committed to the struggle against apartheid.
Aims. The search for solutions to the problems of apartheid from within South Africa.

Islamic Assembly (IA)
Majlis ash Shura al Islami
Conservative religious body, spear-headed by the MJC [see below] in the mid-1960s, with the aim of tackling Muslim educational and social problems.
Leader. Shaikh Shakir Gamildin (president).
Aims. The association's president advocates migration (*hijra*) for any South African Muslim dissatisfied with apartheid.
Publications. Majlis.

Islamic Council of South Africa (ICSA)
Moderate Muslim political organization established in 1975.
Leader. A. Najaar (president).

Islamic Da'wa Foundation (IDF)
Created in 1985 with headquarters in Johannesburg.

Muslim Assembly (Cape) (MA—Cape)
Conservative Muslim organization representing upper-class Muslim professionals, founded in the mid-1960s under the leadership of H. M. Kotwal.

Muslim Judicial Council (MJC)

Founded in the mid-1960s as an organization for traditional Muslim scholars (*ulama*), although its members also include individuals with no juristic training; became an affiliate of United Democratic Front (UDF) in 1983.

Leader. Most of the organization's leaders were dispersed in the mid-1980s; they included Shaikh A.G. Gabier (chairperson); Shaikh Faiq Gamildin; (assistant Secretary) and Shaikh Hassan Solomon.

Muslim Youth Movement (MYM)

Radical youth organization founded in 1970 as a religio-cultural movement; it has, since the late 1980s, assumed an increasingly active role in resisting apartheid. Although the MYM describes its politics as centrist, it is known to have close links with Muslim fundamentalist organizations, including the *Jamaat-e-Islami* in Pakistan and the *Ikhwan-al-muslimun* (Muslim Brotherhood) in Egypt.

Leader. A.R. Omar (president); S. Manjra (vice-president).

Membership. Support for the organization is concentrated in the black township of Soweto, in the Transvaal, the Western Cape and Natal.

Aims. The establishment of "Allah's order in South Africa".

Publications. *Al Qalam* published monthly.

Affiliated organizations. Assalam Educational Institute; Association of Muslim Accountants and Lawyers; Islamic Da'wa Movement founded in 1984 with headquarters in Durban; Islamic Press Movement; Jaame Investments; Muslim Students Association, founded in 1974; South African National Zakat Fund; Women's Islamic Movement.

Spain

Most Muslims in Spain, estimated at around 300,000 in 1991, are first or second-generation immigrants or temporary economic migrants.

Of foreigners legally resident in Spain in 1988, about 12,000 were Moroccans, with smaller numbers from the other Muslim countries of north and north-west Africa.

Total freedom of religious worship was guaranteed in theory in 1967 and has been exercised in practice since 1975. The Constitution does not recognize any religion as the State religion.

Islam reached Spain in 711. The invaders, of Berber and Arab race, known in Spanish as *los Moros* (Moors), established Muslim rule over much of the Iberian peninsula. This period of Moorish cultural hegemony ended with the *Reconquista* of the 13th century as the Christian princes of the north reasserted themselves .

While Jews were expelled from Spain in 1492, Muslims were allowed to remain, although suffering a degree of repression, until an order of expulsion in 1609. In 1614 the last of the *Moriscos* (Spanish Muslims who had been coerced into converting to Christianity) were ordered to leave the country.

Despite the country's long association with Muslim culture, the Muslim presence today is small in terms of both numbers and organization, and much less important than in France. There are some 50 mosques throughout the country and numerous local cultural organizations.

In 1985 tighter immigration laws resulted in the refusal of the right of entry to many would-be immigrants and an increase in the flow of illegal immigrants. In October 1990 Spain signed the Schengen Agreement, abolishing border controls within the European Communities (EC), following which further restrictions were imposed on the number of economic migrants entering the country from north Africa.

From 1989 there have been occasional incidents of racist violence against both non-European immigrants and Spanish gypsies.

EB

Islamic organizations

Association of Moroccan Immigrant Workers in Spain
Asociación de Trabajadores Inmigrantes Marroquíes en España
This group represents the largest national group of foreign workers in Spain. In September 1991 it rallied an estimated 300 Moroccans outside the Moroccan embassy in Madrid in protest against what were seen as the excessive sums charged by embassy officials for the processing of passports.

Initiative for Ceuta
Initiative para Ceuta
Founded in December 1990 to represent Ceuta and Melilla, two Spanish-ruled enclaves on the north coast of Morocco with populations of some 70,000 and 58,000. Both are administratively part of the autonomous government of Andalucia and have sizeable Muslim minorities (in 1990 about 17,000 in Ceuta and 20,800 in Melilla) of both legal and illegal residents. Under the immigration laws of 1985, Muslim residents in these territories who applied to regularize their status would be entitled to Spanish nationality within 10 years.
Leader. Ahmed Subaire (also the leader of the Muslim Community Group of Ceuta).
Aims. To represent the interests of Ceuta's Muslims in local elections.

Islamic Community of Andalucia
Comunidad Islamica en Andalus
Founded in the 1980s by young Andalucians seeking to reassert their Muslim identity. It has sections in Seville, Granada, Malaga and Jerez.

Union of Muslim Students' Associations
Based in Madrid and with sections in most large Spanish cities, its members are mainly foreign Muslim students studying at institutions of higher education.

Sri Lanka

Formerly a British Colony, Sri Lanka became an independent state in 1948 as a Democratic Socialist Republic. Three decades of parliamentarianism were followed by a move to a presidential system after 1977. While the 1978 Constitution confirmed freedom of worship, Buddhism was given the foremost place, with state protection, among the country's religions.

Islam forms one of the island's minority religions. According to the 1981 census, Sunni Muslims predominantly of the Shafi school constituted 7.36 per cent of the population, or 1,134,000 people. Of these, 1,057,000 were Tamil-speakers or Ceylon "Moors"; 43,000 Malays; 29,000 Gujarati-speakers or Indian "Moors" and 5,000 Bohras and Memons of the Shia Ismaili sect.

The term "Moors", derived from "Maurs", was used by the Portuguese in the 16th century to refer to the Muslims of Mauritania (Morocco) and was applied indiscriminately to all Muslims with whom they came in contact, including those inhabiting Sri Lanka. Sri Lankan Muslims of Malay origin were, however, considered a separate group, owing to their distinct ethnic background and culture.

Initially a trading community with links to southern Arabia and South India, Muslims had by the early 16th century settled along the south-west coast of the island. Portuguese rule, which entailed the expulsion in the 16th and 17th centuries of Muslims from their traditional settlements, led to the creation of new Muslim colonies in parts of the island free from Portuguese control, including the interior and the northern and eastern coasts. The resulting proximity to South India explains why most Muslims are more fluent in Tamil than in the language of the majority, Sinhala.

By the time British rule had succeeded in rescinding the policy of discrimination against Muslims in 1832, there were already well-established Muslim settlements concentrated along the east coast (Trincomalee, Batticaloa, Amparai) and relatively large numbers present along the north-west coast (Mannar and Puttalam); in Kandy and in the capital, Colombo, where many Muslims of Malay origin are concentrated.

Muslims have tended to lag behind Sri Lanka's other communities in terms of education; the percentage of Muslims in higher education is lower than their national percentage. Muslim schools, like all schools in Sri Lanka, have been nationalised, but the Muslim school section within the Ministry of Education controls some 200 Muslim primary and high schools.

There is one private Muslim school, the Zahira College, established in Colombo in 1892. There is also a government-run Muslim Ladies' College and one Muslim Training College for teachers in the Eastern Province.

In recent years Muslims have been able to secure financial assistance for religious and educational needs from Muslim states in the Middle East, in large measure through the efforts of the Young Muslim Men's Association (YMMA). The existence of a wide range of social, cultural and educational bodies, including the All Ceylon Muslim Educational Conference, the Moors' Islamic Cultural Home and the Ceylon Moors' League, have ensured that Sri Lankan Muslims retain links with their traditional Islamic heritage.

There are an estimated 2,000 mosques in Sri Lanka with over 60 mosques in Colombo alone. Most are administered by the Religious Endowments (*Awqaf*) Board which is a government department. The Quran has been translated into Tamil and Sinhala.

In the late 1950s and 1960s, foreign exchange shortages led to restrictions being placed on foreign travel which limited the numbers of those performing the pilgrimage to Mecca (*hajj*). In the late 1970s, however, the United National Party (UNP) government removed all restrictions on foreign travel including the *hajj*. Muslims are entitled in matters relating to marriage, divorce, inheritance and religious endowment (*waqf*) to be governed by Muslim personal law.

Islam and the state: developments since independence

Since independence Sri Lanka has experienced fierce ethnic tension resulting in a long-drawn-out and bloody civil war. The main division has been between the majority Buddhist Sinhala-speaking community, and the predominantly Hindu Tamil-speaking minority who resent the special status given both to Buddhism and Sinhala. In 1983 a state of emergency was imposed in response to the guerrilla war against government forces led by Tamil groups.

Sri Lanka Muslims have been directly affected by this ethnic strife, partly as a result of their own ethnic origins and partly as a result of their distribution within the country which places large numbers of Muslims in Tamil-majority areas. On the whole, Muslim relations with the Sinhala Buddhist majority have been much better than with the Hindu Tamil minority with whom they share the same language. This is due largely to the desire of Sri Lankan Muslims to preserve their separate identity, which many believe would be threatened by inclusion within a wider Tamil political entity.

As early as the late 19th century, Muslim and Tamil opinion diverged over the need for separate political representation for Muslims. While Muslims argued for it on grounds of their distinct ethnic and religious identity, Tamil leaders maintained that they were merely Tamil converts to Islam. Sri Lankan Muslims, for their part, have tended to disown their Tamil heritage to the extent of supporting Sinhala as the only official language in the country.

Following the 1956 general election, which resulted in a victory for S. W. Bandaranaike's People's United Front (*Mahajana Eksath Peramuna—MEP*), committed to the revival of Buddhist religion and culture, two important Muslim organizations, the **All-Ceylon Moors' Association** (ACMA) and the All-Ceylon Muslim League (ACML), called for a "Sinhala Only" policy. (Between 1947 and 1956 the ACML had supported the policies of the predominantly Sinhala-based UNP.) The move initiated a process of mutual recrimination between Muslims and supporters of the burgeoning Tamil separatist movement who accused the Tamil-speaking Muslims of collaboration with the majority Sinhalese.

Muslim insecurity in the face of the rapidly evolving political situation was compounded by electoral changes introduced under the 1978 Constitution. Until then constituency arrangements had helped ensure that Muslim candidates were returned roughly in proportion to their percentage of the population; there had always been at least one Muslim minority minister in the government, and the Mayor of Colombo had traditionally been a Muslim. However, following constitutional changes in 1978 Muslims were confronted with a system of proportional representation which effectively reduced the chances of Muslim candidates being elected. Muslim response was to depend on majority, predominantly Sinhala, political parties for their representation. This in turn has defined the nature of Sri Lankan Muslim politics which has tended, on the whole, to shy away from separatism, thus inhibiting the development of a national Muslim organization with a claim to represent all Sri Lankan Muslims.

Meanwhile, both the UNP and the Sri Lanka Freedom Party (SLFP) have been keen to make concessions and include Muslims in their governments largely as a counterweight to the Tamil minority even though this has led at times, such as during the mid-1970s, to riots as a result of anti-Muslim sentiment among Sinhala people.

The growing politicization of Sri Lankan Muslims and complaints by Eastern Province Muslims who alleged that they were being dominated by Western Province Muslim politicians (most Muslim organizations had headquarters in the Western Province) led in 1980 to the creation of a new Muslim party, the **Sri Lanka Muslim Congress** (SLMC) which has taken an active stand in defending the Muslim position in recent Tamil-Muslim conflicts.

In April 1985 simmering tension between Muslims and Tamils in the Eastern Province led to a major outbreak of violence which some national bodies, notably the Department of Muslim Religious Affairs, sought to present as primarily a religious clash. As a result, local Muslims were granted official permission to carry arms in order to defend themselves. Such moves have, however, contributed to escalating violence between the two communities, often resulting in atrocities such as those witnessed in August 1990 when more than 350 Muslims were killed in the Eastern Province, allegedly by the Liberation Tigers of Tamil Eelam (LTTE) in retaliation for Muslim support for the security forces. The SLMC responded by calling on Muslims to arm themselves in self-defence, hinting that the government was unable to provide adequate protection.

Recent attempts to create Muslim pressure groups, including the Islamic Socialist Front (which supported the Sri Lanka Freedom Party—SLFP, while it was in power), and to highlight the grievances specific to Muslims in the Eastern Province, have failed to produce a co-ordinated Muslim approach to Sri Lanka's communal problem or to achieve a more visible Muslim political presence. The SLMC gained only three out of 225 seats in elections to the country's parliament held in February 1989.

SA

Islamic organizations

All-Ceylon Moors Association (ACMA)
Leader. A.R.A. Razik (president).

Muslim United Liberation Front (MULF)
Has operated as a national party since September 1988.

Sri Lanka Muslim Congress (SLMC)
Eastern Province-based Muslim organization founded in 1980; has operated as a national party since 1986.
Leader. M. H. M. Ashraff (president).

Sudan

It is estimated that about 75 per cent of the population of Sudan, totalling 24,000,000, are Muslims concentrated mainly in the northern two-thirds of the country. About 10 per cent are Christians who predominate in the southern states of Bahr al-Ghazal, Upper Nile and Equatoria. The remainder follow traditional African animist religions. More than 100 different languages are spoken by at least 50 different ethnic groups.

Most Muslims in the Sudan follow the Maliki school of Sunni Islam, although some 20 per cent are Ismaili Shias. Historically the influence of the Hanafi school, as followed by some of Egyptian Muslims, has also been important. In the 17th and 18th centuries Arab cultural influences entered from the north, expanding southwards as Muslim leaders went in search of slaves to sustain trade and military expeditions.

The anti-Egyptian Mahdist uprising under Mohammed ibn al-Sayyid Abdullah, known as *al-Mahdi*, which represented one of the most important Malikite *jihad* (holy war) movements in north Africa, began in 1881 as attempt to restore "orthodoxy" to Sudanese Islam. Although supporters of the Mahdi, known as the *Ansar* (companions of the Prophet Muhammad) were subsequently defeated by British forces in the late 19th century, the movement was briefly revived in the 20th century by Sayyid Abd al Rahman al-Mahdi.

Indigenous opposition, both political and sectarian, to the Mahdist movement came from the Sufi Khatmiyyah order which had support among the rural population. Divisions between the Mahdists and their opponents were expressed in the two main political formations of the immediate post-war period: the **National (***Umma***) Party**, which was pro-Mahdist and sympathetic to the British, and the *Ashiqqa* Party which was pro-Khatmiyya and sympathetic to Egypt.

Between 1898 and 1956 Sudan had the status of an Anglo-Egyptian condominium. British administrators who accorded recognition to tribal authorities helped slow the spread of Islam southwards, especially in the period 1930-45. The dilution of an Islamic discourse in the nationalist movement owed much to the secular orientation of the Nationalist Union Party (NUP), established in 1952 which, although pro-Khatmiyyah, did not include Sufi leaders who were reluctant to assume an active political role. (This contrasted with the *Umma* Party which relied on the activist stance of its *Ansar* leadership.)

Islam and the state: developments since independence

The first two decades of Sudanese independence (proclaimed in 1956) were dominated by the NUP (renamed the **Democratic Unionist Party (DUP)** in the 1980s), led by Ismail al-Azhari. Predominantly secular, it intermittently had the support of the Khatimiyyah order which continues to be under the leadership of the Mirghani family, whose members now control the DUP. Opposition to the NUP came primarily from the *Umma* Party.

The weakness of parliamentary politics combined with successive military regimes (1958-64, 1969-85, 1989 onwards) have contributed to the use of Islamic discourse by both civilian and military rulers as the basis of political legitimacy.

Sudan's first military ruler, General Ibrahim Abboud, who seized power in 1958, pursued a policy of Arabization and Islamization in the south as a means of pacification. His regime was, however, criticized as irreligious by the Egyptian-influenced **Muslim Brotherhood** (*Ikhwan al-Muslimun*), one of whose leading members at the time, Hasan al-Turabi, argued for a restoration of democracy. (Later, the *Ikhwan* was to maintain that under Abboud's regime the south had seen benefits in the form of the construction of mosques and Quranic schools.)

In 1964 the *Ikwan*-dominated Islamic movement founded the Islamic Charter Front (ICF), later to become the **National Islamic Front** (NIF). An "Islamic charter" was made public, which omitted previous demands made by the *Ikhwan* including a provision that the head of state should always be a Muslim. The charter also upheld the disassociation of citizenship from religion, and advocated political equality for minorities, especially those in the south.

In national legislative elections in April 1965 the ICF won only seven seats, allowing the *Umma* Party and the NUP to form a coalition government. In July 1966 Sadiq al-Mahdi (leader of the *Umma* Party) became Prime Minister with ICF support. Under pressure from ICF, Mahdi attempted to pursue a comprehensive programme of Islamization.

Meanwhile, constitutional debates during 1966-69 revealed growing national divisions, with some northern groups lobbying for an explicitly Islamic code, and others, represented by southern members of parliament, moving towards closer identification with Christian beliefs and/or political alliances with left-wing groups.

The coup, which brought Jaafar al-Numeiri to power in May 1969, was originally staged by sections of the military reported to have left-wing sympathies and opposed to the *Ikhwan*. However, a left-wing coup against Numeiri in 1971 led him to seek new alliances.

Islamist opposition to the regime demonstrated in *Ikhwan*-led protests against the creation of an autonomous Southern Region in August and September 1973 helped to end the civil war in progress since 1955, and was partially calmed by the provisions of a new Constitution adopted in 1973. It stipulated that Islam was the main source of legislation and endorsed a committee (subsequently established in 1977) to bring existing law in line with the *sharia* (Islamic law).

From 1977, the orientation of Numeiri's regime shifted markedly in favour of the Islamists, permitting the newly founded NIF, representing a breakaway group of the Muslim Brotherhood under Hasan al-Turabi, to join the government for the first time. (A less conciliatory group under Sadiq Abd al Majid continued to function as the Muslim Brotherhood.) Sadiq al Mahdi, leader of the *Umma* Party also joined Numeiri's newly-constituted Sudan Socialist Union (SSU) for a brief period in 1977-78.

In September 1983 Numeiri's "September laws" outlined a revision of the penal code in order to link it "organically and spiritually" with the *sharia* (although non-Muslims would be exempt from Quranic penalties except when convicted of murder or theft). Alcohol and gambling were prohibited, and adultery punished in accordance with Quranic injunctions. In June 1984, the first execution under the new laws took place, with the public hanging of a man convicted of theft.

While southern opinion was strongly opposed to the introduction of the new measures, Muslim leaders in the north also expressed reservations. Sadiq al-Mahdi of the *Umma* Party was arrested and jailed in September 1983 for attacking the reforms. In January 1985 the 80-year-old leader (Mahmud Mohammed Taha) of the **Republican Brothers**, a small Islamic group which advocated a liberal interpretation of Islam, was executed for his opposition to the new laws. In March leaders of the Muslim Brotherhood were also arrested for criticizing the scale of the reforms despite their commitment to Islamization.

Growing popular discontent in March 1985, combined with the disillusionment of Numeiri's erstwhile Islamic allies (Turabi had been arrested and detained in January 1985), formed the background of the military coup which overthrew Numeiri in April 1985. Upon seizing power the new military regime proceeded to revoke much of the Islamic penal code (*hadd*), while leaving intact other parts of Islamic law for fear of provoking a fundamentalist backlash.

Elections supervised by the military in April 1986 resulted in the NIF obtaining almost 20 per cent of the total vote in the northern provinces, winning 51 out of a total of 264 contested seats in the National Assembly. The two largest parties in parliament were the *Umma* Party under Sadiq al Mahdi, which won 99 seats, and the DUP under Muhammad Usman al-Mirghani, which won 64 seats. Much of the south failed to participate in the elections due to the resumption of the civil war.

A new Cabinet took office in May 1986 with Sadiq al-Mahdi as Prime Minister for a second time. The NIF, which joined the ruling coalition from October 1988 until March 1989 with control over key portfolios, ensured that the new government was prevented from further dismantling Islamic laws passed under Numeiri or from adopting a more conciliatory approach to the country's southern problem. In its response to the renewed Islamization drive of 1989 the Sudanese People's Liberation Army (SPLA) had stressed military resistance whilst advocating a federal, secular solution for the whole of the Sudan. In March 1989 the NIF withdrew from the government after opposing plans to delay the introduction of a new Islamic penal code in deference to southern opinion. With the steady disintegration of democracy, the NIF turned to cultivate relations with the armed forces.

A military coup in June 1989 suspended the Constitution, dissolved all political parties and instituted a 15-member Revolutionary Command Council (RCC) under Omar Hassan al-Bashir. Like its predecessors, the new regime sought to initiate its own programme of Islamization. Restrictions on women's freedom to travel unaccompanied were introduced, and dismissals of women from posts in the civil service and the legal profession were reported.

From 1991 Bashir's regime, reportedly with the active complicity of the NIF, heightened its profile as an international leader of radical Islam, whilst internally continuing to issue strict Islamic edicts on dress and the role of women. A new penal code introduced in March 1991, heralded as a more authentic version of *sharia* than that introduced by Numeiri, was not applied in the south. (Numeiri's "September laws" had not been applied in the country since 1985.) In January 1992 the Sudan Catholic Bishops' Conference was ordered by the authorities to withdraw a pastoral letter it had issued the previous November in which it had criticized the treatment of non-Muslims in Sudan.

Foreign press reports in 1991-92 suggested that radical Islamic groups in Algeria, Egypt and Tunisia were receiving support from the Sudanese government. In November 1991 the Tunisian press claimed that in May of that year training camps in Sudan had begun preparing activists from Tunisia, Algeria and elsewhere in the use of small arms and explosives. In December 1991 Iran's President Hashemi Rafsanjani visited the country amid reports that Iran had channelled between US$10,000,000 and US$20,000,000 for Sudan's Islamic revolution.

EB

Major Islamic organizations

Arab People's Islamic Congress (APIC)
Address. Presently unavailable.
Khartoum-based radical international Islamic organization founded in 1991 reportedly as a "revolutionary alternative" to the Islamic Conference Organization (ICO).
Secretary-General. Hassan al-Turabi.

Association of Muslims of Southern Sudan (AMSS)
Created in 1982 under the auspices of the Southern Ministry of Education to represent southern Muslims, mainly from the Nuba group. In 1983 the AMSS found itself isolated in its support for Numeri's "September (1983) laws".
Aims. The promotion of cultural and religious development of the minority Muslim community in the south of Sudan.

Democratic Unionist Party (DUP)
Formerly the Nationalist Union Party (NUP—founded in 1952), the party re-emerged under a new name in 1985; it contested the general election in April 1986, emerging as the second-largest party with 64 seats. The organization was banned along with all other parties following a military coup in June 1989.
Leader. Muhammad Usman al-Mirghani (who also heads the Sufi Khatmiyyah order).
Aims. Recognition of Islam in the Constitution and some identification of the state with Islam.

Islamic Call
Ad-Dawa
Missionary, ostensibly non-political, organization established in the capital, Khartoum, in the early 1980s. In the early 1990s it had the support of the Sudanese government in its humanitarian activities.
Leader. Abd al-Rahman Siwar al-Dhahab (chairman of the council of trustees).
Aims. Its aims outlined in Khartoum in August 1991 included "the establishment of a world fund to assist the needy and to fight poverty . . . [and] to assist refugees and displaced persons without bias or discrimination". The organization also supports the lifting of the international blockade against Iraq.

Islamic Charter Front (ICF)
Founded by Hassan al-Turabi in 1964, it was superseded by the National Islamic Front in 1985. As a member of the ruling coalition from 1977-1985, the Front was officially involved in implementing Numeiri's Islamization reforms, although it subsequently left the government in early 1985 amidst charges of being involved in a coup attempt against Numeiri.

Muslim Brotherhood
Ikhwan al-Muslimun
Fundamentalist organization with its origins in the Egyptian movement of the same name. In the 1940s and 1950s the *Ikhwan* in Sudan was led by Ali Talb-Allah, who had earlier belonged to the pro-Egyptian *Ashiqqa* Party. In the 1950s the *Ikhwan* joined with smaller Islamic groups, including the Islamic Movement for Liberation, to form the Islamic Front for the Constitution (IFC), later to become the Islamic Charter Front (ICF). In 1977 the *Ikhwan* split after a break-away group led by Hassan al Turabi, who

later formed the National Islamic Front (NIF), joined the government of Jafar al Numeiri. *Ikwan* leaders were arrested in March 1985 after opposing aspects of Numeiri's Islamization programme. In the elections of April 1986, the *Ikhwan* backed Turabi's NIF. The *Ikhwan* was subject to a ban on all political parties imposed in June 1989.

Leader. Habir Nur-ud-din.

Membership. Membership is reportedly on the decline, with public perceptions of the organization as an isolated movement of intellectuals who lack contact with ordinary Muslims, frequenting mosques and Quranic schools.

Aims. The creation of an Islamic state in Sudan.

National Islamic Front (NIF)

Fundamentalist organization founded in 1985, following the re-organization of the hitherto Islamic Charter Front (ICF), it is reputed to be the third-largest party after the *Umma* Party and the Democratic Unionist Party (DUP). In April 1986 the party contested legislative elections, winning 20 per cent of votes cast and 51 out of 264 contested seats. Although officially banned in common with all other parties since 1989, the Front has reportedly been involved in directing Islamic reforms initiated by the present government under General Omer Bashir.

Leader. Hassan al-Turabi.

Membership. The Front has a strong following in urban centres (it gained 42 per cent of the seats in the Khartoum area in the 1986 general elections), and is strongly represented in students' unions, winning 24 out 28 seats allocated for university graduates in the same elections.

Aims. The creation of an Islamic state based on the *sharia*. The Front denies that it is opposed to democracy, maintaining that Islam is a religion of consensus.

National Party

Umma Party (UP)

Established shortly after World War II as the leading pro-Mahdist party, it succeeded the National Unionist Party (NUP) to emerge at the forefront of Sudanese politics. As the largest party in the country, it led coalition governments in 1966-69, and again in 1986-89 after it emerged victorious in general elections held in April 1986. In 1989, following a military coup which brought the regime of General Omer Bashir to power, the party was banned and remains proscribed.

Leader. Sadiq al Mahdi (president), also communal leader of *Ansar* who formed the backbone of the Mahdist movement in the 19th and 20th centuries.

Aims. The party subscribes to an Islamic programme with some identification of the state with Islam, although it has repeatedly stressed its opposition to the strict fundamentalism espoused by the NIF and its allies in the *Ikhwan*.

Republican Brothers

Modernist Muslim grouping advocating a liberal interpretation of Islam. It rose to prominence in 1985 after its 80-year-old leader, Mahmud Muhammad Taha, was executed for opposing Islamic reforms introduced by Numeiri.

Surinam

Surinam, which has the highest percentage of Muslims of any South American state, was a former Dutch colony which gained its independence from the Netherlands, after a period of autonomy, in 1975. Surinam's post-colonial history has not, however, been one of stability. The original independence Constitution was suspended in February 1980 following two military coups. Constitutional government was resumed in 1987 to be followed by a further military coup in December 1990.

Surinam is characterized by ethnic diversity. The ethnic composition of the population according to the 1980 census consisted of Creoles (34.7 per cent); descendants of East Indians (33.5 per cent); Indonesians (16.3 per cent); Bush Negroes (*Boschneger*) (9.6 per cent); Amerindians, Chinese, European and others (5.9 per cent).

Of the total population, an estimated 42 per cent are Christian, 27 per cent Hindu and between 20 and 30 per cent Muslim, of whom the majority are Sunni adhering to the Shafi school of law. The percentage of Muslims in Surinam has risen dramatically during the last two decades. In 1982 there were estimated to be about 150,000 Muslims, representing about 30 per cent of the total population. Around 90,000 were of Javanese descent and approximately 50,000 of Indian origin, the remainder being of African and other origins.

The increase in the Muslim population (21.4 per cent in 1964) has been attributed to a high birth rate, immigration and conversion to Islam. This increase is believed also to have been boosted by the emigration of non-Muslims; some 63,000 are reported to have left the country between 1964 and 1971, similar numbers migrated abroad after 1974 and following the turmoil of the 1980s.

The first Muslims to arrive in Surinam were slaves of African origin, brought over by the Dutch during the 1660s. The harshness of living and working conditions largely prevented them from preserving their Islamic heritage. However, as in Trinidad and Tobago, there has recently been a revival of interest in Islam among those of African descent.

Muslim immigration in the form of indentured labour began after the abolition of slavery by the Dutch in 1863. From the early 1870s up until 1918, around 34,000 migrants from the Indian sub-continent arrived in Surinam, including 6,000 Sunni Muslims who belonged mainly to the Hanafi school. Some of the descendants of these Muslims went on to join the professional classes and occupy positions in the civil service.

Indentured labourers, many of them Muslims, came also from Java. Between 1850 and 1940 some 33,000 Javanese were brought to Surinam, the great majority belonging to the Shafi school. Many worked as rice farmers, fishermen and labourers in the plantations and bauxite industries; their socio-economic position tending to be less fortunate than that of their Indian counterparts.

Javanese and Indian Muslims have, on the whole, been more successful in retaining their Muslim identity than the descendants of African slaves, perhaps because of their relative economic strength. However, ethnic and linguistic differences have hindered their greater integration reflected symbolically in disagreements centring on the direction of Mecca, the Javanese praying eastward, the Indians, westward.

Between 1969 and 1973 Muslim politicians assumed a prominent role under the aegis of a Hindustani (Asian-descended "East" Indians) government; in 1973 there were two Muslim ministers out of 13, while eight out of the 39 members of the Legislative Council were Muslim. Since then, guerrillas belonging to the **Surinamese Liberation Army** (SLA or Jungle Commando), composed mainly of Bush Negroes (many of whose ancestors were Muslims), have been engaged in continuous confrontation with the government. The SLA has not, however, been known to espouse any features of an Islamic political agenda.

Surinam has around 70 mosques, the oldest dating from 1932 in the capital, Paramaribo, where an estimated 7,000 Javanese are said to reside. There are around 20 Quranic schools and three full-time Muslim schools.

MCB

Islamic organizations

Federation of the Islamic Communities of Surinam
Federatie Islamitsche Gemeenten in Surinam (FIGS)
An umbrella organization designed to oversee different Muslim bodies in Surinam.
Leader. K. Kaaiman (chair).

Surinamese Islamic Council
Surinaamse Islamitsche organizatie
This association was formed in 1978 after a split in FIGS.
Leader. I. Jamaludin (president); C Hasrat (secretary).
Structure. The Council has six branches.

Surinamese Liberation Army (SLA, or Jungle Commando)
A rebel force composed predominantly of Bush Negroes (*Boschneger*) who are the descendants of escaped slaves, many of whom are Muslims, and who live a separate existence in the isolated interior. Motivated by a fear of enforced urbanization and by opposition to the military regime, there is no explicitly Muslim ideology motivating their guerrilla war.
Leader. Ronnie Brunswijk.

Surinamese Muslim Association
Surinaamse Moeslem Associatie
Formed in 1929.
Leader. A. Abdoelbashire (chair).

Sweden

Official estimates released in January 1991 indicated that the number of Muslims in Sweden totalled some 45,000, the majority of whom are migrant workers from Turkey, the Middle East and north Africa. Muslims of Tatar origin form a sizeable minority as do Muslims from Yugoslavia.

In 1948 Muslims in Sweden formed the Islamic Union of Sweden (IUS) which was subsequently re-organized in 1973 and 1975 to form the United Muslim Community of Sweden (UMCS) with branches in Stockholm, Malmö, Göteborg, Eskilstuna, Jönköping, Västeraas, Mariestad and Tröllhatten.

In 1979 Islam was officially accorded the same legal status as other "recognized" religions, entitling Muslims to state assistance in matters relating to Muslim religious instruction in public schools and to emoluments for Muslim religious officials.

The *Imam* of the Islamic League of Sweden (ILS), Haytham Rahman, visited Iraq in October 1990 to convey the support of Swedish Muslims for the Iraqi government's attempts to find a peaceful solution to the Gulf crisis.

FS

Syria

Formerly part of the Ottoman Empire, Syria was occupied by France in 1920 under a League of Nations mandate. It gained full independence in 1946.

Syria is characterized by religious homogeneity. Ninety per cent of the population, estimated in 1989 at 11,719,000, is of Arab origin, with Kurds, Armenians, Turks, Circassians and Assyrians making up the remainder. The vast majority (75 per cent) of the population are Sunni Muslims who follow the Hanafi school of law; around 10 per cent are Twelver Shias (following the *ithna ashariyya* school), and a further 10 per cent are Alawites, a Shia sub-sect whose members control political and economic power [see below]. Druze and Shia Ismaili sub-sects make up the remaining 5 per cent of the population.

Islam and the state: developments since independence

The Ba'ath Arab Socialist Party was founded in 1947 to support social and economic reform and greater Arab unity through the idea of pan-Arabism. A Ba'athist-supported junta seized control in 1963 and the Ba'ath Party has since dominated Syrian politics. The military wing of the party, led by President General Hafez al-Assad, seized power in November 1970.

Ba'athism is avowedly secular, regarding Islam as little more than an earlier manifestation of the Arabist spirit which it celebrates. The Constitution, adopted in 1973, while providing that "Islam shall be the religion of the head of state" (a clause inserted only after public protest forced the amendment of an original draft), makes no mention of Islam as the religion of the state itself. Syria is thus unique among Arab states in not recognizing Islam as the State religion.

The secularist tendencies of the Ba'ath party soon alienated Syria's traditional Islamic leadership, the (*ulama*). In 1967 a leading cleric, Shaikh Hasan Habannakah, president of the League of *Ulama*, who organized demonstrations in protest against an article in an army magazine, denounced the government as "godless". In Aleppo another cleric, Shaikh Muhammad Abu al Nasr al-Bayanuni, founded the militant *Jamaat ad Dharr*. In 1973 Islamic law (*sharia*) court judges fought to introduce Islamic provisions into the Constitution. In turn the regime has sought to tighten its grip on the mainly Sunni Muslim religious establishment through its Ministry of Religious Endowments (*awqaf*) whose personnel grew from 298 in 1962 to 2,759 in 1978.

The strongest political opposition to the regime has come from radical Sunni fundamentalist groups allied to the **Muslim Brotherhood** (*Ikhwan al-Muslimun*). They offered fierce resistance to the regime's attempts to suppress their activities in 1964 and 1965, and again in 1973 and 1976. Resistance was at a peak during 1979, 1980 and, most notably, with the Hamah uprising of February 1982.

Radical Islamic opposition to the regime has stemmed not only from resentment of the Ba'ath Party's monopoly of the higher echelons of the civilian and military bureaucracy, but also from anger at the control of the state and security apparatus by the Alawites.

In the late 1960s and early 1970s the Ba'ath party built up a powerful network extending into trade, agriculture and industry. State-sponsored agricultural and trading co-operatives adversely affected the interests of the large trading and artisan community which by the early 1970s accounted for at least one-sixth of the population. Radical Sunni Muslim groups are believed to have recruited supporters from these urban trading and artisan classes, deprived of a legitimate political platform.

In 1973 *Ikhwan* supporters were involved in bloody clashes with police after demonstrators demanded that the Constitution explicitly recognize Islam as the State religion.

In the mid-1970s, however, Assad embarked on a policy of "rectification" which, while broadening the economy to allow greater business opportunities for the mainly Sunni urban bourgeoisie, resulted in social and cultural dislocation which greatly encouraged Muslim fundamentalist activity. At the same time the regime attempted to counter charges of "atheism" levelled against it by religious parties by securing a ruling (*fatwa*) in 1973 from the spiritual leader of Lebanon's Twelver Shia community, Imam Musa Sadr (later to found the Syrian-backed *Amal* movement), that declared Alawites to be authentic Shias.

From the mid-1970s the *Ikhwan* intensified its opposition to the regime, organizing a series of public protests and strikes in schools and commercial centres in the northern cities of Hamah and Aleppo. Support for the movement increased substantially among the student population, believed to have formed the basis of the movement's "youth wing".

In February 1982 the regime finally, and ruthlessly, clamped down on the movement after it organized a bloody insurrection in Hamah which led to the deaths of thousands of people and the destruction of whole quarters of the city. Although supporters of the movement appealed for sympathizers to stage similar uprisings elsewhere in the country, most areas failed to respond, leading observers to suggest that the *Ikhwan* had been unable to reach beyond the communities of Sunnis in the cities of Aleppo and Hamah.

With the *Ikhwan* effectively decimated, the regime sought the firm implementation of Law 49, making membership of or association with the movement punishable by death. Signs that the *Ikhwan* had partially revived appeared after supporters of the movement were blamed for an assassination attempt on Assad in 1987.

Indications that the regime no longer regards the Muslim Brotherhood as a serious threat appeared to be confirmed in January 1985 when Assad declared an amnesty for some members of the *Ikhwan* imprisoned in Syria and invited those in exile to return to the country. In December 1991 Assad ordered a further amnesty for almost 3,000 political prisoners, many of them activists belonging to the Brotherhood.

EW

Major Islamic organizations

Islamic Front in Syria

Umbrella organization formed in 1980 for independent militant groups including the *Jammat ad Dharr*, the Islamic Liberation Party and sections of the League of *Ulama* as well as the *Ikhwan*.

Leader. Shaikh Ali Sadr ad Din al-Bayanuni. In 1982 the organization split after a group led by Adnan Uqla broke away in protest at the Front's alliance with Iraq which the group deemed to be a secular state in conflict with the only truly Islamic republic.

Aims. In 1981 two documents published by the Front, the Proclamation and Programme of the Islamic Revolution in Syria and the Charter of the Islamic Front in Syria, spelled out its objectives, stressing the creation of a united front to overthrow the Ba'athist regime and the establishment of an Islamic state.

Publication. Since 1980 the *Ikhwan's* organ, *an-Nadhir*, has been used.

Muslim Brotherhood

Ikhwan al-muslimun

Proscribed Sunni fundamentalist group established in the late 1930s as an offshoot of its Egyptian counterpart by Mustafa as-Siba'i. Originally based in the city of Aleppo, the organization moved its headquarters to Damascus in 1944 and formally adopted its present name in 1945. The movement has a consistent record of opposition to the Ba'athist regime which culminated in its brutal suppression following its involvement in an insurrection in the city of Hamah in February 1982.

Leader. Issam al-Attar (who replaced as-Sibai in 1957). A leadership crisis in 1969 split the organization into rival factions: a moderate group based in Damascus and loyal to al-Attar, and a more radical group, based in Aleppo and Ladhaqia and advocating holy war (*jihad*). This latter group elected Adnan Saad ad-Din as general supervisor in 1975, Ali Sadr ad Din al-Bayanuni as deputy supervisor, and Said Hawwa (a leading cleric) as "chief ideologue". Husni Abu headed the faction's military wing until the late 1970s when he was succeeded by Adnan Uqla. (The leadership underwent a similar crisis in the 1960s after a Hamah-based militant leader, Marwan Hadid (d. 1976), won allegiance from *Ikhwan* members as the head of a fighting faction named *al Talia al-Muqatilah*.)

Membership. The movement has strong support in urban centres, including Damascus, Aleppo and Hamah, and is popular among students: out of 1,384 militants arrested by the government between 1976 and 1981 more than 27 per cent were students.

Aims. The creation of an Islamic state. (The leadership has been divided over whether or not this involves a violent holy war (*jihad*) against the Ba'athist regime.)

Funding. Financial support has reportedly come from Jordan, where leaders established headquarters and training camps after fleeing Syria in the 1970s and 1980s. During the 1982 Hamah uprising Iraq provided sanctuary, arms and money to *Ikhwan* activists, while the organization persuaded Kuwait to cut off subsidies to the Syrian government in protest against its crackdown on activists after the Hamah uprising. The Turkish National Salvation Party and the Palestine Liberation Organization are also alleged to have provided financial and material support. During the 1960s Saudi Arabia was a major source of funding.

Publication. an-Nadhir.

Taiwan

The government of Taiwan is derived from that which ruled the Chinese mainland prior to the 1949 Communist revolution; Taiwan maintains its claim to legal jurisdiction of this lost territory and continues to designate itself as the Republic of China.

The majority of the population follow traditional Chinese popular religions and, often at the same time, Buddhism and Taoism. There are less than 60,000 adherents of Islam in Taiwan. However, all religions, including Islam, are generally encouraged by the government in order to contrast with the anti-religious orientation of the Communist mainland.

There are no known Muslim organizations on the island.

DS

Tajikistan

(For a broad survey of Islam in the former Soviet Union see separate entry for the Commonwealth of Independent States)

The Tajik republic was formed in 1929—having been part of Uzbekistan since 1924—following the division of Turkestan. Of the population of 5,100,000, 62 per cent are Tajiks. Minority nationalities include Uzbeks (23 per cent) and Russians (7 per cent). There are smaller minority groups of Tatars, Kirgiz and Ukrainians. The republic has the lowest income per head of all the CIS member states, and the highest birthrate (41.8 per 1,000 population in 1987 compared to 34.8 per 1,000 in 1970). The infant mortality rate is also among the highest at 48.9 per 1,000 births in 1987.

Tajiks are Sunni Muslims of the Hanafi school. They are unique among the Muslims of the Commonwealth of Independent States (CIS) in speaking a Persian rather than a Turkic language. There are some Shi'ite communities among the Mountain Tajiks (Pamirs), living in the Gorno-Badakhshan Autonomous Administrative Region (*oblast*) of Tajikistan (which in January 1992 was attempting to gain the status of an Autonomous Republic).

The number of mosques is growing rapidly; the *Far Eastern Economic Review* of January 1992 estimated that the number of mosques in Tajikistan had grown from 17 in 1989 to 2,870, with new ones opening daily. In contrast, the number of churches has remained a steady 19. This trend has prompted some commentators to suggest that Tajikistan is the most likely candidate for an Islamic state among existing Muslim republics.

Tajikistan shares a border with Afghanistan, where there are some 2,000,000 Tajiks. Refugees from the Afghan war have settled in the Tajik capital, Dushanbe, and the Afghan *mujaheddin* control the entire border with Tajikistan on the Afghan side, posing the threat of Islamic fundamentalist influence for the Tajik government.

Following the attempted coup of August 1991, Tajikistan was the scene of a power struggle between the republican Communist Party of Tajikistan (CPT), which controlled the Supreme Soviet (parliament), the democrats and Islamic groups. Suspicion that the CPT had supported the coup attempt led to a confused period in autumn 1991, as suspension of the CPT was repeatedly imposed and lifted. Meanwhile, pressure by the Union of Democratic Forces (UDF) led eventually to a lifting of the ban on religious parties in the republic, including the **Islamic Renaissance Party of Tajikistan** (IRPT) banned in late 1990. The Tajik branch of the All-Union IRP held its inaugural congress on Oct. 26, 1991, and discussed independent status [see below].

Presidential elections held in November secured a victory (with 58 per cent of the vote) for the former republican CPT First Secretary, Rakhmon Nabiyev, who had served under Leonid

Brezhnev from 1982 to 85. The democratic candidate Davlat Khudonazarov, who was supported by the IRPT after its preferred candidate Qazi Akbar Toradzhon Zadeh withdrew from the contest, came second with 34 per cent of the vote. Suspicion among rival parties intensified after supporters of Khudonazarov, who included the Qazi, contested the outcome of the elections.

Simmering tension between the government and Islamic groups erupted in May 1992 after Islamic demonstrators in Dushanbe called for the removal of the parliamentary Speaker Safarli Kenjayev, a prominent member of the hardline Communist heirarchy. In a move regarded by some observers as significant, Qazi Toradzhon Zadeh was also reported to have come out in favour of the opposition despite his hitherto known reluctance to endorse the Islamic movement in Tajikistan.

By mid-May increasing pressure by opposition forces forced Nabiyev to concede a third of the posts in a newly formed coalition government to opposition parties including the IRP, and to promise fresh elections.

The latest protests also fuelled speculation that the success of the Tajik-led Afghan *mujaheddin* across the border would breed new demands for a "Greater Tajikistan", comprising parts of northern Afghanistan and the republic.

WS

Islamic organizations

Islamic Renaissance Party of Tajikistan (IRPTa)
Nazdate Islamiye Takzhikistan
In existence since June 1990; founding congress of Tajik branch of IRP held in October 1990, after which the party was banned for a year. At its inaugural congress held on October 26, 1991, the IRPT discussed the possibility of assuming independent status.
Leader. Mohammed Sharif Khimmat Zade. Dubbed by his followers as the Gulbuddin Hekmatyar of Central Asia, after the Afghan *mujaheddin* leader, he spent 15 years working underground for the IRP.
Membership. Estimated to be 20,000.
Aims. The protection of Muslim rights and Islamic spiritual revival; to make Islam the state religion by parliamentary means. The IRP's coalition with the non-Islamic Democratic Party of Tajikistan (TDP) is reportedly designed to prevent the emergence of "Islamic Communism" i.e. the endorsement of Islamic politics by ex-Communists in return for their stay in power.

Qaziat
Republican equivalent of muftiyat, headed by Qazi (Tajik—*Kazikalon*) Akbar Toradzhon Zadeh, official leader of Islam in the republic, second only in status to the Mufti of Tashkent in the official Islamic hierarchy, appointed in 1988. A member of the Supreme Soviet, the Qazi is said to have built up an alliance between the *Qaziat*, the IRP and Sufi spiritualists. The Qazi is publicly opposed to an Islamic state claiming the separation of religion from politics.

Rebirth People's Front
Rastokhez
The organization grew out of a discussion group initiated in February; its founding congress was held in January 1991.
Leader. Takhir Abdudjaborov.
Aims. To promote Tajik nationalism.

Tanzania

Tanzania was formed in 1964 by the union of Zanzibar (a former British protectorate, briefly independent in 1963-64) with Tanganyika, itself independent since 1961 (having been a German colony, subsequently a Britishmandated territory and then a UN Trust Territory).

At independence the country's sole legal political party was the Revolutionary Party of Tanzania (*Chama Cha Mapinduzi*—CCM). However, in January 1992 the National Executive Committee (NEC) of CCM, the country's supreme policy-making body, unanimously accepted a proposal to end 27 years of one-party rule and recommended that the Constitution be adjusted to allow for the registration of political parties. It also proposed that legislation on political parties should include stipulations that all parties should be national organizations, embracing both sides of the union (ie. mainland Tanzania and Zanzibar), and that they should not divide people along ethnic, religious or racial lines.

More than 97 per cent of the population of Zanzibar (estimated in 1988 at 625,000) and about a third of the population of mainland Tanzania (estimated in 1988 at 23,372,000) are Muslim. Although Muslims are widely dispersed among the country's numerous ethnic groups, the greatest concentrations are to be found in coastal areas.

The present Muslim population is divided into indigenous Muslims of African origin, and two established immigrant communities of Arab and Indian sub-continental origin. The Muslims of African origin are all Sunni Muslims observing Shafi rites. Among Muslims of Arab origin, those from Oman are Ibadites; the rest are Sunnis who played an important role in the conversion of the local population and helped develop Swahili, the national language, which is a mix of Arabic and local dialects. The majority of Muslims from India and Pakistan are Shia Ismailis (represented by the Ismalia Provincial Church); a minority are Sunni.

Of a number of brotherhoods operating, the Qadiriyyah and the Shadhiliyyah are the two largest, although their importance is minimal compared with their influence in West Africa.

The first evidence of Islam dates from the 10th century when the coast of present-day Tanzania was dominated by a line of Muslim city-states, established as a result of the development of Arab trading routes. However, Islamic penetration into the interior of the country took place only during the colonial period. Under German rule the Muslim coastal population received a degree of education, and by the beginning of the 20th century the influence of these newly-educated Muslim clerks had become evident in the interior.

Islam and the state: developments since independence

Until recently there was little evidence of tension either within the Muslim community or between Christian and Muslim communities. Although Julius Nyerere, the country's President until 1985, was a devout Catholic, Muslims have always been represented in the government, generally occupying at least one-quarter of cabinet places. When Nyerere stood down as President, he was succeeded by Ali Hassan Mwinyi, a Muslim from Zanzibar.

From the beginning of 1992, however, there were indications of Muslim resentment, prompted in part by government plans to reduce public spending by placing the country's health and education system under the control of the Catholic Church. The latest measures also fuelled protests from the radical Islamic group, the **Council for the Propagation of the Quran in Tanzania** (CPQT—*Balukta*), which had risen to prominence as a fierce critic of both Muslim religious establishment and the Catholic Church.

In January 1992 *Balukta* accused representatives of the **National Muslim Council of Tanzania** (NMCT—*Bakwata*) of corruption, and criticized its attempts to promote Islam. *Balukta* members later occupied *Bakwata* headquarters which prompted *Bakwata's* leadership to appeal to President Mwinyi, who eventually backed *Bakwata*.

Conflict within the Muslim community was paralleled by growing friction between Muslims and Christians. In March 1992 a leading mosque in the capital, Dar es Salaam, was reported to have broadcast anti-Christian sermons triggering riots between Christian and Muslims youths.

TJ

Major Islamic organizations

Council for the Propagation of the Quran in Tanzania (CPQT)
Balukta
Militant Muslim organization opposed to the Muslim religious establishment.
Leader. Shaikh Yahya Hussein.

Mosque Council of Zanzibar
Founded in 1981, it is the chief supervisory body responsible for Islamic affairs in Zanzibar.
Leader. Shaikh Ameir Tajo Ameir (Chief Kadhi—*qadi*, judge).

National Muslim Council of Tanzania (NMCT)
Bakwata
Founded in 1969 and based in Dar es Salaam; it supervises Islamic affairs on the mainland only.
Leader. Shaikh Hemed bin Juma bin Hemed (chair); Gen. Alhaj Adam B. Nasib (secretary-general).
Publications. Muslamu, a monthly journal with a circulation of 10,000.

Thailand

Unlike the other states of south-east Asia, Thailand was free from colonial rule. In 1932 a European-educated, civilian-military group carried out a successful and bloodless coup d'etat which removed the country's absolute monarchical system. Thailand has subsequently been ruled by a succession of military governments, interspersed by short periods of democratic civilian rule. In February 1991 the armed forces toppled the elected government of Chatichai Choonhaven in the country's latest bloodless coup.

Thailand is populated by at least 20 different ethno-linguistic groups, of which the Thais are the dominant grouping. Theravada Buddhism is the predominant religion, professed by over 90 per cent of the country's total population.

Of the 2,000,000 or so Muslims, representing about 4 per cent of the population, the majority live in the south, mainly in the provinces bordering Malaysia, namely Yala, Satun, Narathiwat and Pattani. There are also small pockets of ethnic Thais (Thai Islam) in the central region, and groups of foreign, mainly Pakistani, Muslims in Bangkok and other urban centres.

Over 99 per cent of Thai Muslims are Sunni. The head of the Muslim establishment in Thailand, the Shaikh al Islam (*Chularajamontri*), Haji Praset Mohammad, enjoys semi-official status.

Organizational developments in the Muslim community

A Malay-Muslim minority in the south, neglected by the authorities in Bangkok and looking to Malaysia for support, have long sought autonomy or independence. For decades Muslim insurgents in the region have engaged in a low-level war with the Thai army.

During the 1980s the army successfully contained the Muslim threat in the south, virtually eliminating the threat of separatist movements in the region. Muslim opposition in the early 1990s was centred mainly among the poor, the unemployed and young intellectuals.

Muslim disaffection in the south has tended to focus on demands for a fairer share of economic and political benefits rather than on support for outright separatism or a commitment to Islamic principles. (Muslims in the south were largely detached from the economic boom enjoyed by Thailand in the 1980s and resented Buddhist domination of the higher echelons of local administration and education.) Nevertheless, the desire for greater regional autonomy has remained strong, especially in Pattani, and since the late 1980s there has been a renewed interest in Islamic fundamentalism, especially among the young.

A series of protests in the south during the mid-1980s awakened fears over Shia-sponsored separatism. Rallies organized by the Iranian-educated Shia leader, Sorayuth Sakulnasantisat, in Pattani and Yala were attended by large, and often unruly, crowds. Sorayuth, who was alleged to have had links in the past with sections of the army, had reportedly been travelling throughout the southern provinces for two years building up a network of followers. He was reported to have fled to Malaysia in 1982 when a warrant was issued for his arrest after he had delivered a fiery, pro-separatist speech at Pattani's Kruze mosque, itself a source of ethnic and religious conflict.

A number of Islamic separatist movements operated in the southern provinces during the 1960s, 1970s and 1980s. The Thai army launched a series of successful campaigns against the separatists in the 1980s, and by the end of the decade many of the movements had descended into banditry.

The principal Muslim-dominated movement was the Pattani United Liberation Organization, established in 1960, which carried out a daring bomb attack during a visit to Yala province by the King of Thailand, Bhumivol Adulyadej (Rama IX), in 1977.

Other movements included the National Revolutionary Front, the Pattani Islamic Nationalities' Revolutionary Party, the Pattani National Liberation Front, the Thai Muslim People's Liberation Armed Force and the Sabillillah Movement.

DS

Trinidad and Tobago

Trinidad and Tobago, a former British colony invaded by British forces in 1797, became independent in August 1962. A republic, the islands have been members of the Commonwealth since 1962, after being part of an autonomous federation of the West Indies along with Jamaica, Barbados and the Leeward and Windward Islands.

The islands have a tradition of democracy; free elections have been held successfully every five years since 1956.

Trinidad and Tobago is one of the most ethnically diverse societies in the Caribbean region. Around 40 per cent of its population is of African descent, 40 per cent of Indian origin, 14 per cent of mixed races and 3 per cent of Chinese and European origin.

About 6 per cent of Trinidad and Tobago's estimated population of 1,300,000 are Muslims of Asian and African descent. (Some estimates suggest that the proportion of Muslims could be as high as 13 per cent.)

The first wave of Muslim migrants to Trinidad and Tobago came from Africa as slaves. On the whole, descendants of this African community have not retained their allegiance to Islam, although Black Islam is currently enjoying a renaissance [see below]. In 1982 about 10,000 of the nation's 160,000 Muslims were of African origin.

East Indian Muslim immigrants came to the Islands following the abolition of slavery within the British Empire and the subsequent introduction of indentured labour into the colony. This phase of immigration continued from the 1830s and 1840s until the early 20th century. Muslims within this East Indian community have retained their Muslim identity, although most speak English and have integrated into the wider community without great friction. They are concentrated mostly in the Southern part of Trinidad.

At the end of the 19th century the Islands accepted, along with other nations in the Caribbean, Muslim migrants from "greater Syria" (Lebanon and Syria). This group, though not great in number, has a strong entrepreneurial culture.

Islam and the state: developments since independence

As a relatively minor part of the islands' total population, Muslims have not enjoyed great political influence in Trinidad and Tobago since independence. Traditionally the East Indian population, Hindu and Muslim, has lent its support to opposition parties. The United Labour Front (ULF), an alliance of petroleum and sugar workers, as well as the United National Congress (UNC) led by Basdeo Panday, are two opposition groups which have received support from the East Indian rural community concentrated in the south and west of Trinidad.

The People's National Movement (PNM), traditionally the governing party which ruled continuously from 1956-86, has drawn its support from the black Christian majority.

This picture of a relatively apolitical Muslim community, restricted to an East Indian minority, was challenged in the late 1980s by the resurgence of Muslim militancy within the black African community. (Evidence of a burgeoning black power movement had first emerged in April 1970 after members of a group known as "Black Power" were involved in a failed coup attempt.) Emerging as an offshoot of the North American Black Power movement, black Muslim militants sought to marry Islam and black power doctrines. Its most spectacular political manifestation lay in an abortive coup in July 1990, staged by members of the relatively little known messianic group, the **Society of Muslims** (*Jamaat al Muslimeen*).

Members of the sect were alleged to have had links with US Muslim radicals loyal to Louis Farrakhan, leader of the Black Muslim Nation of Islam organization, and with Muslim militant groups in Iran and Libya. Reports indicated, in particular, that covertly supplied Libyan money and arms had significantly encouraged the attempted take-over. Other reports highlighted the influence of black Muslim immigrants from Grenada, following the US invasion in 1984, who had allegedly help radicalize the rebel movement.

The attempted coup of 1990

On July 27, 1990, members belonging to the *Jamaat al Muslimeen*, led by a former policeman and national footballer, Imam Yasin Abu Bakr, attempted to overthrow the government of Prime Minister Arthur Robinson with the intention of establishing an Islamic republic. The failure of black Muslim militants to enlist the support of the East Indian Muslim majority was attributed to the latter's adherence to more orthodox and traditional interpretation of Islamic practices.

A group of around 150 armed men seized the parliament building in the capital, Port of Spain, destroyed police headquarters and occupied the state-owned television station. Some 45 people were taken hostage, including Prime Minister Robinson, Cabinet ministers and members of parliament, and 37 police officers died.

The immediate cause of the coup appeared to be a government plan to spend TT$500,000 on a monument commemorating a former civil servant who had fought against corruption. Pointing to the crippling effects on the lives of ordinary people of severe austerity measures imposed by the International Monetary Fund (IMF), the rebels claimed that the government's planned action constituted "the final straw".

The coup attempt was also reportedly triggered by a long-standing conflict between the government and the *Jamaat*, centring on a religious commune established by the *Jamaat* on land originally granted to East Indian Muslims in the 1970s by former Prime Minister Eric Williams. Claiming that the commune harboured criminals (a total of 34 people had been arrested in 1988 on a variety of charges), the government won a court ruling in early July giving it permission to evict the *Jamaat* from the site.

Other reported causes of tension were the killing of sect members allegedly at the hands of the police; the maintenance of a government-sanctioned military presence near the commune and the refusal by the government to accept a consignment of Libyan medical supplies offered by the sect.

The coup failed; the rebels surrendering on August 1, 1990 after allegedly extracting promises of pardon from President Emmanuelle Carter. In December 1991, the Privy Council in London upheld the legal status of the pardon which Trinidadian government lawyers had argued was invalid as it was given under duress.

The coup, which intensified ill-feelings towards black Muslims, triggered reprisals including the shooting of Bakr's step-son in unclear circumstances during a police raid on the Bakr's house in August 1990.

MCB

Islamic Organizations

Anjuman Sunnat ul Jamaat Association (ASJA)

Founded in 1935 as an umbrella organization covering Islamic societies in Trinidad and Tobago. In 1986 this organization claimed to represent the majority of Muslims in Trinidad and Tobago.

Leader. Z. A. Khan (chairman).

Structure. In 1986 the ASJA was divided into 70 branches in four regions; representatives from each branch elect an Executive Committee.

Aims. The management of mosques (estimated in 1986 to number 80 in Trinidad and one in Tobago), and Islamic schools (estimated in 1986 to number 15 full-time primary and three full-time secondary schools).

Society of Muslims

Jamaat al Muslimeen

Religio-political organization representing Muslims predominantly of African origin. Although it rose to prominence following its involvement in an attempted coup in July 1990, the group was known to have incurred government sanctions over its refusal to vacate land west of the capital, Port of Spain, where it had established a commune.

Leader. Imam Yasin Abu Bakr (a name adopted by Lennox Smith following his conversion to Islam).

Membership. Estimated in July 1990 to be around 300, composed mainly of black Islamic converts.

Aims. The creation of an Islamic state founded on principles inspired by the Black American, Nation of Islam in the USA.

Tunisia

An estimated 7,000,000 people, representing 99 per cent of the population of Tunisia, are Sunni Muslims who observe Maliki rites. A small minority, under 50,000, are Ibadites who were formerly concentrated on the southern island of Jerba, but are now dispersed. Sufi brotherhoods, especially the Shadhiliyyah, the Qadiriyyah and the Tijaniyya orders, once important, have now lost their influence.

Islam reached North Africa with the Arab invaders, who in AD 647 defeated Byzantine forces and in successive years overcame Berber resistance. The area of modern-day Tunisia came under Ottoman rule from 1574 until 1883, when it became a French protectorate.

Islam and the state: developments since independence

Since Tunisia's independence from France in 1956 Islam has been the state religion. Although the Constitution requires the head of state to be a Muslim, Tunisian institutions have steadily been secularized and some key Muslim religious practices, notably the observance of ramadan (the month of fasting), officially discouraged.

Under President Habib Bourguiba, leader of the ruling *Neo-Destour* (New Constitution) Party, there was a concerted effort to dissociate religion from the state. Personal statute laws relating to marriage and divorce were secularized; Islamic law (*sharia*) courts liquidated; land used as religious endowments (*habus*) confiscated; the religious Zaituna University brought under the administrative control of Tunis University and restrictions imposed on other Quranic schools.

Although Bourguiba and the leadership of the new government sought to present the changes as aspects of Islamic reform rather than of increasing secularization, there was a distinct sense of alienation among the less affluent and educated classes of society, many of whom allied with some religious scholars (*ulama*) who led anti-government demonstrations in 1960-61.

By the end of the 1960s growing opposition from left-wing parties and the trade union movement prompted the government to adopt a more conciliatory approach towards its erstwhile critics in the religious establishment by softening its stance on religious observances.

The rapprochement encouraged mosques and religious study groups to become the chief forum of political debate. In 1970 the government backed the creation of the **Quranic Preservation Society** (QPS—*Association pour la sauvegarde du Quran*), which included among its early members Rashid al Ghanoushi, later to found the **Movement of the Islamic Tendency** (*Mouvement de la Tendance Islamique*—MTI).

Enjoying official sponsorship, the QPS won wide support among working-class students at university campuses where it organized public debates. Its critique of the "open door" economic policies of 1970s also made the QPS popular among sections of the declining land-holding classes and small traders whose businesses had been absorbed into state-sponsored co-operatives in the 1960s.

In 1978 the **Movement for the Renewal of Islam** (*Mouvement du Renouveau Islamique—* MRI) was founded as an off-shoot of the QPS by activists drawn from science faculties and institutes of technology who had grown disillusioned with the QPS's penchant for the ideas of the Egyptian Muslim Brotherhood.

Ghanoushi and Shaikh Abd al-Fattah Mouru, who led the breakaway group, applied in June 1981 for legalization of the MTI. Although MTI stressed that it did not seek to question the validity of "Western" concepts of liberty and democracy or espouse violence, it failed to win government recognition and was banned in July 1981.

The ban substantially boosted the popularity of MTI which emerged by the mid-1980s as the principal organization among a diversity of Islamic currents, represented variously by the Islamic Consultation (*Shura*) Party, the Islamic Vanguard Party, the **Islamic Liberation Party** (ILP—*Hizb al-Tahrir al-Islami*) and the **Islamic Progressive Tendency**.

The arrest and intermittent harassment of MTI members came to a head following violent food riots in January 1984—the first serious disturbances since 1978—which ushered in a second phase of official rapprochement with the Islamist movement. In August the government granted a general amnesty to all MTI prisoners and pronounced MTI a moderate political organization.

By 1985, however, relations between the two parties had deteriorated following MTI's boycott of local elections in protest against the government's refusal to grant the party official recognition. Reports in July 1986 indicated that there was renewed pressure from hard-liners in the government, including Bourguiba, to seek death sentences for leading MTI figures.

In 1986 and 1987 a series of bomb attacks on tourist resorts at Sousse and Monastir led to fresh allegations by the government accusing Islamic activists, and in particular MTI, of seeking to destabilize the country. In court those charged with responsibility for the bombings withdrew their earlier statements claiming membership of MTI, saying they belonged to the pro-Iranian **Islamic Holy War** group (*Islamic Jihad*).

Meanwhile, the government intensified its campaign against Islamic militants who had organized student strikes at university campuses in 1986-87. Official measures counteracting the Islamic trend were tightened, including an extension of the ban on wearing the Islamic headscarf (*hijab*) by women on college campuses and in government offices (introduced in late 1981) to factories and all other places of work. In February 1987 the government established the Islamic Council of Ulama, in imitation of the Moroccan Council of Ulama, which served as a channel for official supervision of religious activities.

The trial of Ghanoushi and some 90 other Islamic activists in September 1987 attracted international attention. Seven men were sentenced to death, but Ghanoushi, who in April had been accused of complicity in a plot to seize power with Iranian help, was sentenced to life imprisonment with hard labour. Two death sentences were carried out in October 1987, the rest were halted by Bourguiba's removal from office.

Zine al Abidine Ben Ali, who replaced Bourguiba as President in November 1987, decreed a presidential pardon for 608 MTI militants in December 1987; Ghanoushi was pardoned in the following year. The new government's apparent willingness to make concessions to its

Islamist critics was underlined further by the reinstatement of Zaituna University as an independent institution and frequent allusions to Islam in speeches by government ministers. However, legislation adopted by parliament in April 1988 permitted political parties to seek legalization with the stipulation that "no party has the right to refer in its principles . . . to religion, language or a race".

In February 1989 MTI unsuccessfully sought legalization under the new name of the **Renaissance Party** (*Hizb al Nahda*). In legislative elections held in April 1989 *al Nahda* candidates who stood as independents in 19 of the 25 constituencies nationwide, gained approximately 13 per cent of the votes cast, although the party failed to win any seats as the electoral system favoured the ruling *Rassemblement Constitutionnel Démocratique (RCD)* which won all 141 seats in an enlarged legislature.

Further attempts by *al Nahda* to win official recognition were ruled out in late 1989 after Ben Ali publicly opposed the concept of a religious political party. Earlier in the Spring of 1989 it had been reported that Ghanoushi, who had sought exile abroad, had been replaced as the head of *al Nahda* by Sadok Shourou.

Despite severe restrictions on its activities *al Nahda* took a leading part in mobilizing pro-Iraqi opinion following Iraq's invasion of Kuwait in August 1990. In January 1991 *al Nahda* activists were in the forefront of demonstrations condemning Western military action against Iraq.

Meanwhile, confrontation between *al Nahda* and the government intensified. Three members of *al Nahda* involved in an attack in February 1991 on RCD headquarters in Tunis in which a night-watchman was burnt to death, were sentenced to death and hanged in October 1991. In May 1991 two students, allegedly supporters of *al Nahda* had been killed, reportedly by government troops, on the campus of Tunis University. By late 1991 officials were engaged in a vigourous campaign to implicate *al Nahda* in a fundamentalist plot to overthrow the government.

Reports in early 1992 indicated that *al Nahda* was in the throes of reorganizing its programme by adopting a more moderate stance on Islamization. Meanwhile, the government sought to temper its denunciation of *al Nahda* as a "terrorist organization", by announcing in March 1992 that it intended to create a Ministry of Religious Affairs, aimed at propagating the "tolerant faith" of Islam.

EB

Major Islamic organizations

Holy War
Islamic Jihad
Rose to prominence in the late 1980s after it claimed responsibility in August 1987 for bomb attacks on the tourist resorts of Sousse and Monastir.
Leader. Habib Dhawi.
Aims. Its orientation is broadly described as

"Khomeinist" after Iran's late Ayatollah Khomeini.

Islamic Liberation Party (ILP)
Hizb al-Tahrir al-Islami
Proscribed organization with an allegedly limited following. Iinspired by similarly named organization founded in Jordan in 1952 by a

Palestinian, Shaikh Taqi al-Din Nabhani. In the 1970s and early 1980s it was reported to have infiltrated the Tunisian armed forces prompting government accusations that the party intended to stage a violent revolution. In August 1983, 19 soldiers, three officers and eight civilians stood trial accused of membership of the ILP. There were further arrests of alleged ILP members in 1989.

Aims. The establishment of an Islamic state.

Islamic Progressive Tendency (IPT)

Created in the 1980s after a group preferring to concentrate on "cultural Islamization" broke away from MTI over its alleged commitment to an Islamic government. In 1980 IPT was granted legal status as a political party.

Leader. Shaikh Hamida En-Neifern, an *Imam* at Zeytouna mosque, and Salah ad-Din Jourchi.

Aims. To reconstruct Tunisian society on Islamic lines.

Publications. The party organ is *Revue 15/21*.

Movement for the Renewal of Islam (MRI)

Mouvement du Renouveau Islamique

Founded in 1978 by a politically-oriented group, with close links to QPS, involved in the publication of the review, Al-Maarifa. Its most influential former member was Rashid Ghanoushi (b. 1941); other founders were Abdel Fateh Mourou (b. 1948), Hassan Ghodbani and Habib Mokni (b. 1955).

Aims. The gradual return, through non-violent means, to an Islamic legal system based on the *sharia*; the renewal of Tunisia's Islamic identity; the reorganization of economic life along humanitarian lines; and the return of the inalienable rights and freedoms to the mass of the population.

Publications. Al Maarifa (Knowledge).

Movement of the Islamic Tendency (subsequently renamed Renaissance Party)

Mouvement de la Tendance Islamique (MTI)
Parti de la Renaissance (Hizb al Nahda))

The most important Islamist movement, created in 1981 after a group led by Rashid Ghanoushi and Abdel Fateh Mourou broke away from MRI, reportedly for its stance favouring the Egyptian Muslim Brotherhood (*Ikhwan al Muslimun*). In 1989 MTI was renamed the *Hizb al-Nahda* (Renaissance Party). To date, successive attempts by the party to win official recognition have failed.

In the mid-1980s MTI was actively involved in anti-government student protests and a violent campaign against centres of moral laxity resulting in the arrest and execution of numerous members. *Al Nahda* candidates who stood as independents in legislative elections in April 1989 won almost 13 per cent of the votes, although they failed to win any seats under an electoral system that favoured the ruling party. After a brief period of reconciliation with the government in the late 1980s, the party was allegedly involved in a series of armed attacks against government strongholds prompting official accusations of being a terrorist organization involved in a fundamentalist conspiracy.

Leader. Rashid Ghanoushi (presently in exile and reportedly replaced by Sadok Shourou); Abdel Fateh Mourou (secretary-general).

Membership. The party is reported to have wide support among university students and sections of the middle and lower-middle classes.

Aims. In its early phase MTI stressed that it did not reject modernity, but sought only to "Islamize" it; it was not known to champion the creation an Islamic state. As the Renaissance Party, the movement has stressed a version of pluralism and a democracy which are compatible with Islam. More recently, there have been indications that the party intends to moderate even further its stance on Islamization.

Publications. The party organ is *al-Fajr* (suspended by the government in June 1990).

Affiliated organizations. The Tunisian General Union of Students is reported to be closely allied to *al Nahda*.

Quranic Preservation Society (QPS)

Association pour la sauvegarde du Quran
Created in 1970 by clerics attached to the Zaituna mosque in Tunis. Enjoying legal status, QPS organizes seminars in high-schools and universities and reported to be favourable to the ideas of the Egyptian Muslim Brotherhood and the late Abul Ala Mawdudi, founder of the *Jamaat-i-Islami* in Pakistan.

Aims. To secure additional state funding for the construction of mosques and the exploration of Islamic alternatives to "Western concepts" at the social and cultural level.

Turkey

The Republic of Turkey was declared in October 1923 following the abolition of the Sultanate in November 1922. The Ottoman caliphate (the monarch's position as religious leader) was abolished in March 1924. Although Islam was stated to be the official religion in the Constitution of 1924, an amendment in 1928 removed this privilege. While subsequent governments since 1950 have tried to re-establish links between religion and state affairs, secularity was protected by the revolution of 1960, the 1980 military coup and the Constitution of 1982. All legislative powers are concentrated in the Grand National Assembly (GNA) elected under a system of proportional representation; executive powers and policy-making belong to the President, elected by the GNA, and a Council of Ministers.

An estimated 98 per cent of Turkey's population, which stood at 55,541,000 in 1990, are Sunni Muslims belonging to the Hanafi school of law. The heterodox Shia-related Alevi sect (related to the Alawis of Syria) is concentrated in south-eastern Anatolia along the border with Iran, while followers of the dualistic Yazidi sect are found among some Turkish Kurds. Small communities of Christians and Jews make up the remaining population.

Under the regime (1923-38) of Mustapha Kemal (henceforth Ataturk) Turkey's Islamic traditions were replaced by a far-reaching programme of Westernization and secularization. Sweeping reforms abolished Islamic courts and instituted Western-style civil codes to replace Islamic law (Turk. *seriat*, Ar. *sharia*); all religious instruction, formerly under the control of the dismantled Ministry of *Seriat* and *Evkaf* (Ar. pl. *awqaf*) was prohibited and religious schools and seminaries (Turk. *medreses*; Ar. *madrassah*) placed under the control of the Ministry of Education. Women were emancipated and formally enfranchised in 1934; polygamy was banned and the Gregorian calendar adopted to replace Islamic dates. In 1925 the republican government banned all Sufi orders following a rebellion by the Naqshbandiyyah (Turk. Naksibendi) Sufi order in south-east Anatolia. The Department of Religious Affairs (*Diyanet Baskanligi Isleri*, established in 1924) regulated all matters relating to Islam. In keeping with the regime's stress on Turkey's national as against its Islamic identity, the Arabic call to prayer (Turk. *ezan*; Ar. *azan*) was banned and a Turkish formula adopted.

Ataturk's reforms met with stiff resistance. In December 1930 a large crowd led by Dervish Mehmet Efendi, a prominent leader of the Naqshbandiyyah order, protested in the town of Mememen, near Izmir, calling for the restoration of the Caliphate.

Islam and the state: developments in the post-Ataturk era

The death of Ataturk in November 1938 and the introduction of multiparty politics in 1945 brought to the surface the extent of popular dissatisfaction with the regime's more extreme anti-Islamic measures. Political parties responded by attempting to soften the impact of Ataturk's secularism. In 1949 the Republican People's Party (RPP), founded by Ataturk, repealed some anti-religious legislation by lifting the ban on religious instruction in primary schools, providing foreign exchange for the Muslim pilgrimage to Mecca (*hajj*) and, in early 1950, by re-opening Sufi convents. These concessions did not, however, ensure the future political success of the RPP, which lost power to the Democratic Party (DP) in the country's first free elections held in May 1950.

During its decade in power the DP appeared relatively more sympathetic to Muslim sentiment than its predecessors, notably by lifting the ban on the Arabic call to prayer. However, its unwillingness to rescind some of Ataturk's more fundamental anti-Islamic laws fuelled renewed opposition to the secular state. The permissive political climate rekindled the activities of well-established brotherhoods (*tariqat*) especially the Ticani (Ar. Tijanniyyah) order (responsible for destroying statues of Ataturk), and strengthened the appeal of more recent ones, including the semi-clandestine Nurcu and Süleymançi societies which called for the restoration of Islam as the basis of the state.

The ideas of Said Nursi (1873-1960), founder of the Nurcus, continue to attract a wide following among Turkish Muslims at home and abroad, especially in Germany. (Nursi himself was reported to have been courted by Prime Minister Adnan Menderes in the late 1950s.) The Süleymanci brotherhood, founded by Süleyman Hilmi Tunahan (d. 1959), and now led by Kemal Kaçar, is said to be popular among university students and some Turkish immigrant organizations in the Netherlands.

In May 1960 a military coup ousted the DP government and introduced a new Constitution which permitted ideological politics for the first time. The years that followed witnessed the steady polarization of Turkish politics, with parties of the extreme right such as the National Action Party (NAP—*Milli Harekat Partisi*) seeking to employ Islam as an instrument against parties of the left. It was around this time that the country's sectarian divide between Sunni and Shias assumed new importance with Sunnis choosing to side with the right, leaving left-wing parties such as the Unity Party (*Birlik Partisi*), later the Unity Party of Turkey (*Türkiye Birlik Partisi*) to enlist the support of the Shia minority.

Meanwhile, some Sufi brotherhoods also began cautiously to re-emerge and cultivate links with established political parties. The Naqshbandi brotherhood harboured close relations with Islamist groups who formed the National Order Party (NOP—*Milli Nizam Partisi*), later the National Salvation Party (NSP—*Milli Selamat Partisi*), while the conservative Justice Party (JP—*Adalet Partisi*), created in 1961, was widely known to have the backing of the Nurcus.

Civilian rule restored in October 1961 was marked by a succession of unstable coalition governments until March 1971, when a wave of industrial and student strikes forced the resignation of the JP government under Süleyman Demirel. A general election in October 1973 which formally ended a period of "guided democracy" under military supervision, returned the NSP, formed in October 1972, as the third-largest party with 48 out of 450 seats in the GNA. (The NSP's predecessor, the NOP, had been disbanded by the army in May 1971). The success of the NSP's Islamic manifesto was widely attributed to the dislocating effects of mass rural migration to urban centres and the introduction of large-scale modern industry that characterized Turkey in the early 1970s.

A coalition government led by the now left-of-centre RPP under Bulent Ecevit collapsed in

September 1974 after the NSP withdrew its support in protest against the government's refusal to endorse the Turkish annexation of northern Cyprus. However, fears that the Islamic fervour generated by the NSP would threaten the country's secular Constitution proved unfounded when the NSP's share of the vote in elections held in June 1977 declined from 11.8 to 8.56 per cent. In by-elections held in 1975 the NSP had obtained 3.4 per cent of the total votes, but it improved its performance in by-elections in 1979, when it gained 9.7 per cent of the votes.

Meanwhile, political violence between left and right which had begun in the mid-1970s reached a crescendo in 1978-1979. In December 1978 more than 100 Shia Alevis were massacred and thousands more wounded in the town of Kahramanmara in south-eastern Anatolia after a raid by members of the neo-fascist NAP. Religious politics were fuelled also by the efforts of international Muslim bodies, notably the Muslim World League (MWL—*Rabitat al-Alam al-Islami*) which reportedly financed the activities of Islamic parties and organizations.

Mounting fears of an Islamic backlash gained ground after the NSP (restored to power as a member of a substantially weakened coalition government) organized a mass rally in Konya on Sept. 6, 1980, in which demonstrators clamoured for the establishment of an Islamic state. Gen. Kenan Evren, who seized power on Sept. 12, singled out the Konya rally as one among other compelling reasons for military intervention.

The army's comprehensive ban on political activities which lasted until May 1983 was followed by the arrest and trial of leaders of extremist parties of both the left and the right, including Neçmettin Erbakan, head of the NSP, and 33 of his collaborators. However, the junta's failure to substantiate charges against Erbakan enabled him to regroup his supporters under the **Welfare Party** (WP), also known as the Prosperity Party (*Refah Partisi*), founded in 1983. Meanwhile, the military regime sought to respond to pressure from Islamists by approving a series of measures in 1981-82 making religious instruction compulsory in all secondary schools. At the same time, however, it also pursued a vigorous policy aimed at suppressing Islamic fundamentalism. In November 1982 members of the Turkish offshoot of the Jordanian-based **Islamic Liberation Party** (*Hizb al Tahrir al-Islami*), who were said to be committed to the restoration of the Islamic Caliphate, were arrested during a police operation in Ankara.

Elections held under a new Constitution in November 1983, which the WP along with 11 other new parties were not permitted to contest, resulted in an overwhelming victory for the Motherland Party (*Anavatan Partisi*—ANAP) led by Turgut Özal. Representing a broad spectrum of right-wing political forces, the ANAP included in its midst former members and supporters of the NSP. (Özal had unsuccessfully contested the 1977 general election as an NSP candidate in Izmir, receiving only 1.6 per cent of the votes.) The party itself was reportedly divided between a liberal and an Islamic wing.

In local elections held in March 1984 the WP made substantial political gains subsequently consolidated by its control of three mayoralties in 84 newly formed municipalities in elections held in June 1987. A general election in late November 1987 (following a referendum lifting the ban on participation in politics by politicians active before 1980), resulted in the NSP obtaining 7.2 per cent of the votes but failing to secure any seats in the GNA because of electoral regulations requiring a party to obtain at least 10 per cent of the total votes in order to be represented.

Attempts to cut into the NSP's Islamist constituency combined with growing pressure from its own Islamist ranks led the ANAP government to initiate reforms which reversed key elements of Turkey's secular educational and social policies. These included the rapid expansion of Quranic schools and the growth of state-run schools for chaplains and preachers (*imams*). According to some reports the expansion of religious education in this period far outpaced secular education. (The 1990 census indicated, however, that the expansion of religious training schools at the secondary level had slowed since 1985.) The government also actively sponsored a mosque-building programme; in June 1987 the number of mosques, estimated at 60,161, exceeded the number of schools which stood at 58,455. In December 1988 ANAP deputies in the GNA succeeded in passing a law which permitted the wearing of Islamic headscarves at universities in contravention of constitutional provisions.

The winning of control by the WP over a number of important municipal councils including Konya, following municipal elections in March 1989, galvanized pro-Islamic opinion. In March 1989 thousands of Muslims demonstrated across the country in protest against a ruling by the Constitutional Court which annulled the law permitting the wearing of Islamic headscarves at universities. The demonstrations coincided with attacks against the novel *The Satanic Verses* by the Indian-born British writer, Salman Rushdie. In April Konya city council ordered women students of the local Selcuk University to travel on separate buses, while Muslim extremists agitated to convert Istanbul's St Sophia cathedral (a museum since 1934) into a mosque.

These events and a Cabinet reshuffle in early November 1989 following the election of Özal as President appeared to confirm the growing appeal of Islamic factions. Among those included in the new Cabinet were Mehmet Keçicilar, deputy chairman of ANAP and leader of the so-called "Holy Alliance" within ANAP representing Islamic fundamentalists and right-wing nationalists. (In elections to the managing committee of ANAP in June 1988, 30 of the 50 seats were won by members of the Holy Alliance.) Also included in the Cabinet was Vehbi Dinçler, a member of ANAP's pro-Islamist faction, who as Minister of State for National Education went on record as denouncing Charles Darwin's theory of evolution as anti-Islamic.

Allegations of the government's increasing subservience to Islamic opinion intensified in December 1989 after a presidential order cancelled an article in the higher education law resulting from the Constitutional Court ruling of March 1989 which had re-imposed the ban on the wearing of headscarves at universities. The move came amid a government decision, reportedly prompted by the Keçicilar faction, to increase budget spending on the Department of Religious Affairs by almost 240 per cent.

The early 1990s were notable for a significant rise in Islamic militancy resulting in the murders of prominent public figures opposed to the government's pro-Islamic measures. In January the hitherto unknown **Islamic Revenge Organization** (IRO—also known as the Islamic Revenge Movement) claimed responsibility for the killing of Muammar Aksoy, head of the Ankara Bar Association and a noted critic of the government's headscarves decree. In March the **Turkish Islamic Commandos** was among the groups that claimed responsibility for the murder of the Cetin Emec, a journalist who had spoken out against religious fundamentalism. The latest murder came amid revelations that Turkish police had uncovered evidence in Ankara, Istanbul and Malatya (about 50 km east of Ankara) of a group working for the creation of an Islamic state in co-operation with the **Kurdish Islamic Revolutionaries**. In October 1990 the Islamic Movement (reported in sections of the press as being identical to the IRO which had claimed responsibility for the murder of Aksoy) said that it had ordered the killing of a leading feminist and member of the Social Democratic Populist Party (SHP), Bahriye Uciok, for her opposition to the veiling of women. In October 1991 a group calling itself **Islamic Jihad of Turkey**, which in 1989 had claimed responsibility for an attack on a Saudi diplomat in Ankara, said that it had planted two car bombs which had killed a US military official and an Egyptian diplomat in Ankara. In January 1992 the previously unknown Islamic Resistance Organization claimed responsibility for a bomb attack in Ankara. Evidence of a militant pro-Iranian group emerged in March 1992 after the authorities blamed the allegedly Iran-backed **Turkish Party of God** (*Turkish Hezbollah*) for a grenade attack on a Jewish synagogue in Istanbul. In March the IRO resurfaced to claim responsibility for the killing in Ankara of the security chief at the Israeli embassy, reportedly in retaliation for the killing of Shaikh Abbas Musawi, head of the Lebanese Party of God (*Hezbollah*).

Reports of infiltration by Islamic militant groups into the Turkish armed forces emerged in January 1990. According to Turkish press reports about 300 non-commissioned air force officers had been under investigation since September 1989 on suspicion of having links with clandestine Islamic groups. The Defence Ministry later confirmed that 1,022 people had been expelled from the armed forces since 1980 on charges of violating the secular Constitution; some though not all of those expelled were reported to have had links with religious groups.

Mounting criticism of the government's pro-Islamic policies prompted a major Cabinet reshuffle in June 1991 with a view to boosting ANAP's secular liberal wing. Two notable omissions in the reorganized Cabinet were former Ministers of State Keçicilar and Dinçler, both firmly identified with the party's recent pro-Islamic orientation.

Despite these measures, however, pro-Islamic opinion appeared to have made significant political inroads. In a general election held in October 1991 the WP, in alliance with the neo-fascist Nationalist Labour Party (NLP—*Millyetçi Calisma Partisi*), entered parliament for the first time with 62 seats on an agenda which included Turkey's withdrawal from the North Atlantic Treaty Organization (NATO) and the renunciation of efforts towards Turkish membership of the European Communities (EC). (The alliance between the two parties was dissolved on November 15, the NLP taking about 20 seats.)

The new government under Süleyman Demirel, now deputy chairman of the True Path Party (TPP—*Dogru Yol Partisi*), appointed on November 20, excluded the WP which had refused to co-operate unless an Islamic leader was found to replace Özal. Other demands by the WP in return for co-operation reportedly included greater commitment to religious education, encouragement of Islamic dress for women, an amnesty for anti-secularist offenders, and NSP supervision of broadcasting.

FS

Major Islamic organizations

Islamic Jihad of Turkey
Clandestine group which claimed responsibility in 1989 for the maiming of a Saudi diplomat in Ankara and for two car bomb explosions which killed a US military officer and an Egyptian diplomat in Ankara in October 1991.

Islamic Liberation Party
Hezb al Tahrir al Islami
Clandestine Turkish offshoot of Jordanian-based

organization of the same name uncovered in November 1982 when its alleged members were arrested during a police operation in Ankara.

Aims. Alleged party members were said by the authorities to adhere to a pamphlet entitled *The Islamic Constitution according to the Book of God and the Sunnah of the Prophet,* which called on all Islamic countries to unite as a single state under the leadership of a Caliph.

Islamic Revenge Organization (IRO) (also known as the Islamic Revenge Movement (IRM))

Clandestine militant group which rose to prominence in January 1990 after it claimed responsibility for the murder of Muammar Aksoy, head of the Ankara Bar Association. A related (or possibly the same) group claimed responsibility for the killing in October 1990 of Bahriye Uciok, a leading feminist opposed to the veiling of women. The group resurfaced in March 1992 saying that it had ordered the killing of the security chief attached to Israel's embassy in Ankara.

Kurdish Islamic Revolutionaries

Clandestine group uncovered in March 1990 and said to be working in co-operation with other militant groups, including the pro-Iranian Turkish *Hezbollah*, for the creation of an Islamic state.

Turkish Party of God

Turkish Hezbollah

Allegedly Iran-backed clandestine militant group uncovered in March 1992 after being held responsible for a grenade attack on a Jewish synagogue in Istanbul.

Turkish Islamic Commandos

Clandestine group which in March 1990 claimed responsibility for the murder of the liberal journalist, Cetin Emec.

Welfare Party (WP) (also known as the Prosperity Party)

Refah Partisi

Currently the country's most important Islamic party founded in 1983 as a successor to the National Order Party (NOP) established in January 1971 and disbanded in May of that year and the National Salvation Party (NSP) formed in October 1972 and dissolved in 1980. The WP entered parliament for the first time in October 1991, winning a total of 62 seats in alliance with the Nationalist Labour Party (NLP); the alliance was dissolved in November 1991, the NLP taking about 20 seats.

Leader. Neçmettin Erbakan (chair; formerly leader of the NOP and the NSP).

Membership. The party is strongest in eastern Turkey where it has sought to cut into the Kurdish nationalist constituency by campaigning on a programme opposed to "feudalism, imperialism and fascism".

Aims. The party seeks Turkey's dissociation from NATO and opposes Turkey's application for membership of the European Communities, preferring closer co-operation with the Islamic world. It demands further religious instruction, the encouragement of Islamic dress for women and a general amnesty for anti-secularist offenders. The WP's economic policies, described as "Islamic corporatism", favour greater state direction for industry within a free-market system.

Turkmenistan

(For a broad survey of Islam in the former Soviet Union see separate entry for the Commonwealth of Independent States)

Turkmenistan declared independence on Oct. 27, 1991, following a referendum in which support for republican independence was estimated to stand at around 94 per cent. In the same poll, 93 per cent claimed to support the policies of President Saparmurad Niyazov, despite, or perhaps because of, reports in August 1991 that he had arrested democratic activists for revealing his support for the attempted coup.

Turkmenistan has the smallest population of the Central Asian republics at 3,500,000, but the highest concentration of a titular nationality at 72 per cent. Minorities include Russians and Uzbeks (both 9 per cent of the population). Turkmenistan's economic situation is dire and it has the highest infant mortality rate of all the republics, at 56.4 per 1,000 births in 1987.

The Turkmen are Sunni Muslims of the Hanafi school, with a traditionally strong Sufi element. There are estimated to be 400,000 Turkmen in Afghanistan, 500,000 in Iraq and Iran, and 300,000 in Turkey.

In October 1991 Niyazov was reported to have established a Turkmenistan Council for Religious Affairs (TCRA), chaired by A. Tuliyev, under the Turkmen government to replace the USSR Council for Religious Affairs (USSR-CRA) which had been responsible for the administration of all religions).

The republican Communist Party changed its name to the Democratic Party of Turkmenistan in November 1991, and, in an apparent change of policy, spoke of the mistakes of the past which had resulted in "the traditional way of life of the Turkmen people being consigned to oblivion".

WS

Islamic organizations

Unity Movement
Akzybirlik
The foundation of the movement was announced in September 1989. The movement was banned by the authorities on January 15, 1990, following a demonstration attended by 10,000 people to mark the anniversary of the capture of the Geok-Tepe fortress in 1881 by a Russian general.

Leader. Nurberdy Nurmamedov who heads a 21-member collective leadership.

Aims. Although not overtly Islamic, the organization is the strongest nationalist opposition movement to the Turkmen government.

The **Islamic Renaissance Party of Turkmenistan** (IRPTu) failed to establish a branch in Turkeminstn in early 1991 after being subjected to a ban.

Uganda

The Republic of Uganda gained independence from Britain in 1962. Its history since independence has been punctuated by a number of coups and President Yoweri Museveni came to power in January 1986 as head of the National Resistance Movement. Although political parties exist, political activity is prohibited.

About 6 per cent of the population of 18,800,000 are Muslims. They are dispersed across the country and the largest concentration is in the Baganda group. The hold of Sufi brotherhoods is minimal in comparison with that in West Africa, although the Qadiriyyah order is believed to have pockets of influence.

As in most of East Africa, Islam in Uganda grew from commercial contacts with Arab traders in the 10th century although it was not widely taught and propagated until the mid-19th century. Conversion was individual, rather than directed at entire communities.

Islam and the state: developments since independence

At independence Muslims in Uganda lacked a leader and were divided by minor doctrinal differences, but political leaders gradually began to take an interest in an increasingly active Muslim community.

From the mid-1940s Muslims organized themselves around educational issues. The Uganda Muslim Education Association, established in 1947, successfully lobbied for funds from the colonial administration as well as from the Aga Khan and the Muslim community itself. It made great strides in educational provision for Muslim children and by the time of independence had established several of its own schools.

The regime of President Milton Obote (1965-1971) employed Islamic rhetoric as a means of winning support among the Baganda, the country's largest ethnic group. It established the National Association for the Advancement of Muslims (NAAM) in 1965, and from 1968 recognized it as the sole representative body for all Muslims. The workings of NAAM, however, provoked discord in the Muslim community and by the time of the 1971 coup it had lost considerable support.

Gen. Idi Amin, a Muslim, was keen to heal rifts in the Islamic community and to use it as a power base, and during his regime (1971-79) the Muslim minority became relatively influential. In 1972 Amin backed the creation of the **Uganda Muslim Supreme Council** to replace the NAAM. Although this has made progress in health and welfare matters affecting the Muslim community, and was instrumental in the admission of Uganda to the Islamic Conference Organization (ICO) in 1974, it has been troubled by internal divisions.

While the present regime of President Yoweri Museveni has adopted a policy of non-interference in religious affairs, the President has on several occasions called on Muslim leaders to reconcile their differences and to preach unity.

TJ

Major Islamic organizations

Uganda Muslim Supreme Council (UMSC)

Umbrella organization founded in 1972 on the initiative of Gen. Idi Amin to replace the National Association for the Advancement of Muslims (NAAM). It is based in Kampala.

Leader. Husayn Rajab Kakooza (chief *qadi* (legal expert) and president).

Aims. The provision of a single administrative organ for all Muslims, the promotion of health and welfare matters, and the improvement of relations with Muslims outside Uganda.

Union of Muslim Councils in East, Central and Southern Africa

Regional organization based in Kampala.

Leader. Haji Juma Sebuliba (secretary).

Aim. The strengthening of co-operation between the government and the Muslim community.

United Kingdom

The majority of Muslims in the United Kingdom, of whom over half were born in the country, are South Asian by origin and follow the Sunni Hanafi school. Estimates in 1991 indicated that there were around 1,500,000 Muslims in the UK (about 2 per cent of the total population). This figure is contested by some Muslim organizations which claim that the total number is closer to 2,000,000.

Most UK Muslims are clustered in and around London, Manchester, the West Midlands, Lancashire, South Wales and Yorkshire. Some belong to the professional classes while others have moved steadily into business; the majority, however, are semi- or un-skilled workers, some unemployed, concentrated in deprived areas in the inner cities and around the formerly prosperous mill towns of northern England.

Muslim migration to the UK was intimately associated with the British Empire. Diplomats, traders, seamen and visiting dignitaries typified the small number of early arrivals. From the late 18th century the merchant navy employed Asian and African seamen and the first significant Muslim community was of Yemenis, many of them seamen, who settled around the port of Cardiff where the first mosque was built in 1870. During the inter-war years other Muslim colonies of seamen were established, with large numbers from the Mirpur district in Azad Kashmir, small towns in west Punjab, parts of the North West Frontier Province, and Sylhet in present-day Bangladesh.

The efforts of eminent visitors from India led to the creation in 1889 of the Shah Jahan Mosque in Woking, the UK's oldest mosque. The Central Mosque and Islamic Cultural Centre in Regent's Park in London were inaugurated by King George VI to accommodate the growing numbers of Muslims in the diplomatic community. Today there are an estimated 314 registered mosques in the UK, compared with nine in 1960.

The postwar labour shortage encouraged Muslim migration in the 1950s, which also increased prior to new restrictions introduced under the Commonwealth Immigration Acts of 1962 and 1968. The new Muslim arrivals did not all come from South Asia but included Muslims from East Africa, Iran, Malaysia, Somalia, Turkish Cyprus, Turkey and as well as Arabs of various nationalities. Nor did the new arrivals, many of whom were dependants, expect to return to their countries of origin. This, along with an increase in the number of Muslims born in Britain, contributed to the emergence of a substantial Muslim community.

The most widely represented Muslim sect in the UK is the Indo-Muslim Barelvi sect whose followers lay special emphasis on devotion to the Prophet, Muhammad. Most mosques are run by followers of the Barelvi sect and there are several doctrinal currents within the Barelvi network, the most important being those associated with Pir Maroof Shah of Bradford and Sufi Abdullah of Birmingham. Another *pir* (holy man), Shaikh Abdal Qadir Jilani, exerts influence in London as well as within the Manchester Islamic Association.

There are also nebulous Sufi brotherhoods whose precise following is difficult to assess as their activities tend to overlap with those of other sects, such as the Barelvis. Sufi orders active among young Muslims and recent converts include the Naqshbandiyyah, the Qadiriyyah and the Chishtiyyah.

Sectarian rivalry between Muslims has focused on differences between the Barelvis and followers of revivalist trends. There are several revivalist strands among UK Muslims, the most well-known of which are the *Jamaat Tabligh ul Islam* (also known as *Tablighi Jamaat*), an influential, though non-political, missionary organization which was an offshoot of the Indo-Muslim Deobandi reform movement, and the more puritanical *Ahl-i-Hadith*. Important centres of the Deobandi sect are the Saddam Hussein Mosque in Birmingham and the Whitechapel Mosque in London.

The *Tablighi Jamaat*'s centre is the *Darul Ulum* (Centre for Education) in Dewsbury in Yorkshire while the *Ahl-i-Hadith* are organized around a small number of mosques focused on the Green Lane Mosque in Birmingham.

Also active, and with a marked political agenda, is the fundamentalist Pakistan-based **Jamaat-i-Islami** (JI), with its headquarters in London and branches in most major UK cities. It has considerable influence in prominent Muslim bodies including the UK Islamic Mission, the Islamic Cultural Centre in London and the Islamic Foundation in Leicester.

In the 1980s doctrinal differences between the *Jamaat-i-Islami* and followers of the Barelvi sect were aggravated by Barelvi allegations about the *Jamaat*'s privileged access to funds from Arab governments, particularly Saudi Arabia.

The UK's non-South Asian Muslims also maintain a number of welfare and political organizations. Members of the well-established Sufi Alawiyyah order, strong among Yemenis, administer their own cultural centres which offer Islamic education and are reported to have financial assistance from the Yemeni government. Turkish Cypriots also maintain cultural centres, though those from Turkey have so far failed to do so. British converts are represented by the **Islamic Party of Britain** (IPB).

Organizational developments within the Muslim community

Despite sectarian rivalry, UK Muslims have often succeeded in agreeing on single issues and in banding together under broad umbrella organizations.

Two trends have emerged over recent years. The first is the development of a number of umbrella organizations, including the **Union of Muslim Organizations**(UMO), the **Imams and Mosques Council** and the **Council of Mosques (UK and Eire)**, which aim to co-ordinate Muslim opinion as well as reportedly acting as intermediaries on behalf of Muslim governments seeking to influence Muslim migrants from the Middle East and North Africa.

The other development is the emergence of city-based organizations such as the politically active **Bradford Council of Mosques** and the lesser-known Manchester Islamic Association and Birmingham Muslim Liaison Committee, which have sought to project Muslim opinion on a range of local issues, particularly education.

Muslim organizations, both local and national, have continued to press for the establishment of state-financed Muslim schools with their own curriculum along the lines of Roman Catholic and Jewish schools. The Islamia Primary School in the London borough of Brent is regarded by some Muslims as a model of the kind of institution the community hopes to establish.

Concern over the need to guarantee Islamic education in the UK led many Muslims in 1980 to join the protest against the reinstatement of Ray Honeyford as headmaster of Bradford's Drummond Middle School, whose strongly stated preference for traditional Christian values over multicultural education was regarded by Muslims as an attack on the values of their community.

The campaign in 1988 to ban the novel *The Satanic Verses* by the Indian-born British writer Salman Rushdie enabled national and local Muslim organizations to unite on what is still the single most important issue facing UK Muslims. In December 1988, 8,000 Muslims took part in a protest march in London against the book in what was described as "the largest ethnic minority demonstration ever staged in Britain".

Led by the UMO, the Bradford Council of Mosques and the campaigning wings of the Council of Mosques (UK and Eire) (the UK Action Committee on Islamic Affairs and the Islamic Defence Council), the movement reflected and generated widespread Muslim resentment, famously captured in the public burning in January 1989 of copies of the book in Bradford. The controversy led to petitions, which continue today, to the government by Muslim organizations that the UK's blasphemy laws be extended to cover non-Christian religions, including Islam.

Although few organizations publicly endorsed the death sentence for apostasy imposed on Rushdie by a ruling (*fatwa*) in February 1989 from Iran's late Ayatollah Khomeini, a British Broadcasting Corporation opinion poll conducted among Muslims in October that year showed "significant approval" for the *fatwa*. The extent of Muslim dissatisfaction over the government's refusal to ban the book was seen in the disquiet expressed by several Muslim organizations representing liberal currents, including the Mosques and Imams Council and the **Islamic Society for the Promotion of Religious Tolerance in the UK**, who described the government's response as "insensitive".

Emerging differences over the question of maintaining the *fatwa* against Rushdie in 1990-1991 generated renewed interest in the creation of a national Muslim forum with a well-defined Muslim political agenda. In July 1990 the director of the London-based pro-Iranian Muslim Institute, Kalim Siddiqui, launched a Muslim Manifesto outlining the structure of a **Muslim Parliament**. The Parliament held its first session in February 1992 but has been castigated by some Muslim organizations, including the Bradford Council of Mosques, for being elitist and of little relevance to working-class Muslims.

YS

Major Islamic organizations

Bradford Council of Mosques (BCM)
Bradford-based organization established in 1980 which under its former head, Sher Azam, rose to prominence in the late 1980s as a leading voice in the campaign to ban the The Satanic Verses.

Aims. To facilitate liaison between Bradford City Council and the Muslim community and especially its mosques, presently under the control of different Islamic factions.
Leader. Liaquat Hussain (chair).

Structure. Twenty-two of Bradford's 26 mosques are represented on the Council, in addition to an estimated 18 Muslim organizations. Each mosque and organization has two seats on the Council which is financed by affiliation fees and voluntary contributions.

Council of Mosques (UK and Eire) (COM-UK & Eire)

Established in 1984.
Leader. The post of chair is presently vacant.
Aims. To provide guidance and advice to all members concerning the construction and maintenance of mosques, to assist Muslims in the performance of religious duties, to promote the training of religious leaders (*imams*), and to increase understanding between Muslims and non-Muslims.

Imams and Mosques Council (IMC)

Founded in October 1985, it took a leading part in the campaign against *The Satanic Verses* although it is publicly opposed to the death sentence imposed on Rushdie. It is reportedly financed by Libya and is said to maintain close links with the officially sponsored Libyan organization, *Jamiyyat ad Dawa al Islamiyya* (Islamic Call Society). It has recently initiated the Islamic Renewal Campaign, aimed at countering the Church of England's programme to revive popular interest in Christianity.
Leader. Zaki Badawi (formerly Director of the Islamic Cultural Centre and the London Central Mosque).
Aims. To provide moral and practical support for mosques and religious leaders *imams* and to promote inter-faith relations.

Islamic Defence Council (IDC)

Founded in 1989 as the campaigning arm of UMO.
Leader. Atiqur Rahman Samdhali (chair).

Islamic Party of Britain (IPB)

Formed in 1989 with its headquarters in Bradford. Five candidates from the party unsuccessfully contested seats in Bradford and London during the 1992 general election.
Leader. David Musa Pidcock; Mustaqim Bleher (general secretary).
Membership. The party has 1,000 members but claims to represent the views of what it estimates to be 2,000,000 UK Muslims.
Aims. To put into practice Islamic principles as expounded in the Quran and to establish interest-free home loans through shared equity. It favours the suspension of the *fatwa* against Salman Rushdie.

Islamic Society for the Promotion of Religious Tolerance in the UK

Leader. Hesham el Essawy.

Jamaat-i-Islami (JI)

An offshoot of religio-political party founded by Abul Ala Maudoodi (1903-1979), which has been active in Pakistan since the inception of the state in 1947. The party has an extensive network in the UK with branches in major cities with large Muslim populations including Manchester, Oldham, Rochdale, Liverpool, Blackpool, Blackburn, Walsall, Birmingham, Wolverhampton and Southampton.
Aims. The party's principal goal in Pakistan is the development of an Islamic state; in the UK the *Jamaat* seeks to increase its influence on the Muslim community.
Structure. The party's main evangelical organization is reported to be based at the UK Islamic Mission. The Islamic Foundation in Leicester, founded in 1968, which regularly publishes Maudoodi's works and Islamic literature for use in schools, is also known to have strong links with the *Jamaat*. The *Dawatul-Islam* (Call of Islam), formed in 1976 as a separate organization for the UK Bangladeshi community, allegedly works in close co-operation with the party. The *Jamaat*'s reportedly privileged access to funds from Saudi Arabia is said to have enhanced its influence over

the Saudi-backed Islamic Cultural Centre in London.
Publication. Impact International.

Muslim Institute

Founded in early 1973 by Kalim Siddiqui, an Indian-born Muslim and former journalist, it rose to prominence as a leading voice in the campaign to win UK Muslim support for the ruling *fatwa* issued by Ayatollah Khomeini in February 1989 condemning Salman Rushdie to death for apostasy. In January 1992 the Institute's Director, Kalim Siddiqui, inaugurated the Muslim Parliament, aimed at "defy[ing] any public policy or legislation which we regard as inimical to our interests". The Institute is a registered charity whose annual donations are said to range between £200,000 and £300,000. It is funded partly by property investments and, reportedly, partly by the governments of Iran and Saudi Arabia. The Institute also allegedly receives financial support from Muslim supporters in South Africa who are believed to donate £150,000 annually.
Leader. Kalim Siddiqui (director); Ghayas Uddin Siddiqui (no relation) (deputy director).
Publication. Crescent International.

Muslim Parliament

First proposed in the Muslim Manifesto launched in London by the Director of the London-based Muslim Institute, Kalim Siddiqui, on July 14, 1990. The Parliament was inaugurated and held its first session on January 4-5, 1992 and its second session was held on May 2-3, 1992. Members of the Muslim Parliament (MMPs) normally convene at Kensington Town Hall. The Parliament's claim to speak on behalf of UK Muslims is rejected by other leading Muslim organizations including UMO and the Islamic Society for Promotion of Religious Tolerance in the UK.
Leader. Kalim Siddiqui. Inayatullah Zaigham (speaker).
Aims. To defend and promote Muslim interests

in the UK along the lines of the policies pursued by the British Board of Jewish Deputies; to co-ordinate UK Muslim opinion; and to secure a total ban on the publication of *The Satanic Verses* and the confiscation of all existing copies of the book. The Parliament has formally acknowledged the supremacy of British law and has publicly refrained from calling on UK Muslims to execute the *fatwa* against Salman Rushdie; it emphasises, however, that the *fatwa* is in keeping with Islamic law and therefore supports its execution in any Muslim country.
Structure. Bicameral, with a 200-seat Lower House (which presently has 180 members); the Upper House, yet to be elected, has an unlimited membership, although the total number of members is not expected to exceed 500. MMPs of both Houses are selected by 40 local Muslim Manifesto Groups (MMGs) and/or by Muslim professional bodies including the Muslim Medical Institute, the Association of Muslim Scientists and Technologists, the Muslim Women's Institute and the Muslim Business Group.
Publication. Crescent International, published fortnightly by the Muslim Institute.

UK Action Committee on Islamic Affairs (UKACIA)

Founded in 1989 as the campaigning arm of the Union of Muslim Organizations (UMO).
Leader. Mughram al Ghamdi (convener), a Saudi diplomat who is also Director-General of the Central Mosque Trust and the Islamic Cultural Centre in London.
Structure. The Committee represents the Council of Mosques (UK and Eire), the Union of Muslim Organizations (UMO), the UK Islamic Mission and the Leicester-based Islamic Foundation (the last two of which allegedly maintain close links with the *Jamaat-i-Islami*).

Union of Muslim Organizations (UMO)

Established in 1970 as the first UK umbrella Muslim organization, reportedly with financial assistance from the government of Saudi Arabia through the World Muslim League. In the 1980s it was reported to have received official Iraqi backing.

Leader. Syed Aziz Pasha who also represents British Muslims on the European Community Migrant Forum.

Structure. The organization has two campaigning wings, represented by the UK Action Committee on Islamic Affairs and the Islamic Defence Council.

United States of America

The territory which today constitutes the United States of America (henceforth the US) was colonised by Britain, France and Spain. After achieving independence in 1783 the area covered by the US, consisting initially of only 13 east coast states, rapidly expanded in the 19th and 20th centuries.

Since independence the US has been a federal democracy, with an elected legislature and President. Although originally settled by west Europeans, particularly the British, the racial composition of the US was affected by heavy immigration during the 19th and early 20th centuries.

A key factor in determining the country's racial make up was the importation and breeding of black Africans for use as slaves, prior to the abolition of slavery in the latter half of the 19th century. Currently over 80 per cent of the population are white, 12 per cent black and the remainder of other racial origin, including a rapidly growing Hispanic population.

Although there is a strictly observed constitutional separation between church and state, the predominant culture of the US is staunchly Christian. Roman Catholics form the largest single denomination, although Protestants as a whole outnumber Catholics by a ratio of 3:2. Other important communities include Jews, Orthodox Christians, Mormons, and a substantial minority of Muslims.

Indeed, the Muslim population has grown faster than any other section of the US population. Between 1971 and 1981 the Muslim population grew from 1,000,000 (0.5 per cent of the total population) to about 3,000,000 (1.3 per cent of the total population). Of these some 1,000,000 were of African origin, 900,000 of Arab origin, 450,000 of Indo-Pakistani origin and 450,000 from elsewhere. By early 1992 it was estimated that there was a total of 6,000,000 US Muslims, possibly outnumbering American Jews and thus representing the country's second-largest religion. Although not highly geographically concentrated, the Muslim population tends to be found mainly in the larger US cities.

The first significant influx of Muslim immigrants began arriving in the latter half of the 19th century, from both Europe and Asia. After 1945 Muslim immigrants entered the US from all over the world, but particularly from the Indian subcontinent, Iran, Turkey and Egypt.

In addition to immigration, the Muslim community in the US was swelled in the 20th century by a significant number of conversions to Islam by sections of the hitherto non-Muslim population. Most were of African origin, and the adoption of what many regard as their "original" religion has served as a means of rediscovering a lost identity. In this sense the development of Islam in the US has become inextricably linked with the civil rights struggle of the black population, and the need to eradicate the legacy of slavery and institutionalised racial discrimination.

Despite the weight of the Muslim population swelled by the combined effect of immigration and conversion, its political influence remains limited. There are no Muslim members in the US Congress and the country's most senior Muslim elected official is Charles Bilel, Mayor of Kountze, a small town on the border of Texas and Louisiana.

Muslim welfare organizations such as the **American Muslim Council** (AMC) blame the lack of Muslim representation in public life to the rise of popular anti-Islamic prejudice. According to the AMC the US State Department has never hired a Muslim; of the three Muslims currently employed as part of the 20,000-strong Congressional staff, the AMC claims that one has had to pose as a Christian for fear of discrimination. Recent reports also indicate that the AMC is considering suing several state school boards for dismissing female Muslim members of staff for wearing headscarves to class.

Organizations such as the **Islamic Society of North America** (ISNA) claim that difficulty in encouraging American Muslims to participate in public life stems from the fact that many new Muslim immigrants were born in countries with little or no experience of democratic politics.

Recent moves by informal groups of American Muslims to lobby against un-Islamic legislation have led the US Army to recognize the right of Muslim soldiers to rest at the end of the annual Islamic month of fasting (*Ramadan*). Sections of the black American Muslim community are also known to have been active in the campaign, which some term a holy war (*jihad*), against alcohol consumption (prohibited under Islamic law) and drug abuse.

Meanwhile, there is evidence of growing links between American Muslims and their co-religionists in the Arab world. In February 1992 it was reported that Egypt's leading Islamic educational institution, the Al Azhar University, had accepted the first American Muslim and chairman of the National Council of Young Black Political Leaders, Khaled Ahmed, as a candidate for religious scholarship. Ahmed was subsequently quoted as saying that his ultimate goal was to become the first American Muslim Congressman.

Black Muslim separatism—the Nation of Islam

Although Syrian Muslim immigrants and African American returnees to Islam formed organizations as early as 1912 and 1913 respectively, it was not until the 1950s that there was any significant organization by orthodox Muslims on a national level. In June 1952 the **Federation of Islamic Associations** (FIA) was formed. It aimed to promote the growth of Islam and to facilitate a greater understanding of it by the non-Muslim majority.

Many black Muslims are Bilalians (a name adopted to celebrate the first black Muslim, the Ethiopian slave Bilal who became a caller to prayer (*muezzin*) during the era of the Prophet Muhammad). Regarded by most Muslims as unorthodox, Bilalian Islam arose from a belief system propounded by Elijah Poole (who renamed himself Elijah Muhammad as a symbolic rejection of any name which implied a connection with white American society and its legacy of slavery), before whom Allah allegedly appeared in the person of Master Wallace Farad Muhammad in Detroit in July 1930.

The essence of the Bilalian belief is that there is one God called Allah; that Elijah Muhammad was his last messenger; that heaven and hell are states which exist on Earth and, therefore, that there is no life after death; that it is necessary to pray seven times a day and to fast during the month of December. A further intrinsic element of the Bilalian Muslim movement is black supremacy: an inverted form of racism which characterized the white race as intrinsically evil.

The most significant product of the growth of Muslim-Bilalian beliefs was the **Nation of Islam**, founded in Detroit in 1930 and, following the mysterious disappearance of Master Farad in 1934, led by Elijah Muhammad.

Under Elijah Muhammad's leadership, black Islam became synonymous with an important strand of black nationalism. The Nation preached separate black development, using self-reliance and self-assertion as the only legitimate black response to the segregation, imposed by the white majority. It included the need to create a black economy which was separate from that of white America. This voluntary form of segregation inevitably placed great emphasis on black community consciousness and was aimed specifically at the poor black population in the ghettos of the country's major cities. Combined with a rigorous code of personal morality, the Nation advocated thrift and sobriety and frowned upon all displays of hedonism or frivolity. Its message had a significant impact upon the black population, and in particular upon those in the vanguard of the struggle for civil rights.

Among the most charismatic of the Nation's senior members was Malcolm X, a dynamic figure whose charisma and oratory saw him rise from the slums of the Bronx, via criminality and imprisonment, to become one of Elijah Muhammad's most trusted lieutenants.

Malcolm broke with Elijah in 1963 after causing a storm of controversy by describing the assassination of President John F. Kennedy as a case of "chickens coming home to roost". It became apparent later that a greater direct cause of the split was Malcolm's expression of disapproval of the conduct of Elijah Muhammad. This was provoked by the revelation that Elijah Muhammad had fathered a number of children from illicit relationships with female members of the Nation.

In 1964 Malcolm made a pilgrimage to Mecca and, thereafter, became a Sunni Muslim convert under the name El-Hajj Malik El-Shabazz. He founded the Muslim Mosque, Inc. in New York, and the Organization for Afro-American Unity.

Although his organizations remained closed to whites, Malcolm toned down the vehement anti-white racism of his earlier views. He moved away from the belief that the white race was inherently evil and came to accept the possibility of working with whites on selected issues. His journeys abroad also stimulated his interest in Arab and African independence movements. His revised views were reviled within the Nation as those of an "international hobo". One of his most ferocious critics was a former close friend and student, Louis Farrakhan, who early in 1965 denounced Malcolm as "worthy of death". Malcolm X was assassinated in New York on Feb. 21, 1965.

In the 1970s the Nation began making a greater appeal to the growing black middle class, and there was a significant reduction in the movement's anti-white racism. By this time the movement had spawned a multi-million dollar empire which included 4,200 acres of farmland, a weekly newspaper *Muhammad Speaks*, and nationwide chains of supermarkets, barber shops, restaurants and clothing stores.

Following Elijah's death in 1975, his son, Wallace (Warith) Deen Muhammad, acceded to the leadership and continued this process of reform until 1978. Under Wallace there was a radical relaxation of the Nation's strict codes of discipline and dress, and rules of personal morality noticeably softened. Wallace also dismantled the Fruit of Islam, the force of young men trained in martial arts (and sometimes in firearms) who dealt with all aspects of discipline and "security" for the Nation.

There followed a split between Farrakhan and Wallace, with the latter becoming head of the World Community of Islam (within which the US component was the **American Muslim Mission**—AMM) whilst Farrakhan took over the leadership of the Nation of Islam.

The AMM continued its reformist direction, opening its membership to all races, and moving further away from the concept of separate black development and closer to Sunni orthodoxy. It even reached an accommodation with the US political mainstream having rescinded the earlier prohibition on political participation. Its global outlook also encouraged greater support from the international Islamic community. The effect of this shift was that Wallace came to possess a degree of respectability that earlier black Muslim leaders had never enjoyed.

Meanwhile, the mantle of Elijah Muhammad was passed to Farrakhan, who sought to rebuild the Nation by returning it to its earliest and most fundamental beliefs. He resurrected the Fruit of Islam and its female equivalent, the Muslim Girls Training, and re-emphasised the importance of personal morality. Once again the Nation targeted its appeal to the black underclass of the major cities. Whereas Wallace had played down anti-white racism and the concept of separate black development, Farrakhan flaunted them, returning them to a central position within the Nation's programme.

Although heavily dependent on Farrakhan's personal charisma, the Nation's popularity in the 1980s was assisted by growing trends of racial hostility and economic insecurity within the US. By 1990 the Nation was showing every sign of vitality, and appeared partially to have recovered from the loss of most of its assets (valued at between US$60,000,000 and US$80,000,000) which Wallace had taken with him when he split with Farrakhan.

SL

Major Islamic organizations

American Muslim Council (AMC)

Washington-based lobby group, active since 1989.

Leader. Abdul Rehman Almoudis (executive director). (In June 1991 the US House of Representatives invited one of the members of the AMC's board of directors, Imam Siraj Wahaj of the mosque Masjid-e-Taqwa in Brooklyn, New York, to conduct Islamic prayers as part of its session marked by recitations from Christian and Jewish texts.)

American Muslim Mission (AMM)

Formed in 1978 by dissident members representing a majority within the Nation of Islam, who sought to revise fundamental aspects of the Nation's stance, particularly the vehemence of its anti-white racism. Centred in Chicago, the AMM is open to all races and believes that whites are not intrinsically evil, preferring instead to stress the importance of individual attitudes and the values of an individual, regardless of racial origin. The AMM's move towards a reappraisal of Elijah Muhammad as a great teacher, but not the Apostle of Allah, together with the AMM's staunchly internationalist perspective, has opened the way towards a reconciliation with orthodox Sunni Muslims. The AMM has sought to extend its commitment to religious orthodoxy by sending some of its members to study at traditional centres of learning, including Cairo's Al Azhar University and the Islamic University of Medina.

Leader. Imam Wallace (Warith) Deen Muhammad, the son of Elijah Muhammad, and former leader of the Nation of Islam.

Membership. Estimates of active membership range from over 150,000 to almost 1,000,000; the number of those sympathetic to it, without being Muslim, is thought to be far higher.

Aims. The improvement of the position of Muslims, particularly black Muslims; the erosion of the barriers between the Bilalian and orthodox Islamic traditions; the sponsorship of educational programmes on Islam; greater contact with the international Islamic community.

Federation of Islamic Associations in the US and Canada (FIA-US and Canada)

Founded in 1952. Co-ordinating agency for 45 affiliated organizations. In 1982 the FIA moved into new headquarters in the Detroit area, one of two buildings purchased with a US$100,000 gift from Saudi Arabia's King Khaled.

Leader. Nihad Ahmed (general-secretary).

Aims. To encourage the growth of Islam and expand its teachings; to improve contacts with the Muslim international community and with other religions.

Publications. The Muslim Star.

Hanafi Muslims

A Black American Muslim group which seceded from the Nation of Islam in 1958.

Leader. Hamaas Abdul Khalis, who is reportedly accepted as an authority by around 100 mosques in the US.

Membership. Unknown.

Aims. The adoption of Islam of the Hanafi school of law.

Islamic Mission of America

Founded in 1938; maintains an educational training institution.

Leader. Dr Jaber (chair).

Membership. 15,000 (1991).

Islamic Society of North America (ISNA)

Leader. One of the organization's chief spokesmen is Kamran Memon.

Muslim Students' Association (MSA)

Founded in 1963 by Muslim students at the University of Illinois-Urbana, this ostensibly non-political organization has established wide influence since it opened chapters on campuses throughout the US. It is responsible for sponsoring a number of separate and professional groups including the Islamic Medical Association; the Association of Muslim Scientists and Engineers; and the Association of Muslim Social Scientists.

Aims. The co-ordination of Muslim students and the promotion of Islamic learning and literature.

Nation of Islam

A Bilalian-Muslim organization which retained the name of the parent body (founded in 1930) from which it split in 1978. It maintains that Allah came to Earth in the form of Master Farad Muhammad, and that Elijah Muhammad was the last of the messengers of Allah. Unlike orthodox Islam, Allah is identified as black, and the place of the Prophet Muhammad is taken by Elijah Muhammad. The justification of Elijah's exalted position rests on the fact that he knew Allah personally (in the form of Farad), which constitutes a double heresy in the eyes of orthodox Islam by making God both visible and personified in a human form. The Nation believes in the intrinsic evil of the white race, inverting the long-standing Western tradition of identifying white with good and darkness with evil.

Leader. "Brother" Louis Farrakhan.

Membership. Estimated to be fewer than 50,000.

Aims. The movement advocates greater social and economic justice for all black people. It stands for equality of employment and education; freedom for black prisoners (of whom there are a disproportionate number in the US prison system); black control of black institutions and the rejection of all attempts to integrate with the white community. The Nation has also been linked with demands for a separate Black American state, rich in minerals, for black people, as a form of compensation for the centuries of slavery.

Publication. Muhammad Speaks.

Uzbekistan

(For a broad survey of Islam in the former Soviet Union see separate entry for the Commonwealth of Independent States)

Uzbekistan's population of 19,800,000 makes it the most populous of the CIS Muslim states. Seventy-one per cent are Uzbeks; 8 per cent Russians, and there are small minorities of Tatars, Kazakhs, Tajiks, Karakalpaks and others. The presence of small communities in adjacent republics has sometimes been responsible for outbreaks of ethnic violence in the 1980s. Thus a conflict over land in Kirgizstan in June 1990 in the eastern Fergana valley spread to the Kirgiz capital, Frunze (now Bishkek), and in June 1989 at least 99 people in the Uzbek Fergana valley died in riots between Uzbeks and the Meskhetian Turk population (exiled from Georgia by Stalin). The other Central Asian republics appear to be wary of Uzbek ambitions for hegemony over the region. Approximately 1,200,000 Uzbeks live in Afghanistan, and 18,000 in the Chinese Sinkiang-Uighur Autonomous Region.

The Uzbeks are Sunni Muslims of the Hanafi school. The capital, Tashkent, acts as the headquarters of the Muftiyat of Central Asia and Kazakhstan. In addition to widespread unofficial Islam, especially Naqshbandi Sufism, Wahhabi Islam is reported to be fairly strong in Uzbekistan, especially in the Fergana valley. Its precise extent remains doubtful as the term "Wahhabi" has traditionally been employed in a pejorative sense within the CIS to signify fundamentalist Islam.

The democratic movement regards Uzbekistan's traditional culture, namely Islam, as the solution to Uzbekistan's social and political problems. Steps to recover the native language and thereby the Islamic way of life have been initiated by the Oriental Studies Institute in Tashkent, which in 1992 was undertaking a translation of the Quran into Cyrillic script.

The republic continues to face severe economic difficulties and widespread political repression. In August 1991 the authorities forcibly dispersed a democratic movements' rally. In September 1991 the Communist Party of Uzbekistan, which had broken away from the CPSU after the August coup, was renamed the People's Democratic Party.

Presidential elections held in December 1991 returned the incumbent, Islam Karimov, to power. Among the most important opposition movements only the leader of the Freedom Party (*Erk*), Mohammad Salikh, stood as a candidate. The **Unity Popular Front** (*Birlik*) was not allowed to contest the elections on grounds that it was registered only as a political movement.

Meanwhile, a crisis centring on the removal of the head of the republic's spiritual directorate revealed growing differences between the *muftiyat* and the Uzbek government. In January 1992, the Mufti of Tashkent, Muhammed-Yusuf Muhammed Sadik, was reported to have been removed from office and replaced by his predecessor, Shamsuddinkhan Babakhan. A member of the USSR Congress of People's Deputies, Sadik was accused by what Russian Radio described as the "representatives of various Islamic societies in Uzbekistan and neighbouring states" of co-operating with the State Security Committee (KGB). (Sadik, who had become Mufti in February 1989 after Babakhan had been dismissed on charges of the "violation of Quranic law", reportedly had the backing of a group calling itself Islam and Democracy.)

The latest dismissal followed months of simmering hostility between Sadik and Uzbek President Karimov, during which Sadik accused Karimov of instigating an attempt in July 1991 to secure his removal as *mufti*. However, the head of the Islamic Law Directorate, Abdel Aziz Mansurov, who had briefly replaced Sadik in July 1991, accused Sadik of financial embezzlement and organizing the sale of Qurans donated by Saudi Arabia.

In September 1991 Muslim demonstrators in the Namangan region protested against Karimov's decision to "curb the Muslim spiritual directorate" and called for a new Islamic leadership to resist government interference. In December Muslim activists attempted to seize the Namagan Communist Party headquarters to establish an Islamic centre. In an interview with *Izvestiya* on Jan. 8, 1992, Mufti Sadik condemned the incident, and dissociated himself from the movement for an Islamic state in Uzbekistan. Other reports indicated, however, that Sadik had openly supported the President of Kirgizstan, thus causing further friction between the *muftiyat* and the Uzbek government.

It was reported that the Fifth (extraordinary) Congress (*Kurultai*) of the Muslims of Central Asia and Kazakhstan had on Feb. 26-27, 1992, re-elected Sadik as Mufti of Tashkent.

WS

Islamic organizations

Islamic Renaissance Party of Uzbekistan (IRPU)
Nazdate Islamiye Uzbekistan
Officially banned after its founding congress, held in January 1991, was dispersed by the authorities.
Leader. Abdullo Utayev.
Membership. Estimated by the party to have numbered 20,000 at the time of its foundation. Its support is strongest in Tashkent, Kokand and Namangan.
Aims. The IRP collaborates with *Birlik* in opposing Uzbekistan's republican leadership.
Publication. *Da'wat* (homily), an irregular *samizdat* paper in Uzbek with a circulation of 10,000.

Unity Popular Front
Birlik
Formally established in November 1988.

Leader. Abdul Rehman Pulatov.
Aims. National renaissance through cultural de-russification and a return to the Arabic alphabet. (It is estimated that 5 per cent of Uzbeks can read Arabic.)

Islamic Democratic Party of Uzbekistan
Semi-clandestine organization founded in August 1989 as a remnant of an inter-republican party; first congress held in September 1990.
Leader. Unknown.
Membership. Claims 5,000, but this figure is exaggerated.
Aims. To create united Turkestan through the creation of democratic Islamic states. Support for the party's programme has been harmed by internal conflict and pressure from authorities. More recently, Uzbek nationalism has threatened to supersede the party's inter-republican character.

Islamic Popular Movement of Turkestan
Founding congress held in August 1989.
Leader. Kakhramon Kahamidov.
Membership. It has a membership of at least 1,000, mainly concentrated in Kokand, Tashkent and Osh (in Kirgizstan). Three members of the Uzbek Supreme Soviet belong to the movement.

Venezuela

Venezuela is a Federal Republic consisting of 20 autonomous states, a Federal District, two Federal Territories and 72 Federal Dependencies.

Of a population estimated in mid-1990 to total 19,734,968, *mestizos* (those of mixed blood) form the majority (67 per cent), followed by those of European descent (21 per cent), blacks (10 per cent) and Indians (2 per cent).

The Muslim population is estimated to number roughly 50,000, the majority of whom are Arab Lebanese (estimated to total 20,000), Syrians and Palestinians.

An Islamic Centre was established in 1972.

MCB

Vietnam

The Socialist Republic of Vietnam was proclaimed in July 1976 after North Vietnam-backed communist insurgents had effectively reunified the country in April 1975 by overthrowing the US-supported government of South Vietnam. The Communist Party of Vietnam is described in the 1980 Constitution as "the only force leading the state and society".

The Vietnamese are ethnically related to the southern Chinese and form some 80 per cent of the country's population. Significant ethnic minorities include the Tai in the north, the tribal people of the Central Highlands (whom the French collectively termed Montagnards), the Khmer in the Mekong Delta region and the Chinese in urban areas.

Buddhism is the principal religion. In addition there are sizable Daoist, Confucian, Hoa Hao, Caodaist and Christian minorities.

Most of Vietnam's 30,000 Moslems are members of the Cham ethnic group. Whilst the Constitution guarantees complete freedom of religious belief, the Vietnamese government has been accused of attempting to curb Islam amongst the Cham. There are no official Islamic organizations in Vietnam, and the Cham have no known legal links with overseas Islamic groups. Neither the Muslim pilgrimage to Mecca (*hajj*), nor the printing of the Quran are permitted. In part, such repression derives from government apprehension over allegations of Cham links with Khmer and Montagnard rebels of the United Front for the Struggle of Oppressed Races (FULRO).

DS

Western Sahara

The vast majority of the inhabitants of Western Sahara, who number some 186,000 people thinly scattered over 252,000 square kilometres, are Sunni Muslim. Local dialects of Arabic are spoken. An estimated 50,000 former inhabitants of Western Sahara also live in refugee camps in the south of Algeria, while other Sahrawis live in Morocco and the Canary Islands.

Spain formally relinquished control over Western Sahara (hitherto known as Spanish Sahara) in 1976. Sovereignty over the territory is presently disputed between Morocco and the **Popular Front for the Liberation of Saguia and Rio de Oro** (Polisario Front), which in 1973 declared itself the sole representative of the Sahrawi people and in 1976 proclaimed the Saharan Arab Democratic Republic (SADR).

The nomadic inhabitants of Western Sahara are predominantly Bidan Moors of mixed Berber, Arab and black African descent. As in Mauritania, some tribes are *maraboutic* (saintly), specializing in dispute mediation and other functions, while others are deemed to be "warrior tribes". In contrast to Mauritania, Western Saharan warrior tribes tend to have a higher status than *maraboutic* tribes. Other social groups include a black servant caste and an artisan caste.

Under King Hassan II of Morocco (whose reign began in 1961), the Moroccan claim to sovereignty over Western Sahara has acquired religious overtones. In the mid-1960s Allal al-Fasi, the reformist Muslim leader of the Moroccan *Istiqlal* party who became the country's Minister for Islamic Affairs, maintained that Moroccans had a religious duty to regain the territory of Western Sahara.

The Polisario Front, aimed at securing the independence of Western Sahara from Morocco and Mauritania, was created in 1973 under the leadership of Mustafa al-Ouali. Among Polisario's early figures was Mohammed Said Brahim Bassir, a religious teacher, who in the late 1960s had been one of the organizers of the Islamic movement, *al-Mouslim*, which advocated autonomy from Spain through peaceful methods (independence was not yet an issue). Al-Ouali was said to have been influenced by the ideas of the Egyptian *Ikhwan al-muslimun* (Muslim Brotherhood).

During the 1970s the support of the Algerian and Libyan governments enabled the Polisario Front to increase its attacks against Moroccan forces garrisoned in the territory. In a 1975 ruling, the International Court of Justice (ICJ) at The Hague found that many, though not all, Western Saharan tribal groups were accustomed to pledge allegiance to the Moroccan monarch. The Court ruled, however, that neither Mauritania nor Morocco was entitled to exercise sovereignty over Western Sahara. (In 1974 the Spanish authorities had agreed to hold a referendum on the future of the territory, subsequently pre-empted by the so-called "Green March" leading to the annexation of Western Sahara by Morocco.)

The Green March on Western Sahara, the first part of which took place on Nov. 6, 1975, was described by the Moroccan authorities as a "pilgrimage", and was launched less than 24 hours after the ICJ's decision. Some 350,000 Moroccan volunteers, including 500 doctors and nurses, bearing the Moroccan flag, portraits of King Hassan and copies of the Quran, crossed Morocco's southern border to annexe Western Sahara. In subsequent years King Hassan was to refer to the Moroccan action as a holy war (*jihad*) against the unfaithful.

In February 1976 the National Provisional Council of the Sahara declared in the name of the Polisario Front the "birth of a free independent and sovereign state, ruled by an Arab-national democratic government of progressive unionist orientation of Islamic religion". In November 1976 Spain agreed to the division of Western Sahara between Morocco and Mauritania; in December the Sahrawi tribal assembly, the *jemaa*, recognized Polisario. After an unsuccessful campaign against Polisario guerrillas to win control over its share of the territory, Mauritania withdrew from Western Sahara in 1979 and abandoned all claims to the territory.

Meanwhile Polisario had by 1989 secured diplomatic recognition for the SADR by over 70 countries, principally from the non-industrialized world. The late 1980s also saw the initiation of a United Nations-sponsored peace process, although in December 1991 the holding of a referendum on the future of the territory was once again postponed as the Moroccan government challenged the official lists of those eligible to vote in the referendum.

EB

Islamic organizations

Popular Front for the Liberation of Saguia and Rio d'Oro (Polisario Front)

Founded in 1973 to win independence for Western Sahara from Morocco. In February 1976 the organization unilaterally proclaimed the Saharan Arab Democratic Republic (SADR).

Leader. Mustapha al Ouali.

Aim. The creation of a sovereign state ruled by a democratic government representing Islamic progressive forces.

Yemen

The Republic of Yemen was founded in May 1990 with the unification of the Yemen Arab Republic (YAR) (North Yemen) and the People's Democratic Republic of Yemen (PDRY) (South Yemen). Unification had been on the agenda since the formation of the two states in 1967.

Yemen is characterized by ethnic homogeneity: over 90 per cent of the population, which according to official estimates totalled 11,282,000 in mid-1990, is of Arab origin. Virtually the whole population is Muslim and most are divided along sectarian lines: 59 per cent are Shia Zaydis (or "Fivers", a moderate branch of Shi'ism) and 39 per cent are Sunnis adhering to the Shafi school of law; the remainder, mostly nomadic tribes, are Ibadites.

While allegiance to Islam throughout the whole of Yemen began in the ninth century, Islam has had a much greater political role in the former North Yemen, where Zaydi clerics (*imams*) ruled until the military-led coup of 1962.

Following the formation of the YAR in 1967, the Sunni Shafi majority dominated successive republican governments while Zaydi politicians controlled the national assembly where they opposed measures aimed at unification with predominantly Sunni South Yemen, with which the north Yemeni Shafi elite had close social and economic ties.

Since gaining independence in 1967 South Yemen, 99 per cent of whose population were Sunni Muslims, had been a socialist state in which the expression of religious beliefs was firmly suppressed. Attempts by President Ali Nasir Muhammad between 1980 and 1986 to allow displays of public piety were effectively reversed in the civil war which engulfed the country in January 1986.

Political differences dating from the pre-unification period have heightened the tensions between Islamic traditionalist tribes in the north and left-wing secular activists in the south. While there was some opposition to unification from communists in former South Yemen, the greatest and most vociferous opposition came from religious fundamentalists and tribal *shaikhs* from the former North Yemen.

In April 1990 the head of the Islamic fundamentalist current in former North Yemen and leader of the **Muslim Brotherhood** (*Ikhwan al muslimun*), Shaikh Abd al-Hamid Zaydani declared a holy war (*jihad*) against "the pagans" within the Communist Party of South Yemen. In September that year religious fundamentalists favouring the creation of an Islamic state formed the **Yemen Reform Group** (YRG).

In May 1991 religious fundamentalists, including activists from the YRG and the lesser-known **League of the Sons of Yemen** organized demonstrations in the capital, San'aa, calling for a boycott of the referendum on the unified Constitution on the grounds that it did not recognize Islamic law as the sole basis for legislation.

Greater political liberalization under the regime of the unified state resulted in the formation of up to 30 new political parties during 1990 and has provided Islamic conservatives with a forum for opposition, much of it focusing on the new Constitution. At the same time the regime has sought to contain Islamic opposition by adopting a more conciliatory approach to Islamic reform. A new law on personal status passed in March 1992 legalized polygamy (permitted under Islam) throughout Yemen.

EW

Major Islamic organizations

League of the Sons of Yemen
Founded in 1990, it took an active part in demonstrations against the Constitution in May 1991, demanding that it recognize Islamic law (*sharia*) as the sole source of legislation.
Leader. Abdel Rahman al-Jifri.
Publication. The party organ is *Al Haq* (Truth).

Muslim Brotherhood
Ikhwan al-muslimun
Active in the YAR among university students and Sunni intellectuals, in early 1990 the organization expressed fierce opposition to the unification of the two Yemens and in May 1991 called for a boycott of the referendum on the Constitution on the grounds that it did not enshrine Islamic law (*sharia*) as the sole basis of legislation. The organization is now believed to have been dissolved following the inclusion of most of its members in the recently created YRG.
Leader. Shaikh Abd al Hamid Zaydani.
Aim. The creation of a state founded on Islamic law.

Party of Truth
Al-Haqq Party
Moderate Muslim coalition founded in late 1991.
Leader. Ibrahim al-Wazir; Shaikh Ahmed bin Ali

Shami has also been referred to as leader.
Membership. Supported mainly by religious scholars (*ulama*) who seek a larger role in government and policy-making.
Aim. To organize the state and national politics on the basis of the Quran and the *Sunna* (the example set by the Prophet Muhammad).

Yemen Reform Group (YRG)
Islamic party founded by members of the legislature and other political figures in September 1990 and based in San'aa. In May 1991 it took a leading part in the demonstrations against the new Constitution. The YRG claimed that the referendum which subsequently endorsed the new Constitution had been marred by irregularities and was therefore null and void.
Leader. Shaikh Abdullah Bin Hussain al-Ahmar (a member of the Advisory Council and a leader of the northern Hashid tribal confederation).
Membership. The group is reported to have wide support among members of the House of Representatives.
Aim. Constitutional reform based on Islamic law.
Publications. Party organs are the daily *Al Islah* (Reform) and the weekly *As Sahwa* (Awakening).

Yugoslavia

Nearly 12 per cent of the population of Yugoslavia, estimated in 1991 to total just under 24,000,000, are Sunni Muslims. The majority, nearly 2,000,000, live in the republic of Bosnia-Herzegovina where they constitute some 44 per cent of the population. Just under 2,000,000 ethnic Albanian Muslims live in the autonomous province of Kosovo, while the remainder, about 500,000, are dispersed throughout the provinces of Montenegro, Macedonia and Serbia.

The largest group of Muslims, representing about 50 per cent of all believers, are descended from Slavs who converted to Islam during the Turkish occupation of the Balkans (*Muslimani*). However, because of Islam's wide ethnic spread encompassing Albanians, Serbs, Turks, Macedonians and Montenegrins, it has not, until recently, been identified with any local nationalism.

Muslim religious affairs are normally administered by the Yugoslav Islamic Community (YIC), an umbrella organization of Islamic religious bodies in Yugoslavia, whose reform-oriented Supreme Head, Hadji Jakub Effendi Selimovski, acts also as the spiritual leader of Yugoslav Muslims. In April 1992 Selimovski was quoted as saying that widespread absenteeism in mosques, approximating two-thirds of the Muslim population, suggested that there was virtually no support for religious revivalism among Yugoslav Muslims.

The highest Muslim religious body in each republic is designated a *mesihat* (guidance council); there are *mesihats* in Bosnia-Herzegovina, Croatia-Slovenia, Serbia-Vojvodina, Macedonia, and Montenegro.

Islam and the state: developments in the post-war period

It was not until the early 1970s that there emerged a discernible trend towards a distinct Muslim identity. The lack of such an identity in the immediate post-war period owed much to the fact that the majority of Yugoslav Muslims were a well-integrated community as exemplified, until recently, by the situation in religiously mixed Bosnia-Herzegovina.

The pragmatism underlying communist religious policy, which expressed itself in impartiality towards all religious groups and harsh measures against advocates of "clerico-nationalism", also helped ensure co-existence between Church and State.

Even in the province of Kosovo where Albanian Muslims controlled the momentum of local nationalism, ethnicity rather than religion proved generally to be a greater source of minority identification. The province's leading political organization, **Democratic Alliance of Kosovo** (DAK), is not reported so far to have espoused an Islamic agenda. Nevertheless, simmering ethnic tension has occasionally assumed a religious dimension as in June 1989 when celebrations marking the 600th anniversary of the Battle of the Field of Blackbirds (also the Battle of Kosovo Polje) in which invading Turkish armies had defeated the Serbs, ended in Christian-Muslim riots which were suppressed by federal Yugoslav troops.

The granting of formal recognition to Muslims as a separate "nationality" in 1972 was an important watershed in the development of a distinct Muslim identity. (Previously Muslims were listed as either "Serbian" or "Macedonian" Muslims, and since 1961, as "Muslims in an ethnic sense".) Even these initiatives, however, had less to do with the emergence of Muslim political aspirations than with attempts by Yugoslavia's communist rulers to strengthen the Muslim bloc with a view to pre-empting control of the federation by either Serbs or Croats. The result, not surprisingly, was the politicization of Muslims, firstly in Bosnia-Herzegovina, then in Croatia, and later in the province of Kosova.

The Iranian revolution of 1979 had a marked effect on many Yugoslav Muslims despite their Sunni affiliation. By the early 1980s social and political problems specific to Yugoslavia's Muslims, indicating the resurgence of Islam, had begun to emerge in Bosnia-Herzegovina. In 1983 a group of Muslim activists, including Bosnia's subsequently elected President, Alija Izetbegovic, were sentenced on charges of attempting "to destroy the brotherhood, unity and equality" of the peoples of Bosnia-Herzegovina and of the federation. In March 1986 a Muslim cleric was charged with fomenting religious hatred, and in 1987, in Sarajevo, three Muslims were imprisoned for "propagating Muslim nationalism, demanding the setting up of a purely Islamic state, and inciting *jihad* (holy war)".

Despite these early manifestations of Islamic fervour, Yugoslavia's communist rulers continued to pursue a conciliatory policy towards Muslims, dictated in part by the benefits of lucrative commercial relations with Iraq, Iran and Libya. During the late 1980s the government took an active part in promoting Muslim educational activities, discouraging state interference in religious affairs and granting easy access to land for religious uses, culminating in 1987 with the opening of a major mosque in Zagreb. (Sarajevo's main mosque, Begova Dzamija, was built in 1530.)

By 1990, however, the Muslim question threatened to redefine the shape of Yugoslav politics. Multiparty legislative and presidential elections held in Bosnia-Herzegovina in November and December 1990 were accompanied by tension and outbreaks of violence between Serbs and Muslims. The main Muslim organization, the **Party for Democratic Action**, led by Izetbegovic, emerged as the strongest party giving rise to fears among the province's Serbian and Croatian minorities of an Islamic backlash. By early 1992 the risk of ethnic conflict threatened to destroy the political consensus that had once governed the province.

In March 1992 Bosnia proclaimed its independence from Yugoslavia following a referendum in which Muslims and Croats voted heavily in favour of the republic's secession; the overwhelming majority of Serbs boycotted the referendum or voted against independence. The violent Serbian revolt against independence combined with latent Croatian suspicion about the allegedly fundamentalist aims of their Muslim allies accelerated the slide towards civil war and enhanced Muslim national consciousness.

GR

Islamic organizations

Democratic Alliance of Kosovo (LDK)
Democratski Savez Kosovo
Kosovo's largest party, it represents the province's ethnic Albanians who are predominantly Muslim.
Leader. Ibrahim Rugova (president).
Aims. Seeks independence of Kosovo by peaceful resistance.

Party for Democratic Action (PDA)
Stranka Demokratske Akcije
The main Muslim political party in Bosnia-Herzegovina founded in May 1990. In November 1990 the party won 86 out of 240 seats in elections to the Bosnia-Herzegovina National Assembly; in December 1990 the seven-member State Presidency of the Republic appointed the party's leader, Alija Izetbegovic, President of the Republic. The PDA initiated the move towards Bosnian independence in March 1992.
Leader. Alija Izetbegovic (president); Omer Behmen vice-president).
Membership. Estimated to be between 650,000 and 800,000. The party has branches and, reportedly, supporters in other parts of Yugoslavia, including Serbia and Croatia.
Aims. The party regards its political orientation to be moderate and centrist. Its vice-president claimed in 1992 that the PDA was "not a Muslim party, but a party of Muslims" adding that Islam was to the PDA what Roman Catholicism was to the Christian Democratic parties of Western Europe. Although Izetbegovic has sometimes been charged with advocating an Islamic republic in Yugoslavia, it is understood that he does not publicly favour ideas commonly associated with Islamic fundamentalism, although he is committed to upholding Muslim religious, cultural and political rights.

Moslem Bosnjak Organization(MBO)
Established in September 1990 following a split within the PDA which led to the separation of its liberal wing.
Leader. Adil Zulfikarpasic (formerly PDA vice-president).
Aims. The MBO is opposed to what it sees as the extremism and militancy of some sections within the PDA and proposes a separation between Islam and politics.

Yugoslav Islamic Community (YIC)
Rijaset Islamske Zajednice
Founded in 1882, it is concerned with the administration of Muslim religious affairs and the co-ordination of religious bodies in Yugoslavia.
Leader. Hadji Jakub Selimovski (Supreme Head) who replaced Hadji Husein Effendi Mujic in March 1991 following Mujic's ousting in the wake of a militant grass-roots *imams* (religious leaders) movement in Bosnia-Herzegovina in 1988-89.
Publication. Preporod.

International Islamic Organizations

Economic Co-operation Organization (ECO)

Address. 5 Hejab Av, Blvd Keshavarz, POB 14155-6176, Tehran, Iran.

Islamically-oriented economic grouping originally involving Iran, Pakistan and Turkey; founded in 1964 as the Regional Co-operation for Development (RCD), reactivated and renamed in 1985.

Members. Iran, Pakistan and Turkey; the former Soviet republics of Azerbaijan, Kirgizstan, Tajikistan, Turkmenistan and Uzbekistan were admitted as full members at a summit meeting in Tehran in February 1992. The "Turkish Republic of Northern Cyprus" has associate status.

Secretary-General. General Ali Raza Salari.

Aims. Closer economic co-operation with the ultimate aim of the creation of an Islamic common market involving joint industrial projects and standards, trade, tourism and transport (and including the building of road and rail links, communications and cultural affairs).

Activities. A joint postal organization, the South and West Asia Postal Union, was established in 1988, and a joint Chamber of Commerce and Industry in 1990. A ministerial meeting in February 1992 considered plans for the reduction by 10 per cent of customs duties on a list of goods, and the establishment of a joint investment and development bank.

Islamic Development Bank (IDB)

Address. PO Box 5925, Jeddah 21432, Saudi Arabia.

Formally inaugurated in October 1975; plans for the IDB were approved at a meeting of Finance Ministers of the Islamic Conference Organization (ICO) in Jeddah in 1973.

Members. 45: Afghanistan, Algeria, Azerbaijan (June 1992), Bahrain, Bangladesh, Benin, Brunei, Burkina Faso, Cameroon, Chad, Comoros, Djibouti, Egypt, Gabon, The Gambia, Guinea, Guinea-Bissau, Indonesia, Iran, Iraq, Jordan, Kuwait, Lebanon, Libya, Malaysia, Maldives, Mali, Mauritania, Morocco, Niger, Oman, Pakistan, Palestine Liberation Organization, Qatar, Saudi Arabia, Senegal, Sierra Leone, Somalia, Sudan, Syria, Tunisia, Turkey, Turkmenistan (June 1992), Uganda, United Arab Emirates, Yemen.

President. Ahmad Muhammad Ali (Saudi Arabia).

Structure. Each member is represented on the Board of Governors chaired by the President of the Bank; there is also an 11-member Board of Executive Directors.

Aims. To encourage the economic development and social progress of member countries and of Muslim communities in non-Muslim countries in accordance with Islamic law (*sharia*).

Activities. The Bank adheres to the Islamic principle forbidding usury and does not grant loans or credits for interest. Its methods of financing are interest-free loans (with a service fee); equity participation in industrial and agricultural projects; leasing operations and instalment sale financing; and profit sharing operations. A statement issued by the Bank in June 1992 said that it would finance projects worth US$184,700,000 in member states during the calender year 1992. In February 1992 the Bank awarded US$280,000 to the Islamic University of the Philippines in Marawi, Mindanao, for the promotion of Islamic studies. In March 1992 the five Islamic republics of the former Soviet Union were offered US$12,000,000 as economic and social support. *Affiliated organizations.* Islamic Research and Training Institute, founded in 1962, to provide training for staff involved in development activities in the Bank's member countries.

Islamic Conference Organization (ICO)

Also referred to as the Organization of the Islamic Conference (OIC)

Address. Kilo 6, Mecca Rd, POB 178, Jeddah 21411, Saudi Arabia.

Founded in May 1971; plans were finalized during a meeting of Muslim Heads of State in Rabat, Morocco, in May 1969 and of Islamic Foreign Ministers in Jeddah in March 1970, and in Karachi, Pakistan, in December 1970.

Members. Afghanistan (membership suspended January 1980, restored to the exile Afghan Interim Government (AIG) March 1989); Algeria, Bahrain, Bangladesh, Benin, Brunei, Burkina Faso, Cameroon, Chad, Comoros, Djibouti, Egypt (membership suspended May 1979, restored March 1984), Gabon, The Gambia, Guinea, Guinea-Bissau, Indonesia, Iran, Iraq, Jordan, Kuwait, Lebanon, Libya, Malaysia, Maldives, Mali, Mauritania, Morocco, Niger, Oman, Pakistan, Palestine Liberation Organization, Qatar, Saudi Arabia, Sierra Leone, Somalia, Sudan, Syria, Tunisia, Turkey, Turkmenistan (membership granted June 1992), Uganda, United Arab Emirates, Yemen. (Mozambique, Nigeria and the "Turkish Republic of Northern Cyprus" have observer status.)

Secretary-General. Hamid Algabid (Niger).

Structure. The supreme body of the ICO is the Conference of Heads of State which meets every three years to determine general policy; to date the ICO has held six Heads of State summit conferences: in Rabat, Morocco (September 1969); in Lahore, Pakistan (February 1974); in Mecca, Saudi Arabia (January 1981); in Casablanca, Morocco (January 1984); in Kuwait (January 1987); and in Dakar, Senegal (December 1991). The Secretariat, which acts as the ICO's executive organ, is headed by a Secretary-General (elected by the Conference of ICO Foreign Ministers for a non-renewable four-year term), and four Assistant Secretaries-General (similarly appointed).

Aims. To promote Islamic solidarity among member states; to consolidate economic, social, cultural and scientific co-operation among member states; to eliminate racial segregation; to support international peace and security; to safeguard the Muslim Holy Places and support the movement for the liberation of Palestine; to strengthen the national rights of all Muslim people; to promote co-operation and understanding among member states.

Activities. The ICO has taken a number of measures aimed at furthering economic, cultural and political co-operation and providing humanitarian assistance. An agreement in 1981 provided for the establishment of joint investment and trade projects; in February 1982 ICO Trade and Industry Ministers agreed to promote industrial co-operation; in December 1988 a committee of experts was delegated to draw up a plan of action for assistance in science and technology to developing countries (mainly in Africa). An Islamic Solidarity Fund created in 1974 has helped establish Islamic universities in Niger, Uganda, Bangladesh and Malaysia. In March 1989 ICO Foreign Ministers denounced as an apostate (though refrained from passing judgment on) the Indian-born British writer, Salman Rushdie for his controversial novel *The Satanic Verses*, demanded the withdrawal of the book and urged member states to boycott publishing houses which refused to comply. The ICO's political activities have been wide-ranging and have included calls for the withdrawal of Soviet troops from Afghanistan and an end to fighting in Chad and Lebanon (1987); the creation of an Islamic Peace Committee to end the war between Iran and Iraq (1980); the launch of a non-military holy war (*jihad*) for the liberation of Palestine (1981); the boycott of Israel (1982); the condemnation of Iraq's invasion of Kuwait (1990) and the upholding of international sanctions against Iraq (1991). The ICO has provided humanitarian assistance to Muslim communities affected by war and natural disasters with Burkina Faso, Cape Verde, Chad, The Gambia, Guinea, Guinea-Bissau, Mali, Mauritania, Niger and Senegal receiving particular attention.

Institutions within the ICO system. International Islamic News Agency (founded 1972); Islamic Development Bank (founded 1975); Islamic Educational, Scientific and Cultural Organization—ISESCO (founded 1982; publications include *ISESCO Bulletin*; *Islam Today*; *ISESCO Triennial*). The decision in January 1981 to establish an International Islamic Court of Justice has not as yet been implemented.

Subsidiary organizations. Al Quds Fund (founded 1976); International Commission for the Preservation of Islamic Cultural Heritage (founded 1983); Islamic Centre for Technical and Vocational Training and Research (founded 1979); Islamic Foundation for Science, Technology and Development (founded 1981); Islamic Jurisprudence Academy (founded 1982); Islamic Solidarity Fund (founded 1974); Research Centre for Islamic History, Art and Culture (founded 1979); Statistical, Economic and Social Research and Training Centre for the Islamic Countries (founded 1978).

Affiliated organizations. International Arab-Islamic Schools Federation; International Association of Islamic Banks; Islamic Cement Association (founded in 1984 but not yet in operation); Islamic Chamber of Commerce, Industry and Commodity (founded 1979); Islamic Committee for the International Crescent (founded 1979); Islamic Shipowners' Association; Organization of Islamic Capitals (founded 1978).

Islamic Council of Europe (ICE)

Address. 16 Grosvenor Crescent, London SW1 XEP.

Founded in 1973 as a co-ordinating body for Islamic centres and organizations in Europe; an autonomous Council collaborating with the Secretariat of the Islamic Conference Organization (ICO) and other Islamic organizations.

Secretary-General. Salem Azzam.

Aims. To develop a better understanding of Islam and Muslim culture in the West.

Muslim World League (MWL)

Rabitat al Alam al Islami

Address. POB 537, Makkah al Mukarramah, Saudi Arabia.

Founded in 1962 with a reported official annual budget of around £2,000,000. Dependent on funding from the government of Saudi Arabia, the MWL has been reported as acting as a financial pipeline for Saudi-backed radical Sunni Muslim groups in Asia, Africa and the Middle East).

Secretary-General. Abdullah bin Omar Nasseef.

Structure. It has 30 offices throughout the world; the MWL's European section, concerned with the promotion of mosque-building, is based at the Islamic and Cultural Centre of Belgium (Centre Islamique et Culturel de Belgique).

Aims. To advance Islamic unity and solidarity, and to provide financial assistance for education, medical care and relief work in Muslim countries.

Publications. *Majalla al Rabita* (monthly, Arabic); *Akhbar al Alam al Islami* (weekly, Arabic); *Journal* (monthly, English).

Affiliated organizations. World Council of Mosques; World Assembly of Muslim Youth, based in Riyad.

Glossary

Abbasids. Dynasty of caliphs ruling from Baghdad between AD 750 to 1258 although with little actual power after AD 945.

Ahmadiyyah. Heterodox sect founded by Mirza Ghulam Ahmad (1835-1908) in the Punjab, India. Followers of the sect are known for their energetic proselytizing and mosque-building programmes abroad.

al jamaa al-Islamiyya ("Islamic Society"). Often used by Islamists to emphasise their doctrinal unity; used by others to refer to various Islamic movements.

Alawi. 1. The name of the Moroccan royal family. 2. A Sufi brotherhood, the Alawiyyah, also known as the Shadhiliyyah, widespread in North Africa and throughout the Arab world. 3. A religion, "followers of Ali", professed by an ethnic group of the same name, found mainly in Syria, but also in Lebanon and parts of Turkey where they are called Alevis.

Alevi. See *Alawi.*

amir. Commander, chief or prince.

awqaf (sing. *waqf*). Religiously endowed property entrusted to clerics; in modern Islamic states the administration of *awqaf* is generally assigned to a government ministry.

Ayatollah (Ar. "sign of God"). Honorific title for high-ranking Shi'ite religious authority regarded as "a reference of emulation" (*marja at-taqlid*).

bay'a. Pact between ruler and subjects concluded at the time of the installation or recognition of a ruler in his office.

caliph. See *khalifa.*

caliphate. See *khilafa.*

dar al Islam. Abode of Islam or lands where Islam is dominant.

da'wa. Literally "call"; also signifies proselytization, missionary or propaganda work with the intention of spreading and confirming the Islamic message.

Druze. A heterodox sect which developed in the 11th century as an offshoot of Shia Ismailism; concentrated in parts of Israel, Lebanon and Syria.

evkaf. Turkish for *awqaf* [see above].

fatwa. Religio-juridic ruling or verdict issued by a recognized Islamic scholar.

habus. Term synonymous with *awqaf* [see above], used in Maghreb countries.

Hadith. Sayings attributed to the Prophet Muhammad.

hajj. The canonical pilgrimage to Mecca, one of the "five pillars" of Islam in addition to the affirmation of the creed ("there is no god but God and Muhammad is His Messenger"); fasting in the month of *ramadan* [see below]; prayer; and *zakat* [see below].

halal. That which is permitted under Islamic law.

haram. That which is proscribed under Islamic law.

Hanafi. One of the four recognized juridic schools of law, sometimes referred to as "rites", of Sunni Islam founded by Abu al Hanifah (d. AD 767); regarded as the least "fundamentalist" of the four schools, it has a majority of adherents and is dominant in most countries formerly part of the Turkish empire and in India.

Hanbali. One of the four recognized schools, sometimes referred to as "rites", of Sunni Islam, initiated by Ahmad ibn Hanbal (d. AD 855); observed in Saudi Arabia and Qatar, it is known for its strict adherence to the Quran and the "genuine" Hadith [see above].

hijra. Emigration or (immigration); the most significant *hijra* in Islam is that of the Prophet Muhammad from Mecca to Medina in AD 622.

Hujjat al-Islam, also *Hojatoleslam* ("Proof of God"). Honorific title for Shi'ite religious authority with a substantial religious following, second in rank to Ayatollah [see above].

hudud (sing. *hadd*). Islamic penalties.

Ibadites, also *Ibadis.* The only surviving branch of the radical Kharijite sect [see below], they form a majority in Oman which is their historical centre and are found also in East Africa, Zanzibar, Libya, the island of Djerba in Tunisia, and the region of the M'zab in Algeria.

ijtihad. Independent reasoning with regard to religious issues.

imam. Literally "model" or exemplar"; among Sunnis the term refers generally to the leader of prayer; among Shias it has acquired a special significance of an intercessor, unique and predestined to the age, who must be recognized and followed for the community to be saved.

Ismaili. See *Shi'ism.*

ithna ashariyyah. See *Shi'ism.*

jihad ("effort"). Holy war to extend Islam into the *dar al-harb* (the non-Islamic territories), or to defend Islam from danger.

khalifa (caliph). "Successor", though not of his prophetic mission, to the Prophet Muhammad.

Kharijite. Members of a radical sect that arose in the mid-seventh century in opposition both to Sunni and Shia orthodoxy. For hundreds of years they were the source of insurrection against established authority embodied in the Caliphate; they survive today in a more moderate form among Ibadites [see above].

khilafat (caliphate). The institution of Islamic government after the Prophet Muhammad.

Maliki. One of the four recognized juridic schools of law, sometimes referred to as "rites", of Sunni Islam, founded by Malik ibn Anas (AD 716-795); dominant in the Arab west and in west Africa.

marabout. A French word derived from the Arabic *marbut*, "attached", in the sense of being bound to God. A term used in north and west Africa for a saint or venerated descendant of a saint.

mujaddid. Renewer of the faith.

mujahid, pl. *mujaheddin.* One who engages in *jihad* [see above].

Ottomans. Turkish dynasty which ruled the Muslim empire and parts of south-east Europe, using Istanbul as the capital after AD 1453. The caliphate was abolished by the Turkish Republic in 1924.

ramadan. The ninth month of the Arab and Islamic calendar; fasting during the month is one of the "five pillars" of Islam in addition to the affirmation of the creed ("there is no god but God and Muhammad is His Messenger"), prayer, *hajj* [see above] and *zakat* [see below].

riba. Usury; describes most interest charged by or received from modern banks; prohibited under Islamic law.

salaf (lit. "ancestors"). The first generation of Muslims.

Salafiyyah. Modernist Muslim movement founded at the end of the 19th century.

Shaf'i. One of the four recognized juridic schools, sometimes referred to as "rites", of Sunni Islam founded by Muhammad ibn Idris ash-Shafi (d. AD 820); dominant among Muslims in south-east Asia.

sharia, also *shar'* (adj. *shar'i*). Originally "path" or "way"; body of detailed Islamic law based on the Quran and Sunna [see below].

Shia (adj. *Shi'i*). "The Party of Ali" who believe that leadership of the Muslim community after the death of the Prophet Muhammad should have gone to Ali (the Prophet's cousin and son-in-law) and his family.

Shi'ism. Branch of Islam comprising 10 per cent or less of all Muslims. It is divided into three main groups, namely, the *ithna ashariyyah* or Twelve-Imams ("Twelvers") representing the largest division and constituting the official religion of Iran; the Zaydis or Five-Imams ("Fivers"); and the Ismailis or Seven-Imams ("Seveners") one of whose branches is led by the Aga Khan. All Shia sects have their own school of law, with the "Twelvers" following the Jafari school named after the eminent religious scholar Jafar as Sadiq (AD 699-765).

shura. Non-binding consultation sought by the ruler from the Muslim community or its representatives.

sufi. Religious mystic.

Sunna. The sayings, ways and "traditions" of the Prophet Muhammad.

Sunni. The mainstream majority of Muslims.

tariqa (literally "path"). School or brotherhood of Sufi mystics. The first *tariqa* to emerge was the Qadiriyyah; other important brotherhoods include the Naqshbandiyyah, the Shadhiliyyah and the Tijaniyyah.

ulama (sing. *alim*). Muslim religious scholars.

umma. Muslim community.

Wahhabi. Sect founded by Muhammad ibn Abd al-Wahhab (AD 1703-1787) dominant in Saudi Arabia and Qatar. It gained footholds in India, Africa and elsewhere at the beginning of the 19th century. Wahhabism is said to be grounded in the rigid Hanbali [see above] school of Sunni Islam and is noted for its emphasis on the strict observance of Islamic religious duties and on the enforcement of public morals to a degree not found elsewhere.

waqf. See *awqaf.*

zakat. Obligatory alms-giving; one of the Muslim's five ritualistic duties in addition to the affirmation of the creed ("there is no god but God and Muhammad is His Messenger"), fasting, pilgrimage and prayer.

Zaydi. See *Shi'ism.*

Bibliography

Ayubi, Nazih N., *Political Islam: Religion and Politics in the Arab World*. Routledge, London, 1991.

Dessouki, Ali, ed., *Islamic Resurgence in the Arab World*. Praeger, New York, 1982.

Esposito, John L., ed., *Voices of Resurgent Islam*. Oxford University Press, Oxford and New York, 1983.

Etienne, Bruno, *L'Islamism radicale*. Hachette, Paris, 1987).

Carré, Olivier, and Michaud, Gérard, *Les Frères Musulmans, 1928-1982*. Éditions Gallimard, Paris, 1983.

Clarke, Peter, ed., *The World's Religions: Islam*. Routledge, London, 1990.

Gerholm, T., and Lithman, Y. G., *The New Islamic Presence in Western Europe*. Mansell, London and New York, 1988.

Kettani, M. A., *Muslim Minorities in the World Today*. Mansell, London, 1986.

Piscatori, James P., *Islam in the Political Process*. Cambridge University Press for the Royal Institute of International Affairs, London, 1986.

Youssef, Michael, *Revolt against Modernity: Muslim Zealots and the West*. E. J. Brill, Leiden, 1985.

Index

Banna, Hassan al- 15, 66
Banna, Seif al Islam Hassan al 68
Bano, Begum Shah 95, 97
Baoan 52
Baqar, Ahmed 138
Bara 168
Barbados 47, 243
Bardhi, Reshat Baba 9
Barelvi 186, 261
Bariba 34
Barisan Jam'aah Islamiah Sa-Malaysia (Berjasa)
  151
Barisan Nasional 149
Barreau, Jean-Claude 76
Barzani, Adham 112
Bashir, Alhaj Muhammad 190
Bashir, Omar Hassan al- 227
Bashkirs 201
Bashkortostan 57, 60, 201
Basmachi movement 201
Basri, Hassan 104
Bassir, Mohammed Said Brahim 278
Batak 99
Battalion of as-Sadr 115
Battle of Kosovo Polje 283
Battle of the Field of Blackbirds 283
Bauchi 176
Bayanuni, Shaikh Ali Sadr ad Din al- 235
Bayanuni, Shaikh Muhammad Abu al Nasr al- 233
Baz, Abdulaziz bin Abdullah bin 208
Bazargan, Mehdi 107
Beafada 89
Beeharry, Imam S. M. 158
Beheshti, Ayatollah 106, 107
Behmen, Omer 284
Beijing Islamic Association 53, 54
Beira 163
Bektashi 8
Belau 183
Belgian Royal Commission for Immigration 32
Belgium 30
Belhadj, Shaikh Ali 12, 14
Bello, Ahmedu 175
Ben Ali, Zine al Abidine 247
Ben Badis, Shaikh Abd al-Hamid 10
Ben Bella, Ahmed 10
Ben Youssef University 160
Bengali 165
Benin 34, 35
Benjelloun, Omar 162
Benkiran, Abdellilah 162
Bennabi, Malik 15
Berber 278
Beri 173
Berlin 81

Bermuda 47
Berri, Nabih 141
Beshkesia Islamike Shqiptare 9
Bharatiya Jana Sangh 94
Bharatiya Janata Party 96, 97
Bhojpuri 168
Bhumivol Adulyadej (Rama IX), King of Thailand
  242
Bhutto, Benazir 185
Bhutto, Zulfiqar Ali 185
Bialystok 197
Bida Yan Izala 176
Bidan Moors 155, 278
Bilal 268
Bilel, Charles 268
Bini 175
Bint al-Huda 113
Bir Zeit 119
Birlik 59, 273
Birlik Partisi 252
Birmingham Muslim Liaison Committee 262
Bissa 41
Biya, Paul 44
"Black Arabs" 43
Black Brigades 137
Black Islam 243
Black Moors 156
"Black Power" 244
Blacks 276
Bleher, Mustaqim 264
Bloc Démocratique Sénégalais 211
Bohras 184, 222
Bolkiah, Sultan of Brunei, Sir Hassanal 37
Bonnet law 76
Borkou 48
Boschneger 230
Bosnia-Herzegovina 282
Boudiaf, Mohammed 13, 14
Boumedienne, Houari 11, 13
Bourguiba, Habib 246
Bouyali, Mustafa 11, 13
Bozo 153
Bradford Council of Mosques 262
Brahui 1
Brazil 36
Brazilian Catholic Inquisition 36
Brent, London borough of 263
Brezhnev, Leonid 57, 237
British Board of Jewish Deputies 265
Brunei 37, 164
Brunswijk, Ronnie 231
Buddhism 126, 148, 222, 236, 277
Buddhist 42, 99, 152
Buddhist Moghs 165
Buddhists 25, 184

310

Shwebo 165
Siba'i, Mustafa as- 235
Siddiqui, Ghayas Uddin 265
Siddiqui, Kalim 263, 265
Siddiqui, Raees 126
Sidya, Ould Shaikh 155
Sierra Leone 214
Sierra Leone Muslim Congress 214
Sierra Leone Muslim Men and Women's
  Association 215
Sikhism 148
Sikhs 1
Singapore 148
Sinhala 222
Sipah-i-Sabahah-i-Pakistan 187
Sirbil, Shaikh Ibrahim 129
Slavs 282
Smith, Lennox 245
Social Democratic Party 21
Social Democratic Populist Party 255
Social Democratic Republican Party 156
Social Educational Group 136
Social Reform Group 136, 137
Socialist Arab Union 144
Socialist Labour Party 67
Socialist Party of Albania 8
Sociedade Mussulmana de Chile 51
Society for Expansion of the Majority 187
Society for Social Reform 24
Society for the Unity of Clergy 189
Society for the Victory of Islam 175
Society of Compamions [of the Prophet
  Muhammad] 37
Society of Combatant Clergy 108, 110
Society of Indian Scholars 93
Society of Muslims 244
Society of Overflowing Islam 179
Society of Qom Theological Teachers 108
Society of Religious Elders 187, 188
Society of the Call 24
Society of the Muslim Brothers of Palestine 128
Society of Young Muslims in Nigeria 179
Sofala 163
Soglo, Nicéphore 34
Sokoto Caliphate 175
Soldiers of the Imam 115
Soldiers of Truth 32
Solomon Islands 183
Solomon, Shaikh Hassan 218
Soltani, Shaikh Abdellatif 11
Somalia 124
Somalis 65, 72
Somono 153
Songhay 153, 173
Sorush 116

South Africa 216
South African National Zakat Fund 219
South and West Asia Postal Union 285
South Lebanese Army 141
South Vietnam 277
South Yemen 280
Soviet Union 81, 159
Spain 220
Spirit of '46 150
Spirit of 1946 151
Spiritual Directorate in Baku 20
Spiritual Directorate of Muslims of the Soviet Union
  57
Sri Lanka 222
Sri Lanka Freedom Party 224
Sri Lanka Muslim Congress 224
Stalin, Joseph 58
State Law and Order Restoration Council 165
Statistical, Economic and Social Research and
  Training Centre 287
Stranka Demokratske Akcije 284
Students' Islamic Movement 98
Students' Islamic Movement of India 96, 97
Students' Society 189
Studies and Investigations 116
Subaire, Ahmed 221
Sudan 12, 225
Sudan Catholic Bishops' Conference 227
Sudan Socialist Union 226
Sudanese People's Liberation Army 227
Suharto, General 100
Suhrawardi 184
Suhrawardiyyah 93
Sukarno 100
Sulaiman, Alhaji Ibrahim 176
Sulawesi 100
Sulaymanci 30
Suleymanci 81, 172, 252
Sultan of Sokoto 175
Sultan Suleiman 53
Sultan, Khaled al- 137
Sulu 193, 195
Sundanese 99
Sunnis 1, 8, 16, 22, 30, 36, 38, 41, 45, 52, 61, 62,
  63, 65, 66, 72, 81, 87, 89, 90, 93, 105, 127, 136,
  139, 144, 152, 155, 159, 160, 168, 169, 180, 199,
  210, 214, 222, 225, 230, 241, 246, 251, 278, 282
Superior Islamic Council 12
Supreme Assembly of the Islamic Revolution in Iraq
  109, 114
Supreme Council for Islamic Affairs 176
Supreme Council of Islamic Affairs 66
Supreme Council of Kenya Muslims 134
Supreme Council of Muslims 32
Supreme Council of Sufi Orders 66

313

Warriors of Islam 106
Warsaw 197
Wasoqi, Alhaj Shaikh Ali Wasoqusalam 5
Way of the Revolution 115
Wazir, Ibrahim al- 281
Wazzaniyyah 10
Wei Wuer 52
Welfare Party 83, 253
West Bank 119
Western Australia 19
Western Sahara 156, 278
Western Samoa 183
Western Thrace 85
White Guards 96-98
White Revolution 106
Whitechapel Mosque 262
Williams, Eric 244
Wolof 155, 210
Women's Islamic Movement 219
World Assembly of Muslim Youth 123, 287
World Community of Islam 270
World Council of Elders of the Bektashis 9
World Council of Mosques 123, 287
World Muslim League 83, 166, 206, 266
Wormser, André 78
Wosoqi, Alhaj Shaikh Ali Wosoqusalam 5

Xanthi 86
Xhosa 216
Xinjiang Uygur 52

Yakdasta, Qari 6
Yala 241
Yan Tatsine 175
Yang di-Pertuan Agong 148
Yao 163
Yaoundé 44
Yasawiyyah 57
Yaseen, Haji S.M. 91
Yassein, Shaikh Ahmed 120
Yasser, Abu 16
Yassin, Abdessalam 161
Yayia, Ould Siddi 156
Yazidi 111, 251

Yeltsin, Boris 20, 131
Yemen 280
Yemen Reform Group 280, 281
Yoruba 34, 175
Young Men's Muslim Association 120
Young Muslim Association of Nigeria 176, 179
Young Muslim Men's Association 223
Young Muslims 117
Youth of Islam 179
Yugoslav Islamic Community 282
Yugoslavia 75, 81, 282
Yunnan 52
Yunus, Muhammad 167

Zade, Mohammed Sharif Khimmat 238
Zade, Zardusht Ali 21
Zadeh, Akbar Toradzhon 238
Zadeh, Qazi Akbar Toradzhon 238
Zaghawa 48
Zahar, Mahmoud al 123
Zahira College 222
Zaid, Abu 115
Zaigham, Inayatullah 265
Zain, Pehin Dato Dr Haji Mohammad 37
Zaituna University 246
Zaker Party 29
Zambezi river 163
Zambézia 163
Zangon-Kataf 177
Zant, Abdul Munim Abu 128
Zanzibar 239
Zaria 177
Zawi, Sheikh Al-Tahir Ahmad al-, Grand Mufti of
    Libya 145
Zaydani, Shaikh Abd al Hamid 281
Zaydani, Shaikh Abd al-Hamid 280
Zaydi 65, 105, 111
Zaydis 280
Zia, Khaleda 27
Zoroastrians 105, 184
Zubaydi, Hamza al- 112
Zulfikarpasic, Adil 284
Zulu 216
Zummur, Abbud al 70